FUNDRAISING

for Social Change

KIM KLEIN

Fourth Edition, Revised & Expanded

JOSSEY-BASS
A Wiley Company
www.josseybass.com

Published by

JOSSEY-BASS
A Wiley Company
989 Market Street
San Francisco, CA 94103-1741

www.josseybass.com

Jossey-Bass books and products are available through most bookstores. To contact Jossey-Bass directly, call (888) 378-2537, fax to (800) 605-2665, or visit our website at www.josseybass.com.

Substantial discounts on bulk quantities of Jossey-Bass books are available to corporations, professional associations, and other organizations. For details and discount information, contact the special sales department at Jossey-Bass.

We at Jossey-Bass strive to use the most environmentally sensitive paper stocks available to us. Our publications are printed on acid-free recycled stock whenever possible, and our paper always meets or exceeds minimum GPO and EPA requirements.

ISBN: 0-7879-6174-4

FOURTH EDITION

PB Printing   10 9 8 7 6 5

THE CHARDON PRESS SERIES

Fundamental social change happens when people come together to organize, advocate, and create solutions to injustice. Chardon Press recognizes that communities working for social justice need tools to create and sustain healthy organizations. In an effort to support these organizations, Chardon Press produces materials on fundraising, community organizing, and organizational development. These resources are specifically designed to meet the needs of grassroots nonprofits—organizations that face the unique challenge of promoting change with limited staff, funding, and other resources. We at Chardon Press have adapted traditional techniques to the circumstances of grassroots nonprofits. Chardon Press and Jossey-Bass hope these works help people committed to social justice to build mission-driven organizations that are strong, financially secure, and effective.

Kim Klein, Series Editor

For Stephanie

Contents

PREFACE vii

ACKNOWLEDGMENTS ix

INTRODUCTION 1

SECTION 1 — FUNDRAISING FRAMEWORK 3

    1. Philanthropy in America 5

    2. Principles of Fundraising 13

    3. Matching Fundraising Strategies with Financial Needs 19

    4. Making a Case for Your Organization 27

    5. The Board of Directors 35

SECTION 2 — STRATEGIES TO ACQUIRE AND KEEP DONORS 51

    6. Using Direct Mail 53

    7. How to Conduct Special Events 89

    8. Fundraising by Telephone 135

    9. Personal Solicitation 151

    10. The Thank-You Note 171

SECTION 3 — STRATEGIES TO UPGRADE DONORS 177

    11. Major Gifts Programs 179

    12. Pledge Programs 189

    13. Major Gifts Campaigns 197

    14. Capital Campaigns 207

    15. Planned Giving 219

    16. Using Donor Analysis 237

SECTION 4 — OTHER METHODS OF FUNDRAISING 251

    17. Voluntary Fees for Service 253

    18. Payroll Deduction Programs 259

    19. Door-to-Door Canvassing 265

    20. Setting Up a Small Business 273

    21. Religious Institutions, Service Clubs, and Small Businesses 279

    22. The Internet 285

SECTION 5 — FUNDRAISING MANAGEMENT 291

    23. The Fundraising Office 293

    24. Managing Information 295

    25. Managing Time 301

    26. Recordkeeping 307

SECTION 6 — YOU THE FUNDRAISER 315

    27. Hiring a Development Director 317

    28. Hiring a Consultant 325

    29. Making Fundraising Your Career 331

    30. Dealing with Anxiety 337

    31. Working with the Executive Director 341

SECTION 7 — BUDGETING AND PLANNING 345

    32. Developing a Budget 347

    33. Creating a Fundraising Plan 355

    34. What to Do in Case of Financial Trouble 363

SECTION 8 — SPECIAL CHALLENGES 367

    35. Raising Money in Rural Areas 369

    36. Fundraising in a Coalition 375

    37. When Everyone Is a Volunteer 379

    38. Being Brand New 381

    39. The Perennial Question of Clean and Dirty Money 385

RESOURCES 389

THE FOUNDATION CENTER COOPERATING COLLECTIONS NETWORK 395

INDEX 399

Preface to the Fourth Edition

In order for a publisher to claim that a book is "revised and expanded," more than one-third of the text must be changed. With a book on fundraising, this is not difficult to do. In fact, there is no way to rewrite a how-to book on fundraising every few years without changing it substantially. New technologies for fundraising and office management, changes in the economy, the shifting role of government, the trend toward globalization, and the sheer number of nonprofits all contribute to a continually changing landscape with one constant need for nonprofit groups — more money.

To keep up with all that affects the art and process of fundraising, this edition of *Fundraising for Social Change* has several new chapters. Moreover, all the old chapters have been rewritten, some only slightly and some almost entirely.

In the previous editions, I have noted two tenets of fundraising that haven't changed and probably won't:

1. If you want money, you have to ask for it.

2. If you ask enough people, you will get your money.

Certainly, the first statement will never change. As Millard Fuller, founder of Habitat for Humanity, often says, "I have tried raising money by asking for it and by not asking for it, and I always got more by asking for it."

The second statement, too, is still true. But the number of people you must ask in order to get the money you need to do your work is greater than ever. The cost of doing business has gone up dramatically, as small organizations strive to make employee salaries and benefits equitable, as rent costs rise, and with each "must have" technological innovation. Further, the number of nonprofits raising money has increased exponentially in the last ten years, so thousands more organizations are fundraising from a population that has more and more demands on its money, particularly as wages of working and middle-class Americans have not grown as much as they need to in order to meet the needs of nonprofits.

You can address these problems by working harder or by working smarter. Since most people reading this book would be hard-pressed to work any harder than they do already, I recommend the latter. This book will give you the tools you need to get more money out of the work you are already doing.

An organization that is financed by a broad base of individual donors is in a strong position to advocate for the structural changes our society needs to make. As management guru Peter Drucker points out, "Every important idea for social change has come from the nonprofit sector." For each of those ideas to become reality, they must be well supported by the time and money of dozens, hundreds, or thousands of people. If you are serious about educating your community and organizing your constituents to advocate for change, the number of donors you have will be as important as the amount of money you raise.

This book will tell you how you can find and reach those donors so you can get the money you deserve.

Acknowledgments

Thank you to the thousands of people and organizations around the world that I have been privileged to work with over the past two-plus decades. In making sure that everything I write or say about fundraising actually works, I use the criteria that either I have done it myself or seen it done in enough detail that I feel confident writing about it. If I haven't tried some of the techinques presented in this book myself, I have worked closely with groups that have.

Fundraising for Social Change was first published in 1988; since then it has sold 22,000 copies in three editions. Each time I rewrite and add to it, I am amazed at how much more I have learned and how many wonderful people I have learned from, or more often, learned with, as we worked together to figure out what fundraising plan would work best.

Some of the information in this book first appeared in article form in the *Grassroots Fundraising Journal,* a bi-monthly periodical that I have been publishing since 1981. The *Journal* is the best expression of my commitment to capturing and writing down the vast oral tradition that is grassroots fundraising.

I thank also two people who have made this book one of high quality both to read and to look at. The first is my dear friend, Nancy Adess, who has been my editor and production manager for all the years I have been writing. She has an extraordinary ability to make all concepts clearer and more accessible. The second is our designer, Cici Kinsman, who is that most rare combination in a graphic artist of a talented creative artist and an unfailingly patient and responsive listener as I add my many back-seat designing suggestions.

A very special thank you to the staff of Chardon Press, especially our finance manager, Nan Jessup, my assistant, Shelana deSilva, and our Web master, Taylor Root, for their good humor, hard work, and extraordinary competence.

Gary Delgado has given Chardon Press a home at the Applied Research Center and provided opportunity and encouragement for me during my whole career, for which he has my enduring thanks.

All the young people in my life, particularly my nieces, Emma and Alexanna Ashley-Roth, and my friends Sari and Molly Firestein-Bilick, remind me that successful fundraising is mostly about asking often and saying thank you.

My dog, Brooklyn, and my cat, Jack, couldn't care less about fundraising and won't feel the least bit flattered that their names are included here. They and all their animal colleagues remind me that while my work is important, it is not everything.

And, as always, my thanks to my life and business partner, Stephanie Roth, for all she has done for me and for our business, and for her constant commitment to working for justice.

Introduction

This is a how-to book. Its goal is to provide organizations that have budgets of less than $1 million (including much less than that) with the information they need to establish, maintain, and expand a successful community-based fundraising program. Building a broad base of individual donors gives organizations maximum freedom to pursue their mission. They can then use foundation, corporate, or government grants for special programs, start-up costs, technical assistance, capital or endowment projects, or other time-limited needs.

Organizations with small budgets, particularly those working for social change, need to keep in mind that the context in which their fundraising efforts take place is different from that of large organizations, such as universities, well-established museums, or multi-pronged social service agencies.

First, the name of your group is not a household word. And even when they hear about you, many people will not understand what you are trying to do. Many of those who do understand may disagree with you, particularly if you are trying to challenge the status quo. Even those in sympathy with your mission may think your aims are hopelessly naïve or idealistic; you may often be told to "face reality."

Second, you probably have little or no front money and not enough staff; therefore, you cannot afford to invest in large-scale fundraising strategies, such as large direct mail campaigns or fancy interactive Web sites. Without a cushion of money, you are either just holding your own financially or falling behind.

Third, your board of directors, volunteers, and staff are likely to be unfamiliar with fundraising strategies and may not be comfortable with the idea of asking for money.

For grassroots groups such as yours, traditional fundraising strategies need to be re-thought and translated into workable terms. This book does that. All of the strategies explained and recommended here have been successful for small groups. Not every strategy will work for every group, but the discussion of each strategy will allow you to decide which strategies will work for your group and how to expand the strategies you are already using.

Fundraising without planning, without a strong, committed group of volunteers to help, without a workable organizational structure, or without understanding the basic components of all fundraising plans is practically impossible. The appropriate staff, whether paid or unpaid, of every organization should read the first two sections of this book to learn the context for successful fundraising.

The next sections present detailed descriptions of how to carry out strategies to acquire, retain, and upgrade donors to your organization. These proceed from the most impersonal — direct mail appeals and special events — to the most personal — solicitation by telephone and in person. The book gives special attention to the difficulties most people have asking for money, and offers concrete ways to overcome these difficulties. Other types of strategies, such as starting a business, using the Internet, payroll deduction plans, and other income streams are explored. Finally, the book covers how to create a budget and a fundraising plan and the rudiments of setting up a fundraising office, keeping records, working with an executive director, and hiring fundraising staff or consultants. Special circumstances for fundraising are also discussed, such as raising money in rural communities or raising money for a coalition of groups.

If you find this book helpful, I encourage you to buy my other books and to subscribe to the *Grassroots Fundraising Journal,* a bimonthly publication that will help you keep up with fundraising strategies and developments in the field. I also encourage you to buy my training videotapes and use them with your board. All that helps me, and it will help you. (See the Bibliography for a complete listing.)

But ultimately, after you have read how to raise money and gone to workshops on how to do it, the only thing left is to do it. Like driving a car or learning to swim, all the theory and explanation will not help until you get behind the wheel or into the pool and try it for yourself.

Few people give money without being asked. Make this your motto: "Today somebody has to ask somebody for money."

Fundraising Framework

When I hand out the agenda for a fundraising workshop, participants are often surprised to see that the section on personal solicitation is in the afternoon. Many have said, "I came to learn how to identify prospects and ask for money, not how to create a case statement or run a board of directors." Successful fundraisers know, however, that fundraising doesn't start with asking for money; it starts with understanding how philanthropy works and what an organization needs to have in place before it can begin asking for money.

This first section starts with what, for me, are the two most important facts I ever learned about fundraising: The bulk of money given away to nonprofits comes from individuals, and the majority of people who give are not rich. The corollary to these facts is this: Fundraising starts with who you know, and you already know all the people you need to know to begin your fundraising efforts.

The section continues by describing what a group must have in place before it can begin asking anyone for money and finishes with a discussion of the group of people that are going to be most key to a successful fundraising effort — the board of directors.

A friend of mine who is now in her nineties once told me that she learned to drive in the countryside. When she drove into town for the first time, she realized she didn't know a lot of things about driving; she knew only how to start the car, stop it, and steer it in a forward direction. She did not know how to shift into reverse, how to do parallel parking, how to use a turn signal, or how to interpret the actions of other drivers. Driving on country roads and the roads that led from one field to another of her parents' farm had not required those skills.

Fundraising is a lot like this — you can know enough to get by in certain circumstances, but if you are serious about developing your skills in fundraising, you have to take time to learn a lot more or you will be limited in how far you can go. Those who want to take their organizations as far as they can go will read this section with great attention.

one

Philanthropy in America

The word *philanthropy* comes from two Greek words meaning "love of people." In modern times, this goodwill or humanitarianism is often expressed in donations of property, money, or volunteer time to worthy causes. Similarly, the word *charity* comes from a Latin word meaning "love" in the sense of unconditional loving-kindness, compassion, and seeking to do good. The roots of these words remind us of the fundamental reasons for the work of most nonprofit organizations.

The United States of America has the largest system of organized private philanthropy in the world. In this country, non-governmental organizations have been created — and funded through private sources — to provide services that countries with greater government commitment to social welfare provide directly and fund through taxation. If nonprofits in the United States were a single industry, they would rank as the nation's largest industry, accounting for more than 10% of the workforce, and about 5% of the Gross Domestic Product. As of 2000, more than 1,100,000 organizations have been recognized by the Internal Revenue Service as tax-exempt. Several million more small, grassroots organizations that are doing important charitable work are not registered with the government and have no formal tax status. These groups include organizations just getting started; organizations that use very little money, such as neighborhood block clubs; organizations that come together for a one-time purpose, such as cleaning up a vacant lot or protesting something; and those that don't wish to have a structural relationship with the state or federal government.

Because of the size and growing sophistication of the nonprofit sector, it has increasingly drawn the attention of the government, researchers, academics, and many members of the general public. Some agencies and organizations want to regulate how nonprofits function, while others believe that increased public awareness and voluntary compliance with accepted ethical standards of accounting, personnel, and fundraising practice will provide sufficient self-regulation. Nonprofit status is a public trust and tax exemption is, in effect, a public expense. Even if an organization has no formal tax status, if it seeks to raise money from the public it has the same moral duty as registered nonprofits to operate ethically, be truthful with donors, and provide the highest quality of services to clients.

The Foundation/Corporation Giving Myth

As with many endeavors that are critically important and use the resources of millions of people, it is not surprising that a number of misconceptions have grown up about philanthropy and charities.

The most serious misconception people have is that most of nonprofit funding comes from corporations and foundations. The truth is far different: most charitable dollars come from government programs (collectively known as "the public sector"). This fact holds true despite the extensive cutbacks in government funding of nonprofits that characterized the 1980s and early 1990s. Following government dollars, more money is given to nonprofit organizations by individuals than by any other source, including corporations and foundations combined. This book focuses almost entirely on how to raise money from that enormous market of individual donors.

The American Association of Fund Raising Counsel (AAFRC) publishes a report every year called *Giving USA* that identifies economic and social trends in American philanthropy. Every year since 1935, Counsel authors have calculated just how much money was given away to nonprofits and by whom. They have identified four sources of gifts from the private (non-governmental) sector: living individuals, bequests (a cash or other donation an individual arranges to be given to a charity upon their death), foundations, and corporations. Their research shows that the proportion of giving from each of these sources remains constant, varying from year to year by only two or three percentage points, with gifts from individuals (living or deceased) exceeding the rest by nine to one.

Another research and advocacy group, The Independent Sector, also studies trends in giving and volunteering in the United States and periodically publishes their findings in a book called, oddly enough, *Giving and Volunteering in the United States*. They note that 82% of the money given away by individuals is given by people living in families with incomes of less than $60,000. This is, of course, because families living on incomes of $60,000 and less comprise the majority of American families. Many studies have also shown that poor and working-class people tend to give away more money as a percentage of income than upper-middle-class or wealthy people, probably because the need is so much clearer to them.

In 1999, the latest year for which figures are available, giving from these sources totaled $190.16 billion.

SOURCES OF CONTRIBUTIONS

CONTRIBUTIONS FROM	AMOUNT (IN BILLIONS)	PERCENT OF TOTAL
Individuals	$143.71	75.6%
Foundations	$ 19.81	10.4%
Bequests	$ 15.61	8.2%
Corporations	$ 11.02	5.8%

Given these facts, an organization should have no trouble knowing where to go for money: individuals provide the vast bulk of support to nonprofits. Foundations and corporations, which have the false reputation of keeping charity alive, are over-rated as a source of funds and the help they can provide is often misunderstood. While foundation and corporate giving will always play a vital role in the nonprofit sector, the limitations of that role must be clearly understood.

Foundations

Foundations have relatively little money and that money is in very great demand. Many of the larger foundations report receiving one hundred proposals for every two they are able to fund. As more information about foundations is easily available, the demand is increasing. Guidebooks to foundations by state or by subject proliferate, as do databases to help potential grantees identify more and more sources. Many foundations now post their guidelines and annual reports on the World Wide Web. Some progressive foundations have adopted a standard grant application form, allowing grantees to submit exactly the same proposal for many different foundations. The very things that thus make foundations more accessible also make them inundated with requests.

While many nonprofits, especially new or small organizations, think foundation funding would be the answer to their money problems, in fact foundation funding is designed to be used only for short-term projects. These include the start-up of a new organization and its first few years of operation, special capital improvements, endowments (very rare), one-time projects such as conferences, or for help through a particularly rough period in the life of an organization for which it has a good excuse and a recovery plan.

If an organization has come to rely on foundation funding, decreasing reliance should be an important part of its financial planning. If an organization has never relied on foundation funding, it should plan not to, and not make the mistake common to many small organizations of seeking more foundation funding as the years pass rather than less.

Corporations

Corporations are different from foundations in a key way: unlike foundations, whose job is to give money away, corporations exist to make money. Giving money away is primarily an activity that a corporation hopes will directly or indirectly help it to make more money. In fact, only 11% of corporations give away any money at all, and the average amount these companies give away is 2% of their pre-tax profits, although they are allowed to give up to 10% of those profits. Corporations generally give money to the following types of organizations or activities:

- Organizations that improve the life of the community where their employees live (symphonies, parks, museums, libraries)

- Groups that help their employees be more productive by addressing common employee problems (alcohol and drug rehabilitation, domestic violence)

- Organizations that provide volunteer opportunities for employees, or to which employees make donations

- Research that will help the company invent products or market existing products (various departments in universities get much of their funding for such research from corporations)

- Education programs for young people to ensure an adequate workforce for the company in the future (literacy programs, innovative schools, scholarships)

More frequent and generous is corporate giving to match employee donations. While many corporations have had matching programs for some time, the scale of today's matching programs has come to be called "employee-driven philanthropy."

Corporations also make valuable donations besides money, such as expertise (loaning a worker to help a nonprofit with accounting, marketing, personnel), space (free use of conference or meeting rooms), printing, furniture, office equipment (computers, fax machines, copy machines), building materials, and so on.

The past couple of decades have seen many corporations joining with charities in "cause-related marketing" efforts, in which a corporation donates a certain percentage of its profits or a certain amount of each sale to its partner charity. The nonprofit group and the corporation advertise the arrangement and encourage people in choosing among similar products to choose the one that also benefits the charity. Variations on this theme include corporations that offer to give a percentage of profits to a certain kind of organization (environmental, progressive, feminist) or who allow customers to nominate groups that should receive corporate funding. Cause-related marketing has benefited many organizations by allowing shoppers to feel that their shopping can also serve a charitable purpose, but it does not serve to build a donor base because the loyalty of the donor is not primarily to the organization and the motive of the donor is not solely to give to the organization, but also to buy this product.

Many organizations using this book will not be able to get corporate funding because their work is too controversial; and many others will not seek corporate funding because they wish to avoid appearing to endorse a corporate product or a particular corporation's way of doing business.

The Power of Individual Giving

A broad base of individual donors provides the only reliable source of funding for a nonprofit year in and year out, and the growth of individual donations to an organization is critical to its growth and self-sufficiency. Further, relying on a broad base of individuals for support increases an organization's ability to be self-determining: it does not need to determine program priorities based on what foundations, corporations, or government agencies will fund.

Recipients of Charitable Giving

To really understand private-sector giving, we must look at not only who gives this money, but also who receives it. Again, with only a few percentage points of variation from year to year, AAFRC's recordkeeping has demonstrated a consistent pattern of giving. Nearly half of all the money given away in America goes to religious organizations, with education a distant second, followed by health, human services, the arts, and four other categories that receive small percentages of giving.

1999 USES OF CONTRIBUTIONS

CONTRIBUTIONS TO	AMOUNT (IN BILLIONS)	PERCENT OF TOTAL
Religion	$81.73	43.0%
Education	$27.46	14.4%
Health	$17.95	9.4%
Human Services	$17.36	9.1%
Gifts to Foundations	$15.11	7.9%
Arts, Culture	$11.07	5.8%
Public/Society Benefit	$10.94	5.8%
Environment	$ 5.83	3.1%
International Affairs	$ 2.65	1.4%

(Source: *Giving USA*, 2000)

Giving to Religion

Religion as a category receives almost half of every charitable dollar, yet only a small percentage of giving to religion is from foundations and virtually none of it is from corporations. Because of the constitutional separation of church and state, religious activity receives no government funding either, although with religious organizations filling in many of the social services previously provided by government agencies, religious groups do sometimes receive government contracts for specific work. The vast majority of funding that religious organizations receive is from their own members. We can learn a lot by examining what makes fundraising for religious institutions so successful.

At first glance, many people think that religious institutions receive so much money because of their theology: the reward of heaven, the blessing of giving, the threat of eternal damnation. While these may play a role in some people's giving, it is clear that in the wide variety of religious expression, these motives are not enough. Many religious traditions do not believe in any form of eternal life; some don't even believe in God. Even in traditions that have some of these beliefs, it is trivializing of mature adults to think that their behavior is based simply on a desire for rewards or a fear of punishment.

So, why do religious organizations receive almost half of private-sector dollars? While religious institutions offer ideas and commitments that are of great value, there are two reasons they get money: they make up half of all nonprofits and — and this is key to understanding successful fundraising — they ask for it.

Let's take as an example a Protestant or Catholic church. (If you come out of a different religious tradition, compare your own tradition to what follows.) Here is how they raise money:

- They ask every time worshippers are assembled, which is at least once a week.

- They make it easy to give: a basket is passed to each person in the service and all gifts are acceptable, from loose change to large checks. Everyone, whether out-of-town visitor, occasional churchgoer, or loyal and generous congregant, is given the same opportunity to give. The ushers are not concerned about offending someone by asking. They would never say, "Don't pass the basket to Phyllis Frontpew — she just bought the new carpet," or "Skip over Joe — he just lost his job."

- They make giving easy even if you are not a regular congregant. Once a year, they will have some kind of stewardship drive or all-member canvass and someone will come to your house and ask you how much you will be pledging this year. You can pay your pledge by the week, month, or quarter or give a one-time gift. The option of pledging and paying over time allows people to give a great deal more over the course of a year than most could in a single lump sum.

- They provide a variety of programs to which you can give as you desire. If you are particularly interested in the youth program you can give to that; you can buy flowers for the altar, support the music program, or help fund overseas missions. Many churches have scholarships, homeless shelters, food banks, or other social programs. And of course, if you are a "bricks and mortar" person, you can contribute to any number of capital improvements — new hymnals, a new window, a better organ, or a whole new sanctuary.

Finally, religious institutions approach fundraising with the attitude that they are doing you as much of a favor to ask as you will be doing them to give; in other words, they recognize that fundraising allows an exchange to happen between a person who wants to see a certain kind of work get done and an institution that can do that work. If one of your values and beliefs is that a house of worship is important, then in order for that institution to exist, you will need to help pay for it. Giving money allows you to express your desire and commitment to be part of a faith community and allows your commitment to be realized.

All organizations should institute the diversity of fundraising that characterizes most religious institutions. In the chapters that follow, I will show you how.

two

Principles of Fundraising

If one were to ask, "What is the purpose of fundraising?" many people would think, "What a stupid question," and would answer, "To raise money." But, in fact, the only way you can raise money year after year is by developing a broad base of individual donors who feel very loyal to your organization. The purpose of fundraising, then, is to build relationships — or more simply put, instead of raising money, the purpose of fundraising is to raise donors.

Focusing on building a donor base rather than on simply raising money means that sometimes you will undertake a fundraising strategy that does not raise money in the first year, such as direct mail, or for several years, such as planned giving. It means that you will relate to your donors as individual human beings rather than as ATM machines that you engage when you want money but ignore otherwise. It means you will plan for both the short term and the long term and look at the results of any fundraising strategy for both the next month and the next few years.

Diversifying Sources

Focusing on raising donors means that an organization systematically diversifies its sources of funding, builds the number of people helping raise money, and diversifies their skills. The need for diversity is not a new lesson. People with only one skill have a more difficult time finding employment than those with a variety of skills. Investors put their money in a variety of financial instruments rather than in just one kind of stock. In the 1980s and early 1990s, thousands of nonprofits were forced to severely curtail their services or close their doors because the government funding they were so heavily reliant on ceased to be available.

Yet many organizations continue to look for the ideal special event that will fund their entire budget, or they search for one person, foundation, or corporation to give most of the money they need, or they try to hire the perfect fundraiser who will bring in all their income without anyone's help. These groups reason that if they could use one fundraising strategy that was absolutely certain and tried-and-true, their money worries would be over. Unfortunately, no fundraising strategy or person fits that description. In fact, only if it maintains a diversity of sources will an organization survive for the long term.

An organization could lose 30% of its funding and probably survive, though it would be difficult, but the loss of more than 30% of funding would be catastrophic for all but the biggest organizations. That's why organizations should not receive more than 30% of their funding from any one source for more than one or two years. This guideline means that while you could have more than 30% of income coming from membership (and many groups do), you cannot have one member providing 30% of this money. (The IRS recognizes this principle with its "one-third rule," which states that an organization with one-third or more of its total income from one person, foundation, or corporation for more than three years does not meet the test of a public charity and risks losing its 501(c)(3) status. This rule underscores that public charities are to be supported by a broad spectrum of the public and that tax exemption is not appropriate for hobbies or forums for any one person or corporate entity.)

There is no set number of sources that constitutes healthy diversity. Much will depend on the size of your budget, your location, and your work. However, the more people who give you money, and the more ways you have of raising money, the better.

Why People Give

Approximately seven out of ten adults regularly make donations to nonprofits. Of those, most support between five and eleven organizations, giving away a little more than 2% of their personal income. All fundraising efforts should go toward trying to become one of the groups that these givers give to, rather than trying to become the recipient of the first charitable donation of a previous non-giver. People who give money are not denying themselves food or shoes for their children; these people are dedicated givers, and your group's job is to become one of those they give to. To do that you must carefully examine what makes a person a giver.

Appealing to Self-Interest

There are many reasons that people give to nonprofit organizations. The most common reasons vary from consumerism to tradition to deeply held beliefs. Some people give because they like the newsletter or because they receive a free tote bag, bumper sticker, or some other tangible item. Some give to a certain group because everyone in their social circle gives to that group or because it is a family tradition. Some give because it is the only way to get something the organization offers (classes, theater seats, access to a swimming pool).

At a more altruistic level, there are more reasons for giving. People give because they care about the issue, they believe in the group, and they think the group's analysis of a problem and vision of a solution are correct. Often people give because they or someone they know was once in the position of the people the group serves (alcoholics, abused women or children, unemployed, homeless) or because they are thankful that neither they nor anyone they know is in that position.

Sometimes people give because they feel guilty about how much they have or what they have done in their own life, or to feel more assured of salvation and eternal life.

People give because the group expresses their own ideals and enables them to reinforce their image of themselves as a principled person — for example, feminist, environmentalist, pacifist, equal rights advocate, good parents, concerned citizen, or whatever image is important to them. Through their giving, they can say in truth, "I am a caring person," "I want to make a difference," "I am helping others."

Most often people give because they are asked, and being asked reminds them what they care about. When they are asked personally by a friend or someone they admire, in addition to feeling good about giving to the organization, they get to show themselves as principled and generous people to someone whose opinion they value.

Although these motivations for giving are what impel most people to give, most nonprofit organizations appeal to two other motives that are not very persuasive. These are "We need the money" and "Your gift is tax deductible." Neither of these reasons distinguishes your organization from all the others. All nonprofit organizations claim to need money, and most of them do. The fact that the gift is tax deductible is a nice touch, but gifts to several hundred thousand other nonprofits are tax deductible too. Neither need nor tax advantage makes your organization special.

The 70% of Americans who give away money pay nonprofits to do work that can only be accomplished by group effort. There is very little one person can do about racism or gay bashing or sexual assault. Only as part of an organization can an individual make a difference in these or any other pressing social problems.

Certainly one person cannot be a theater or a museum or an alternative school. Donors need the organization as much as the organization needs them, and the money is given in exchange for work performed. In a very important way, donations are really fees for service.

Anyone Can Do It

Finally, and most important for small organizations, it is critical to understand that fundraising is easy to learn. In the past 20 years, there has been an increasing emphasis on fundraising as a "discipline." Colleges and universities now offer courses on various aspects of fundraising, sometimes as part of degree programs in nonprofit management, and professional organizations offer certification programs in fundraising. There are more and more people who are professional fundraisers. All of these things are important and contribute to the health and well-being of the nonprofit sector. But a course, a degree, or certification is not required for a person to be good at fundraising and they will never take the place of the only three things you really need to be a fundraiser: simple common sense, a commitment to a cause, and a basic affection for people.

No one says at the age of 12, "When I grow up, I want to be in fundraising." Instead, a person is drawn to an idea or cause and an organization working on that issue. The organization needs money in order to pursue the cause, so they decide to help with fundraising even though it is not their first choice of how to be involved and even though they have at first found the idea slightly distasteful or a little frightening. With time and experience, many people find that fundraising is not as difficult as they had imagined and they may even begin to like it. They realize that people feel good about themselves when they give money to a cause they believe in, and that to ask someone for money actually means to give that person an opportunity to express traditions or beliefs that are important to them.

People asked to raise money often confuse the process of giving money and the process of asking for it. In fact, there is a significant difference between the two. People feel good about giving money, but rarely do people feel good when they ask for money until they get used to it. People asking for money for their cause tend to project their own feelings of discomfort in asking onto the potential donor, and then describe the donor in words such as these: "I really embarrassed that person when I asked him," or, "I could tell she wanted to leave the room when I asked her," or, "They were so upset that they just looked at each other and finally said yes, but I know they wanted to say no." These descriptions of what supposedly happened to the donor (embarrassed, humiliated, upset) are more likely to be descriptions of what was happening to the asker. The potential donor was more than likely flattered, pleased to be included, thinking about what amount he or she could give, or wondering if the asker was feeling all right.

The feelings of discomfort in asking for money are normal, and in Chapter 9, Personal Solicitation, we will talk about them and how to deal with them. For now, simply be clear that asking and giving are two very different experiences, even when they happen in the same conversation. When people are recruited to ask for money, they must reflect on what they like about giving, not on what they hate about asking.

When an organization has a diversity of ways to raise money, it can use the talents and abilities of all the people in the group to help with fundraising. As volunteers and board members learn more about fundraising and experience success, they will be willing to learn new strategies and they will begin to like asking for money. Further, an organization that has only one or two people raising its money is not much better off than an organization that has only one or two sources of money. Many small organizations have suffered more from having too few people doing the fundraising than from having too few sources of funds. In the chapters that follow, I discuss identifying appropriate strategies and building a team of volunteer fundraisers.

three

Matching Fundraising Strategies with Financial Needs

Organizations have three financial needs: the money they need to operate every year, called "annual needs"; the money they need to improve their building or upgrade their capacity to do their work, called "capital needs"; and a permanent income stream to ensure financial stability and assist long-term planning, the source of which is called an "endowment."

Annual Needs

The vast majority of time in grassroots organizations is spent raising money for the program needs of the current year. This kind of fundraising is often referred to as the "annual fund" or the "annual drive" or, to cover all tracks, the "annual fund drive." The annual fund drive uses several strategies, such as direct mail, special events, phoning, and personal visits. The purpose of the drive is to get donors to give over and over.

Because the overall purpose of fundraising is to build a base of donors who give you money every year, it is helpful to analyze how a person becomes a donor to an organization and how, ideally, that person increases in loyalty to the group and expresses that increased loyalty with a steady increase in giving.

A person goes through three phases in moving from not giving at all to a particular group to giving regularly several times a year. The first phase starts when a person hears or reads about a group that they like or believe in and decides on the spur of the moment to make a donation. That first gift is called an "impulse" gift. Even if an impulse gift is fairly large, it will not reflect what the donor could really afford, and it generally reflects little knowledge of and a shallow commitment to the organization. After the donor is thanked for that gift, he or she will be asked for another gift for a different aspect of the organization's work (see Chapter 6, Using Direct Mail, for how often to ask and what to ask for). We call people who give over and over for more than two years "habitual" donors. These people see themselves as part of the organization, even though probably not a big part. Some habitual donors have a bigger commitment to the organization than their gift reflects and have the capacity to make a bigger gift. Identifying and asking these people to increase their gift form the basis of a major donor program. Once a donor is giving a larger gift than he or she gives to most other groups, this donor is called a "thoughtful" donor. Instead of just giving what they are in the habit of giving, they must think about what they can afford and what a large gift to a group will mean for their other giving. The process of moving people from non-donor to donor, habitual donor, and thoughtful donor is the main focus in planning the annual fund. Every year, an organization has to recruit a certain number of new donors, upgrade a certain number of regular donors into major donors, and give all their donors three or four chances to give extra gifts.

A group can expect to retain about two-thirds of their individual donors every year, with the greatest proportion of their one-third loss being people who give once and not again. In planning fundraising strategies, then, you need to have a few strategies for the sole purpose of replacing lost donors. Groups that lose less than one-third of their donor base do not have enough donors. Groups that lose more are not doing enough to keep their donors, and in the case of most grassroots organizations, it usually means they are not asking donors for money often enough. You also need to have a few strategies designed to cultivate a group of habitual donors — people you can turn to every year, and sometimes several times a year, for gifts.

And, finally, you need to have some strategies to get current donors to give more money — these are called upgrading strategies. Sections Two and Three discuss a wide variety of these strategies and their uses.

Capital Needs

In addition to planning how much money your organization needs each year and what strategies will be used to raise that money, organizations occasionally need to raise extra money for capital improvements. Capital needs can range from new computers to the cost of buying and refurbishing an entire building. Most donors who give capital gifts have usually given thoughtfully to an annual fund. They know your organization, they believe in your cause, and they have the resources to help you with a special gift. These resources could be a computer they are not using, land they donate for a building, or a large gift to build the building. These gifts are given only a few times in a donor's lifetime, and are almost always requested in person (see Chapter 14, Capital Campaigns).

Endowment

An endowment is a glorified savings account in which an organization invests money, and uses the interest from that investment to augment its annual budget; the invested amount, or principal, is not spent. Endowment funds are raised in many ways, but most often through planned gifts such as bequests. A gift from a person's estate is in some ways the most thoughtful gift of all and usually reflects a deep and abiding commitment to an organization. It also reflects the donor's belief that the organization will continue to exist and do important work long after the donor is dead. The idea of making an endowment gift can be introduced to donors in a variety of ways, but generally a person making such a gift has a personal relationship with the organization (see Chapter 15, Planned Giving).

Three Goals for Every Donor

An organization has three goals for every donor. The first goal is for that person to become a thoughtful donor — to give the biggest gift he or she can afford on a yearly basis. The source for an annual gift is the donor's annual income. The second goal is for as many donors as possible to give capital or special gifts. These do not have to be connected to capital improvements, but are gifts that are unusual in some way and are only given a few times (or possibly only once) during the donor's lifetime. Capital gifts are usually given from the donor's assets such as savings, inheritance, or property. A donor cannot afford to give assets every year and so will only give these gifts for special purposes. The third goal is for every donor to remember the organization in their will or to make some kind of arrangement benefiting the organization from their estate. An estate gift is arranged during the donor's lifetime but wholly received by the organization upon the donor's death. Obviously, these gifts are made only once.

Most small organizations will do well if they can plan a broad range of strategies to acquire, maintain, and upgrade annual gifts, but over time organizations need to think about capital and endowment gifts and learn to use fundraising strategies that will encourage such gifts. Grassroots organizations do receive bequests and gifts of property, art, appreciated stock, and the like. Only by asking will you find out what your donors might be willing and able to do for your group.

MATCHING ORGANIZATIONAL NEEDS TO DONOR GIVING

ORGANIZATION'S NEEDS	DONOR HELPS USING
Annual	Yearly income
Capital	Assets (savings, property, stocks)
Endowment	Estate

THE STORY OF GINA GENEROUS

To understand how a person might move from not giving at all to becoming a thoughtful donor and then to leaving the organization a bequest, consider the following story.

Gina Generous comes home from work tired and frustrated. It's been a long day. She feeds her cats, kicks her shoes off, and sits down to leaf through her mail. Most of it she characterizes as "junk" and throws away, but one piece of direct mail catches her eye. It's not fancy or even very well designed, but it is from a shelter for homeless women and Gina generally supports women's causes. She opens the letter, reads it quickly, and decides to send a small gift. As she waits for her dinner to cook, she writes out a check for $15 and puts it in the return envelope that came with the appeal. She mails it the next day, then soon forgets about the group.

This impulse gift does not represent Gina's true giving ability or say very much about her commitment to that group. Now the homeless shelter must try to move Gina to the next level, that of a habitual donor, and they do.

In a few days Gina again comes home tired, and again feeds her cats and reads her mail. In it, she has received a short personal thank-you note from the shelter. "Wow. How nice," she thinks. She again feels good about her gift and the name of the group is more firmly planted in her mind.

Over the next few months, Gina receives a copy of the shelter's newsletter. One day she drives by the shelter. About three months later, Gina receives another letter from the shelter. This letter thanks her again for her previous gift and asks if she can make a special, extra gift to help buy some playground equipment for the children of the women at the shelter. Gina is touched by the request and sends $25. Again, she is thanked. Three months later, she is asked again for a special, extra gift — this one to help defray the costs of a job training program that will partially be funded by the city. While Gina thinks this is important, she has also had to replace two tires on her car, so sends nothing. Three months after this — now nine months since her first gift — she is invited to an open house at the shelter. She attends and is given a tour of the facility and meets the director and some board members. Everyone who attends the open house is asked to leave a check in a jar by the door if possible. Gina gives another $15.

By now, Gina has moved from being an impulse donor to being a habitual donor to the shelter. Whenever they ask, she gives unless she really can't afford to. She feels she is a part of this organization and may even mention it to friends from time to time.

After a year or two of giving small gifts two or three times a year, either by mail or at a special event, Gina receives a personal letter signed by a board member asking her to consider upgrading her gift to $250. The letter thanks her for her past support, talks again about how important the shelter is, and asks her not to make a decision until the board member calls her. Gina now has to think about the organization: How important is it to her? Can she afford it? Does she care enough to send $250 to this group? What will she want to find out from the board member to help make her decision?

Whatever her decision, Gina has moved to the next level of donor, which is a thoughtful donor. She may thoughtfully decide to give $250, or she may decide to give $100, or she may continue to give small gifts a few times a year, but she has had to think about her giving. She gives $250.

Over the course of the two years, Gina's relationship to the shelter went from impersonal giving by mail to a little more personal (attending events) to very personal (being solicited by a member of the board).

Over the next few years, Gina is asked to give again and to give more. After five years of being a regular donor to the shelter, she is giving $500 a year. That year, the shelter decides to buy a new building. The building will cost $500,000 and will become a model shelter, allowing them to conduct their many programs on-site. They receive some state and federal funding for the purchase and $75,000 from a foundation; they must raise $100,000 from individuals. They launch a capital campaign to ask each of their donors for a capital gift in addition to their annual gift. Gina is asked to serve on the capital campaign committee because she has given so regularly and steadily for five years. She comes to events and is acquainted with several board members. Gina agrees to serve and decides to give $5,000 that she inherited from an aunt. She is happy to find a meaningful way to use this money that she did not expect to receive.

After the campaign is completed, Gina becomes a regular volunteer at the shelter and later serves on the board. When the shelter institutes a planned giving program, Gina changes her will so that the shelter is the beneficiary of the bulk of her estate.

The progression to this stage of highly committed donor is natural, and feels good to Gina, but it is the result of careful planning on the part of the shelter and its commitment to developing relationships with donors.

Three Types of Strategies

Because all strategies are directed toward building relationships with funding sources — whether these sources are individuals, as this book stresses, or foundations, corporations, or government — it is important to understand the types of strategies that create or improve relationships with donors. There are three broad categories of strategies: acquisition, retention, and upgrading. They directly relate to the cycles that donors follow: giving impulsively, giving habitually, and giving thoughtfully.

1. Acquisition strategies. The main purpose of these strategies is to get people who have not given to your group before to give for the first time. Direct mail is probably the most common acquisition strategy. Acquisition strategies seek impulse donors, and the income from them is generally used for the organization's annual fund.

2. Retention strategies. These strategies seek to get donors to give a second time, a third time, and so on, until they are donors of habit. The income from retention strategies is also used for annual needs.

3. Upgrading strategies. These strategies aim to get donors to give more than they have given previously — to give a bigger gift regularly, and later to give gifts of assets and a gift of their estate. Upgrading is done almost entirely through personal solicitation, although it can be augmented by mail or phone contact or through certain special events. Upgrading strategies seek to move habitual donors to being thoughtful donors. The income from thoughtful donors is used for annual, capital, and endowment needs, depending on the nature of the gift or the campaign for which the gift was sought.

As you create a fundraising plan, note beside each strategy you intend to use whether you are using it for acquiring, retaining, or upgrading donors, and make sure it is the best strategy for that purpose.

You Can't Save Time

For small organizations, the ultimate reason to be thoughtful about fundraising strategies is to work smarter, not harder. The group in the house party example raised 400% more money in their second year of house parties by spending a little more time thinking about the strategy more thoroughly. There is a Buddhist saying, "We have so little time that we must proceed very slowly." This applies to fundraising and especially to the fundraising programs of small organizations with tight budgets, which have little room for errors that result from carelessness and lack of thought.

It is clear to me from years of working with nonprofit organizations that you can never save time. You can put time in on the front end, planning, thinking things through, and doing things right, or you can "save time" on the front end, only to have to put it in later, clearing up the mess, handling disgruntled donors, and having to do more fundraising because what you have done did not raise the money you need. This book will help you be a front-end time user!

HOW ONE ORGANIZATION LEARNS
TO USE A STRATEGY CORRECTLY

Eastside Senior Advocacy decides to hold some house parties to raise money. Seven board members will invite friends to their homes and ask them for money for the group. The remaining five board members who don't want to have a party at their house will help with invitations, food, clean-up, and so on.

No thought is given to the purpose of these parties beyond the goal of raising money. No one thinks about whether these parties should be used for acquiring, keeping, or upgrading donors. Consequently, each board member has a hodgepodge of people at the event — some are donors, some never heard of the group but came because a friend asked them, and some came because they are neighbors and it looked like there would be free food. Many people are invited to more than one house party because there is no attempt to sort lists ahead of time and many of these board members travel in the same circles.

The parties make about $6,000, so they are not a waste, but some donors complain about being invited to so many events and many non-donors come to the parties but do not make a gift.

The following year, the organization decides to use the same strategy but to segment the parties and be more thoughtful in their fundraising approach. First, they compile a master list of everyone who is going to be invited to ensure that no one is invited to more than one party, unless that person would like to go to more than one party or would give at more than one party. Then they designate some parties as being only for people who have not given before, with a sprinkling of current donors to encourage the non-donors to give.

One board member charges people $25 to come to his party so that every person who is there will have made a donation, and he does not do another pitch at the party. Another feels that her friends will give more if she gives a pitch at the party and she aims for first gifts of $50 to $100 from most of the guests. One board member with a particularly fancy house has an elegant party for current donors; this party is used specifically as an upgrade strategy. The donors who are invited are capable of giving more than they currently do. They are introduced to members of the board and given an opportunity to discuss a political issue related to this group and make recommendations for action. The party is limited to 15 people; in a follow-up solicitation after the party, each person is asked for $500.

By determining which parties are for which purpose, the organization now increases its earnings from these parties by 400% to $24,000, acquires 40 new donors, upgrades 15 donors, and does not receive any complaints. As an unexpected side benefit, three donors offer to give their own house parties.

four

Making a Case for Your Organization

The previous two chapters discussed the framework for fundraising, the logic of the fundraising process, and the fact that an organization will ultimately be supported not so much by money itself, but by relationships with individuals who give money because of their increasing commitment to the group. This chapter presents the first step in successful fundraising — creating a case statement.

Before you can begin to raise money, your organization must state clearly why it exists and what it does. This is done in a written document that describes in some detail the need an organization was set up to meet, the way the organization will meet that need, and the capacity of the organization to do so. This document is called a "case statement." It is an internal document for use by staff, board, and key volunteers. Although it will be too long and cumbersome for use in approaching the general public, parts of it will be used in brochures, proposals, direct mail letters, and the like. Everyone close to the organization will agree with the information presented in the case statement and nothing that is produced by the organization will contradict it.

THE CONTENTS OF THE CASE STATEMENT

The case statement includes the following elements:

- **A statement of mission** that tells the world why the group exists
- **A description of goals** that tells what the organization hopes to accomplish

over the long term — in other words, what the organization intends to do about why it exists

- **A list of specific, measurable, and time-limited objectives** that tells how the goals will be met
- **A summary of the organization's history** that shows that the organization is competent and can accomplish its goals
- **A description of the structure of the organization** discussing board and staff roles and what kinds of people are involved in the group (such as clients, organizers, teachers)
- **A fundraising plan**
- **A financial statement** for the previous fiscal year and a **budget** for the current fiscal year.

Having this information in one document, with key people in the organization having copies, saves a great deal of time and helps guarantee that information and philosophies that are presented by board members, staff, or volunteers in their personal fundraising letters, in speeches, or in conversations with funders or donors are consistent. Further, it reminds people why they are raising money — to do the important work of the organization. A good case statement rallies people to the cause and reinvigorates staff and volunteers. Parts of the case statement, such as objectives and budgets, change every year. The entire document should be reviewed at least annually to ensure that everyone is still in agreement with its premises and that the words used still accurately describe what the organization is doing. Many organizations open their board meetings with a recitation of the mission statement and goals, a practice that they find helps keep the meeting on track and focused.

Here is an explanation of each of the components of the case statement.

The Mission Statement

The statement of mission, sometimes called the "Statement of Purpose" or the "Preamble to the Principles of Unity," answers the questions, "Why does your organization exist?" or "What is your basic premise?" or "What is the one thing that unites everything you do?" People in an organization will often claim, "We know why we exist," and then describe their programs, but it may not be clear to a listener that the programs meet any particular need or that there is a problem to be solved. For example, an organization that buys run-down or abandoned apartment buildings and then fixes up and rents each unit well below market rates to elderly poor people has this mission statement: "We believe decent, affordable housing is a right and not a privilege, yet thousands of seniors have inadequate or substandard housing, and an increasing number have no homes at all. Housing for Seniors seeks to rectify this problem." At this time, their goal is to buy buildings and convert them. However, their mission statement allows them to have a wide variety of goals, such as advocating with the city to provide housing, helping seniors stay in their homes, educating the public about the housing shortage, or providing loans to seniors for housing. They intend to pursue all these goals as they grow, and they will not need to change their mission statement as the reach of their work expands.

An education organization that primarily teaches economic literacy has this lofty mission: "Authentic human freedom begins with every person living free of economic compulsion. Understanding how economic forces work and how they can be changed is fundamental to this freedom." Their goals include teaching people how unsafe workplaces, wage discrimination, toxic dumping, substandard housing, and poverty itself are not necessary for an economy to be healthy and how society could be restructured to eliminate these injustices.

A mission statement should be only one or two sentences long, and its purpose is to attract someone's attention by giving a passionate and global sense of why the organization was founded.

Keep in mind that when you talk or write to someone about your organization, they, like you, have a lot on their mind. Your group and its needs are not foremost, at least at the beginning of a conversation. Further, we live in a world of constant messages — advertising, warnings, directions, prompts, signals. Study after study in publications such as *American Demographics* and *Advertising Age* show that people living in urban areas who drive to work, listen to the radio, and watch TV will be exposed to 2,000 messages in a day! Our conscious mind doesn't even take in most of these. We are constantly screening and filtering messages. Your mission statement is one of those messages. In order to be noticed, it has to be brief, compelling, and intriguing. It has to make a person with a lot on their mind stop thinking about all their other cares and focus on your group.

In fact, a good mission statement does only two things: It is a summary of the basic belief of the organization and the people in the organization, and it makes the person hearing or reading it want to ask for more information ("Well, that's very nice, but how are you going to accomplish that mission?"). This question allows the organization to describe its goals.

A hint about writing a mission statement: Missions often start with "Because" or "Whereas" or with a noun, "People," "Rights," "The future." Avoid using any infinitive verbs such as "to do," "to provide," "to help." Infinitive language is goal language.

Goals

Goal statements tell what your organization is going to do about the problem and indicate the organization's philosophy, which may be expanded in the section on history. The goals are what really distinguish one organization from another, since organizations may have similar missions but very different agendas. For example, two organizations whose missions concern the health of children have opposite goals. Their mission statements are remarkably similar: "We believe that whatever promotes children's health and well-being is the best public policy," and "We believe the health of our children should be the highest priority."

The first mission statement belongs to a group that documents the large number of children who are not immunized, particularly poor children and children of undocumented workers. Despite the fact that immunization is free in their state, some parents are afraid to take their children for inoculations because one clinic had been raided by the INS; other parents do not understand the immunization process. This group works to have inoculations administered in schools, houses of worship, and in a mobile van that travels to migrant communities. They feel this will ensure that all children are immunized. They believed that immigration status should not be questioned in the context of immunizing children.

The other group was organized by a woman whose child was brain damaged as a result of a reaction to an immunization (this happens in about 1 out of 20,000 cases). She organized a group opposed to all immunization, saying that diseases such as diphtheria, typhoid, or polio are so rare in the United States that the risk from immunization is higher than the risk of contracting the disease.

Two organizations with the same concern about children's health, with many goodhearted and thoughtful people working for them, and with opposite goals.

Goal statements almost always start with infinitives: to provide, to ensure, to monitor, to educate. For example, "To ensure that old-growth forests in Humboldt County are protected forever from logging," or, "To teach conflict resolution skills to all elementary school children in Logan County," or, "To find a cure for breast cancer."

Objectives

Objectives are specific, measurable, verifiable, easy-to-evaluate, and time-limited statements of how the group intends to accomplish its goals. Goals last as long as they need to, but objectives last for one year at the most. Objectives are evaluated yearly or in whatever time frame is specified in the objective. For example, here is an objective from the economic literacy group: "We will teach ten weekend courses aimed at teenagers. Two courses will be in Spanish, one in Cantonese, and seven in English. Each course will have a minimum attendance of 15 and maximum of 25.

A pre-test and post-test will be given to document learning and the curriculum will be modified throughout the year as needed."

History

The history section summarizes when the group was formed and by whom, and relates the group's major program accomplishments, including any major program changes. In describing your accomplished objectives, you have the chance to provide further documentation of the need your group was set up to meet. The more specific your objectives are, the more dramatic your history will be.

Two examples: "In 1993, Ourtown was shocked by an outbreak of smallpox. Ten children developed the disease and three died. This is when we discovered that children can be admitted to school without proof of immunization. Since then, Children's Health First has immunized 4,000 children in and around Ourtown and provided ten in-service trainings each year for educators and parents on the importance of immunization." Or, "Homes for Seniors originally focused on providing living accommodations for homeless seniors until we discovered that hundreds of seniors live in substandard housing, often without electricity or running water. Every year since our founding in 1990, we have refurbished or upgraded 20 to 30 housing units that were already inhabited and are continually expanding our programs to upgrade substandard housing." The groups can then go on to describe their work in more detail.

There are no set rules for the length of the historical piece. Again, common sense would dictate that you strike a balance between telling the whole story and risking boredom from too many details.

Structure

The structure shows that the way a group is organized is consistent with its overall mission. This section discusses staffing and board size, composition and governance. Some examples: "We have four staff who work collectively," or, "Our board of 11 members is entirely composed of clients and former clients so that all decisions about the organization are made by people most knowledgeable and most affected by them."

This section should be long enough to explain a complicated or non-traditional structure, but brief if the organizational structure is fairly straightforward. The way an organization is structured is a key to its accountability. For example, someone reading about an organization that claims it is committed to full participation of all members of a multi-racial community but has only white people on its board might question the organization's understanding of what community is. An organization that claims to organize in low-income communities but whose structure consists of a board of well-paid professionals, with no one from the communities the organization serves, raises questions about the organization's philosophy of power.

More and more, donors request information on structural issues to help determine if the group understands the implications of its mission and goals. This section can also include brief biographical sketches of board members, resumes of staff, and numbers of members, volunteers, and chapters, if applicable.

Fundraising Plan

The fundraising plan shows whether the organization has a diversity of funding sources and an understanding of the fundraising process. The fundraising plan shows all the sources of income and describes in a narrative fashion how this income will be raised or how these financial goals will be reached. Like the section on structure, the fundraising plan will show whether the organization is consistent with its mission. For example, an environmental organization primarily supported by oil or timber corporations or an organization working in the poverty pockets of an inner city with only major donor fundraising strategies both raise questions about how their financing can be consistent with their mission.

Financial Statement and Budget

A financial statement provides proof that the organization spends money wisely and monitors its spending — both in total amount by category. The financial statement consists of an annual report and an audited financial report, if available, or a balance sheet. The budget is an estimate of expenses and income for the current fiscal year and should include a description of how finances are monitored, such as "The finance committee of the board reviews financial reports monthly, and the full board reviews such reports quarterly."

ELEMENTS OF THE CASE STATEMENT

SECTION ON	ESTABLISHES
Mission	Why the organization exists
Goals	What it will do about why it exists
Objectives	How it will accomplish the goals
History	A track record, showing which objectives have been accomplished already
Structure	Consistency of composition and governance with regard to the goals
Fundraising plan, financial statement, and budget	That the organization intends to exist into the future and is planning and managing its finances appropriately; also shows that salaries, benefits, rent, and other costs are consistent with the mission

DEVELOPING THE CASE STATEMENT

A case statement is usually developed by a small committee, but the board, staff, and key volunteers must all agree on its contents, particularly the statement of mission and the group's future plans. If the people who must carry out the plans don't like them or don't believe they are possible, they will not do good work for the group. Therefore, it is worth spending a good amount of time on developing the case statement. Hurrying a statement of mission or a set of goals through the board process to save time or get on with the job will come back to haunt you in the form of commitments not kept and half-hearted fundraising efforts.

five

The Board of Directors

In the United States, nonprofits play a critical role. They provide almost all social services, arts and other culture, education, advocacy, religion, pro bono legal services, and free health care. In addition, nonprofits are leading the charge, and in many cases, are the only organizations working on saving the environment, ending racism, protecting civil rights and civil liberties, and promoting full acceptance and recognition of the rights of women, sexual minorities, people with disabilities, and seniors. In general, then, almost everything that is creative, humane, and promoting of justice is brought to us by a nonprofit.

The government recognizes that a nonprofit cannot exist in a for-profit, capitalist economy without a lot of help. Over the past several decades, laws have created a series of subsidies that make it possible for nonprofits to exist. As a result, nonprofits registered as 501(c)(3) organizations are exempt from many corporate taxes, can offer donors tax deductibility for their gifts, have access to foundation and corporate funding that individuals and small businesses do not, receive lower rates for sending bulk mail at the post office, and enjoy a host of other tax exemptions at both the federal and state levels. Because these tax exemptions and subsidies cost all taxpayers money, the government has also set up a way to hold nonprofits accountable for the money benefits. The group of people that is responsible to the government for the actions of the nonprofit is the board of directors.

The broad purpose of a board of directors is to run the organization effectively. To qualify for tax-exempt status, an organization must file a list of the names of people who have agreed to fulfill the legal requirements of board membership. The board members are bound to ensure that the organization:

- Operates within state and federal laws

- Earns its money honestly and spends it responsibly

- Adopts programs and procedures most conducive to carrying out its mission.

The best summary of a board member's responsibility is contained in the state of New York's Not-for-Profit Corporation Law (the language of which has since been adopted by many other states). According to this law, board members must act "in good faith and with a degree of diligence, care, and skill which ordinarily prudent people would exercise under similar circumstances and in like positions."

Board members, in effect, own the organization. They are the final policy makers and they employ the staff. They are chosen because of their commitment to the organization and long-term vision for it. As the Council of Better Business Bureaus points out, "Being part of the official governing body of a nonprofit, soliciting organization is a serious responsibility, and should never be undertaken with the thought that this is an easy way to perform a public service."

The responsibilities of board members fall into several broad categories. How any specific organization chooses to have board members carry out these responsibilities will depend on the number of board members, the number of paid staff, the sources of funding, and the history of the organization. There are few right or wrong ways to manage an organization, but there are ways that work better in some groups than in others.

With that in mind, let's look at board member responsibilities.

RESPONSIBILITIES OF THE BOARD

Board members are responsible for the following:

1. Ensuring organizational continuity. The board develops leadership within both board and staff to maintain a mix of old and new people in both spheres.

2. Setting organizational policy, reviewing and evaluating organizational plans. The board ensures that the organization's programs are always in keeping with its statement of mission, and that the statement of mission continues to reflect a true need.

3. Doing strategic planning. The board forms long-range plans with reference to the case statement, focusing on the following types of questions:

- Where does the organization want to be in two years, five years, ten years? How big does the organization want to become?

- If it is a local group, does it want to become regional or national?
- What are the implications of world events for the group's work, and what is its response?
- How can the group become more pro-active, rather than reactive?

These and other questions can be answered during an annual strategic planning retreat. Some organizations find it helpful to have a board-level strategic planning committee that raises and researches appropriate questions and brings recommendations to the retreat for discussion and decision-making.

4. Maintaining fiscal accountability. The board approves and closely monitors the organization's expenses and income. The board makes certain that all the organization's resources (including the time of volunteers and staff) are used wisely, and that the organization has enough money to operate.

5. Personnel. The board sets and reviews personnel policies, hires, evaluates, and, when necessary, fires staff. For staff positions other than the executive director, these tasks are often delegated to the executive director. She or he then takes the place of the board in personnel matters. The board hires the executive director and evaluates her or his performance regularly. The board is also the final arbiter of internal staff disputes and grievances and is ultimately responsible for maintaining good staff/board relationships.

6. Funding the organization. The board is responsible for the continued funding and financial health of the organization. With regard to fundraising, board members have two responsibilities: give money and raise money.

BOARD STRUCTURE AND SIZE

There is no evidence that any particular board structure works better than another. Each structure will have its strengths and weaknesses. The structure your organization chooses will probably stem from past history and the experience and desires of the present board members. Some groups work best with a collective structure, including open meetings, informal discussion, and decision by consensus. Other groups do better with a hierarchical structure, a parliamentarian who will help the group follow *Robert's Rules of Order,* and a formal method of discussion and decision making. The only rule is that everyone has to understand the structure you have. If one person thinks that she should raise her hand and wait to be called on before speaking while another person simply shouts out what he thinks, the board will have communication problems.

The size of the board also depends on the group, but there is evidence that the ideal size is between 11 and 21 members. A board of fewer than 11 members will probably have too much work, and one of more than 21 members is likely to be unwieldy, with work divided unevenly. If you already have a large board, work can be most effectively accomplished through small committees, having few full board meetings. A small board can also be divided into committees, which can be fleshed out with non-board representatives recruited to participate.

STATEMENT OF AGREEMENT

For a board to operate successfully each member must understand and respect the organization's structure and decision-making process, as well as the mission of the organization, and must feel that she or he can participate fully in it. One technique that many groups have found helpful to achieve this understanding is to develop a statement of agreement for board members. This statement serves as a job description and clarifies board responsibilities and authority. On the next page is a generic example of such a statement.

This kind of agreement defines understandings that may never before have been articulated; it also helps channel board members' motivation to serve the organization.

Once a board has developed this type of contract, it can be read at regular intervals to remind people of their commitments. It can also be used for internal evaluation and to recruit new board members.

Such an agreement also improves relations between board and staff. It enables staff to know the limits of board responsibilities so they will not make demands that exceed those limits. Board members know when they can say, "No, this is not my responsibility."

STATEMENT OF AGREEMENT

As a board member of _____ , I believe in the mission of the group, which is
_____ . I understand that my duties and responsibilities include the following:

1. I am fiscally responsible, with the other board members, for this organization. It is my duty to know what our budget is and to take an active part in planning the budget and the fundraising to meet it.

2. I am legally responsible, with the other board members, for this organization. I am responsible to know and approve all policies and programs and to oversee their implementation.

3. I am morally responsible, with the other board members, for the health and well-being of this organization. As a member of the board, I have pledged myself to carry out the goals of the organization, which are as follows: (summarize goals here). I am fully committed and dedicated to the mission and goals of this group.

4. I will give what is for me a significant financial donation. I may give this as a one-time donation each year, or I may pledge to give a certain amount several times during the year.

5. I will actively engage in fundraising for this organization in whatever ways are best suited to me. These may include individual solicitation, undertaking special events, writing mail appeals, and the like. There is no set amount of money that I must raise because I am making a good faith agreement to do my best and to bring in as much money as I can.

6. I will attend (#) _____ of board meetings every year and be available for committee work, where appropriate, and phone consultation. I understand that commitment to this board will involve a good deal of time and will probably require a minimum of _____ hours per month.

7. I understand that no quotas have been set, that no rigid standards of measurement and achievement have been formed. Every board member is making a statement of faith about every other board member. We are trusting each other to carry out the above agreements to the best of our ability, each in our own way, with knowledge, approval, and support of all. I know that if I fail to act in good faith I must resign, or someone from the board may ask me to resign.

In its turn, this organization is responsible to me in the following ways:
1. The organization will send me, without request, quarterly financial reports that allow me to act in good faith and with a degree of diligence, care, and skill that ordinarily prudent people would exercise under similar circumstances and in like positions.

2. Paid staff will make themselves available to me to discuss programs and policies, goals, and objectives.

3. Board members and staff will respond in a straightforward and thorough fashion to any questions I have that I feel are necessary to carry out my fiscal, legal, and moral responsibilities to this organization.

THE BOARD AND FUNDRAISING

The reluctance of board members to take responsibility for fundraising can usually be traced to two sources: 1) Board members don't understand the importance of taking a leadership role in fundraising, and 2) they are afraid of asking for money. Board members cannot give themselves wholeheartedly to the process of fundraising unless these two problems are resolved.

The reason that board members must take a leadership role in fundraising is simple: they own the organization. They are responsible for the well-being of the organization and for its successes. Furthermore, their supporters and potential supporters see board members as the people most committed and dedicated to the organization. If they, who care the most about the group, will not take a lead role in fundraising, why should anyone else? When the board does take the lead, its members and the staff can go to individuals, corporations, and foundations and say, "We have a 100% commitment from our board. All board members give money and raise money." This position strengthens their fundraising case a great deal. Both individual donors and foundations often ask organizations about the role of the board in fundraising and look more positively on groups whose board plays an active part.

Board members are often reluctant to participate in fundraising activities because they fear they will be required to ask people for money. It's true that many fundraising strategies require board members to make face-to-face solicitations. This is a skill and thus can be learned, and all board members should have the opportunity to attend a training session on asking for money (see Chapter 9, Personal Solicitation).

In a diversified fundraising plan, however, some board members can participate in fundraising strategies that do not require asking for money directly. While some can solicit large gifts, others can plan special events, write mail appeals, market products for sale, write thank-you notes, stuff envelopes, enter information into a database, etc. Everyone's interests and skills can be used. Board members inexperienced in fundraising can start with easy tasks ("Sell these 20 raffle tickets") and then move on to more difficult fundraising tasks ("Ask this person for $1,000"). Some fundraising strategies will use all the board members (selling tickets to a dance), whereas others will require the work of only one or two people (speaking to service clubs or writing mail appeals).

People often bring to their board service two myths that hamper their participation in fundraising. First, they feel that since they give time they should not be called on to give money. "Time is money," they will argue. Second, if an organization has paid development staff, board members may feel that it is the staff's job to do the fundraising. Let us quickly dispel both of these myths.

Concerning Time and Money

While a person's time is valuable, it is a very different value than their money. Time is a non-renewable resource — when a day is gone, you cannot get it back. Money is a renewable resource. You earn it, spend it, and earn more. Further, you cannot go to the telephone company and ask to volunteer your time in order to pay your phone bill. You cannot pay your staff or buy your office supplies with your time. Further, everyone has the same amount of time in a day, but people have vastly unequal amounts of money. Finally, people are rarely nervous to ask someone for their time, but most are very reluctant to ask someone for their money, even though for many people, time is their most precious resource. In training, I often use this example: "If a board member is assigned to call three people and tell them about a meeting on Wednesday night, he or she will do it. If two people can come to the meeting and one can't, the board member does not take this personally and feel like a failure. However, if this same board member is assigned to ask these same three people for $100, he or she will probably need to be trained in how to ask for money before being comfortable doing that." I have conducted thousands of trainings in how to ask for money, but have never been asked to lead a training in how to ask for time. Comparing time and money is like comparing apples and asphalt. Board members must understand that contributions of time and money are very different, although equally important, parts of their role.

The Role of Paid Staff

Paid staff have specific roles in fundraising. These are to help plan fundraising strategies, coordinate fundraising activities, keep records, take care of routine fundraising tasks such as renewal appeals, and assist board members by writing letters for them, form fundraising plans with them, accompany them to solicitation meetings, and so on. Fundraising staff provide all the backup needed for effective fundraising. It is clearly impossible, however, for one person or even several people to do all the work necessary in a diversified fundraising plan. Just as it is foolish for an organization to depend on one or two sources of funding, it is equally unwise for it to depend on one or two people to do fundraising.

The final reason for all board members to participate in fundraising is to ensure that the work is evenly shared. Fundraising is rarely anyone's favorite task, so it is important that each board member knows that the other members are doing their share. If some members do all the fundraising while others only make policy, resentments are bound to arise. The same resentments will surface if some board members give money and others don't. Those who give may feel that their donation "buys" them out of some work or that their money entitles them to more power. Those who do not give money may feel that they do all the work or that those who give money have more power. When board members know that everyone is giving their best effort to fundraising — including making their own gift — according to their abilities, the board will function more smoothly and members will be more willing to take on fundraising tasks.

COMMON BOARD PROBLEMS AND SUGGESTED SOLUTIONS

While each board of directors will have its own problems and tensions to be resolved, many boards have a number of problems in common. They are discussed here, along with some solutions.

1. Board members are overworked — too much is expected of them. Nonprofit organizations use all of their volunteers to augment paid staff. The smaller the organization, the more responsibility volunteers will have, becoming more and more like paid staff. To a certain point this is fine. But there comes a time when board members are taking on much more work than they had agreed to. Overload can result when board members are given new work by staff, or when board work takes longer than originally planned. When board members find themselves attending three or four meetings each month and spending hours on the telephone, they begin to dread calls and meetings and to count the days until their term is up.

This dynamic can be changed or averted altogether by adhering to the following principles:

- Board members should understand that they can say no to tasks that go beyond their original commitment.

- Staff and board members should ensure that tasks given to the board have a clear beginning and end. Thus, when additional work is essential, board members should be assured that extra meetings will last no more than a month or two and that once that task is accomplished they will not be asked to do more than the minimum for a few months.

- A careful eye should be kept on what the whole board does with its time. Board members (particularly the executive or steering committee) should ask, "Are all these meetings necessary? Can one person do what two have been assigned to do or two people what four have committed to do?"

- Boards should not be asked to make decisions for which they are unqualified. Sometimes consultants need to be brought in to make recommendations, or the board needs to be trained to handle tasks related to management and fundraising.

2. Individual board members feel overworked. This problem can arise either because the person was given the wrong impression of the amount of work involved beyond attending regular board meetings, or because they are already overcommitted in the rest of their life. In the latter case he or she cannot fulfill the expectations of any one part of their life, and feels overworked even while not doing very much for the organization.

A clear and precise statement of agreement, as discussed earlier in this chapter, will help with this problem. The statement can be used to screen out people who are overextended and to call current board members into accountability.

3. The board avoids making decisions. In this instance the board constantly refers items back to committees or to staff for further discussion and research. The whole board never seems to have enough information to commit themselves to a course of action. This problem is generally the result of inadequate board leadership. The board chair or president must set an example of decisiveness. He or she needs to point out that the board can never know all the factors surrounding a decision and yet must act despite factors changing on a daily or weekly basis.

The person facilitating a meeting should always establish time limits for each item on the agenda. This can be done at the beginning of the meeting. Close to the end of the time allotted for an item, the chair should say, "We are almost at the end of time for discussion on this item. What are the suggestions for a decision?" If the chair or facilitator of the meeting does not take this role, individual board members should take it upon themselves to call for a time limit on discussion and a deadline for a decision.

Very few decisions are irrevocable. Decisions can be modified, expanded, or scrapped altogether once they are made and put into action.

4. The board makes decisions, notes them in the minutes, and then forgets about them. As a result of this process the board both fails to implement their decisions and ends up discussing the same issue again in a few months or years. Further, board members feel that they are not taking themselves seriously and that their work is for nothing. Three methods can be used to avoid this problem. One method is to appoint a member to keep track of decisions and remind the board of them. The secretary of the board can serve this function, or someone designated as "historian." A second complementary method is for decisions from board meetings to be written up and kept in a notebook available at every board meeting (as distinct from meeting minutes). The notebook can be indexed so that decisions can be easily found. The chair and executive committee should stay familiar with this book. Finally, each board member should read and keep a copy of the minutes of every meeting. Then, each member can help remind the whole of decisions made.

5. A few board members do all or most of the work. When this happens, those who do the work resent those who are not carrying their share. Those who don't work resent those who do because they imagine them to have all the power. Inevitably, some people will work harder than others, and some will work better.

Nonetheless, the board should plan for work to be evenly shared and for everyone to take an active role, assuming that all members will work equally hard and equally effectively. People rise to the standards set for them. Mediocre work should not be accepted. Above all, board members must value everyone's contribution. The person who stuffs envelopes is as valuable as the person whose friend gives $5,000.

6. Staff members don't really want the board to have power, or some board members don't want to share the power evenly. Sometimes people take and keep power because they enjoy having power and building empires. More often, though, they take power because they are afraid to let go — afraid that others will not do as well as they have. This is particularly true when some board members have served for many years or when a person on staff has seen the board turn over several times. Whoever perceives that someone is hoarding power or refusing to delegate tasks (either staff or board) should address their concerns to the appropriate committee or the board chair. That person should use examples, so that people can have a clear sense of what they are doing wrong and change their behavior accordingly. Generally, people will share power in the organization as others prove reliable.

All of the dynamics described above, as well as others including personality conflicts, deep political disagreements, or staff-board conflicts, can be serious enough to immobilize an organization. The board and staff may not be able to resolve the problem themselves. Sometimes they can't even figure out what the problem is. Board or staff members should not hesitate to seek help in that case. A consultant in organizational development or a mediator can help the group articulate and solve its problems. Although for a board to find itself in such an extreme situation is unfortunate, it is usually no one person's fault. Not to ask for help in getting out of the situation, however, constitutes a failure of board or staff members to be fully responsible.

Some conflict can be creative, and board members and staff should not shun difficult discussions or disagreements. There is built-in tension between program and finance committees, new and old board members, and staff and board personnel. As Karl Mathiassen, a veteran board member and consultant to organizations for social change, states in *Confessions of a Board Member*, "My own feeling is that if you go to a board meeting and never during that board meeting have a period during which you are yourself tense and your heart beats and you know that something is at stake — if you lack that feeling two or three meetings in a row, there is something wrong with the organization."

RECRUITING AND INVOLVING NEW BOARD MEMBERS

Once an organization has a clear sense of the board's roles and responsibilities, has defined the type of structure it wants (collective, hierarchy, or other form), and has developed a statement of understanding or similar agreement, it can begin the formal process of recruiting additional board members. Two key tenets of board composition are 1) board members, while sharing a sense of commitment to the organization's mission and goals, also need to represent a diversity of opinion and skill; and 2) ideally, the combination of all the people on the board will provide all the skills required to run the organization.

To recruit board members, the current board should appoint two or three people to form a "nominating committee." (In some organizations this becomes a standing committee of the board.) This small group will assess the present board's strengths and decide what skills or qualities are needed to overcome the board's weaknesses. The following chart is an example of a way to evaluate the current board and quickly spot the gaps. Each group should fill it in with the board membership criteria it has established.

CURRENT BOARD EVALUATION

BOARD NEEDS	NAME OF BOARD MEMBER			
	Montoya	Murphy	Hong	Burger
Demographic:*				
Women		X	X	
Men	X			X
GLBT			X	
Latino	X			
African American				X
White		X		
Asian			X	
Other				
Budgeting			X	
Financial management				X
Personnel		X		
Fundraising:				
Personal asking	X	X		
Events				
Planned giving				
Marketing				
Web design				
Evaluation			X	
Public policy				
Organizing				X
Other:				

*Many groups think through how many people from any demographic criteria they want. Of course, it is important to keep in mind that one or two people will not represent a whole constituency.

There is a common belief that a board should include "movers and shakers." Bank presidents, successful business people, politicians, corporate executives, and the like are thought to be people with power and connections, making them ideal board members. An organization needs to define who are the "movers and shakers" *for its work.* Many of the people perceived to be the most powerful in a community would be terrible board members, even if they would agree to serve. There are hundreds of successful organizations whose board members are neither rich nor famous and who have no access to the traditional elite, but whose connections are exactly what the organization needs. Belief in the mission of the organization and willingness to do the work required are of far greater importance than being successful or wealthy.

First and foremost, board members and new recruits must understand, appreciate, and desire to further the goals and objectives of the organization. Enthusiasm, commitment, and a willingness to work are the primary qualifications. Everything else required of a board member can be learned, and the skills needed can be brought by a wide variety of people and taught to others on the board.

In assessing what skills and qualifications your board lacks, then, don't just go for the obvious recruits. For example, suppose that no one on your board understands budgeting. An obvious solution would be to recruit an accountant, MBA, or corporate executive to meet this need. If you know someone in one of these areas who shares the commitments and ideals of your group, then certainly invite her or him to be a board member. But if you don't know anyone whose profession involves budgeting, use your imagination to see what other kind of person might have those skills. In one organization, a self-described housewife does all the budgeting and evaluation of financial reports. Her experience of managing a large family has taught her all the basics of financial management; she is completely self-taught. Anyone who has to keep within a budget may have excellent budgeting skills: ministers, directors of other nonprofit organizations, small business persons, seniors living on fixed incomes.

Another example: If the gap on your board is in getting publicity, an obvious choice would be someone who works in the media or has a job in public relations. However, as many groups know, anyone willing to tell his or her personal story of experience with a group or who is articulate about the issues can get media attention if a staff person lays the groundwork. A staff member can arrange an interview, send a press release, and put together a press packet. A volunteer can then do the follow-up required to get the media coverage.

The Recruitment

Prospective board members are found among friends and acquaintances of current board members, staff members, former board and staff members, and current donors and clients. Ideally, a prospective board member is someone who already gives time and money to the organization.

The chair of the board should send a letter to each prospective board member asking the person if he or she is interested in serving on the board and giving a few details of what that would mean. The letter should state that someone will call in a few days to make an appointment to discuss the invitation in detail. Even if the prospect is a friend of a board or staff member or a long-time volunteer, a formal invitation will convey that being on this board is an important responsibility and a serious commitment and that it is a privilege to be invited. Whoever knows the board prospect can follow up the letter by talking to the person about being on the board. If no one knows the prospect, two people from the board should meet with the person. If the prospective board member does not have time to meet and discuss the board commitment, this is a clue that he or she will not have time to serve and should be removed from the list of prospects.

Whoever meets with the prospective board member should go over the board's statement of understanding point by point. The current members should share their experiences in fulfilling their commitment and discuss what others have done to fulfill theirs. It is particularly important to discuss the amount of time board participation requires as well as the area of fundraising. Do not make the board commitment sound easier than it is. It is better for a person to join the board and discover that it is not as much work as they originally thought than to find that it is much more work and resent having had the commitment misrepresented.

The contact person should feel free to ask the prospective board member how he or she feels about the group or what experience he or she has in working with people of other classes, races, sexual orientations, and so on (depending on the composition of your board). Asking someone to be on the board is as serious as inviting someone to be a partner in a business, finding a new roommate, or interviewing staff. Do not expect people to change once they are on the board. What you see is what you get. Take it if it is good, leave it if it is not.

Tell the person why you are asking them to be on the board. Let them know that the nominating committee has given a great deal of thought to this choice. Give the person a few days to think it over. Ask them to call for more information or with further questions. Let this be an informed and considered choice. It is better for ten people to turn you down than to get ten half-hearted new board members.

Orienting the New Board Member

After a person has accepted nomination to the board and been elected, a current board member should be assigned to act as the new person's "buddy." The buddy should bring the new board member to the first meeting, meet with him or her (perhaps for lunch or dinner) once a month for the first two or three months, and be available for discussion. New board members have many questions that they are too embarrassed or shy to ask at the full board meeting. They will be incorporated into the life of the organization much faster if they can easily get the answers they need.

Before their first meeting, new board members should receive a packet of information, including a copy of the statement of agreement, the organization's bylaws, the case statement, and anything else that would be helpful to their understanding of the organization such as an organizational chart, the current annual budget, brochures and other promotional information, and the names, addresses, phone numbers, and profiles of the other board members and of staff members.

Board members work best when they feel both needed and accountable. They will be more likely to keep their commitments when they know that is expected and that others are doing so. When this tone is established at the beginning, the board will function smoothly.

A NOTE ON ADVISORY BOARDS

In addition to a board of directors, small organizations often find it helpful to form "advisory boards" made up of people who can help with various parts of the organization's program, including fundraising. Having an advisory board can be a helpful strategy, although it involves a good deal of work and does not take the place of a board of directors.

In some ways an advisory board is an administrative fiction. Unlike a board of directors, an advisory board has no legal requirements, no length of time to exist, and no purposes that must be fulfilled. Such a board can consist of 1 person or 200.

Advisory boards are variously named depending on their functions. They may be called community boards, auxiliaries, task forces, committees, or advisory councils. Some advisory boards meet frequently; others, never. Sometimes advisory board members serve the group by allowing the organization to use their names on the organization's letterhead. In at least one case an organization's advisory board was called together, then met for the first time and disbanded all in the same day, having accomplished what they had been asked to do.

You can form an advisory board for the sole purpose of fundraising. Since this board has no final responsibility for the overall management of the organization, its members can be recruited from anywhere. Furthermore, the advisory board can be completely homogeneous — something a group tries to avoid in its board of directors.

People like to be on advisory boards. It gives them a role in an organization without the full legal and fiscal responsibilities of a member of the board of directors.

The Fundraising Advisory Board

Organizations sometimes see an advisory board as a "quick fix" to their fundraising problems. They may reason, "Next year our group has to raise three times as much money as it did this year. Our board can't do it alone and we don't want to add new board members. So, we'll just ask ten rich people to be on a fundraising advisory board and they'll raise the extra money we need."

There are several problems here. First, finding "ten rich people" is not that simple. If it were, the group would already have a successful major gifts program. Second, a wealthy person doesn't necessarily have an easier time asking for and getting money than someone who is not wealthy. Nor will he or she necessarily be more willing to give your group money than a "not rich" person.

These are the conditions under which an advisory board is a solution to a fundraising need:

1. Although the board of directors is already doing as much fundraising as it can, it is not enough. An advisory board works best when it is augmenting the work of an active and involved board of directors.

2. An organization has a specific and time-limited project that needs its own additional funding. This can be a capital campaign, an endowment project, or a time-limited program requiring extra staff and other expenses. The advisory board commits to raise a certain amount of money overall or a certain amount every year, usually for no more than three years.

3. An organization needs help to run a small business or put on a large special event every year. The type of advisory board that runs a small business is usually called an "auxiliary" as it does not have a time-limited function.

4. An organization wants help in raising money from a particular part of the private sector, such as corporations, businesses, service clubs, or houses of worship. The advisory board, composed of representatives from these particular sectors, plans the campaign and the members solicit their own colleagues.

Forming the Advisory Board

If you decide that an advisory board is a good tool for your group, be sure to write out clearly your expectations of this group. Use the same specificity and thoroughness here as in drawing up a statement of agreement for your board of directors. In terms of fundraising, set an amount that you want the group to raise as a goal, the number of hours you expect them to work (per month, per event, etc.), and the number of meetings they need to attend. Also suggest ways for them to raise money. (Sometimes you won't know what to suggest, which may be why you are forming this board. In that case, be clear that there is no staff expertise to guide advisory board members.)

Be straightforward with prospects for your advisory board. Tell them your goals and choose those who can work to meet those goals.

Use the same priorities in choosing members as when forming a board of directors. Of primary importance is the members' commitment to your organization and their willingness to express that commitment by fundraising.

Once you have formed an advisory board, the staff of the organization must provide back-up as needed and guide the board as much as necessary. The chair or designated representative of the board of directors should receive reports from the advisory board and frequently call or write the advisory board's chair to express the organization's appreciation for the advisory board's work. Advisory board members should receive minutes of every meeting, be phoned frequently, and generally be treated like major donors to the organization (which they are).

Allow the advisory board to develop a direction. The first few months may be slow, but once an advisory board begins to work well and carry out its commitments, its members can raise a substantial amount of money every year.

Strategies to Acquire and Keep Donors

The work of asking people who have never given to our organizations to give once and then, if they give, asking them to give again and again forms the bulk of what fundraising is about. Building a donor base is labor-intensive work and requires persistence and minute attention to detail, along with a healthy sense of risk and willingness to spend money in order to make money.

The strategies I discuss in the next five chapters are those most commonly used to acquire and retain donors: direct mail, special events, asking on the phone, and asking in person. The final chapter of this section is on writing thank-you notes, including how to make them varied and interesting. I devote an entire chapter to this topic because thanking people for what they give to your organization is the best way, besides running your organization soundly and honestly, to get them to give again.

six

Using Direct Mail

Direct mail is a strategy of sending a form letter that asks for money to hundreds, thousands, or even millions of people by bulk mail. The letter contains a self-addressed envelope, making it easy for the donor to return a gift, and is possibly the most common fundraising strategy in use today. Letters that are addressed to an individual, "Dear Ms. Smith," or letters sent first class are not technically considered direct mail pieces, although these more personalized letters may borrow from direct mail principles in their look or style of writing and identical text may be going to dozens — or thousands — of recipients. However, because the salutation is different for each letter, the post office will not process them as bulk mail. Direct mail letters are sent in minimum quantities of 200, pre-sorted by ZIP code for the post office; at the post office they receive bottom priority for processing.

Direct mail solicitation (often derisively called "junk" mail) has been in wide use for about the past 30 years. It was first used by a secular organization in 1964 for the Barry Goldwater for President campaign. For the next 15 years direct mail fundraising became a popular method; many organizations derived the bulk of their income from it. Over time, as the market has become saturated with it, its effectiveness has decreased. People have become accustomed to receiving direct mail, making letters from groups one never heard of no longer as interesting to open.

To get a sense of the volume of direct mail, consider that 40% of the total mail in the world is domestic mail and 40% of that mail is direct mail, both from commercial and nonprofit sources. This means that about one out of every six pieces of mail worldwide is direct mail. For many Americans, far more than one out of six pieces coming through their mail slots is an unsolicited fundraising letter.

Some fundraising professionals (and probably thousands of consumers) have questioned whether direct mail continues to be an effective fundraising strategy. Despite all the bad publicity it gets, however, direct mail remains the least expensive way to reach the most people with a message that they can hold in their hands and examine at their leisure. A well-designed and well-written direct mail piece sent to a good list (more on all of this later) can still yield a 1% response — though small, this is far greater than any other way of reaching large numbers of people who do not know about your group. Many groups also use direct mail letters to communicate with current donors and to ask for additional gifts. Used properly, direct mail is one of the most powerful strategies a small nonprofit can have.

THREE FUNCTIONS OF DIRECT MAIL

Direct mail soliciting has three functions and, along with special events, is one of the most versatile strategies for developing closer relationships with donors. The three functions overlap with the strategies discussed in the previous section: donor acquisition, retention, and upgrading.

1. Get someone to give for the first time. Donor acquisition is the primary purpose of using direct mail and direct mail does it better than any other strategy. To see how it works, consider the experience of People for Good. People for Good trades 2,000* names of their donors for 2,000 names of donors to another group, Friends of Progress. People for Good compares the names they got from Friends of Progress with their own donor list and pulls out anyone who already gives to both groups. To the remainder of the Friends of Progress list, People for Good sends a direct mail appeal asking for a donation to their work. They get a 1% response or 20 gifts. Their cost was .50 cents for each piece of mail (including postage, printing, paper, and the use of a mail house) or $1,000 total. Most of the 20 donors give $35, which is the suggested donation, and two give $50. People for Good brings in $750 on the mailing, giving them a net cost of $250 ($750 income subtracted from their $1,000 cost) or $12.50 for each of the 20 donors they acquired. These donors will now be moved to the next stage.

2. Get donors to repeat their gift. Once a person becomes a donor, the organization tries to get the donor to give routinely. The best way to do that is to thank the donor within 72 hours of receiving their gift, and then to ask the donors

---

*2,000 names is considered by most experts to be an appropriate test sample size. The idea is that if you get a 1% or better response on 2,000 names, you should send the appeal to the whole list. If the response is less than 1%, you can change the appeal or abandon the list. To take advantage of direct mail rates, you only need 200 names, but 200 is not considered statistically significant for predicting future response on that or a similar list.

for money more than once a year. Small organizations should ask their current donors for money at least two or three times a year, either through the mail or with a combination of mail, phone solicitations, and special events. This frequency of asking will not offend people and keeps the name of your group in the donor's consciousness. It also enables you to take advantage of the ups and downs of each donor's cash flow situation. Every time you ask your donors for an extra gift by mail, you can expect that about 10% of them will respond. In this phase you make back the money you spent acquiring these people. You will probably even show a profit.

3. Get donors to renew their gift. To be considered an active donor (as opposed to a lapsed donor), a person must make a contribution at least once a year, thus renewing their commitment to the organization. Most organizations have a renewal rate of about 66% — enough to generate a nice profit.

DIRECT MAIL PLAN: ONE ORGANIZATION'S RESULTS

INCOME

ACQUISITION MAILINGS

10,000 pieces of mail × 1% response – 100 donors – @ average gift of $35 .... $3,500

Three more mailings to those who gave asking for extra gifts:
10% response per mailing from 100 donors: 30 extra gifts × average gift of $25 .... $750

RENEWAL MAILINGS

One renewal mailing to these 100 donors; 66% renew at average gift of $50 .... $3,300

Total revenue **$7,550**

EXPENSES

ACQUISITION MAILINGS (renting or exchanging lists, printing postage, etc.)

10,000 pieces at $.50 .... $5,000

Further mailings to 100 donors:
3 mailings × 100 × $.60 .... $180

RENEWAL MAILINGS

One to all 100 donors and a second to those who did not respond to the first
150 letters × $.60 .... $90

Total expenses **$5,270**

Net gain: 66 donors .... $ 2,280

Net income per donor $35

Large organizations that frequently send direct mail appeals often have a fund of $5,000–$50,000 that they constantly reinvest in these appeals. Money coming in from one appeal is invested in the next until the fund is depleted. Organizations spending that kind of money often hire direct mail consultants to design their appeals and to handle all the details of writing, printing, and mailing them.

By now, you are probably thinking, "Well, that counts my group out. We don't have the money, we don't have the lists, and we can't wait a year or two for the repeat gifts and renewals to start making money."

Don't despair. There is a way for even small groups to use mail appeals effectively. To do so, they must decrease the risk by decreasing the amount of money spent on each mailing. At the same time, they must try to increase the response rate, so that they at least break even on first-time mailings to a list and with luck, make money.

These goals can be achieved in two ways: by mailing to more carefully selected lists and by mailing to fewer people at one time. In the example above, we used the conventional estimate of a 1% response from a new list, which, to be safe, is what you should use in making predictions and planning costs. However, with smaller, targeted mailings, a response rate of 2% or even 3% is not unusual. Let's look at the scenario again but on a much smaller scale and with much more targeted lists.

DIRECT MAIL PLAN: A SMALLER SCALE

INCOME

ACQUISITION MAILINGS

5 mailings of 200 pieces each × 2% response – 20 new donors – @ average gift of $35 .... $700

Three requests for extra gifts to 20 people × 10% response = 6 extra gifts ×
average gift of $25 .... $150

RENEWAL MAILING

Renewal mailing to 20 people at 66% response = 13 gifts × average gift of $50 .... $650

Total income **$1,500**

EXPENSES

1000 pieces of mail × $.50 .... $500

60 letters asking for extra gifts @ $.60 .... $36

Renewal letters, including second mailing to those not responding: 30 letters × $.60 .... $18

Total Expenses **$554**

Net gain: 13 donors $946

Net income per donor $71

As you can see, the average net income per donor from smaller mailings to truly warm lists is much higher and the risk much lower than with larger, less targeted mailings. However, neither set of income figures is particularly impressive given all the work involved, and one wouldn't enter a direct mail program if this was the only kind of income you could expect. A group must be prepared to take the donors it has acquired and identify and then ask those who can to become major donors and to ask long-term donors to include the organization in their will. Direct mail illustrates more than any other strategy the fundraising principle of building relationships: If you are not willing to keep track of your success so that you know which lists work and which don't, if you are not willing to ask donors over and over, and if you are not willing to ask some donors for very large gifts, then you might as well not acquire them at all. The cost of acquisition and the income from retention by themselves are not worth the effort.

DEVELOPING LISTS FOR MAIL APPEALS

The cornerstone for the success of any mail appeal is the list of people who receive it. Compile or choose lists carefully. Make sure that each person's name is spelled correctly and that the address and ZIP code are correct. People tend to be miffed when their name is misspelled, and a wrong ZIP code will mean the letter won't be delivered.

Lists are divided into three categories of expectation, which describe the likelihood of people on that list making a donation. These categories are hot, warm, and cold.

A hot list consists of people who have already made some kind of commitment to your organization. In order of decreasing heat, these people are your current donors, from whom can you expect a 10% – 66% response to a mail appeal; lapsed donors from the past two years (5% –10% response); volunteers and board members who are not yet donors (various response rates depending on the group, however it should not be lower than 5% and could be as high as 100%); and finally, the close friends and associates of all of the above people who are not yet donors (2% –5% response).

A warm list consists of people who have either used or heard of your services or are donors to organizations similar to yours but have not heard of your group. These lists should yield a 1% – 3% response.

A cold list is any list that is more than a year old, or any list of people about whom you know little or nothing. The phone book is an example of a cold list.

Hot Lists

The hottest list of people for any organization is its list of current donors. The second-hottest list includes friends of current donors, because most people's friends share their values and commitments. Therefore, to find new hot names to send appeals to, send current donors an annual mailing with a form on which to send the names and addresses of friends they think would be interested in your organization.

Some people will send only one or two names and most people will not send any, but others will send in dozens of names. With a mailing list of 1,000 donors, you can be assured of getting at least 200 names from this type of appeal. Many organizations regularly remind their current donors to send in names of potential contributors by including a coupon in their newsletter and a request for names in other appeals.

Another source of hot prospects are board members, volunteers, and staff. On a yearly basis these people should also be asked to provide a list of names, which can be compared to the current mailing list; anyone who is not already a donor can be solicited. Of course, any board member, staff person, or volunteer who isn't already a donor is a hot prospect as well.

Some statisticians claim that every person knows 250 people — relatives, school friends, colleagues, neighbors, and so on. Of this number, perhaps only 10 to 20 will be suitable prospects. Nevertheless, with each volunteer or member contributing some names, you will soon have the 200 needed for a bulk mailing.

Warm Lists

If your organization gives people advice, referrals, or other service over the phone or through the mail, create a system to gather the names of people served. A notebook to log the needed information can be kept by each phone. When people call, respond to their request and then ask if you can send them more information about your organization. People who don't want an appeal will decline to give their name. Names from information requests that come through the mail can be transferred directly onto carrier envelopes; every time you have compiled 200 envelopes you can send an appeal by bulk mail. Some groups prefer to send appeals by first-class mail as the names come in. This ensures a hotter prospect, as people are more likely to open first-class mail, but is more expensive because of the postage cost.

People who buy any of your organization's products, such as booklets, educational materials, T-shirts, etc., are also prospects for a mail appeal. Certainly, their names should be kept to advertise any new items you produce, and some of them will become members of your organization. The same is true of people who attend conferences, seminars, or public meetings that you sponsor.

People who attend special events who are not donors should receive an appeal soon after the event. Pass out a sign-up sheet, or conduct a door prize drawing to get names and addresses. People who previously gave your organization money, but no longer do, constitute a warm list if you have correct addresses for them.

Renting and Trading

The other type of warm lists are lists of people who belong to organizations similar to yours. To get these names requires renting or trading mailing lists. No one actually buys a mailing list outright. By renting it, they acquire the right to use the list one time. Many organizations with large mailing lists (5,000 or more names) rent their lists as a fundraising device. You may have noticed that if you give to one organization you will receive appeals from several similar organizations within a few weeks. Your name has been rented because you are a proven "buyer" through direct mail.

You rent mailing lists either from a mailing list broker or from another organization. Professional mailing list brokers have a wide variety of lists available, which are used by both nonprofit organizations and businesses. Most brokers will send you a free catalog of the categories of names available and the number of names in each category. The variety is astounding. A quick glance through one catalog shows these possible offerings: sports medicine doctors, corporate secretaries in corporations with budgets over $250,000, earthquake research engineers, season ticket-holders to dance performances, donors to animal shelters, women in the press, or even the fascinating category, "super-wealthy women" (236,000 nationally).

These lists come to you in ZIP code order. The lists generally cost $75–$125 per thousand names, with a minimum rental of 2,000 to 5,000 names. For a small additional fee, you can have lists crossed with each other, yielding the names, for example, of all the super-wealthy women who are donors to animal shelters or of earthquake engineers who are donors to historic preservation projects.

To find mailing list brokers, look in the Yellow Pages under Mailing Houses, Mailing List Brokers, or Fundraising Services and Consultants. Also, ask organizations that use direct mail services for their recommendations.

Many low-budget organizations trade mailing lists with other organizations for a one-time use. Usually, lists are traded on a name-for-name basis: 200 names for 200 names and on up. A group can also trade names for as many names as they have and rent the rest. If your organization has 500 donors and you want another group's list of 2,000 donors, trade your 500 and pay for the remaining 1,500.

Depending on your relationship with the other organization, it may rent the list to you simply for the cost of producing the list on labels or the cost of the labels plus handling, or it may seek to make some profit.

If you almost never rent your list, each of your names may be worth two and up to five names of an organization that rents their list more often. If you have a little-used mailing list of 200 names, you may be able to trade for a list of 1,000.

Do's and Don'ts of Sharing

Organizations often feel reluctant to share their donor lists with other organizations. Some fear that their donors will prefer the other groups and stop giving or give less to their group. Studies of donors show that this is not true. In fact, donor loyalty to the first group they give to in a series of organizations with related goals is increased as they learn of similar organizations. In other words, if a person gives to an environmental organization and then is solicited by several others, he or she may think, "I already support a group that does good work on the environment," or "I've been concerned about environmental degradation for a long time, and it's good that a lot of groups are working on it." Furthermore, most people who give to charity give to a number of them — usually between five and eleven. Often most of the charities are similar: they may all be arts organizations or environmental groups, or they may be civil rights and civil liberties causes, but there will be some similar theme in all five charities. People change one or two charities each year, dropping one and taking on a new one. You are going to lose some donors every year, but you will not lose donors simply by sharing your list.

Sometimes organizations fear that their donors will take offense at being solicited by so many groups. To ensure that this does not happen, simply include a line in your newsletter or on your reply device that says, "From time to time we make our mailing list available to other organizations that we feel would be of interest to our members. If you would rather we did not include your name, please drop us a line (or "check here" on the form) and we will make sure that you do not receive any of these mailings." You can publish this announcement in every issue of the newsletter to be sure that every donor sees it. Very few people will actually write in with this request. Many people like to get mail, and although they grouse about how much direct mail they get, they also feel important and needed because of the volume of mail that comes to them.

Do not steal mailing lists or use mailing lists that are marked "members only." Because mailing lists are fairly easy to compile and acquire, once you have the systems in place there is no need to be underhanded with others' lists. Further, your group's reputation may suffer. Almost all mailing lists, particularly those rented from commercial firms, have a certain number of "dummy" names: names that are placed to identify the use of that list. The letter addressed to a "dummy" name goes to the source of the list. Suppose you have "liberated" the list of members of a service club that has given your organization a donation. John Q. Jones is on that list. "Q" is his code for service club, and when he gets a letter using that initial, he knows it came from the service club list. He is also in a position to know or discover that no one gave your group permission to use the list. The situation can then become unpleasant and counter-productive to your fundraising efforts, especially if Jones announces at the next meeting of the club that members should not join your group.

A final rule about list acquisition and development: Do not save mailing lists. On a list that is more than three months old, 7% of the addresses will already be inaccurate. After you have used a list twice (if you have permission to do so), you have gotten 90% of the response you are going to get from that list. Throw away the names of people who have not responded. Concentrate your efforts on getting new names and refine your systems so that the names are as "hot" as possible. The quality of the list is pivotal to your direct mail success.

THE DIRECT MAIL PACKAGE

A direct mail appeal needs to be conceived of as a package rather than as simply a letter in an envelope. The work of your organization is only one variable in determining the success of your appeal. The appeal is "wrapped" in a certain way to entice the donor to open the letter, then to read the letter, then to fill out a check and put it in the return envelope. This is a lot of pressure on a few pieces of paper with no power of their own.

The standard package has four parts: the "carrier" or outside envelope, the letter itself, the reply device, and the return envelope.

Each part of the package is complementary to the others, and all the elements work as a unit to have the maximum effect on the person receiving the appeal. We will examine each element separately and then discuss putting the elements together.

The Carrier (Outside) Envelope

Many mail appeals fail because although much attention has been spent writing an effective letter, it is enclosed in an envelope that no one opens.

First-class personal and business mail can be sent in a plain envelope with great security that the person receiving the letter will open it. In the case of first-class mail, the envelope is simply a convenient way to carry the message.

In a fundraising appeal sent by bulk mail, however, the outside envelope has an entirely different purpose. It must grab the prospect's attention and then intrigue them enough that they want to open it and see what's inside. The envelope in this case is like gift wrapping. Everyone wants to know what's inside a present. In fact, gift wrapping works so well that even when you may know what the gift is, there is still the thrill of discovery in removing the wrapping.

That thrill and that curiosity is what you should strive for with mail appeals. Make the prospect want to know what is inside the envelope.

Getting Personal

The main idea is to make the envelope look as though it contains a personal letter. There are two ways to make that happen: 1) make the envelope look like it was sent by first-class mail, or 2) make it different from other mail appeals the prospect will be receiving.

The methods you choose to accomplish this purpose will depend on how many volunteers you have to help with the mailing, your judgment about whether this is the best use of their volunteer time, how many pieces you are actually sending, and your goal for the mailing.

The best way to make a mail appeal look as if it came by first class is to hand-write the address. If you have an appeal going to fewer than 750 names, this is not too arduous a task.

In addition to or instead of writing or typing the address, you can use a pre-cancelled bulk-mail stamp in place of the more common postal indicia. These stamps may be purchased at the post office where you send your bulk mail. The rules for sorting and handling the mail are the same as for any other bulk mailing.

Consider the rest of the envelope. If you are in a major metropolitan area where a lot of mail appeals originate, don't put your name and return address in the upper left-hand corner. Either put it on the back flap of the envelope or use only your address without your organization's name in the upper left-hand corner. In either case, the prospect asks, "Who is this from?" and opens the envelope to find out.

On the other hand, if you are in a rural area, it is likely that the people receiving your appeal will open all letters that originate in their county or small town. In that case, you want your return address to be fairly prominent on the front of the envelope.

Most mail appeals are sent in standard business-size envelopes (called No. 10). Your appeal will stand out if it arrives in a smaller or an odd-size envelope. Personal letters are not generally sent in business-size envelopes, so to make your appeal look more personal, send it in a No. 6-3/4 or No. 7-3/4 envelope, or in an invitation-style envelope. If you use smaller envelopes, make sure your return envelope is smaller yet, so that it will fit into the carrier envelope without needing to be folded, and remember that odd-size envelopes and letters may run up your printing costs. Check first with the post office about costs.

The least effective strategy is "teaser copy" on an envelope. However, it should not be totally disregarded. "Teaser copy" is text. a drawing. or a photograph on the envelope that intrigues the reader or causes some emotional response that will make them open the envelope. So many direct mail appeals use teaser copy that it will not make your envelope stand out unless yours is very unusual or provocative.

You may wish to experiment with various styles of outside envelopes to find which methods work best for your organization. Save mail appeals that you receive and are moved to open, and figure out what about the envelope caused you to want to look inside. The more creative you can be in designing the outside envelope, the greater chance you will have of the prospect reading your appeal.

The Letter

Because of the cost and volume of direct mail, it has been studied very carefully for upwards of 30 years. A few simple principles about writing a direct mail letter have emerged. In thinking about these principles, keep in mind that a direct mail appeal is not literature. Because of this fact, many good writers are not good writers of direct mail letters. The direct mail letter is not designed to be lasting, or to be filed away, or to be read several times with new insights emerging from each reading. It is disposable, part of a culture acclimated to disposable goods of all kinds — from diapers and cameras to contact lenses. The function of the fundraising letter is simply to catch the reader's attention and hold it long enough for the person to decide to give. The recipients of fundraising letters most often read these letters on their own time. It is not their job to read the letter, and if the letter has its intended result, they will wind up paying money for having read it.

Also keep in mind how adults respond to input: When reading, watching TV or a movie, listening to a lecture, or even to a lesser extent listening to someone they care about, they subconsciously go back and forth between two questions. The first question is, "So what?" If this question is answered satisfactorily, they move to the next question, which is, "Now what?" This seesaw is a strong screening device for filtering out trivia, boring details, and rhetoric. To be sure, what is trivial and boring to one person may be profound or lifesaving to another, so the answers to these questions will vary from person to person. However, details about when your organization was founded or the permutations of your organizational structure will not pass the "So what?" test, and the myriad problems that led to your current budget deficit will only bring on a fit of "Now what?" questioning.

As you write your letter, then, imagine the reader asking at the end of each sentence, "So what? What does this have to do with me, people I care about, or things I believe in?" If the sentence stands up under that scrutiny, then read the next sentence while asking, "Now what?" Does this sentence offer a solution, provide more information, inspire confidence in the group?

Using the "so what — now what?" spectrum as the foundation, build your letter on the following principles:

1. People have very short attention spans. A person should be able to read each sentence in your letter in 6 to 15 seconds. Each sentence must be informative or provocative enough to merit devoting the next 6 to 15 seconds to reading the next sentence.

2. People love to read about themselves. The reader of the letter wonders, "Do you know or care anything about me?" "Will giving your group money make me happier, give me status, or relieve my guilt?" "Did you notice that I helped before?" Therefore, the letter should refer to the reader at least twice as often and up to four times as often as it refers to the organization sending it. To do this requires drawing the reader into the cause by saying, "You may have read…" "I'm sure you join me in feeling…" "If you are like me, you care deeply about…."

When writing to someone who is already a donor to solicit another gift or a renewal, use even more references to what they have done. "You have helped us in the past," "Your gift of $50 meant a great deal last year," "I want you to know that we rely on people like you — you are the backbone of our organization." Using the word "You" makes your letter speak *to* the reader rather than *at* them.

3. People must find the letter easy to look at. The page should contain a lot of white space, including wide margins, and be in a font that is clear and simple. Break up paragraphs so that each is no more than two or three sentences long, even if such breaks are not absolutely dictated by the content. Use contractions (won't, you're, can't, we're) to add to the informal style. This is a letter, not a term paper. Do not use jargon or long, complex words.

4. People read the letter in a certain order. First, they read the salutation and the opening paragraph, but then, no matter how long the letter is, they read the closing paragraph and then the postscript. Sometimes people read the P.S. before reading the closing paragraph. Up to 60% of readers decide whether or not to give based on these three paragraphs and will not read the rest of the letter. The other 40% will read selective parts of the rest of the letter, usually parts that are easy to look at, such as facts set off in bullets or underlined phrases. Only a small number of people will read the entire letter.

The Opening

Use the opening paragraph to tell a story, either about someone your group has helped or some situation your group has helped to rectify, or about the reader of the letter. There is a saying in fundraising: "People buy with their hearts first, and then their heads." Programs and outcomes need to be described in "people" terms (or animals, if that is your constituency). Remember that Americans have read a lot of stories in direct mail appeals and newspapers, and have seen even more on TV. They are used to being entertained by stories, but at the same time they are skeptical of their veracity. So make sure that your story is true, even if facts have been changed to protect someone, and that it is credible and typical. (You don't want someone saying, "What a sad story, but that could only happen once, so I'm not going to give.") Finally, have the story resolve itself positively because of the work of your organization. Here are some examples.

Someone the group has helped:

> Tony has been homeless for two years, moving in and out of shelters. Like nearly half of the homeless people in our community, Tony works full time, but she has not been able to save the money she needs for the security deposit on an apartment. This week, because Homes Now has paid Tony's security deposit, she will be able to move into an apartment of her own.

The paragraph ends here. The body of the letter goes on to explain how many working people are homeless and how this group helps homeless people with housing, job training, and child day care.

A situation the group helped to change:

> To some people it looked like a vacant lot, full of weeds, old tires, and paper trash. So when Dreck Development proposed paving it over for a parking lot, few people objected. After all, it is in a poor neighborhood and a parking lot would be useful to commuters who work in the Industrial Park a few blocks away. To Joe Camereno, however, the lot looked like a park. He called Inner City Greenspace and asked us how to go about protecting this vacant lot. Today it is Camereno Park. How did this come about?

The opening ends here. The rest of the letter lets people know how Inner City Greenspace can help them transform vacant lots, treeless streets, and abandoned buildings into more livable community spaces.

Where the reader is part of the story:

> As a resident of Rio del Vista, you were probably as shocked as I was to learn of the toxic waste dump proposed for Del Vista Lake last year. Working together, we were able to save the lake, but now a dump is proposed for Del Vista Canyon. We've got another fight on our hands.

The letter goes on to explain why Rio Del Vista is often targeted for these projects and what can be done about it.

Any of these styles of opening can be effective. The one you use will depend on your list and the stories available or what the role of the reader in the situation described.

The Length

There is has been much debate about the length of a direct mail letter. Many people claim that they never read a long letter and object to groups wasting trees to print them. Direct mail consultants, on the other hand, advise their clients to send four-to-six page letters. In fact, the evidence is overwhelming that a two-page letter will get a better response than a one-page and even that three to four pages will often get a better response than two pages. It is also true that consumers don't read these long letters — in fact, most of them only read the opening, the closing, and the postscript.

So why do longer letters work when people don't read them? Because a longer letter makes it look as though your organization has more to say, and therefore more substance to its work. It says to the reader, "We know you are not some slouch that will give to just anything, so we will explain ourselves." And it allows the organization to take the space it needs to make a case for itself without jamming words onto the page.

The Closing Paragraph

The next paragraph people read, which is the last paragraph of the letter, suggests the action you want the reader to take. It is specific and straightforward:

Send your gift of $25, $50, $75, or whatever you can afford. Use the enclosed envelope and do it today. A gift of $25 will help us reach 200 people. For your gift of $25, we will send you our quarterly newsletter, "Community Views," which will keep you posted on our progress. Your gift is a critical part of our efforts to provide health care to uninsured people.

If your group has several different membership levels, only the simplest description is used in the letter. This last paragraph is a short paragraph, with the full details of the benefits explained on the reply device.

The Postscript

This is the final sentence people read and, in a small but significant percentage of cases, the only sentence. The P.S. is most commonly used to suggest action: "Don't put this letter aside. Send your check today." Sometimes it offers an additional incentive for acting immediately: "Every gift we receive before April 15 will be matched by Nofreelunch Foundation," or, "We have a limited supply of *Excellent Book* by Important Author. Send your gift of $50 or more as soon as possible to be sure that you get one." The P.S. can be used to tell a story:

> P.S. An independent study showed that the quality of our schools has improved because of Community Concern. It also showed that we have a long way to go. For the sake of the children, please make your donation today.

Or it can make the reader part of the story:

> P.S. You cared enough to come to our community meeting last week. We hope you will join us in our critical work by making a donation now.

The Rest of the Text

The rest of the letter tells more of your history, discusses your plans, tells more stories, gives statistics, and lists accomplishments. To break up the text, use devices other than straight paragraphs. These devices might include bullets:

> Because of us:
> • In 1999, a city ordinance banning the distribution of birth control to teenagers was repealed as unconstitutional.
> • All teenagers in this community receive sex education as a part of their biology courses.
> • We remain the only independent clinic providing referrals and birth control to anyone who needs them, regardless of their ability to pay.

Or underlining:

> When it got up to 10 <u>drive-by shootings</u> in one month with <u>half of the victims children,</u> the neighborhood association had had enough!

Or using handwriting very selectively by adding a brief note that looks handwritten:

> *You can help!*

Or:

> *Every gift makes a difference. Send yours today.*

Who signs the letter is not critically important. If a famous person can be found to sign the letter, then the letter should be from that person. "I am happy to take time out of my busy movie schedule to tell you about Feisty Group." Otherwise, the chair of the board or the executive director can sign. The letter should be signed, however, and it should not be signed by more than two people or it begins to look like a petition. The person who signs the letter should have a readable, straightforward signature.

The Reply Device

Many years ago when fundraising was in its infancy, the reply device was called "the little card that people send in with their check." This little card is now known as "the reply device."

In the letter, the organization refers to the reader using the word "You." The reader reads about her or himself. In the reply device, the reader responds to the organization while continuing to read about him or herself. The reader is asked to respond by saying, "Count me in" or "I agree" or "I'm with you."

More and more, when people open mail from groups they have heard of, or causes they believe in, they move right to the bottom line — how much will it cost to join? For this, they look to the reply device. If the reply device holds their attention, they may return to the letter, or they may just give without referring to the letter at all.

The reply device may be the one piece of paper the donor keeps from the mail appeal, as happens when someone reads an appeal letter, decides to give, then puts the return envelope and reply device into their "Bills to be Paid" file and throws the letter away. Two weeks later, the reply device must rekindle the excitement that the letter originally sparked, using a fraction of the space. For this reason, the design of the reply device is crucial.

The reply device is usually printed on card stock cut smaller than a return envelope (this is important) so that it fits easily with a check into the return envelope. Another option is the "wallet flap" style of envelope; in that style the reply device is the back flap of the envelope itself. However, wallet flap envelopes are more expensive to print. A reply device separate from its envelope allows for one or the other to get lost without the person losing the address of your group, and you can use the return envelopes for other things you may want people to return.

The Design

If possible, the reply device should display the logo of the group and have a catchphrase to remind prospects of what the group stands for or its mission. Some organizations put a brief description of their group or their project on the back of the card. Be sure the group's return address is somewhere on the card.

Probably the trickiest part is wording the donor categories and benefits briefly. Many organizations use a simple series of boxes with differing amounts of money, with the benefits the same for any amount of money.

If you have more elaborate benefits of membership or incentives for giving, put the amount first, then describe the incentive. For example:

> $35: includes newsletter
> $50: newsletter, plus free T-shirt (specify color and size below)
> Pledge ($10 per month minimum): newsletter, plus *Very Good Book* by our own Roberta P. Activist

Unless you have really clever names or really good incentives, naming your membership categories is not worth that much. "Patron," "Benefactor," "Friend," all have little or no meaning, and inevitably reflect a hierarchy of giving that is just as well avoided.

The rest of the card must have room for the name, address, and phone number of the donor, or a place for a label, and a statement about how to make out the check. Because many corporations will match the gifts of their employees, you may want to add a line for the donor to indicate whether his or her employer has a matching gifts program. Make sure the response you want is obvious and easy to comply with: Note on your reply device to whom to make the check payable, and whether or not the contribution is tax-deductible.

People will read the suggested amounts until they find a number they are comfortable with, but all else being equal, people will generally choose the second option in a line of numbers. So given a choice such as:

☐ $25   ☐ $35   ☐ $50   ☐ $100   ☐ other ___

most people will choose $35. Put the amount of money or the membership option that you want most people to choose, and that makes the most sense, in the second slot and build your categories around that. Sometimes your numbers will not be in order of ascending value, as in:

☐ $35   ☐ $25   ☐ $50   ☐ $100   ☐ other ___

You may wonder, why not start with high numbers or put a large number in that second slot? Because people will not pay more than they can afford, and you don't want to scare them off. A group with this sequence:

☐ $100   ☐ $50   ☐ $35   ☐ $500   ☐ other ___

may wind up giving a message that small gifts are not encouraged.

On the other hand, do not suggest an amount you would rather not receive, such as $5. If someone wants to or needs to send only that much, they can check "other." By suggesting it, you will get it from people who could have given a lot more.

When it comes time to evaluate your appeal, you will want to be able to distinguish one appeal's response from another's. You do this by coding the reply device for each appeal in some way. If you have access to inexpensive printing, you could print each reply device in a different color, add a number or date to a bottom corner, or change them in some other way. If you don't have a way to have the reply devices printed differently, a cheap and easy method is to put a dot with a colored marker on each reply card and note which color you are using for which mailing.

The Return Envelope

There are two styles of return envelopes: business reply envelopes (called BREs) and plain, self-addressed envelopes. With a BRE, the organization pays the cost of the return postage, which is about twice as much as a first-class stamp, but is only paid on those envelopes that are returned. With a plain, self-addressed envelope, the donor affixes a stamp.

For small organizations, BREs are not necessary, and, organizations have ceased using them as consumers have become aware of the cost. Unless you are working with a sizzling hot list of current donors, do not put a first-class stamp on the return envelope. Your response rate will be too small to justify this expense. On the other hand, do not try to save money by omitting an envelope. Your percentage of response will decline significantly if you do not use a self-addressed envelope of some kind.

Other enclosures

The letter, reply device, and return envelope are all that is necessary to make an excellent mail appeal. There are some additions you can use if you wish. Whether they will increase your response rate depends on many other variables, but they might.

The lift-out note. This is a small note equivalent to the notes in commercial direct mail packages that say, "Read this only if you have decided not to buy our tires." This note usually appears to be handwritten, or at least done in a different font than the letter. It is from someone other than the signer of the letter and provides another compelling reason to give. For example, a letter signed by Judy Blacetti, director of an organization concerned with police brutality, had this lift-out note,

> Emmett Smith, whom Judy writes about in the enclosed letter, is my son. I had often told Emmett, "A policeman is your friend." I still believe that should be true. Join us, please. Don't let there be another Emmett Smith."
>
> Lois Smith

Of course, most people will read the lift-out note first, even though it reads as though you would read it after the letter. People's curiosity is aroused and they now read about Emmett Smith in the letter.

A newspaper article. If your organization has received positive press, reprint the article. If possible, reprint it on newspaper-quality paper so that it looks as though you cut the article out of the paper. People tend to think that if something was in the newspaper it is more true than if you say it yourself.

An internal memorandum. Similar in theory to a lift-out note, these documents give readers the impression that they are learning something that they would not normally be privy to. For example, an organization working to feed starving people in the Sudan used this internal memo:

> To: Joe (the director, who signed the letter)
> From: Fred Smythe, Comptroller
> Re: Recent food shipment
>   Joe, we can't continue to send this much food without a lot more money. I'm way over budget already and getting more and more requests from the field. There is no way we can send medical supplies as well. You have got to cut back.

Joe then scrawls on the memo,

I received this memo just as I was about to send you this letter. Please help with as much as you can as soon as you can. Lives hang in the balance.

Fact sheet. A well-designed, easy-to-read fact sheet highlighting exciting facts about your organization can take the place of one page of your letter. Many organizations now use a fact sheet with a two-page letter with their results as good as using a longer letter. Even though the number of pages are the same, a fact sheet is handy because the same one can be used with several different letters. A fact sheet should be on your organization's stationery. Among the "facts" should be that you depend on donations from individuals, and with what minimum donation a person can become a member of your organization. This reinforces the message of the letter, reaches those people who only read the fact sheet and not the letter, and allows you to use the fact sheet in other kinds of mailings or give it away by itself at rallies, house parties, or other events.

Brochure. Surprisingly, using a brochure in a direct mail appeal will almost always decrease your response. Brochures are more complicated to look at than fact sheets or newspaper articles and require more of the reader's attention. Because a brochure does not generally emphasize giving, it can wind up holding attention but not achieving the purpose of the mailing. Brochures are designed to be given away at special events or to people writing for more information, and to be sent with personal letters asking for money.

Putting the Package Together

Be sure that your letter and enclosures are free of typographical errors. One typo can change the meaning of a sentence or, more often, render it meaningless; typos give a bad impression of your group's work. Although the letter itself is in a clean, readable font, the carrier envelope, reply device, and return envelope generally should be done in a larger, bold font. Remember, the only impression that donors recruited by mail will have of your group will be from what they get in the mail.

Be sure that the envelope color and the paper stock for your letter do not clash. Avoid strong colors such as bright yellows or reds or any dark-colored paper. People with vision problems have a difficult time reading type on dark-colored paper, and you don't want to lose a prospect because he or she couldn't read the letter. Use sharp contrast in your type and paper color so that the words are easy to read. Use recycled or tree-free paper and soy ink whenever possible and if you do, put the recycle logo on your letter so that people will know you have used environmentally friendly paper. Even if you have to pay a little more for this kind of paper, you will make it up in goodwill from your donors and in a higher percent of response to your mailing. Ditto for using a union printer.

Do a spot-check of all the printed materials before they are mailed. Sometimes a printer's mistake may make the middle 25 letters smeared or blank. While you can't look at every piece individually, you may be able to stop a mistake from being sent out. Double-check that your reply device fits into your return envelope. The card should not have to be folded to fit into the envelope. Put your return address on everything: the reply device, the letter, and the return envelope. That way if someone loses the return envelope, she or he can still find you.

Fold the letter so that the writing appears on the outside rather than on the inside, as would be the case with a normal letter. A person pulling the letter out from the envelope should be able to begin reading it without having to open it or turn it around.

Some states have laws that require you to send a copy of each appeal to a government agency for approval before sending it out or to list your federal identification number on everything you send. Be sure to investigate and comply with these laws.

A Note on Time of Year

There is a saying among direct mail consultants that the best time of year to send an appeal is when it is ready. There is much truth in this saying, because there are no really bad times of year and no really excellent ones; the best time will always be when the appeal is fresh and exciting. However, all things being equal, there are some months when donors may be more responsive than others. In order of effectiveness, they are:

- **January – February**
- **September – November 15**
- **November 15 – December** (If your program feeds the hungry, houses the homeless, or is a religious organization, these may be your best months.)
- **March**
- **May**
- **June** (This is a particularly bad month for people with children in school because their attention is on end-of-year school functions and their own and their children's summer vacations.)
- **April** (Again, Christian organizations may do very well here, but most people have their mind on taxes.)
- **August**

Every organization needs to adjust the timing of its direct mail appeals according to its constituency. Farmers have very different schedules from schoolteachers.

Your constituency's religion and how fervently they practice it will affect some timing; elections will affect timing; even the activities of other organizations your constituents belong to may have an impact.

RENEWAL AND EVALUATION

The final use of direct mail is to renew gifts on an annual basis. There are many ways to set up renewal programs, but a simple, tiered renewal program based on size of gift works well. First, categorize your donor base according to their giving as small, mid-range, and major donors. You may want to do this with a code. Small donors are people giving gifts that total $100 or less in one year. Mid-range donors are people giving $100–$250 annually, and major donors are people who annually give $251 and up. (You can adjust these numbers as you wish — the point is to create three categories of donors who are treated in somewhat different ways.)

At renewal time, all donors of small gifts should receive a form letter asking them to renew their gift, all donors of mid-range gifts should receive a personalized letter, and all major donors should receive a personalized letter followed by a phone call, or a letter followed by a phone call and a visit. If you have a very small donor base (fewer than 200 donors), you may wish to personalize all your renewals. Though this means more work, your renewal rate and your income from these donors will be higher.

Direct mail renewals are only used with small donors. The list of small donors is divided into four categories according to when the person gave — spring, summer, autumn, winter. Once each quarter, the names of donors needing to renew in that quarter are generated from the database and they are sent a renewal letter with a reply device and return envelope. This is much easier than trying to write to people on the anniversary date of their gift and much more effective in terms of renewal rates and cash flow than writing to everyone once a year regardless of when they gave.

The renewal letter follows the format of direct mail appeals. It starts with a sentence or two about the donor, affirming the importance of individual donors to the health and work of the organization. The letter goes on to list a few of the group's accomplishments during the previous year and asks for a renewal gift, requesting that the donor increase their gift if possible. While a renewal letter need be no longer than one page, do not jam the letter onto the page. Do not try to save space by saying so little that you wind up being cryptic.

The reply device should be designed specifically for renewals, so the donor feels that they are a part of a group being asked to give again, rather than a new person being asked to give for the first time. In addition to their renewal, you can use the renewal reply device to ask for other things such as:

□ Here are the names of three people I think would be interested in Name of Group:

_____

_____

_____

You may use my name when writing to them.

□ I would like membership information to send to (#)____ friends. Please send me membership packets to give them.

□ I would like information about planned giving.

□ I would like to volunteer. Please get in touch with me at the following phone number/ e-mail address: _____

Don't put more than one or two of these other options on the reply device, and vary them over time. After six to eight weeks, generate a list of any donors who haven't renewed yet and send them a shorter and firmer letter:

In your busy day, you may have forgotten to renew your commitment to Good Group. Please don't put this letter aside. Renew today.

Most organizations find it effective to send three renewal notices over a six- to eight-month period before taking people off their mailing list. Lapsed donors are then allowed to miss one or two newsletters before a fourth notice is sent out which says something like:

We miss you. We need you. I'd like to send you our next newsletter so you can know all the important work people like you are making possible with your gifts. Please use the enclosed form to send in a gift or let us know why you are not contributing at this time. Thanks.

People who don't respond to this final notice are archived or deleted from the mailing list.

Most social change organizations allow people to receive the newsletter or stay on the mailing list without paying if the person is interested in the group but can't afford to join or subscribe. This is certainly appropriate; however, you don't want to keep people on your list whom you never hear from. Many times these people do not read your newsletter or your appeals and don't even remember how they got on your list. Since I teach fundraising to hundreds of groups a year, I get a lot of newsletters and mailings. One organization, to which I have never and will never donate, has been sending me their newsletter since 1981! I have moved to three different states and nine different addresses during this time. I have written asking to be taken off the list, I have called, I have sent the newsletter back marked "return to sender." This is a waste of resources, and, unfortunately, I know from speaking with other people, this kind of waste is not unusual. Make this your general rule:

To be considered an active donor and stay on your mailing list, a person must show their interest in a tangible way every 12 to 16 months. They need to make a donation, indicate that they want to stay on the list even if they cannot donate, or volunteer. A quarterly renewal system for small donors will help you keep your mailing list clean and up-to-date and ensure that you are not spending money, paper, printing, and staff energy on people who are not going to respond.

In Chapter 2, Principles of Fundraising, I noted that a normal renewal rate is 66% — that is 66% of people giving you a gift in one year can be expected to give you a gift the following year. The remaining 34% will not renew. No matter how often you appeal to people and how wonderful your organization is, some people will only give once and not again, or will give two or three times and not again. This probably has little to do with you and more to do with them changing jobs, marrying, divorcing, moving, getting sick, changing their giving priorities, etc. This means you must attract enough new donors every year to replace 34% of your donor base.

If your renewal rate is less than 66%, you are probably not doing enough to keep your donors. Examine your program to ensure:
- You are writing to donors more than once a year asking for money.
- You are thanking donors promptly with a personal note.
- You are sending at least two renewal notices.
- Your records are accurate and up-to-date.

If your renewal rate is more than 66%, your organization does not have enough donors. Any organization can have an 80% to 90% renewal rate if they are only working with a handful of donors. A 66% renewal rate is a sign of health. It means you are bringing enough people into your system to ensure that you will have a decent number of major donors, if you work with the other strategies in this book. The donor pyramid gets smaller as your donors move up from first-time to habitual to major donors. There are fewer and fewer at each stage. In order to have an adequate number at the top, you need an adequate number at the bottom.

What to Do with the Responses

There are few things as thrilling as receiving gifts from a successful mail appeal. When you go to your mailbox and pull out all these return envelopes that you know have checks in them, it is tempting to just cash the checks, spend the money, and go home early. But receiving the checks brings on a whole new set of tasks.

First, all donors must be thanked, preferably within 72 hours of their gift arriving and certainly within seven days. Sometimes you will not be able to meet this time frame, so remember that a late thank-you is always better than no thank-you. (See also Chapter 10, The Thank-You Note.)

The gift must also be recorded (for additional detail, see Chapter 26, Recordkeeping). Use the following steps:

1. Photocopy the check before cashing it. This is a bookkeeping basic, but also helps with fundraising, as a lot of information is on a check.

2. Note in the database the day the check arrived, what appeal it was responding to, and when the thank-you note was sent out. Also note new information that should be transferred from the check to the database, such as a new address, the name of a foundation, or other information.

3. Cash the check as soon as possible.

Evaluating Your Appeal

In order to know if your appeal has been effective and which of your appeals are the most effective and why, you must "track" and evaluate them. Without evaluation, all fundraising is simply shooting in the dark. To get maximum benefit from a mail appeal program, evaluation is essential. The process of tracking is simple: You want to find out how many people responded to a particular appeal and how much money it brought in.

As responses come in from each appeal, or each section of an appeal, note each response on a tally sheet. The heaviest response will come during the first four weeks after you could reasonably expect most people to have received the mailing (always send one to your organization in order to get a sense of how long it takes to arrive). Ninety-five percent of the responses will be in by the end of two months.

At that time, add up the responses and the money earned and evaluate the appeal in these categories:

• Total number of gifts received and amount given

• Number of donors by category (less than $25, $26–$50, $51–$100, etc.)

• Percent of response (Divide the number of responses by the number of pieces mailed.)

• The gift received most often (Note—this is not the average gift; it is the mode gift.)

• Cost of mailing

• Ratio of income to expense (Divide the amount of money you received by the money you spent.)

• Any narrative comments, such as "Send earlier next time," or "Joe's Printing said he would do free printing next time."

The percent of response and the mode gift are the most important aspects of the evaluation. The percent of response tells you much more important information than the amount you earned from the mailing. For example, one organization's appeal to

1,000 names generated only two responses (.002%); one response was for $10 but the other was for $1,500! The board was told that the mail appeal had generated $1,510 but not the percent of response. They decided to do more mailings to similar lists and quickly spent all their profit because the lists were virtually worthless and their original response (which was extremely poor) only appeared successful because of the chance response of a very major gift.

Similarly the mode gift gives you usable information, whereas the average gift, which many groups spend time figuring out, is a virtually meaningless number. For example, if you received 25 replies to a mail appeal and 24 were for $25, but one was for $1,000 (given by the mother of the board chair), your average gift would be $64. That doesn't tell you anything. But knowing that the mode gift is $25 tells you this is a good amount to ask for and the majority of people responding from that list feel comfortable with it.

After you finish your evaluation, place the mail appeal with all its components and the evaluation in a file folder. If you decide to repeat the mailing, you will have all the information you need in one place.

After several mailings, you can pull out all the evaluation forms and see what they have in common. Do some types of lists seem to respond better than others? Did the mailing offering a special benefit do better than the one without? Does one set of facts or one particular story seem to stir more people to give?

Remember to test only one variable at a time. You cannot find out if more people respond to one benefit or another in a mailing that is also testing a lift-out note and a letter against a letter alone. Also, you must use portions of only one list to test responses. You cannot test one variable on a list to a service club and another on a list to a group of health activists.

If you have mailed fewer than 2,000 pieces, your evaluation will not be statistically significant. However, using your instinct and what information you are able to garner, you should be able to make some educated guesses about what is working and why.

VARIATIONS ON THE MAIL APPEAL PACKAGE

The previous sections discussed in detail the purposes of direct mail and how to put an effective direct mail package together. This section presents a number of variations on the direct mail appeal to make your mail appeal package not look like a mail appeal at all. These suggestions will not work for every organization, and not all possible variations are explored here. The point is to suggest a number of options for using the principles of direct mail fundraising. Some of these may inspire you to create other variations on the theme.

A Gift Catalog

A gift catalog is a mail appeal in which the organization lists items it needs and their costs. People then either donate an item or — more usually — the money to purchase an item for the group. In the latter instance the donor's gift is "earmarked" for a particular item.*

Gift catalogs work particularly well for groups such as shelters, land preservation organizations, clinics and other health services, and the like, whose shopping list can inspire donations more readily than can that of the organization that simply needs office supplies.

A land conservancy, for example, successfully uses a gift catalog in their efforts to preserve ecologically significant land. A sampling of the items contained in their catalog includes:

- Binoculars: four pairs, $200; one pair, $50
- Classroom visits: 10 visits, $400
- Scholarships for docent trainees: cost per docent, $50
- Gates for fences: one gate, $100
- Hand lenses: 25 hand lenses, $32
- Research grants for various projects (which are described, with amounts for each)
- Weather monitoring equipment: complete cost, $450

The catalog itself may be only a few pages long. It should include an "order form" that is a variation on the direct mail reply device. People can then "order" more than one item.

Some organizations have used this concept to raise money for intangible program components, such as client care, or provision of services. A nonprofit therapy collective listed these items in their gift catalog:

- Scholarship for one family therapy session: $60
- Complete six-week therapy program: $360
- Parent effectiveness training:
  - Full scholarship: $200
  - Partial scholarship: $50
- Day care for children of parents in therapy: $10/hr. (indicate number of hours you wish to donate)

The actual gift catalog can be fancy or plain. It can include illustrations of the needed item or photographs of people using the services. It can be laid out like a

---

* There is an important difference between the terms "earmark" and "designate" in fundraising. An "earmarked" gift is to be used for the purpose indicated until that need is filled; after that, it can be used at the organization's discretion. A "designated" gift can only be used for the purpose for which it is designated, even if that need has been filled. Organizations are advised to stay away from the term "designated."

regular mail order catalog or simply list the needed items on a sheet of paper.

Generally, using your imagination in layout and adding drawings and illustrations will make your catalog more effective. Laying it out in the form of a newsletter or booklet will give it the air of a catalog and make it stand out from regular mail appeals.

Your Newsletter as a Mail Appeal

If you have a newsletter or magazine that contains useful articles or information that people cannot easily obtain elsewhere, send a sample copy of portions of your publication to people not familiar with your organization with information on how to subscribe. You can have a special cover made for one issue of the publication or make up a special issue for promotional purposes, with the best of your previous issues.

In this variation, the cover becomes the mail appeal. The front or back inside cover includes a return form to be torn off, which is essentially a subscription form. A return envelope stapled into the newsletter will increase your returns. This appeal is not sent in an envelope.

If your newsletter is long (12 pages or more) and expensive to produce, consider making up a special short edition. This piece might be four to eight pages and contain one or two excellent articles plus a listing of articles and information that people would receive by subscribing. Include a subscription form, either as part of the cover or somewhere in the newsletter.

Whatever style you use, make sure it is clear that this issue is complimentary and where to find information about subscribing.

Some groups have found it effective simply to stamp "Complimentary copy—please subscribe" on their newsletter and send these complimentary copies to people whose names they have acquired. These can go with their regular mailing of the newsletter or as a separate mailing. If the newsletter is good enough, that simple message can be enough to generate donations.

Phantom Event

In a phantom event people are invited to a special event that is not going to happen. What will not happen is described in detail, and the prospects are invited to stay home and miss it. The appeal is sent in the style of an invitation, with the RSVP as the return form. (See sample on the next page.)

Phantom events work because they catch people off guard, they amuse them, and they appeal to the many people who don't enjoy large social events.

> ### *The Board of Directors of Youth Organizing for Peace*
>
> invites you to their first annual gala nonevent. We will not be at the event.
> We do not wish to look for parking and drink wine out of plastic glasses.
> We invite you to join us in staying home. You will not have to mingle
> with people you barely recognize. You will not have to eat soggy
> hors d'oeuvres, buy a fancy outfit to appear in, or travel after dark.
>
> #### PLEASE JOIN US IN STAYING HOME
> TIME: 6–10:30 • DATE: You pick it
> COST: $59.95
> Send us $50 and keep $9.95 to buy a bottle of wine to share with a loved one.
>
> We look forward to not seeing you.
>
> RSVP by June 1, using the enclosed card

The Brief Message

Organizations working on issues that are familiar to most people, or whose mission is totally self-evident, can use the brief message format. Your appeal and return form are all on the same piece of paper, and a return envelope is enclosed.

The brief message format conveys the following ideas: "I am not going to use a whole sheet of paper and precious minutes of your time. You know who we are. You read the paper and hear the news. Join us. We need you." Brief messages are effective when the group or the group's work is well known and requires little explanation. The brief message must use the word "you" effectively.

Groups working on specific health issues such as arthritis, cancer, asthma, or groups working on easy-to-understand programs such as homeless shelters or stop-smoking clinics can avail themselves of this method. An excellent example of the use of the brief message is an appeal from the UNC Fund (formerly the United Negro College Fund), which pictures a young African-American man looking depressed, and contains this brief message: "His math got him into college. Economics may keep him out. Give to the UNC Fund." The reader is pulled in quickly and asked to decide almost before there is time to think about it.

Pictures

Organizations that serve animals or people in distress can often express their message more poignantly through photographs or drawings than with words. A picture can take the place of many pages of text. Pictures can be part of a letter or a separate enclosure. For pictures to be effective they must be real and they must not be sentimental or patronizing. Photographs must not demean the people or animals in them.

Sometimes photographs are used to jar people's sensibilities. This can be effective when done carefully. Showing an animal caught in a leg-hold trap, for example, is far more moving than a wordy description of the trap and its effect. A picture of the bodies of people killed by death squads provides vivid evidence of a situation that many people find hard to believe.

Drawings, such as an artist's rendering in an appeal for a capital campaign of a new building, are usually used to augment the text of a letter. Again, the drawing must depict something real and be well done. It does not generally replace as many words as a photograph.

Promotional Items

Many long-established organizations use promotional items to draw in donors. The method works because people open the envelope to get what's inside — stamps, bumper stickers, pencils, address labels, seeds, etc. It also works by generating a feeling of obligation to reciprocate with a donation. Because these items are expensive it is generally better to use them as part of a thank-you package, if it all. With the exception of groups that have always used these items, they do not seem to increase the rate of response relative to their cost.

Use of Benefits and Premiums

An organization that intends to have a large base of donors who repeatedly give small gifts must establish a workable benefits program. The purpose of a benefits program is to give donors something tangible for their donation. Benefits are important for the simple reason that Americans are consumers. We are accustomed to getting things for our money, and even nonprofit organizations compete for the consumer dollar on this level.

The psychology of a benefit is this: The donor sends a gift, and your organization, in gratitude for the gift, sends a *free* benefit. The donor is not buying the benefit, which costs much less than his or her donation.

Although supporting the work of the group gives the donor a feeling of goodwill, this feeling lasts only a little while, and the donor needs a reminder of their gift and of the work of the group. A thank-you note is the first reminder. It should go out within 72 hours of receipt of the gift. The second reminder is the item or items that the group will send the donor regularly, such as a newsletter.

In setting up a benefits program, the organization must define what relationship their donors will have to the organization. If you want your donors to have a feeling of ownership and involvement in your organization, you should consider establishing a membership program. Each donor is then called a member. If your bylaws already specify the rights of members, and if you do not wish to give donors voting or other rights specified by your bylaws, amend your bylaws to include a class of nonvoting members, number unlimited. If you do not wish to have members, you might establish giving categories such as "friend," "supporter," "benefactor," and the like. Or you can create giving categories that do not convey any sense of relative importance by calling them "A," "B," "C."

After you decide what to call your donors, you must decide what you are going to give them and whether donors who give more money will get more attention. Most organizations find it useful to have three donor categories to reflect greater contribution amounts. Each category has incentives to join at that rate. The categories might be:

- Basic: $25–$100 — includes basic benefits package

- Larger: $101–$499 — includes basic package plus a book, T-shirt, or other incentive

- Major Donor: $500 and up — includes the above, plus regular reports on the progress of the organization and individual attention.

Generally, you will be seeking smaller gifts through the mail. A major donor requires a more personal approach, such as a personal phone call or a face-to-face meeting.

The Basic Benefits Package

The most common benefit is a newsletter. Appropriately, this benefit regularly reminds donors of your group, raises their level of awareness about your group's work, and provides information not available elsewhere or a point of view not generally expressed in the mass media. Other possible basic benefits include a T-shirt, bumper sticker, membership card (which doesn't have to entitle the member to anything), discounts to special events, or other educational materials.

There are two guidelines for choosing benefits for donors: 1) the fulfillment costs (that is, how much money it costs your organization to produce and send the item you promised) should never be more than one-fifth of the lowest membership category, and 2) while you can always add benefits, it is far more difficult to take them away.

In deciding on a benefits package, then, start with small benefits that you know your organization can continue to afford, and that you have the staff or volunteers to provide. The difference between a bimonthly newsletter and a quarterly one will not be nearly as important to the donor as it will be to your budget, staff, and volunteer time.

If you decide to have incentives for larger donations, try to find something that promotes your organization. A book about the work you do or that is related to a topic you address is good. Books can usually be purchased directly from the publisher in quantities of 10 or more for 40% off the cover price. Paperback volumes are fine. Paperweights, tote bags, bookmarks, bumper stickers, T-shirts, and the like are all acceptable as well. Specialty merchandising firms can send you catalogs of available items on which they can print your logo or message at a low cost.

The problem with books or any other benefit, however, is that it may not be easy to find a new one every year, which is why many groups use premiums to encourage people to give, but infrequently for renewals and upgrades.

Premiums

Premiums are additional thank-you gifts for donating within a specified time period. Announcement of a premium is often included in the mail appeal letter at the postscript, whose main purpose is to move the donor to act.

> P.S. Send your gift by December 1 and we will send you a special edition of a calendar created by a local artist for our group.

Or,

> P.S. We have a limited number of signed lithographs that we will send to the first 50 donors. Join today.

You don't want the renewing donor to put your appeal in the pile of bills to be paid later or to lose the appeal, so you offer them a premium for acting promptly.

Premiums are particularly useful in securing upgraded gifts. The majority of these donors are probably going to give anyway; the premium simply encourages them to give sooner and more: For example, letters to people who gave $25 could entice a higher gift with "Gifts of $40 or more receive two free tickets to the spring concert."

The best premiums from your organization's point of view are ones that you already have. For example, suppose you are doing a concert and ticket sales are slow. Offer renewing donors a free ticket for renewing by a certain date. Or suppose you have had too many calendars printed and cannot possibly sell them all before the beginning of the new year. Offer them as a premium.

In using premiums for acquiring new donors, remember to add the cost of the premium when figuring the cost of the mail appeal. This will lower your net income, but if you gain even one or two percentage points in response, the cost will be offset.

You can also use premiums when you don't wish to commit yourself to a regular benefit — just send the premium item when you have it.

Appealing to Current Donors

Once your organization has acquired donors, it should appeal to them several times a year. Too often, appeals to current donors are overlooked. Years of testing have proven that some donors will respond every time they are asked, another group will give less automatically but more than once a year, and that donor renewal rates are higher for all donors (even those who do not respond to extra appeals) when they receive several appeals a year.

Many groups have discovered that they can raise enough money from their current donors with repeated appeals that they can scale down their recruitment of new donors. Many large organizations appeal to their donors 8 to 12 times a year, which tends to have a saturating, and in the case of many donors, alienating, effect. Experience with hundreds of grassroots social change organizations shows that two to four appeals a year will raise significantly more money and increase renewal rates without irritating your donors. Since most people who give or buy by mail get upwards of 1,200 pieces of bulk mail a year, two to four appeals a year will barely make a ripple in the volume of mail most of your donors are receiving.

Repeated appeals are successful for a number of reasons. First, a person's cash flow can vary greatly from month to month. A person receiving an appeal from a group he or she supports may have just paid car insurance and so throws the appeal away. If the organization were to ask again after two more months the person might have more money available and make a donation.

Second, different people respond to different types of appeals. Sending only one or two appeals a year does not allow for the variety of choices donors want. Organizations often discover that donors who regularly give $25 a year will give $50, $100, or more when appealed to for a special project. People who respond to specific project appeals are often called "bricks and mortar" people. They "buy" things for an organization: media spots, food for someone for a week, a job training program, a new building.

We rarely know why people don't respond to appeals. Despite this lack of knowledge many people are willing to make the assumption that the donor doesn't want to give, when any of the following might be true:

- The donor has been on vacation and mail has piled up, so anything that is not a bill or a personal letter, including your appeal, gets tossed.

- The donor is having personal problems and cannot think of anything else right now, even though he or she might be quite committed to your group.

- The appeal is lost in the mail, or the donor meant to give but the appeal got lost or accidentally thrown away before it could be acted on.

Donors do not feel "dunned to death" by multiple appeals. On the contrary, they get a sense that a lot is happening in the organization. Their loyalty is developed when they know that their continuing donations are needed. Most important, they have an opportunity to express their own interests when a particular appeal matches their concerns.

Once an organization has accepted the idea of sending appeals throughout the year, they often wonder what they are going to say in each one. The following section contains 12 ideas to help you choose some approaches. Some of these appeals are taken from or modeled on specific groups' letters. Some will suit one organization better than another, but almost any organization should be able to find one or two ideas that they could modify and use for their group.

Seasonal Appeals

1. End-of-year: "As you close your books for this year, please remember _____ (name of organization). We have many more clients this time of year, and your additional support can ensure uninterrupted service."

2. Beginning-of-year (written as a testimonial): "One of my New Year's resolutions was to give more money this year to _____ (name of organization). I realized that, like many of my resolutions, this one could fade if I didn't act now. So I sent an extra $25 on January 5. I imagine that many of our members made a similar resolution. Perhaps you did. If you are like me, time may pass without action. So join me, and send that extra donation now."

Holiday Appeals

1. Lincoln's Birthday: "President Lincoln was only one of the more famous people to be killed with a handgun. I know you want to end this senseless violence. An extra donation from you, sent today, will give us the extra funds we need to work on (special program) against handguns/crime in the street/to strengthen our community organization activities/escort people who are alone across campus."

2. Valentine's Day: "Do you often think of important people on Valentine's Day? Do you remember them with flowers, candy, or cards? I know I do. This year,

I thought of other important people in my life — the people at _____ (name of organization). They really depend on us, their members, for the financial support they need. Will you join me in sending an extra donation? You can send flowers or candy as well. Simply use the enclosed card."

3. Labor Day: "A time to take the day off. But what about all the people who want to work — the part of the population that is unemployed? For them Labor Day is another reminder of their joblessness. Our organization is providing training to thousands of people so that they can get good jobs in areas needing workers. Remember the unemployed this Labor Day with a gift to _____ (name of organization)."

4. Columbus Day: "Columbus discovered America. This is one part of American history almost everyone knows. The problem is that this is only a half-truth: Columbus discovered America for white people. There were already people here — our people. We are Americans. Yet our history since Columbus has been one of genocide, displacements, and oppression. At the Indigenous People's Organizing Project, we are determined to reclaim Columbus Day. You have helped us in the past. Will you help us, on this holiday, to continue our vital work?"

5. Thanksgiving Day: "We would like to make Thanksgiving Day a little brighter for hundreds of people in our city who cannot afford to buy food. With your donation of $14.50 we will provide a family with a turkey and all the trimmings. Please give whatever you can."

6. Christmas/Hanukkah/Winter Solstice/end-of-year: "We are just $700 short of our goal to buy a new furnace for our runaway house/send our staff person to the state capitol to press for the bill we have been working so hard on/ distribute thousands of leaflets telling seniors how to get their homes insulated for free. Can you help us meet our goal with a special end-of-year donation?"

Old Standbys

1. Anniversary: "Our organization is now entering its third/fifth/fiftieth anniversary of service to the community. Celebrate with us by sending $1/$10/$100 for each year of our existence. For your gift we will be pleased to send you a special anniversary parchment, suitable for framing. In addition, for those donating $1,000 or more, there will be a special reception honoring Famous Person, who has been so helpful to our cause."

2. Famous Person: "I'm Very Famous TV Star. You may have seen me on television. In my personal life, I am very concerned about birth control/tenants' rights/public education. I believe that Good Organization defends our rights in this area. Please join me in supporting them." (Famous person can be truly famous, such as a movie star, or someone well known only in your community and widely respected there.)

3. Another member: "My name is _____. I have been a member of _____ (name of organization) for five years. In that time, I have witnessed the continuing erosion of our rights and the seemingly malicious efforts of our leaders to take what little we have left. All that stands between them and us is Good Organization. In the past five years, our organization has succeeded in _____ and _____. That's why I am giving a little extra this year. Thirty dollars is not a lot, but it really helps, and if everyone gave just $30, $50, or even $100, it would really add up. Will you join me?"

4. Urgent need: "We have an urgent need to raise $2,000 to alert the public to the hazards of chemical dumping being proposed for the east side of town. This little-known bill, which has the support of our supervisors, will bring unwarranted health hazards to more than 1,000 people. The town council is trying to slide this bill through without our knowledge; we must protest. Help us stop this outrage now, with an extra donation of $25, $35, or whatever you can send."

seven

How to Conduct Special Events

Special events, also often called "fundraising benefits," are social gatherings of many sorts that expand the reputation of the organization, give those attending an amusing, interesting, or moving time, and possibly make money for the organization sponsoring the event. The variety of special events is practically limitless, as are the possibilities for money earned or lost, amount of work put in, number of people participating, and so on.

Because of their variety and flexibility, special events are excellent strategies for acquiring, retaining, or upgrading donors, and organizations serious about building a broad base of individual donors need to have at least one or two special events every year. Special events are both the most common fundraising device used by small organizations and the most misunderstood. They can do things for an organization that no other fundraising strategy can do as well, yet what they can best do is often the last thing that is expected or wanted.

Special events should have three goals:
• To generate publicity for the organization
• To raise the visibility of the organization
• To bring in (new) money.

Generating publicity means getting a particular audience to pay attention to the organization for a limited time by means of advertising the event and by the quality of the event.

Enhancing visibility raises the overall profile of the organization in the community. Visibility is the cumulative effect of publicity. With each successive event, and in combination with other fundraising and organizing efforts, the organization becomes known to more and more people. Eventually the organization becomes known to all who should know about it. The visibility of your group can be assessed by asking this question: Of the people who should know about you, what percentage do? This percentage is called your "visibility quotient." Assessing a visibility quotient requires thinking through what types of people should know about your organization and what mechanisms reach those potential donors. For example, if you are regularly featured in the local newspaper, you may be well known to those who read the paper, but you may also need to reach people who don't read the newspaper. In that case, getting more print publicity will not help you, and you may need to move to radio, speaking engagements at houses of worship, or a door-to-door canvass in order to reach new constituencies. Events are excellent publicity-generating tools because they give the media a "hook" around which to focus attention on the group. A newspaper or radio station may be interested in discussing or even doing a profile of the actual event — an auction, self-defense class, or concert — and will mention the sponsoring group's name, thus raising visibility.

Raising money is a secondary goal for a special event because there are many faster and easier ways to raise money than this one. An organization that simply needs money (perhaps from being in a cash flow bind, or having an unexpected expense) will find that the slowest ways to raise that money are seeking foundation funding or having an event. On the other hand, an organization that wants to raise its profile, bring in new people, and possibly make money will find a special event an ideal strategy. In many cases special events can lose money or barely break even and still be successful because of the publicity and visibility they produced.

TYPES OF PEOPLE WHO ATTEND SPECIAL EVENTS

There are two categories of people who attend events: those who come because of the event itself and those who come both for the event and to support your group. In the first category are people who would come to a particular event no matter who sponsored it. These people attend flea markets, dances, movie benefits, decorator showcases, auctions, and the like. Many times these people will not even know the name of the group sponsoring the event. In a similar vein are small businesses or corporations that will buy ads in an adbook, donate raffle prizes, buy tables at luncheons, or even underwrite an event, but would not give the organization money under any other circumstance. They want the advertising and resulting goodwill the event gives them, and the chance to target a specific audience cheaply. Raising money from a person or a business that would not give you money otherwise does not constitute donor "acquisition" but it is a smart use of an event, given that the event should also be designed to draw people who are interested in your group. For organizations in rural communities or serving a very small constituency, and unable to build a large base of donors, events that draw people to the event rather than the cause will be imperative.

The second type of people who attend events are both interested in the event and believe in your group's work. They may not have heard of your organization before learning of this event, or they may already know of your organization and want to support it while getting something important to them. For example, women wanting to take a self-defense class may choose one sponsored by the local rape relief program rather than a commercial gym in order to support the rape relief program. After the classes, some of the participants may want to join the program as volunteers and paying members. People who buy all their holiday presents at a public radio crafts fair, or enter marathons sponsored by groups they believe in, are good prospects to follow up with direct mail.

Among the second type are people who appreciate your organization's work but can't afford or don't want to give more than a small amount. For them, buying a $1 raffle ticket or attending a $6 movie benefit is a perfect way to show their support.

CHOOSING A FUNDRAISING EVENT

Several criteria should be considered in choosing a fundraising event, including the appropriateness of the event, the image reflected on the organization by the event, the amount of volunteer energy required, the amount of front money needed, the repeatability and the timing of the event, and how the event fits into the organization's overall fundraising plan.

Appropriateness of the Event

To decide if an event is appropriate, ask yourself, "If people knew nothing about our organization except that it had sponsored this event, what would they think of our group?" If you think the answer is "neutral or good," then the event is appropriate. If you think that you would want them to know more about the group than just what the event implies about it, you should think again. Examples of inappropriate events abound. In the extreme, if you are the symphony you don't sponsor a pie-eating contest; if you run an alcohol recovery program you don't have a wine tasting. Often, however, the question of appropriateness is subtler than in those examples. The following are two case studies.

A QUESTION OF CONSISTENCY

An organization working to end sweatshop conditions in garment factories around the world plans a luncheon to which they will invite 1,000 people in hopes it will be attended by 500 of them. The development director asks a large print shop employing more than 75 people to print their invitations and adbook as an in-kind donation. He then finds out from a worker at the print shop that the working conditions at this business are not good. The workers are exposed to toxic fumes, they are paid minimum wage with no benefits, and they are laid off during slow periods, then rehired when business picks up. A union has been trying to organize the workers at the printshop. A member of the union calls the development director of the anti-sweatshop organization and asks him not to use this shop. She explains the terrible working conditions and points out the lack of consistency for an organization whose mission is to stand up for workers everywhere. However, the lure of free printing for 1,000 invitations and 750 adbooks, saving the organization upwards of $2,000, is too much to pass up. The development director thanks the union organizer for her comments, but says that his using this print shop will not worsen conditions there and that not using it will not improve conditions.

The union knows that this organization's events get a lot of publicity and often attract a cross section of powerful people. They decide to organize an "information" line outside the event. The line is not a picket line and they don't ask people to boycott the event, but union members and volunteers do hand out information about the printshop outside the hotel where the event is held. The workers at the hotel, members of a different union, spontaneously decide to join the information line. As a result, the event becomes a public relations nightmare from which this group is still recovering. They learned the hard way the importance of political consistency.

A QUESTION OF JUDGMENT

A women's health organization in a large West Coast city offered as a top raffle prize a case of very fine, expensive wine. During their promotion, a number of studies were released showing the high rate of alcoholism among women. An internal debate ensued over whether it was appropriate for a group working to prevent dangerous drugs and devices from being given to women to offer alcohol — a potentially dangerous drug — as a raffle prize. Proponents argued that only 10% of the population is alcoholic and that alcohol does not harm most people who use it. The chance of an alcoholic winning that prize was slim compared to how many people would be attracted to the raffle because of this prize. However, opponents swayed the group by reasoning that they would not approve of a contraceptive that hurt 10% of its users. The group withdrew the prize, not wanting to promote a drug with any potential for harm.

Image of the Organization

In addition to being appropriate, the event as much as possible should be in keeping with the image of the organization or should promote the image the organization wishes to have. Although considerations of appropriateness sometimes include those of image, image is also a distinct issue. Many events that are appropriate for a group do not promote a memorable image of it. For example, a library would choose a book sale over a garage sale, even though both are appropriate. An environmental organization would use a whitewater rafting trip over season tickets to the ballet as a door prize, even though both are nice prizes. An organization promoting awareness of the problem of high blood pressure might choose a health fair over a dance. The idea is to attract people to your event who might become regular donors to your organization by linking the event to your mission.

Energy of Volunteers

Looking at the volunteer energy required to plan and mount an event involves several considerations. How many people are required to put on this event? What would these volunteers be doing if they were not working on this event? Do you have enough volunteers who have the time required to produce this event — not only to manage the event on the day of its occurrence but to take care of all the details that must be done beforehand?

Volunteer time is a resource to be cultivated, guided, and used appropriately. For example, don't use someone with connections to major donor prospects to sell T-shirts at a shopping mall on Saturday afternoon. Similarly, a friendly, outgoing person who loves to talk on the phone should be the phone-a-thon coordinator or the solicitor of auction items and not be asked to bake brownies for the food booth at the county fair. Obviously, what the volunteer wants to do should be of primary concern. People generally like to do what they are good at and be involved where they can be most useful.

Front Money

Most special events require that some money be spent before there is assurance that any money will be raised. The front money needed for an event should be an amount your organization could afford to lose if the event had to be canceled. This money should already be available — you should not, for example, use funds from advance ticket sales to rent the place where the event will be held. If the event is canceled, some people will want their money back. Events that require a lot of front money can create a cash flow problem in the organization if the need for this money is not taken into account.

Repeatability

The best event is one that becomes a tradition in your community, so that every year people look forward to the event that your group sponsors. Using this criterion can save you from discarding an event simply because the turnout was small the first time you did it. Perhaps you got too little publicity and only a handful of people came. If each of those people had a great time and you heard them saying, "I wish I had brought Juan," or "I wish Alice had known about this," then it may be worth having the event again next year. To decide if an event is repeatable, evaluate whether the same number of people working the same number of hours would raise more money producing this event again.

Timing

You need to find out what else is happening in your community at the time you want to hold your event. You don't want to conflict with the major fundraising event of a similar organization, nor do you want to be the tenth dance or auction in a row. If you are appealing to a particular constituency, you need to think of their timing. Farmers are mostly unavailable during planting and harvest seasons; Jews will not appreciate being invited to a buffet on Yom Kippur; gay men and lesbians may not come to a silent meditation scheduled during the Gay and Lesbian Pride Parade, and so on.

The Big Picture

The final consideration is the place of the event in the overall fundraising picture. If you find that the same people attend all your organization's events as well as give money by mail, you are "eating your own tail" and need to rethink how you are using events. If you cannot seem to get publicity for your events or you are unable to find an event to reach new constituencies, then maybe special events is not the right approach. If, after analyzing your donor base, you decide that your organization needs to build its number of thoughtful donors, then you won't do as many events whose main purpose is acquisition. In other words, the results of special events (new names, publicity, new volunteers) must be fed into the overall effort to build a donor base or the effort of the event will have mostly been wasted.

HOW TO PLAN A SPECIAL EVENT

Special events require more planning time than one would imagine. Because so much can go wrong, and because many things often hinge on one thing so that one mistake can throw off weeks of work, events must be planned with more attention to minute detail than almost any other fundraising strategy.

The Committee for Special Events

There must be a small committee of volunteers overseeing the work for the event. Using paid staff time to organize a special event is expensive and does not help to train or involve volunteers in substantive fundraising tasks.

The job of the committee is to plan and coordinate the event, not to do every task. After planning the event, most of the committee's work is delegating as many tasks as possible. Large committees can be unwieldy and counterproductive. With a larger committee planning the event, it is likely that some important element will be left out, that the planning process will take longer, that the committee meetings will be like special events themselves, and that the committee members will quickly burn out.

Each special event should have its own committee, although there can be overlap from one event to another. Special events are labor intensive, however, and people need to have a rest period between events and a chance not to participate in every one. The committee must have staff and board support, and everyone must agree that the chosen event is a good idea.

Tasks of the Committee

There are three simple steps a special events committee should take to ensure the success of the event: Detail a master task list, prepare a budget, and develop a timeline.

1. Detail a master task list. On a piece of paper, make four columns labeled What, When, Who, and Done (see example on next page). Under "What" list all the tasks that must be accomplished. Include everything — even those things you are sure no one would ever forget, such as "Pick up tickets at printer" or "Send invitations to the board." Every minute detail should be on this list. Under the "When" column, note beside each task when it must be finished. Now put the list into chronological order, so that you have a list of things that must be done and the order in which to do them. After completing steps two and three, you will complete the "Who" column — to whom the task is assigned — and note the date the task is completed under "Done."

MASTER TASK LIST

WHAT	WHEN	WHO	DONE

2. Prepare a budget. On a piece of paper or in a spreadsheet program, make two sets of three columns as shown below:

BUDGET

INCOME	ESTIMATED	ACTUAL
Item	$	$
Item	$	$
Item	$	$
Total income	**$**	**$**

EXPENSES	ESTIMATED	ACTUAL
Item	$	$
Item	$	$
Item	$	$
Total expenses	**$**	**$**

Net	$	$

Look at the master task list you just created. Put anything that will cost money in the column marked "Expenses." Anything that will raise money is put in the column marked "Income." When you have listed everything, subtract expenses from income to find the projected "net income," or financial goal, of the event. The budget should be simple but thorough, so that all costs are accounted for and planned on.

As you budget, remember that an estimate is not a guess. If someone says, "The estimate for food is..." or "The estimate for printing is..." it means he or she has called several vendors for prices, bargained, and is satisfied that the estimate will be the price or very close to the price. As costs are incurred they can be noted under the column marked "Actual." As much as possible, put off paying for anything until after the event is over and be sure you work in cancellation clauses for rentals or other contracts. For example, if a hall rents for $600 with $300 required as a deposit, try to reserve the right to get all or part of that $300 back, if necessary, as close to the date of the event as possible.

Ideally, of course, you will aim to get as many things as possible given as in-kind donations, but don't budget to get anything free. Always put down a price in the budget. This will protect you in case you do have to pay for something you had planned to get donated, and also give you a cushion in case you have an unexpected expense.

3. Create a timeline. To ensure that you have thought of everything that should be done, and that you have allowed enough time to do everything, think "backwards" from the target date of your event. If you want to have a dance on August 10, what would you have to do on August 9? To do those things, what would you have to do in early August? What would have to be in place by July 15? And so on, back to the day you are starting from. By this "backward planning," the committee may find out that it is impossible to put on the event in the time allowed. In that case they must either modify the event or change the date. Thinking through each week's tasks for the timeline may also surface expenses you hadn't thought of, or additional tasks. Add these to your task list and budget.

As you plan, remember to take into account that, although there may be 90 days between now and the event, there may be only 60 "working" days because of schedule conflicts. For example, if a number of your volunteers have children, you should check a school calendar to make sure you don't need anything done on the first or last day of school, or during a vacation, or on commencement day. Few organizations can have a New Year's party as a fundraiser simply because they cannot get anyone to work during the two weeks preceding New Year's Day.

Establish "go/no go" dates. On your timeline, you will notice that there are periods of intense activity and lulls throughout the time leading up to the event. The periods of intense activity, where several tasks must be accomplished and each is related to the other (i.e., design, layout, proofread, print, and mail invitations), are called "task clusters." These groups of tasks must be accomplished as projected on your timeline. The date by which each cluster must be accomplished is a "go/no-go" date. At those dates, evaluate your progress and decide if you are going to proceed with the event or if you are too hopelessly behind or too many things have gone wrong and you should just cancel or modify the event. Go/no-go dates can also be set for goals to determine if the event will be successful, such as how many tickets you should have sold, or how many ads in the adbook you should have acquired, or how many underwriters you should have lined up.

Once the committee has prepared the task list, the budget, and the timeline, they are ready to assign tasks to other volunteers. When you ask volunteers or vendors to do things, give them a due date that is sooner than the one in the "When" column of your task list. That way, in the best case you will always be ahead of your schedule; in the worst case — if the task is not completed — you will have some time to get it done.

What Not to Forget

Here is a checklist of commonly forgotten items in planning an event:

• Liquor license

• Insurance (on the hall, for the speaker, for participants). Contracts vary on this, but check it out. It often happens that a hall or auditorium is inexpensive because insurance is not included but is required of the renting organization. A one-night insurance policy or a rider on an existing policy can cost upwards of $2,000.

• Logistics of transporting food, drink, speakers, performers, sound equipment, and the like to and from the event

• Lodging for performers or speaker

• Parking: either in a well-lit lot or available on well-lit streets

• If there is going to be food: platters, plates, utensils, and napkins. Don't forget things like salt and pepper, hot and cold cups, cream and sugar.

• Heat or air conditioning: Is it available, does it cost extra, will you need to bring your own fans or space heaters?

• Receipt books for people who pay at the door or who buy anything sold at the event

Here are some questions you need to ask before the event:

• Is the venue wheelchair accessible? Make sure that all rooms are accessible, especially both the men and women's bathroom doors, stalls, toilet paper dispenser, sinks, etc. Sometimes a building will be labeled "wheelchair accessible" when only the front door and one area of seating are actually accessible.

- Where and how to dispose of trash? Are there clearly marked recycling bins and trash cans?

- Will you allow smoking? If so, where, and is that clearly marked?

- Does the invitation's reply card fit into the return envelope?

- Has everything been proofread at least five times?

- Is the organization's address, Web site, and phone number on the reply card, flier, poster, invitation, everything else?

- If appropriate, is the event advertised on the Web site and is there an announcement of it on your answering machine?

- Are the price, date, time, place, directions, and RSVP instructions for the event on all advertising?

- Have you considered the necessity of child care or language translation?

- How safe is the neighborhood? Will women feel safe coming alone?

- Can you see and hear from every seat? (Sit in a number of seats to make sure.)

- Who will open the room or building for you? Do you need a key?

- Where are the fire exits?

- Do you know how all the lights work?

- What has to be done for clean-up?

The Evaluation

The final step in planning a special event is evaluation. Within a few days after the event, the planning committee should fill out an evaluation form, as illustrated on the next page. Save this evaluation along with copies of the advertising, the invitations, and any other information that would be useful for next year's planning committee.

The evaluation will allow you to decide whether or not to do the event again, and will also ensure that the same number of people working the same amount of time will raise more and more money every year. It should not be necessary to create the planning documents described above more than once. Once you have created them, every year a new committee can modify and add to them, but each committee is building on the knowledge and experience of previous committees.

SPECIAL EVENT REPORT (EVALUATION FORM)

Approximately how much time did the committee spend on this event? (In evaluating this, try to subtract time spent fooling around and be sure to count time members spent driving around on errands and on the phone.) _____

Did this event bring in any new members? _____ How many?_____

Can people who came to this event be invited to be members? _____

Did this event bring in new money? _____

Does this event have the capacity to grow every year? _____

What would you do exactly the same next time? _____
_____

What would you do differently? _____
_____

List sources of free or low-cost items and who got them and indicate whether these items will be available next year, in your opinion:

_____   _____
_____   _____
_____   _____
_____   _____

What kind of follow-up needs to be done? (For example, thank-you notes written to people who went out of their way to help you, bills paid, prizes sent to those who weren't there at the drawing, tablecloths or platters returned to those who loaned them, etc.)

_____   _____
_____   _____
_____   _____
_____   _____

Which committee members did what work?

_____   _____
_____   _____
_____   _____
_____   _____

Which committee members would be willing to work on this event next year?

_____   _____
_____   _____
_____   _____
_____   _____

Other comments: _____
_____

SOME SPECIAL EVENTS IN DETAIL

This section discusses two events: a house party and an annual dinner. It also covers two important components of many events, which could also be held as independent events: a raffle and an adbook. These four activities have been chosen because they are relatively easy to organize in the sense that they follow a formula and, taken as a whole, they demonstrate all the principles of fundraising that are discussed in this book. The next section contains an annotated glossary of special events — a quick look at 24 events, their possible net income, and the time it takes to organize them.

How to Do a House Party

One of the easiest special events, and sometimes one of the most lucrative, is the common house party. In some ways, it seems ludicrous to describe how to do a house party since anyone who has ever put on a birthday party, school picnic, anniversary celebration, let alone a small wedding or bat mitzvah, already knows most of what there is to know about putting on a house party. However, because sometimes the seemingly most simple events are fraught with pitfalls, I want to describe the obvious and not so obvious details about giving a house party.

First, the basic definition of a house party: A person or persons involved in a nonprofit group invites his, her, or their friends to a party at their house. The purpose of the party is to educate the friends about the work of the nonprofit group and ask them to make a contribution.

The party is also a place for those attending to meet people, see old friends, and eat good food, so it sets up a cordial atmosphere for the request. Finally, a house party allows someone not familiar with the group to learn a lot about it, ask questions, and get some personal attention without being obligated to give. People can either give a very small gift or not give at all without embarrassing themselves, and they can attend the house party without having to pay to get in.

House parties are a useful venue for an organization to explain a complicated issue to many people at once, allowing them to ask questions and get more information. A house party can be used to see what questions friendly people may have about an issue or strategy, and thus help prepare the group for less friendly audiences. House parties have been widely used over the past 30 years to raise money for the United Farmworkers, anti-apartheid work, gay and lesbian organizing, as well as hundreds of political initiatives and candidates.

In addition to explaining an issue, a house party can also be the venue for a group of people to meet someone famous or important, or someone who brings interesting information about the issue your group is working on. Recently released political prisoners, journalists who have witnessed atrocities, workers from sweat-shops, or activists of various kinds can tell their stories to an audience that is then moved to help amend the situation. The host then describes what people can do to respond (vote, give money, boycott, give money, demonstrate, give money).

No matter what else you ask people to do, ask them to give money. It is the only thing they can do right on the spot, and it is usually the most passive action, requiring the least amount of work. The final use of a house party, which underlies all the other uses, is to expand the organization's donor base.

There are five steps to putting on a house party:

1. Find the person who is willing to host it at his/her house and take on other responsibilities related to the event.

2. Prepare the list of people to be invited.

3. Design the invitation.

4. Choreograph the event, particularly the pitch.

5. Evaluate and follow up.

Find a Host

The host of a house party has several responsibilities, the least of which is providing the house and the food. The host invites anyone he or she thinks might be interested in the organization or the topic being discussed. At the party, the host or another person gives an appropriate description of the organization and the issues. Then the host makes a pitch for money.

The host must be a donor who has contributed a gift, regardless of size, that was significant to her or him. The donor asks the guests to join him or her in making a significant gift of their own. In some cases, the host cannot bring him or herself to make the pitch. In that case, the host needs to introduce the person making the pitch in such a way that the audience knows the host has made a gift. A staff person or another board person will then ask the guests for money.

The ideal host is someone close enough to the organization to understand the importance of the group and to be willing to conquer their fear of asking friends for money, but not so close as to have all their friends already be donors. A major flaw of house parties is that the same people attend several house parties for the same organization. Those people may enjoy each party, but wind up feeling "nickel-and-dimed to death" and the donor base of the group is not expanded.

Prepare the List of People to Be Invited

Once someone has volunteered to host the party, the organization's staff must help that person decide who should be invited. A house party can have any number of people, but generally works best when there are at least 12 guests and not more than 50. Figure out how many people the house can comfortably accommodate. If you are planning a presentation, you will need to make sure most of the people can sit down at that time. If the pitch is to be short, then having enough seats will not be so important.

Generally you need to invite three times as many people as you want to attend. There should be one person from the organization such as a board member, volunteer, or staff for every five to eight guests, so include them in the numbers.

Obviously, start with the host's friends. Don't forget neighbors. Sometimes, a house party is also a way to meet neighbors. For example, a member of a group working for peace in the Middle East had a house party at his apartment. Knowing how emotional some people can be about a Palestinian homeland being proposed as part of a just peace, he was nervous to invite people he didn't know well. Nevertheless, he decided to take a risk and invite his entire apartment building. A Jewish neighbor from another floor, whom he had never met, gave $5,000 that night! Suggest that the host think about people at church, synagogue, social clubs, work, and relatives. Except for those people specifically invited to mingle and r epresent the organization, don't include very many people who are already donors. If you invite donors and use this opportunity as an upgrade strategy, focus on those who could be asked to give more money than they currently do.

Design the Invitation

The invitation does not have to be fancy, and it can be printed at an instant-print copy shop, so expense shouldn't be an issue. For groups with access to desktop publishing programs, good-looking invitations can be turned out very inexpensively.

The invitation should reflect something about the host and about the crowd being invited. This will make people want to attend. Whether your invitation is serious or light, educational or assuming knowledge on the part of the invitee, always include the following:

- An indication that people will be asked for money. "Bring your checkbook" is the most direct way to make this known. You might also say, "Bring your questions and your checkbook," or, "Find out how your contribution can be instrumental in starting/stopping/ending/creating/propelling/saving/helping _____." One lighthearted invitation said, "Of course, you'll be asked for money. Come anyway. The worst thing that will happen is you'll have to listen to something you don't agree with, but you'll get free food!"

- A way for people to give without coming to the party. On the invitation's return card include the option, "I can't come, but I want to help. Enclosed is my donation."

- Encourage people to bring friends. Require an RSVP so you will know how many people are coming.

- Give people clear directions to the house. If finding the place is at all confusing, draw a map. Include the phone number of the host.

Choreograph the Event

Where most parties fail is in not having thought through exactly how the event will go. To avoid this danger, imagine yourself a guest at the event and play over in your mind what will happen.

You walk or drive up to the house. Is it obvious where to park? (This can be important if the host shares a driveway with people not attending the party, if there is a hidden ditch near the house, or if the neighbors are the kind that are likely to call the police about a guest parked too near the crosswalk.) Is the house obvious? Is there a porch light? Is there a sign saying, "Marvin's house party here"? This is especially important in rural communities where homes can be hard to see, and in big apartment complexes where it may be confusing to find the right number.

You come in to the house or apartment. Is it obvious where to put your coat? If not, someone needs to be stationed at the door to provide that information. Ditto for the bathroom. Is there a place where people will sign in and that has literature about the group? There should be a guest book for everyone to sign their name and provide their address and phone number.

You look around for people you know and make your way to the food. Is there a traffic jam at the food table? Pull the table out from the wall, so people can serve themselves from all sides of it. Put the drinks on a separate table removed from the food table to force people to move on from the food or from the drinks. If possible, have several small platters of food, rather than two or three large platters. Are the plates big enough? You don't want people to have to have five helpings to get full, or stay hungry because they are too embarrassed to keep going back for more food. People returning to the food table create a traffic jam, and people feeling hungry create a non-money-giving atmosphere. If the house allows it, there can be several food tables in different rooms serving different kinds of food. Serve things that are easy to eat while standing up — finger food rather than things that need a fork and knife. Don't serve anything that would be a disaster if spilled (such as red wine on light-colored carpeting, chili on the couch).

Once you get your food, you look for a place to sit. Are there enough chairs?

Make sure no chair is sitting alone or obstructing people coming in and out of the entrance or the bathroom or kitchen. When you are done with your food, where will you put your empty dish? Make sure there are several trash cans around for disposable dishes and utensils, an obvious table or plastic tub for dishes needing to be washed, and a container for recyclable beverage bottles and cans.

TWO HOUSE PARTIES FOR ONE GROUP

An organization of Catholics advocating the ordination of women had two house parties. Each party was geared to a different audience and everything from the invitations to the pitch reflected that difference.

One party was given by three Catholic nuns who live in a group house. They invited other sisters as well as people from their local parish who they thought would share their belief that women should be able to be priests. These women are well known in the community for being outspoken and courageous. Most of the people they invited were Catholic. Their invitation was on a standard sheet of paper, on the top of which was the slogan, "If you won't ordain women, don't baptize them." Further down was a description of the group, the list of the party's hosts, and the date, time, and place of the event. The page concluded with "Eat, drink, and bring your checkbook." It was simple, direct, and appealed to a group of people who were familiar with the issues.

At the party there was no formal presentation besides the pitch. The party attracted about 50 people, raised a little over $1,500, and signed on 20 new members. Almost everyone attending made a donation.

The second house party was given by a married couple who are members of the parish and active in the organization. They invited people from their workplaces (the husband works in a shelter for homeless people, the wife for a public interest law firm handling mostly sex discrimination cases), from other churches, and from the neighborhood. Most of those invited were not Catholic and some were probably not religious. Many have been active in women's organizations. Their invitation was done in a card format, with a quote from one of Paul's letters in the New Testament on the front: "In Christ there is neither male nor female, Jew nor Greek...all are one...." The inside described the organization and invited people to hear a talk about the history of women in the Catholic Church and the importance to the women's movement of the push to ordain women. The speaker was one of the nuns who gave the first party.

More than 40 people came to this party. Many asked difficult questions about the priority of this effort in light of the many needs of women, the point of being ordained into a patriarchal and hierarchical church, why the women didn't seek ordination in a different denomination, and so on. The discussion was lively and sometimes heated. At the end, the wife of the couple explained her commitment to this cause and asked everyone to join her and her husband in giving $100 or more. Twenty people gave $100 or more, including one new donor who gave $1,000; another ten people gave less than $100 for a total of $3,100. Of the 30 who gave, 25 people had never given to this organization before. About a dozen people did not give at all, but the hosts reported that several of them gave later, and for everyone the party had been important in raising consciousness on the issue.

Orchestrate the Special Moment: The Pitch

Everything at the house party should be built around the pitch. Make arrangements ahead of time with at least two and not more than four people that when the host says, "I hope you will make a donation," they will pull out checkbooks or hand over checks to members of the organization. They don't have to be ostentatious about it, but a few people have to break the ice and show that this is the time to give money.

Some people object to this practice, claiming that it imposes too much pressure. However, a little more thought will show that it is the considerate thing to do. Few people have the self-confidence to be the first to do anything. When the host asks for money, many people are prepared to give, but everyone has a brief attack of anxiety, "Perhaps this isn't when you give the money," or, "Perhaps I am the only person in the room who believes in this cause," or, "Perhaps everyone else already turned in their money and I will look odd if I give my money now." Having some people go first gives permission for everyone else who wants to give to do it now. Much like ushers at plays who show you your seat without being asked, or clerks in clothing stores who hand you the appropriate accessory (without you having to reveal that you wouldn't have known what to put with that outfit), the people planted to make the first donation show that giving is the right thing to do at this time.

Time the pitch so that the most people will be there when it is made. This is usually 45 minutes to an hour into the party. The host calls for people's attention. The members of the organization discreetly get envelopes ready and the two to four "plants" space themselves around the room. The host introduces him/herself and welcomes everyone. If there is a presentation, the host introduces the presenter. (If there is more than one host, such as a couple, or a group, they should take turns talking so it is clear that both or all are involved.)

After the presentation, the host should be the one who gives the pitch. If the presenter is a famous person or somehow special to the work of the group, that person can sometimes make a formal request for money, followed by the host saying, "I hope you will join me in helping this important cause." It doesn't matter if the host is nervous or doesn't like asking for money. Your proceeds will be cut in half (at least) without a pitch, or at least a strong indication of support, from the party sponsor.

Sometimes people argue that doing the party — loaning the house, arranging for the food, giving up the time — should indicate the host's interest. Indeed it does. It shows that the host helped save the group the cost of renting a conference room at a hotel. But, in order for the guests to give money, the host must also say that he or she gives money and wants anyone who agrees with him or her to do the same.

How the pitch is made determines how the money will be collected. This is also decided ahead of time. The best way to get the most money at the party is to pass around envelopes immediately after the host speaks. If you would prefer, the host can say, "Please put your donation in the basket over there," and point to a place. Or the host can say, "You can hand me your check, or give it to any of the people wearing an 'End the Death Penalty' T-shirt." In any case, tell people how and when to give the money.

After the pitch is made, the host should remain standing in front of the group and give people a few moments to write their checks. A very effective method is to say, "Let's just have a moment of silence right now so that everyone can write a check or make a pledge. For those who have already given, just sit quietly for a moment while everyone else has a chance to catch up with you." Then wait a minute and say, "When you have finished writing your check and putting it in the envelope, pass it to _____" and then tell people who to give their envelope to. This method ensures that no one who wants to give will leave without making a gift, but gives those who do not wish to give a way to sit quietly without being embarrassed.

House parties often fail at the moment right after the pitch. For example, at one house party, the host said, "I hope you will all think about making a gift to this group, which is my favorite." Then, without missing a beat, he said, "Now that the fundraising part is over, eat up and drink up! Let's have fun." People did exactly as they were told. For a few seconds they thought about giving a gift, then headed for the food. No envelopes were present, and no method of collection was obvious.

At another party, the hosts showed a videotape about the group, then took the tape out of the VCR and went into the kitchen. People sat around chatting about the tape, then got up to get drinks and food. After a while, the hosts re-emerged and went on with the party. People could be heard asking, "Are we supposed to give money?" or, "What are you supposed to do with the money?" Perhaps out of fear of being rude, they did not ask the hosts.

In those cases, the parties raised almost no money and left people feeling that house parties are a waste of time. They are if not done properly.

Evaluate and Follow Up

After each party, take some time to evaluate what went well and what could have been done better. Particularly if you have a regular presentation, think about the length, the relevance, how to get a discussion going and so on.

Be sure to write thank-yous to everyone who gave money, and put them on the organization's mailing list. If the host failed to make a pitch, then immediately send the guest list an appeal letter. If people gave, go over the list of donors with the host and if there are people missing from it who the host thinks would have given but didn't take the opportunity or forgot, he or she should call them. If the host does not want to do that, then send them an appeal letter as soon as possible.

Like all fundraising strategies, house parties only work if someone actually asks for the money. Otherwise a house party is just a party — fun but no funds.

How to Do an Annual Dinner

I have mentioned that one of the criteria for an event is that the event is repeatable. Many organizations find that creating an event that is associated with them and happens every year is the most lucrative way to use the strategy of special events. This annual event becomes their "signature" event. They may or may not do other events during the year, but they will always do this one. A relatively easy and malleable signature event is the annual dinner.

An annual dinner is a large banquet generally held at a hotel or other very large venue. During the dinner, the organization will present a short program of some sort, often honoring someone, or having a great speaker, comedian, or singer, and certainly bragging briefly about their accomplishments. The dinner may include a silent auction or dancing afterwards, but the main reason that people come is that they have come every year. Many of the people who come know each other. They bring new friends with them and have the most fun when the program is brief and the time for mingling and eating is long.

An annual dinner takes two or three years to really reach its stride, but is worth the investment. The first year people close to the group come and have a good time. Perhaps there are only 50 people at the dinner. The next year, many of them bring friends and the ranks grow to 100, and the following year to 150, then 200. When the event draws an audience of 200 to 300 people, it does not need to grow and does not need to rely on all of the same people coming back every year. There are dozens of grassroots organizations that have 500 people come to their signature event: Some come every year, some every two years, some have come once and continue to give to the event, some always bring friends, some always say they are going to come and don't show up, and so on.

A really well-done annual dinner takes at least six months to organize. It is a lot of work, but the work is predictable and generally proceeds in the following pattern:

Form an Annual Dinner Committee

Identify four or five volunteers who will shepherd the event. They will set a date for the event and prepare the master task list, budget, and timeline as detailed earlier in this chapter. The ideal members of the committee include at least one or two volunteers who have organized an event of comparable complexity in the past. It could have been a small wedding or commitment ceremony, grand opening of a business, or the like — it does not have to have been for a nonprofit, but it should have been a large event with a lot of details. People with this experience know the importance of keeping on schedule and they expect that some things will not go according to plan so they are able to be flexible and solve problems quickly. In addition, people on this committee need to be able to spend time on weekdays on the event: making calls, visiting venues, interviewing caterers, and the like.

If the income stream for the event includes other mini-events, such as a raffle or adbook (described below), silent or live auction, or reception ahead of time, the committee will need to form subcommittees to take care of each of these components. In other words, the Dinner Committee will serve as the Master or Oversight Committee and then there will be an adbook committee, a raffle committee, and so on. These subcommittees operate fairly autonomously, but must be included in the overall planning so that they don't step on each other's toes in arranging prizes, underwriting, or auction items, and must work to ensure that the designer and the printer are not expected to produce all the materials for all the different components in the same week. The first year of an annual dinner, there should not be more than one other component than the dinner.

Recruit Volunteers

Once the Master Committee has completed the task list, budget, and timeline, and the board of directors or whoever has the authority to do so approves those items (a process that can take a full month), they are ready to begin recruiting the small army of volunteers that will ensure a successful event. If the event is well organized and the Master Committee has recruited enough volunteers, the process of working on the event will be fun, which will guarantee that at least some of the committee members will be willing to serve the following year.

This army of volunteers will include the following committees:

Honorary Committee. This is a group of people who actually do very little. They are well known in the community you want to attract to the event and so they loan their names to your event. You can use their names on your invitation and possibly use their names in soliciting gifts. Honorary Committee members also make a donation to the event (usually significant, such as buying a large ad or a table), and give the event committee names of people or businesses who should be invited to buy tickets, tables, or underwrite the event in some way. Often, members of the Honorary Committee don't come to the event and that should not be a requirement.

Publicity Committee. This small committee of two or three people is in charge of publicizing the event in all media. Media obviously include radio, newspapers, and possibly TV, but this committee also needs to think about where your constituency gets information about what is going on in their community. Church bulletins, posters at every laundromat and supermarket, and announcements at service clubs or union meetings can often attract more people to the event than newspaper coverage.

Arrangements Committee. This committee is in charge of the many details that make or break an event: food, drink, flowers, valet parking, sound systems, child care, translation, and the like. They work with the Master Committee to identify what arrangements they are in charge of, and they should not be seen as a catch-all committee to do whatever other people don't want to do.

Materials Committee. This committee is in charge of writing and designing the invitation and any other materials required for the event such as a program, posters, flyers, and so on. Having one committee take care of all materials ensures a uniform look to the materials and a uniform message.

Invitation Committee. This committee is responsible for getting all the lists for the invitations and getting them mailed in a timely way. They generally are not in charge of designing the invitation.

Sponsorship or Underwriting Committee. This committee is in charge of soliciting businesses, corporations, or even major donors to buy a table or pay a chunk of the event's cost in return for having their name prominently displayed at the event.

Cleanup Committee. This committee is responsible for bringing or locating garbage bags and trash and recycling receptacles after the event is over, and knowing where the cleaning tools — brooms, mops, cloths — are kept or providing them. They are responsible for putting chairs and tables away, returning platters, vases, and the like to their rightful owners, and knowing what the rules of the venue are for adequate cleanup. Because there is generally a cleaning and security deposit involved, someone from the Master Committee will want to be on this committee.

In addition to all these, the Master Committee may want a small group to handle all the logistics for the night of the event — decorations, registration, seating, problems.

Balancing having enough committees to get the work done with not having so many that they are impossible to keep tabs on is a constant struggle. Building in regular reporting times and deadlines helps a great deal, as does having the committees be as small as possible while still able to get the work done.

Get the Money Ahead of Time

The ideal event is paid for and the cash is in hand well before the night of the event. Sponsors have sent in checks, attendees have sent in money for tickets, adbook ads are paid for, and so on. Any money that is raised the night of the event is extra. That way, if something goes wrong the night of the event such as an earthquake or chemical spill, you may be able to negotiate keeping most of the money you have raised even if you have to cancel or postpone the event. If something goes wrong at the event — the Master of Ceremonies is ill, the speaker can't be heard because the sound system is bad — you can apologize and continue with the event without worrying that people aren't going to pay.

The most important thing is to have a lot of decent quality food and drink. If people have enough to eat, they will generally be satisfied.

The Day of the Night of the Event

The Master Committee and a representative from each subcommittee meet together and review the master task list, which has now become the master checklist. These lists should be almost grimy because of how often they have been reviewed, added on to, and modified. The purpose of this meeting is to walk through the event one last time to make sure every detail has been thought of. From the point of view of someone attending, what does the event look like?

The person arrives at the venue. Parking is clearly marked or easy to find. When she enters the venue, there are signs pointing her to the event. She checks in at a table where four or five people keep the process quick and the lines to get in short. The check-in sheet shows that she has paid and that she has asked to sit at the Morgan table. The check-in person welcomes her warmly, tells her where the Morgan table is, and invites her to go to the drink table and enjoy some hors d'oeuvres. Once she has her drink, she can stop by a literature table nearby where she can chat with a person there about what good work the group does, and buy a T-shirt or a raffle ticket, if a raffle is part of the event. Once she and most people are seated, but before the dinner begins, board members circulate and greet people. They introduce themselves to people they don't know and thank them for coming. They point out the program books (which are really adbooks) at each place.

The MC introduces herself or himself, welcomes people, gives a brief overview of the program, and then tells people how they will get their food. Either people are served at their table or — more often and less expensive — they serve themselves from a buffet. The MC points out the buffet lines (of which there are at least four), and where to get drinks. With a really big crowd, it is best to call people up table by table.

The food is served efficiently and the Morgan table is impressed. As they are finishing and their plates are being cleared, the program begins. Everyone who needs to use the microphone knows how to work with it, as they have been shown ahead of time. The program proceeds. It is entertaining, moving, and concise. There are no long gaps between the time someone's name is mentioned and when they arrive at the stage because a stage manager is constantly cuing people. A discreetly placed timekeeper sits in a front table and cues speakers with signs that say, "Five Minutes," "Two Minutes," and "STOP NOW." None of the guests know that there is a STOP NOW sign because no one has had to use it.

At the end of the program, the MC or other designated person gives a pitch for more money. Envelopes are on each table along with the adbooks, and people are encouraged to make an extra donation right then and there and turn it in to the people circulating with baskets. (Depending on the nature of the event and how much people have paid to get in, the pitch can raise a few hundred to a few thousand dollars.) At the end of the program, people are encouraged to get dessert from the buffet table and to stay and have fun. If there is a raffle drawing, that happens after dessert; if there is a silent auction, successful bidders are announced after the program. Many people leave shortly after the program, but a critical mass stay for quite a while longer, talking and having fun. Finally, as all plates, food, tablecloths, and so on are cleared away, the last of the crowd leaves. The Cleanup Committee does whatever needs to be done and the event is over.

If the walk-through looked like that, you have thought of everything that can be thought of. If, as you walked through, you realized you had not built in a time for dessert to be served, or did not have a designated timekeeper, you have time to take care of those details.

The committee in charge of the event evening arrives at the site at least two hours early. They help with decorations, putting out adbooks and contribution envelopes on each table, and taking care of any other details that can only be taken care of right before the event.

If the group is as prepared as I have recommended, even if something happens at the event you have not prepared for, there are enough of you to figure out a plan. If you are running out of food, you will notice ahead of time and race out and buy some more. If you have a shortage of chairs, you will go around asking all board members and staff to give up their chairs, and you will try to borrow more chairs from a nearby place. You have upwards of two dozen people who have put a lot of time and effort into this event. They will help, as will people attending.

After the Event

Write up a final report as indicated in the first part of this chapter. Count your income and pay your bills. Write thank-you notes to everyone who did anything to help, and take yourselves out for a nice meal to celebrate a job well done.

How to Do a Raffle

A common, easy, and fun way to raise almost any amount of money is a raffle. Almost everyone is familiar with raffles, having bought tickets for them, perhaps even won a prize in one.

Because raffles are so common, most people don't realize that they can be complicated; when you are organizing a raffle, you can make your life more difficult by not paying attention to the myriad of details that a raffle involves.

The first fact to keep in mind is that raffles have to be organized carefully so that they don't violate gambling laws. Clearly, laws against raffles are rarely enforced, but it is important to organize your raffle so that you are within the bounds of the law. In addition to federal and state laws, you need to find out the laws in your own community. Sometimes you will need to register with the Sheriff's Department, and in some towns, laws against raffles are strictly enforced, and you simply will not be able to do one. We will discuss how to set up your raffle so that you will be within the laws of most states. Ironically, states with their own lottery tend to be more likely to stop a raffle from taking place than states without a lottery.

Raffles basically appeal to people's desire to get something for less than it is worth. Your organization gets some gifts donated, which are used as the prizes. These gifts can vary from straight cash to services such as child care for an evening or having your windows washed, to trips, microwaves, VCRs, and so forth. Generally, there are five to ten prizes, one of which is a grand prize. Tickets are sold for somewhere between $1 and $10 each. Many more tickets are sold than prizes available, so a person's chances of winning are small. At an appointed day and time, all the tickets are put into a barrel or other container, stirred up, and a neutral person (such as a small child) draws out the winning tickets. The organization makes money from the number of tickets sold. There is no other source of income in a raffle. The costs can be kept low — ideally the only costs are printing the tickets and getting the prizes to the winners. As a result, most of the income is profit.

There are three parts to a successful raffle, each requiring three steps:
• Organizing the raffle
• Selling tickets
• Holding the raffle drawing

Organizing the Raffle

Step One: Get the Prizes

Bring together a small committee (two or three people) to decide when the raffle will be held and what the prizes are going to be. It is helpful if the prizes have a theme, such as "vacations" or "services" or "household" or "restaurants." Make a list of all the vendors who might give you a prize, and list specifically what you want from them such as dinner for two, a weekend cabin, etc. Remember that people who own small businesses, particularly storefronts, get asked to donate raffle prizes a lot. They may have policies against doing it; they may donate to five charities and are not taking on anymore; they may be having a hard time in their business and not be inclined to give you anything. Have at least twice as many places to seek prizes as prizes needed.

The small committee then goes out and solicits the prizes. Be sure to stress to each merchant how many people will see the tickets, how much other publicity you are going to do, how you will not ask for another item this year, or whatever is true for you. Merchants must think about how giving your organization an item is good for their business, and you must help them in that thinking.

Step Two: Get the Workers

While you are soliciting prizes, start calling your volunteers to ask how many tickets they are willing to handle. Some people hate raffles — don't push them into taking tickets; they will resent it, and probably won't sell their tickets. Give the tickets to people who work in large office buildings or unions, or who have large families or large circles of friends. Have one prize for the person who brings in the most money for the raffle.

Keep track of who said they would distribute tickets. Raffles are a good opportunity to get some peripheral people involved, so don't just go to your reliable volunteers who already do everything else. Ask each person if they know someone who would be good at getting people to buy tickets. People's spouses or lovers, neighbors, business partners, etc., can be recruited for this effort.

Step Three: Get the Tickets

Once they have the prizes, the committee decides which prizes will be the grand prize, the second prize, and so on. They decide on the date of the raffle drawing. Raffles should go on for at least one month, and can go on for up to six months without losing momentum. The ideal time for a raffle is two to three months.

Printing the tickets requires attention to detail. (See illustration for the points discussed.) First of all, it is with the tickets that groups usually run afoul with the law. This is because raffle tickets cannot actually be "sold." We speak of "selling" tickets but technically what we should say is that the ticket is free, but a donation of $1.00 (or whatever the price is) is requested. Technically, someone can ask for a free ticket and not give you any money. If you were to turn down that request, it would be clear that you are selling the ticket, and that is against the law. In this chapter, we refer to "selling" the tickets, because that is the common shorthand; however, keep in mind that we are not truly selling anything.

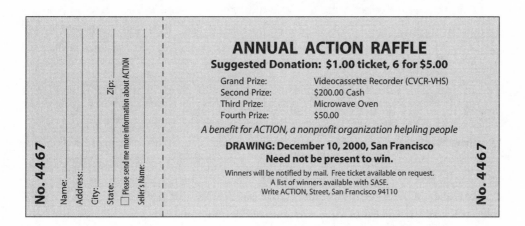

You must print on the ticket how a person can get a free ticket, and that a list of winners will be available. This is to help ensure that the prizes are actually awarded. To increase sales, indicate that the donor doesn't have to be present to win.

The tickets must be numbered so that they are easy to keep track of. Although it costs more for the printer to number the tickets, it is worth it. Many organizations try to save money by not having numbered tickets or by numbering the tickets themselves. This is a foolish use of time. It is also critical that the ticket stub be perforated so it can be easily separated from the body of the ticket. Don't save money by printing cheap raffle tickets. Your volunteers will not distribute them as easily, and donors will be reluctant to give their money when the ticket does not appear properly done.

Not all printers can print raffle tickets. Find a printer who can, even if you cannot use your regular printer. Needless to say, seek to have the printing done for free, but don't scrimp on print costs. They should be your only cost.

Notice in the illustration that the seller is asked to sign his or her name on the ticket stub. This is another incentive that you can build in to your raffle: giving a prize to any person who sold winning tickets. You are obviously more likely to win such a prize if you have sold a lot of tickets.

To promote the organization, offer people a box to check to get more information about the group's work. If you do make such an offer, be sure you go through every ticket and pull out those with the box checked.

To know how many tickets to print, add up how many tickets the volunteer workers are willing to take, and note what your goal is for the raffle. Always print at least 200 more tickets than your financial goal, because some tickets are bound to be lost or mutilated.

One final word concerning the law: many groups send raffle tickets to possible donors through the mail. This is against postal law and, if caught, your letters will be sent back. If you send the tickets by bulk mail, you risk having your bulk mail permit revoked.

In any case, raffles are not mail appeals. If you want to use the mail to raise money, do so, but do not combine raffles and mail appeals.

"Selling" Ticket

Step Four: Distribute and Keep Track of the Tickets

Make a list of everyone selling tickets and the numbers of the tickets they take. Keep track of the tickets as they are returned. Have a date by which the tickets and the donations are to be turned in. Call volunteers with unsold tickets to remind them of this deadline.

Step Five: Encourage the Workers

Call your volunteers at least once a week to see how they are doing with their tickets. Remind them of the deadline and to send in their stubs and cash. To encourage competition, tell them who is winning the "most sold" prize so far. The job of the small committee is not to sell tickets, but to keep other people selling them. A raffle works best when organized like a pyramid, with the most tickets being sold by a large number of workers, and the smaller number of workers distributing the tickets to others. Raffles fail when there are not enough people out selling tickets, or when the people who take tickets don't sell them. Be sure to have a lot of people selling tickets, and keep reminding them of due dates, praising those who are doing their job, and pressuring those who aren't. Every volunteer ought to be able to sell a minimum of 25 tickets. Most people who live in a town or city can sell 50 tickets in two or three weeks with no difficulty. Some people will be able to sell 100 to 500 in one or two months.

Step Six: Round Up the Tickets

Surprisingly, most people find the most difficult task in a raffle lies not in getting the prizes and not in getting the workers, but in getting the tickets and the cash back.

Some volunteers will be careless with their ticket stubs, or return stubs and promise cash later, or claim to have sold tickets when they really haven't. If you have encouraged people to turn in money and stubs as they go along, you will have less difficulty than if you wait until just before the drawing. Final submission of stubs and cash should be due at least three days, and preferably five days, before the drawing. That way, you can ensure that you have all the tickets accounted for well ahead of time. People should turn in unsold tickets as well so that all numbers are accounted for.

The problem with a raffle is that all the transactions are in small amounts of cash. Someone sells three tickets to a co-worker, puts the stubs and dollar bills into their wallet, then goes to lunch and uses that cash for lunch without thinking. Later, they turn in more stubs than cash, and, without a careful recordkeeping system, this error might not be caught.

Another advantage of getting ticket stubs in well ahead of time is that some people try to make their stub into the winning one by bending down a corner, sticking something on the back, or tearing it nearly in half and then taping it together. Workers will sometimes fold ticket stubs or spill stuff on them. These stubs cannot be used, and new stubs must be written. This is, in part, the use of the 200 or so extra tickets. For the drawing, the stubs must be as uniform as possible.

Holding the Raffle Drawing

Step Seven: Set Up the Drawing

Some organizations hold the raffle drawing as part of another event, such as a dance or auction. Using a raffle as a part of another event increases your profit, even though it involves organizing the other event as well. You don't need to have another event — it is fine to have a small party for all those who worked on the raffle and sold tickets and do the drawing there. The drawing is held on the date printed on the ticket. If you have good food and drinks, the drawing is then a celebration and a reward for a job well done, as well as a way to ensure that all the sold tickets are turned in on time.

Step Eight: Hold the Drawing

Get a big box or barrel for the ticket stubs. Be sure to mix and re-mix the stubs thoroughly after each prize is drawn. Start with the bottom prize and work up to the grand prize. Have a blindfolded adult or small child do the actual drawing to guarantee neutrality.

After the prizes are drawn, announce the prizes for top salespeople and award these. Many organizations give several prizes to their salespeople. In addition to the person who sold the most tickets, they award a prize to the person who got the most prizes donated, to the person who got the most other people to sell tickets, to the person who sold the most tickets in a week or to a single person, and so on. Having a lot of prizes for salespeople is a good motivator for those who are competitive during the selling process, and a nice reward at the end.

After the drawing, sort through the tickets for people who checked that they were interested in getting more information about your group. Many organizations also keep the ticket stubs and use them for a mail appeal later. It can be labor intensive to sort through the ticket stubs, eliminating current members' names, and making sure that you only have one ticket stub for each person, even if they bought 20 tickets. However, this is an easy way to build a good mailing list.

Step Nine: Send Out the Prizes, Thank-Yous, and Evaluate

Arrange for the winners to get their prizes, either by picking them up at your office, or receiving them in the mail.

Send thank-you notes to each person who sold tickets and to all the merchants and others who donated prizes.

Count your money. Note how many tickets were unsold and where the problems were with the workers, the merchants, the tickets themselves, etc. Make a file with all the information about the raffle, including a list of winners, a list of people donating items, and a list of volunteers; add notes about timing and other issues. Next year, it will be much simpler to do the raffle if a committee can pull out a file and benefit from the previous year's experience.

How to Do an Adbook

An adbook provides a way for your organization to raise money from businesses and corporations by selling them advertising space in a booklet, program, menu, or other printed item. The adbook is then distributed to people who are coming to an event and who will be likely to patronize the businesses that advertised there. Businesses whose owners may not care about the issues you represent may still buy an ad because they know your constituents use their business or want them to do so.

Adbooks are a superb fundraising strategy if they are done well and on a regular basis. Some organizations use this concept as a way to underwrite conventions, luncheons, concerts, or any special event where a program or printed agenda would be appropriate.

Adbooks are lucrative because the business buying the ad is paying 200% to 1,000% more for the space than its actual design and printing cost. An adbook can be as simple as a folded sheet of paper with ads on both sides, or as complex as a full-scale paperback booklet printed in color. An adbook can also include coupons. Most businesses spend more on advertising than on charitable giving and can more easily support your group by buying an ad than by making an outright donation.

One advantage of adbooks is that they train volunteers to ask for money face-to-face while giving the donor a concrete value for his or her money. Some volunteers who are reluctant to ask for outright monetary donations are willing to approach business people to buy ads. They know that business people want and need to advertise and that they are always looking for creative ways to reach more people. The advantage to the advertiser is that the cost of space in your adbook is always less than the cost of an ad of comparable size in a newspaper. Even though a newspaper reaches more people, if the advertiser's goods and services are particularly useful to your audience, your adbook reaches more targeted prospects. Further, the publicity over the past ten years about corporate responsibility has created a large group of consumers who prefer to buy from businesses and corporations that are perceived to be involved in the community. The Social Venture Network and Businesses for Social Responsibility have reported numerous studies that show that a customer will choose a product made by a company that supports nonprofits over a similar product from a company where that information is not known. To appear in an adbook is good business, particularly if that adbook will be seen by a large number of people.

Planning Distribution and Design

An adbook, like all fundraising strategies, requires careful advance planning. The first step is to plan the distribution of the adbook, what the book will look like, and the cost of the ads. If it is an adbook for a special event, the distribution will be simple: All those attending will receive one. However, if the adbook is to be distributed widely, you need to decide if you will send one to all your donors, put stacks of them in stores, hand them out in your neighborhood to people on the street, or use some other distribution strategy. In order to sell ads, you need to know what shape and size the adbook will be so you can determine the size of the ads and their price. The final number of pages will depend on the number of ads you sell.

Pricing Ads

There are no set formulas for determining how much ads should cost. Check with other groups in your area that have done successful adbooks and see what they have charged. The price of the ads will depend in large part on how widely your adbook will be distributed and how fancy it will be. If it is being given out to 200 people, ads will be less expensive than if 3,000 people will get one. If it is printed on glossy paper, for example, or in color, the ads will cost more than if it is simply printed in black and white. There should be some variation in price between ads on the inside cover of the adbook and those on inside pages. Cover-page ads (including the back cover and the two inside covers) are usually at least twice the price of ads within the book because the exposure is so much better. Some groups charge more for ads in the centerfold as well, since they too will have more exposure.

The ads are sold either by dimension in inches ("display ad") or by the number of words ("classified ad"). A display ad is prepared by the advertiser and sent to you, either in hard copy or as a digital file, "camera ready," that is, ready to go to the printer. For a classified ad, the advertiser sends the ad copy and you have the message designed for inclusion in the book. Display ads can be sold in full-page, half-page, one-third page, quarter-page, and sometimes one-eighth page sizes (depending on how big one-eighth of a page would be). Some groups choose only to have display ads so that they will not have to design classified sections. If you give people the option of sending you copy that you design in a display ad, then you can charge a design fee that covers your cost and gives you a small added profit.

It is a good idea to give businesses and individuals the option of buying a single line in your book and listing those advertisers as "friends" or "sponsors." These listings are less expensive — $15 to $25. They do not advertise a person or business but they do show that the person or business is supportive of your organization. People pay proportionately more for smaller ads than bigger ones because it is much less work for you to have two dozen big ads than 50 small ads. The price of an ad can include one or two free tickets to the event, or some other type of recognition at the event, such as a large poster on which all advertisers are listed.

Once you have the dimensions of your adbook and set prices for the ads, prepare sample pages to be given to volunteers selling the ads. A sample layout for an 8-1/2" × 11" two-page spread is shown on the next page.

SAMPLE AD PRICES

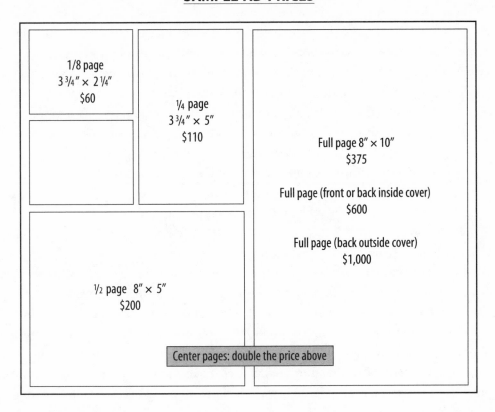

1/8 page
3 ¾" × 2 ¼"
$60

¼ page
3 ¾" × 5"
$110

Full page 8" × 10"
$375

Full page (front or back inside cover)
$600

Full page (back outside cover)
$1,000

½ page 8" × 5"
$200

Center pages: double the price above

Setting a Timeline

The next step is to set a timeline for ad sales. If the adbook is for an event, the event will be the distribution point. The deadline for final sales must be at least one month before the event to allow for design, layout, proofreading, and printing of the book.

Prepare the timeline in the same way as for a special event, with a master task list and a budget. A large adbook will require about an eight-week sales period. Two weeks before sales begin will be needed for planning and preparation of materials and training the sales force. Four weeks at the end of the sales period will be needed for layout, proofreading, and printing. Thus, the total timeline will cover 14 weeks.

Getting Ready to Sell

Make a list of businesses and individuals who might want ads. Ask all volunteers, board members, and staff to list all the businesses they patronize, companies they work for, companies their spouses and friends work for, and businesses that would serve a large cross-section of your donors. (For example, a women's organization would be sure to include women's clothing stores, beauty salons, and women's magazines.) To help people recall all the possible businesses they patronize, give them a list of suggestions, including banks, restaurants, vegetable stores, supermarkets, butchers, clothing stores, bakeries, liquor stores, and such people as your doctor, dentist, lawyer, mechanic, therapist, hairdresser, chiropractor, accountant, and plumber. Include in the final list all of the vendors your organization uses as well as other nonprofits with whom you have worked over the years, unions, friends and family of staff or board, politicians, and even major donors.

Set up a database with the name, address, phone. and a contact person for each potential advertiser. Include the name of the person who uses the business and any other information that will be helpful to the salesperson. (For example, Joe's Auto Supply, Joe Jones, owner, 512 Main St., 835-4692. He is board president's brother-in-law; also, Sally buys everything for her motorcycle there.)

Print out a master list of prospects and have volunteers sign up for as many prospects as they feel comfortable taking. Don't skip this step. You want to make sure that one business isn't approached by two people, and that the best person makes the request for the ad. Most important, you need a master list to keep track of how the volunteers are doing. Ideally, you will be able to enter the name of the volunteer who will be asking into the database record of each business, then print out a list for each volunteer of their prospects. If you are a neighborhood or community group, you may also wish to have some volunteers simply approach every store on a square block of the neighborhood, in addition to any other businesses you may be approaching.

In addition to their prospect lists, the volunteers each need a supply of brochures describing the work of your organization, sample ad sheets with order forms to give each business, instructions for how camera-ready ads are to be sent, return envelopes in case the business owner wishes to mail in their ad or payment, and receipt books to record payments received at the time of sale.

Prepare the volunteers for difficult questions they may encounter, and provide possible answers including convincing arguments. Each volunteer should stress how many good prospects the adbook will reach, how inexpensive the ad is, and how much members of your organization enjoy the business, store, or service where the volunteer is selling.

Selling the Ads

Depending on the type of business you are soliciting and the general style of your community, volunteers may first want to call the business owner or manager and make an appointment. In soliciting ads from corporations or large firms, sending a letter then following up with a phone call and visit will be imperative.

Two or three volunteers should act as "team leaders" for the rest of the sales force. The team leaders play the same role as the planning committee for a special event. While they should sell ads, their main function is to encourage people on their team and to make sure that volunteers are making their calls. Volunteers must understand that they will be turned down more often than not. It will take from five to eight solicitations for every sale. As is the case when soliciting major gifts, you rarely know exactly why you were turned down. Don't spend a great deal of time thinking about it; simply go on to the next prospect.

As sales are made, a progress chart should be posted at the office and progress reports should be given to salespeople to encourage them. Once a week every salesperson should be given a list of the businesses that have already bought ads. They can take this list with them on solicitations; business owners may be persuaded to buy an ad when they see the names of colleagues who have done so.

Thank businesses immediately after they send in their ads and their money. When the adbook is produced, send them a copy. Encourage your members to support the business they see in your adbook and to thank them for supporting your organization. Some businesses will not send payment until the adbook is published. Careful records will show which bills remain outstanding, and those businesses can be billed again after they receive a copy of the adbook. Because they have filled out and signed an agreement specifying the size and wording of the ad, it is extremely rare for businesspeople not to pay.

Producing the Adbook

After all the ads are in and the sales period is over, the book must be produced. Once the sales force has done their task, a second set of volunteers handles the production and distribution details. A graphics designer or person with layout skills should be asked (or paid) to help ensure that the ads are laid out straight, that all the ads fit properly on each page, and that all the ads fit in the book. Layout can be done by hand, or using a graphics program on a computer. Attention should be paid to putting ads that look nice together on the same page and to having some "white space" on each page so that the ads don't look crowded. Great care should be taken to proofread all copy and to keep the display ads and all the copy clean.

Besides the ads, several pages are devoted to the group and the event, either throughout the adbook or in a specific section of it. These include the conference agenda or program notes of the event, information about your group, and a membership form. Many organizations also include a brief history of their organization, a page listing and thanking all their donors, and short biographies of board and staff. If the event you are doing the adbook for is a tribute or awards dinner, then include a profile of the persons, ideas, or groups being honored. High quality, good contrast pictures are very nice inclusions in an adbook.

When the book is ready for printing, someone who knows about paper stock and the printing process should help select the paper and ink and specify the printing process. Print enough copies to give one to everyone who comes to the event, everyone who gave to the event but did not come, all advertisers, and foundation funders, to have a supply to hand out over the course of the year, plus enough for next year's sales force to show the people they solicit.

The first year you produce an adbook is the most difficult. Businesses are taking a chance that you will do what you say in terms of quality and distribution of the book. If your adbook is successful and people patronize the businesses they have read about there, repeat sales will be easy to get. New businesses will be able to see exactly what they will get for their money. If they like what they see, they will be more inclined to buy.

Adbooks can be lucrative, both because the ads bring in much more money than the cost of printing them and because they are a repeatable commodity. They are good for training volunteers in fundraising techniques and for building community relations with businesses. They should only be done, however, when the group has the lead time, the number of volunteers required who can devote time to the adbook and are not also organizing the rest of the event, and access to the design and printing expertise required.

A POTPOURRI OF SPECIAL EVENTS

This section presents a collection of special events and what is needed to put them on. This small sampling represents the major types of special events that small nonprofit organizations hold. Most other events are variations on these.

The following 24 events are divided into three categories according to the time required to accomplish them: those that can be done in one month, those that can be done in three months, and those that require five or more months of preparation. Needless to say, some of the events that can be done in one month with several people working on them would take much longer if only one or two people were available, or could be much bigger if more time were taken. Conversely, some of the events requiring more preparation could be done in a considerably shortened time with the help of paid staff or more volunteers. Although, as has been repeatedly emphasized, special events should not be held primarily to raise funds, they do play an important part in the plans of low-budget, grassroots organizations as a fundraising strategy.

Each event listed is followed by a brief description of the event, the number of planners and other volunteers needed, and the principal costs of the event. All of these descriptions assume little or no involvement of paid staff. "Planners" are the volunteers in charge of the special event who then delegate as many tasks as possible to other volunteers.

Events That Can Be Done in One Month

Summertime Barbecue

Choose any weekend or holiday, find a park or beach, and invite as many people as you want to an "all-you-can-eat" barbecue. Volleyball, softball, and games for children round out this afternoon event.

Planners: 2 or 3. Tasks: Reserve a space for the barbecue (city parks generally need to be reserved through City Hall or the park commissioner); prepare and distribute advertising flyers or invitations; plan the food and table items needed.

Volunteers: 2 or 3. Tasks: Help with publicity; cook and clean up on the day of the barbecue.

Main Costs: Permits for the barbecue; plates, cups, utensils, and other table items; advertising flyers. Food can be an expense, but often one or more stores will donate some or all of it if you promise that a large sign at the picnic will note their donation.

Charge: Adults, $12; children under 12, $6; under 5, free.

Dinner in a Private Home

A board member, staff person, or volunteer who lives in a nice or unusual home or setting and/or is a gourmet cook invites 10 to 25 people (depending on what the house will hold) to a sit-down dinner.

Planners: 1 or 2. The person doing the event may be the only planner. Tasks: Compile guest list; send the invitations; cook the food for the event.

Volunteers: 2 or 3. Tasks: Address invitations, tabulate RSVPs; help prepare the house, serve, and clean up the night of the event.

Main Costs: Invitations, which should look fancy or elegant (but can be produced with a computer or color printer) and postage. Generally, the person putting on the event donates some or all of the food and drink; if not, food and drink will be the only other large cost.

Charge: $35–$50 per person/$50–$80 per couple. Children are not generally included in such an event.

Garage Sale

On a small scale, garage sales are easy to organize and reasonably lucrative. Simply ask 5 to 10 people to clear out their closets and bookshelves and bring their donations to a garage or yard located on a street with a lot of traffic.

Planners: 1. Tasks: Call the donors (usually board or staff members), determine the location of the sale.

Volunteers: 4. Tasks: Prepare signs noting the place and time of the sale; help price the items for sale; transport and set up the sale tables and items; secure boxes for money and change for early large bills; staff the sale, collect money, refold clothes, answer questions of prospective buyers, and clean up, taking leftover items to Goodwill or other community thrift store.

Main Costs: None. Everything is free.

Charge: Price items well below their actual worth and attempt to sell everything that has been donated. Be prepared to bargain with buyers. In the last two hours of the sale, mark everything down 50%.

Pancake Breakfast

Serve an all-you-can-eat breakfast from 7:30 A.M. to 11 A.M. on a weekend morning at a public location, such as a church or service club.

Planners: 2 or 3. Tasks: Find a place, set a date, prepare advertising.

Volunteers: 6. Tasks: Distribute flyers and help with any other invitations; cook, set up, and clean up.

Main Costs: Food, eating utensils, and advertising. The volunteers should seek donations or discounts on food.

Charge: Adults, $6; Children, $3. Try for volume of people, and make the charge low enough for a family to afford to go out for breakfast.

Progressive Dinner

This event starts at one person's house for drinks and appetizers, moves to a second house for dinner, and a third house for dessert. Two more stops could be added, one for soup and salad, and a final stop for coffee and liqueur after dessert. The houses need to be near each other, and the guests should carpool or be transported from house to house, then returned to the starting place.

Planners: 3. Tasks: Line up the homes; help plan the menu, solicit food donations or cooking services of local chefs. Generally, the three planners are also the people in whose homes the various courses of the dinner take place.

Volunteers: 5. Tasks: One or two people send invitations and help to set up each house. Two or three people at each house serve and clean up. Possibly one or two people drive the guests from house to house, if houses are not within walking distance.

Main Costs: Food, if the hosts or caterers do not wish to donate it; invitations and postage; any decorations or needed materials, such as rented wine glasses.

Charge: $25–$50 per person; more if the food is very fancy or the homes very elegant or unusual, or if entertainment, such as music, is offered at one or more of the homes.

Events That Can be Done in Three Months

Book Sale

The same idea as a garage sale, but only books are for sale.

Planners: 3 or 4. Tasks: Collect and store the books; arrange a place for the sale and publicity. Usually a mailing to all local donors asking for books will bring in a large number. Ask people to bring books to a central location, or offer to pick them up if you have volunteers to do that.

Volunteers: 6 to 12, depending on the number of books. Tasks: Sort the books, secure and set up tables and books, staff the sale; clean up. Books should be sorted into hardbound and paperback and usually into broad categories such as fiction, travel, self-help, cookbooks, children's books, religion, philosophy, history, etc. Someone familiar with books should pull out rare ones, such as first editions, old books, and out-of-print books. These should be displayed on a separate table and bring higher prices. Usually, a set price for paperbound and hardback books makes accounting easier and encourages sales. Set the price of non-rare books low (such as $.50 for paperbacks and $1 for hardbacks) so that you sell as many as possible.

Main Costs: Advertising.

Charge: No admission charge, various prices for the books.

Cocktail Party

Hold an early evening event in an attractive setting and, possibly, with someone of note as the guest of honor.

Planners: 3 or 4. Tasks: Secure a place; find the person to honor; design and print the invitation, arrange for the drinks and the food.

Volunteers: 3 or 4. Tasks: Send the invitations; help set up the site; welcome people as they arrive, and, unless you have hired bartenders, serve the drinks.

Main Costs: Renting the place, if it is not someone's house, the invitations, liquor, and finger food.

Charge: $15–$25 per person. As with a house party, you can decide not to charge and to give a pitch at the event after the person of honor has given a moving speech.

Crafts Fair

Give local artists a chance to display their wares while promoting yourselves to the public.

Planners: 3. Tasks: Identify a place to hold the fair; set the date; design the publicity. The place should be big enough for the number of crafts booths needed and in a high-traffic area, preferably with its own parking lot. A church or community center is an excellent site.

Volunteers: 5. Tasks: Send out invitations to artists to display at the fair; advertise the fair to the general public; help set up the showroom; clean up afterwards.

Main Costs: The place for the fair, the invitations, and publicity.

Charge: Varies. Generally artists are charged a booth fee and there is a small admission charge for the general public. Artists can be asked to give a percentage of their sales for that day to the organization.

Haunted House

For Halloween, convert a house, community center, or church activity hall into a haunted house. Supply cardboard or plastic skeletons, plastic spiders, and the like, and set up lighting and sound systems for appropriate scary ambience. Some volunteers should dress up as mad scientists, vampires, witches, and so forth, and make occasional unannounced appearances to groups touring the house. Two or more volunteers must lead group tours of the house, telling a scary story about the various parts of the house or objects in it.

Planners: 3 to 4. Tasks: Find a site, plan the publicity and the house setup.

Volunteers: 6 to 10: Tasks: Advance publicity; set up the house, including lighting and sound; dress in costume to lead groups through the house; collect the entrance fees; and return the house to normal at the end of the evening or the next day.

Main Costs: Publicity and sound and light systems, unless they can be hooked up to stereo and light fixtures already installed.

Charge: $1.00–$2.00 per person, less for children under 7. The price should be low enough that children and their parents can take several tours through the house during the day.

Movie Benefit

A theater donates an afternoon or evening to your group.

Planners: 2 or 3. Tasks: Find the theater and work with its staff to select a movie; design publicity in cooperation with the theater.

Volunteers: 2 or 3. Tasks: Help get publicity out and, depending on your arrangement with the theater, collect tickets or work the concession stand.

Main Costs: Publicity.

Charge: The same price as the movie theater normally charges, or more. Bill it as a donation.

Open House

Invite donors and prospects to your office to meet the staff and board. An open house is not technically a fundraiser, but you can prominently display donation cans and envelopes and sell your organization's products. You can also add a no-host bar.

Planners: 2. Tasks: Set the date; prepare the invitations.

Volunteers: 2 to 4. Tasks: Send the invitations; bring in refreshments (usually finger foods, soft drinks, and wine); set up, welcome guests, sign up new members; clean up before and after the event.

Main Costs: Food and publicity.

Charge: No charge at the door. Have things for sale (T-shirts, bumper stickers, etc.) and encourage people who are not already donors to join. Have a lot of membership information available and a person whose only task is to answer questions and enroll new members.

Tasting

An exotic, sophisticated, or popular food or drink is offered in many guises or varieties for tasting. Wine, chocolate, liqueurs and cordials, fancy candy, and ethnic foods all lend themselves to this format.

Planners: 2 or 3. Tasks: Find a place, decide on a theme, and prepare advertising.

Volunteers: 4. Tasks: Solicit donations of the food or drinks to be tasted (manufacturers or distributors can gain a great deal of publicity through this event); distribute advertising; mail invitations; set up the place; keep the food and drinks replenished; collect money at the door.

Main Costs: Advertising. You may have to provide snacks at a wine tasting, or coffee and tea for a chocolate or candy tasting.

Charge: Varies depending on what you are serving, but usually at least $8 per person. Children are generally not encouraged to come to such an event.

Tour

A guided tour of a historic part of town or architecturally interesting buildings (houses, churches, or other places) or a nature walk.

Planners: 1 or 2. Tasks: Find someone to lead an appropriate tour, design the advertising.

Volunteers: 1 or 2. Tasks: Greet people as they arrive, provide refreshments at the end of the tour.

Main Costs: Advertising. Possibly an honorarium for the tour guide.

Charge: $5–$15 a person, depending on how exotic the tour is or how knowledgeable the tour guide.

Workshop or Class

Offer a learning experience on almost any topic that people want to know about for which you have a qualified teacher. Topics might include organic gardening, sewing, knitting, fundraising, tennis, judo, computers, designing Web pages, auto mechanics, aerobics, etc.

Planners: 1 or 2. Tasks: Find the teacher; get a place; design publicity.

Volunteers: 1 or 2. Tasks: Help with publicity and registration; introduce the teacher at the start of the class; clean up after the class.

Main Costs: The place and publicity. Try to get the teacher to donate his or her time and try to get a free place.

Charge: The going rate for similar classes; usually between $25 and $150 a person. Depends on the class and how well known or in demand the instructor is.

Events Requiring Five or More Months of Planning

Auction

Invite the public to bid on items that have been donated for the purpose.

Planners: 3 to 5. Tasks: Find a place, secure an auctioneer, design publicity, help get items to auction.

Volunteers: 10 or more. Tasks: Get good items to be auctioned; get publicity; prepare a list of items to be auctioned to give to each participant, including value and minimum bid; the day of the auction, provide food and drink at the event, set up chairs, collect money, arrange for delivery of auctioned items, clean up.

Main Costs: The place and the publicity. You may also have to pay a professional auctioneer, although usually a volunteer can be found.

Charge: Charge a nominal admission price and charge for food and drink. The bulk of the money is made from the auctioned items.

Bingo

You may be able to be a one-night beneficiary of an ongoing bingo game. Check with your community's laws to ensure compliance.

Planners: 1 to 4. Tasks: Set up the bingo game, which generally means renting out an evening of an ongoing bingo game; advertising; recruit volunteers to manage the game. Some organizations prefer to pay the person running the game.

Volunteers: 2 or 3. Tasks: Run the bingo game; collect money, set up, and clean up. However, if you are the beneficiary of an ongoing game, you may only need volunteers to do publicity.

Main Costs and Charge: Varies from community to community. Check with other groups doing bingo as a fundraising device.

Concert

One of the most common fantasies of a grassroots group is the idea of having a concert with a famous performer. This is one of the most difficult fundraising events to carry out successfully.

Planners: 5. Tasks: Find the performer (this can take months of research and cultivation); coordinate a time and place with the performer's schedule; prepare publicity.

Volunteers: Unlimited number. Tasks: Distribute publicity, sell tickets, take tickets at the event, set up food and drink at the performance hall (if allowed), sell T-shirts, CDs for the performer; clean up. Many organizations choose to pay someone to handle the details of planning and implementing.

Main Costs: Rental of the performance space, publicity, and the performer's expenses (assuming that their fees are waived, you will still be charged for plane fare, local transportation, hotel, food, etc. Remember that many performers expect to fly first class, travel with an entourage, have very specific food requirements and so on, so the cost of a performer who is donating their time may be very high.)

Charge: Whatever is the going rate for similar performances, or more.

Conference

An expanded version of the workshop or class discussed earlier. A conference of one or more days is held on a particular topic and can include a series of speakers and workshops. Ideally offers some continuing education credits.

Planners: 4 or 5. Tasks: Decide on the theme; arrange for conference space; contact speakers and workshop leaders; plan publicity; create packets for conference attendees.

Volunteers: 12. Tasks: Advertise the conference; mail packets to conference participants; set up and clean up; pick up speakers at airport, bus station, etc.; register attendees; answer questions, solve problems, and act as runners for any items needed at the last minute.

Main Costs: Advertising and conference materials, honoraria for speakers, rental of conference space.

Charge: Depends on the number of days and the type of conference. Charge the going rate for similar conferences. Do not undercharge.

Dance

Invite the public to a dance with a special theme.

Planners: 3 or 4. Tasks: Decide a theme, find a space, hire performers, and plan advertising.

Volunteers: 8 to 10. Tasks: promote the dance; arrange for decorations, food, and drink the night of the dance; get liquor licenses; take money at the door, staff the food and drink booths; set up and clean up.

Main Costs: The performers (unless donated), hall rental, security guard(s), publicity.

Charge: Depending on how popular the dance band is, charge at least $5 per person. Some groups charge $8 to $10 and include free munchies and one free drink. (This encourages people to buy more drinks, and is a lucrative strategy.)

Decorator Showcase

A large, architecturally elegant or unusual house or one belonging to a famous person submits each room to be decorated by a different interior designer. Charge people to come through the house.

Planners: 5 or 6. Tasks: Details seem almost infinite for this event. The main ones are to line up the house, the decorators, and plan publicity. There is a tremendous amount of work involved in coordinating the schedules and the homeowners and the decorators and giving the decorators time to do their work with minimum inconvenience to the homeowners (who must move out during this time).

Volunteers: Unlimited numbers can be used. Tasks: promote the showcase, collect money, conduct the tours, arrange for parking for people coming to the showcase, assist the planners in coordinating the whole thing.

Main Costs: Publicity and invitations.

Charge: $15–$50 per person, depending on how fancy the house and the decorations are.

Dinner-Dance

An elegant affair usually held at a hotel, with a fancy dinner and excellent dance band.

Planners: 4 to 5. Tasks: As with the decorator showcase, details are everything here, and a comprehensive task list is imperative. Aside from the obvious details of renting the hotel, the band, etc., soliciting sponsors for the invitation is important. The invitation thus comes from 25 to 100 socially prominent people who join in inviting the rest of the community to a dinner-dance in honor of your organization.

Volunteers: Again, as many as possible to send out the invitations, collate the RSVPs, make a seating chart for the dinner, coordinate with the hotel's catering service, and oversee setup and cleanup.

Main Costs: The room rental, food, invitations, and performers' fees. This is a costly event. Get as much underwritten or discounted as possible.

Charge: $50–$250 per couple.

Fashion Show

Put on a traditional fashion show — models displaying the latest fashions — or, for more fun, do a takeoff on that idea. Variations abound, such as a "working woman's fashion show," which would show professional-looking but comfortable fashions for upwardly mobile working women, or an around-the-world fashion show that would feature clothes from other countries, or a spoof on a fashion show, that might model clothing that is out of fashion, what never to wear in public, cyber fashion, etc. The models can be professionals or, for fun, board and volunteers, or politicians and well-known people in the community.

Planners: 2 or 3. Tasks: Plan the theme; find appropriate models and clothing, find a place; plan publicity.

Volunteers: 4 or 5 (not including models). Tasks: Help with publicity; coordinate the show itself; write up descriptions of the fashions, announce the models and what they are wearing; set up and clean up. If food and drink are sold, volunteers need to staff those booths.

Main Costs: Hall rental and publicity. If the models are paid that will be a main cost.

Charge: Depends on the theme of the fashion show and the intended audience; at least $10.

Tribute Luncheon

A fancy luncheon, usually held at a hotel, honoring one or more people and featuring a well-known speaker.

Planners: 4 to 5. Tasks: Decide whom to honor and why; find an appropriate speaker; solicit a "committee" of 50 to 100 people whose names will be used on the invitation as joining in inviting the community to the luncheon; design the invitation.

Volunteers: As many as needed. Tasks: Reserve the hotel room; arrange the food; send out invitations, collate responses; solicit corporations and businesses to reserve tables at the luncheon; arrange the seating; and see that things go smoothly the day of the luncheon. Many organizations add an adbook as an additional source of funds.

Main Costs: The hotel, food, and invitations, all of which are very expensive. Like others in this section, this event is heavy on front money and must be planned with great care.

Charge: $50–$500 per person, depending on how fancy it is and who the audience is. Encourage corporations or wealthy donors to "buy" whole tables for a set price, which is usually more than just buying that number of seats. The idea is that a corporation gets more publicity for reserving a whole table and then all the people from that workplace can sit together.

Walk-Jog-Bike-Rock-Read-a-Thon

Participants collect pledges for every mile they walk, jog, or bike, or every hour they rock in a rocking chair, or for some other measurement of endurance or accomplishment.

Planners: 2 or 3. Tasks: Plot the course of the event; get any required permission from the police department or City Hall for using the streets; attract dozens or hundreds of people to participate; design publicity.

Volunteers: 12 or more. Tasks: Help with publicity; monitor and mark pledge sheets of participants as they go by their checkpoints; collect money from participants (who must collect it from their pledges); provide first aid in case of injuries.

Main Costs: Publicity, permits, and prizes (usually a T-shirt or certificate of participation) for those who participate.

Charge: There is usually no charge to enter, unless the 'thon is done as a race among participants, in which case an entry fee is charged. Participants get whatever they can for each mile; usually a minimum pledge of 25 cents is suggested.

eight

Fundraising by Telephone

Imagine that you are sitting on your couch after a long day's work. You are sipping a delicious cup of hot tea, with your cat on your lap, watching TV or reading a good book when suddenly the phone rings. The cat flies off your lap. You think it could be important, curse yourself for not having the phone beside you, and get up to answer the call. A pleasant but slightly smarmy voice says, "Hello, is this Jane Smith?" and pauses for your answer. If affirmative, the voice continues, "Jane, how are you this evening? I hope you are well, because, Jane, did you know that there are 2,532 people in our community that are very, very sick tonight, and Jane, you can help them…."

This scenario is played out night after night in millions of homes in America. The fundraising phone call interrupts dinner, putting the kids to bed, or just relaxing. People complain about it incessantly and some states have even attempted to stop the use of the phone for sales or fundraising.

Yet, it works. Phone-a-thons continue to pull a greater percent of response than direct mail, and they are an excellent way of reaching a large number of people with a (somewhat) personal message.

Like direct mail, phone-a-thons can be modified for small organizations in a way that allows them to both raise money and not offend donors. The two modifications small organizations make are to use very warm lists (such as lapsed donors, current donors, and friends of board members, staff, and current donors, or lists of donors to very similar organizations) and to use only volunteers to do the calling. Even if a person is annoyed to be phoned during dinner, they will be less annoyed by a volunteer, who is giving their time and doesn't sound as smooth or insistent as boiler-room professionals.

A basic fundraising axiom is that the closer you can get to the prospect, the more likely you are to get the gift. Phoning, as the ad says, is "the next best thing to being there."

BASIC TECHNIQUE OF THE PHONE-A-THON

In its simplest terms, a phone-a-thon involves a group of volunteers calling people to ask them to support your organization with a donation. A phone-a-thon is an excellent way to involve volunteers in fundraising because it teaches them how to ask for money while being less intimidating than soliciting donations in face-to-face situations.

Phone-a-thons can be good moneymakers. They are usually inexpensive to produce and have a high rate of return. Between 5% and 10% of the people reached will contribute, and possibly more if you are calling lapsed donors. Compared to a direct mail campaign's response rate, which is considered good at 1% to 3%, a phone-a-thon has much greater potential for raising money. The costs involved include printing and postage, any toll-call charges, and food and drinks for volunteers doing the calling. If you haven't already, arrange for your organization to be able to accept credit cards. You will get larger gifts and have a smaller loss of pledges using credit cards.

A phone-a-thon can be organized by one or two people. It takes several hours of preparation followed by a five-hour block of time for the event. Several people are needed to make all the calls. (See the formula in #5 below.)

Preparation

To prepare for a phone-a-thon, the organizers take these steps:

1. Prepare the list of people who will be called

These potential donors are people who have either expressed an interest in your organization, have benefited by something you have done for them, or are past or current supporters of your organization. People attending community meetings you have organized, alumnae or former clients, and members of and donors to similar organizations are all prospects. Get their names and look up their phone numbers. (Organizations in small towns or rural communities or organizations that serve a specific neighborhood or geographic constituency may be able to use the phone book as their source of names, but generally this is too "cold" a list.)

Create a card for each person with their name, phone number, code (L = lapsed, FB = former board member, CL = client, etc.) and any information you will want the telephone volunteer to record, as shown in the following example:

JANUARY PHONE-A-THON: PEOPLE TO BE CALLED

Name: _____   Phone: _____   Code : _____

Address: _____

Were they home? ☐ Yes ☐ No   Donation made? ☐ Yes ☐ No
    Message left? ☐ Yes ☐ No   Credit card type & number _____

                                       _____

Need more information? ☐ Yes ☐ No
    Was it sent? ☐ Yes ☐ No   Address verified? ☐ Yes ☐ No

Thank-you sent? ☐ Yes ☐ No   Other: _____

2. Set a date for the phone-a-thon

Pay attention to other events in your community — don't call, for example, on an evening when everyone will be at an anniversary party or benefit auction for another group. Most people find that calling on a Tuesday, Wednesday, or Thursday night between 6:00 and 9:00 P.M. at the beginning of the month (near payday) works best.

Some groups call on weekends with success, but calling on a sunny weekend afternoon may bring people racing in from their yard or interrupt them while entertaining and may irritate more people than necessary. No one is sitting in the sun on a Wednesday evening at 8:00. Also, pay attention to what's on television: Don't call during the Super Bowl, on an election night, or during the Academy Awards.

3. Write a script for volunteers to read as they phone

Generally volunteers can "ad lib" after the second or third call, but initially a script gives them a feeling of security. The script should be brief and to the point:

"Hello, my name is Jill Activist, and I am a volunteer with Good Organization. May I speak with you for a minute?" (PAUSE for answer.)

"Thank you. I am calling tonight as a part of a phone-a-thon. Are you familiar with our work?" Or, "Did you read about us in the *Daily Blab*?" Or, "Did you receive our recent appeal?" (PAUSE for answer.) If the answer indicates little familiarity with the organization's work, say, "We are a group of concerned people working on..." and give a two-sentence or 15-second summary of your work. (PAUSE.)

If there is no reaction or a positive reaction from the person being called, continue: "Our goal tonight is to raise $ _____. We are asking people to help us with a gift of $35 or more. As a way to thank you for your gift, we will send you our quarterly newsletter (or other benefit). So far, ____ people have pledged and we have $ _____ toward our goal. Would you care to make a donation?" (PAUSE for answer.)

If the answer is positive, continue: "We are trying to keep track of how much we have raised. What amount may I put you down for?" (PAUSE for answer.) "Thank you so much. Will you be able to pay by credit card?" If YES, then get the credit card number and whatever other information you have been instructed to get for credit cards. If the prospect is hesitant to give you a credit card number, then say, "If you prefer, I can send you an envelope for you to use in tonight's mail. Let me just verify your address." (Read the address.) "Thank you again. Good night."

In addition to the script, write up a list of questions that volunteers may be asked, with suggested answers. Include questions and statements such as, "Why haven't I heard of you before?" or, "I sent you guys money and never got anything."

4. Prepare three letters and appropriate enclosures

A. *A letter for people who say yes*

Dear _____ ,

Thank you so much for joining Good Organization with your gift of $ _____ this evening.

As you probably know, Good Organization is primarily supported by donations from people like you. Your gift will help us continue our work of _____. (Describe in two or three sentences.)

Please fill out and return the enclosed card with your check or your credit card information in the envelope provided. You will begin receiving our newsletter in two weeks.

            Sincerely,
            Name of volunteer

Return card format:

Name _____

Address _____

☐ Enclosed is my pledge of $ _____. I look forward to receiving the newsletter and other benefits of membership.

☐ Please charge my VISA/MC $ _____

Card #_____

Name as it appears on card_____

Expiration date _____

Make checks payable to: Good Organization

Mail to: Our Address

(The return envelope should have a first-class stamp affixed.)

B. *"Sorry we missed you" letter to people who weren't home:**

Dear _____ ,

Sorry we missed you this evening. We tried to call you because we wanted to ask you to join/renew/tell you more about Good Organization.

Good Organization is ... (brief summary of not more than three to five short sentences). Our main program goal for this year is _____.
(The exact language of this paragraph will depend on whether you are asking for a renewal or a new gift.)

I hope you will want to join us in our important work. For a gift of $ _____, we will be pleased to send you our quarterly newsletter, *The Right-On Times.* For a gift of $100 or more we will include a beautiful/important book/calendar/picture.

Please take a moment to read the enclosed fact sheet, then fill out the membership form and send it with your check or credit card information today.

Sincerely,

Name of volunteer

P.S. For more information and to sign up for our free electronic newsletter, check our Web site at www.goodgroup.org.

If you have the capacity to take donations online, you will want to note that in your letter also.

C. Letter to people with questions about the organization:*

Dear _____ ,

Thanks for talking with me this evening.

I am enclosing the information we discussed, which I hope will answer your questions. Please feel free to contact our office to discuss our organization further if you wish, and check out our Web site at www.goodgroup.org.

I hope that after reading this information you will decide to make a donation. I am sure once you read about us, you will agree that our work is very important. Please support us in whatever way you can.

An envelope and membership form are enclosed for your convenience. I look forward to hearing from you.

Sincerely,

Name of volunteer

Enclose with both the second and third examples a reply card or form that the donor will fill out (similar to those used with direct mail, see pages 67–69), a fact sheet or brochure about your organization, and a return envelope. It is not necessary to put a postage stamp on any of these envelopes.

To decide the quantity of each letter to have printed, count the number of people you will be calling and assume that one-third to half of them will answer. Of this number, 5% to 10% will say yes and need the "yes" letter; another 10% to 15% will say, "Send me more information," and need the letter described in (C); and the

---

If these letters go by bulk mail, each one must be exactly the same. In that case use the salutation, Dear Friend.

rest will say no. The other one-third will need the "Sorry we missed you" letter described in (B). Much depends on how good your list is, but this formula should give you enough letters without having lots of them left over. (You could also photocopy the letters as you go along, if you have access to a high-quality copier. If you are working with a small list, you could print each letter off your computer.) If you do not date the letters and avoid using any reference to a month or day, you can use the same letters at other phone-a-thons throughout the year.

5. Determine how many phones and how many volunteers you will need

To do this, estimate that one person can make about 40 phone calls in an hour (although they will talk to no more than 15 people) and that people will call for no more than three hours. Therefore, one person can make about 120 calls in an evening (including calls to people who aren't home) and fill out the appropriate follow-up letters.

To get by with fewer phones, people can work in teams of two to a phone. In this arrangement, as soon as one person has made a call and is filling in the appropriate letter, the other person begins a call. This way the phone is always in use. Sometimes a phone team agrees that one person will do all the talking and the other will do all the writing. Phone teams can make about 30 calls an hour or 15 per volunteer per hour. Since most people will not call for three hours straight, you will need one or two extra volunteers to make maximum use of the phones available.

Suppose you have 600 names to call. If one person made all the calls it would take 15 hours (600/40). If each person has his or her own phone it will take five volunteers with four or five phones to get through the calls in one evening, plus one or two extra volunteers to relieve people (15/3 hours of calling).

In addition to the calling, allow two to three hours (or one or two extra volunteers) for stuffing envelopes, making sure all the needed information is recorded, and cleaning up.

You may wish to conduct the phone-a-thon over two nights. This has two advantages: You can call more people or use fewer volunteers, and you can call people on the second night who weren't home on the first night.

6. Find a place

You will need one room or a suite of connected rooms with one or more telephones in each one. Depending on the number of telephones in your organization's office and the number of volunteers you have, you may have enough lines there. Real estate offices, travel agencies, law firms, large social service organizations, mail order businesses, and so forth are good candidates to let you borrow their telephones for the evening. You will be trusted not to disrupt or take anything, to clean up before you leave, and in most cases, to pay for any long-distance or toll calls.

Sometimes small organizations decide to conduct a phone-a-thon with each volunteer working from their home. While there is nothing wrong with this method and just as many calls can be made, it is more fun and generates more momentum to have everyone in the same office. That way, successful calls or rude responses can elicit immediate praise or sympathy, as appropriate. A group effort is also helpful in keeping track during the evening of how much is being pledged. (If you have to use individual homes, have at least two people at each home.)

7. Recruit volunteers

Use the phone-a-thon as an opportunity to bring in some new volunteers. Often people who have limited time or who cannot volunteer during the day can be recruited to work one evening on a phone-a-thon. It is a straightforward commitment for a short time period and does not require preparation outside of a training session 30 minutes before phoning begins.

THE NIGHT OF THE PHONE-A-THON

The person or committee planning the phone-a-thon should arrive at the place where the phoning will take place 30 minutes before everyone else. Be sure that desktops or tabletops where volunteers are to sit are cleared off so that your papers do not get mixed up with the papers of the person who uses that desk during the day. On each desk, put a stack of the three different letters, their enclosures, the return envelopes, the mailing envelopes, and a couple of pens. Put a list of names to be called and a script by each phone.

Bring in juice, coffee, and snacks. Pizza, sandwiches, or other simple dinner food should be provided if volunteers are arriving at dinnertime. The food should be kept in one part of the office, and volunteers should be discouraged from having food by their phones. Pay attention to details like bringing in napkins, plates, and eating utensils. In a borrowed space, take out your own trash. Do not serve alcohol.

After all volunteers have arrived, been introduced to each other, and had a chance to eat, go through the phoning process step by step. Review the script and make sure people understand and feel comfortable with it. Review difficult questions they might receive and simulate a few phone calls (one from each of the response categories: yes, maybe, no). Be sure people understand the different letters, know what to write on each, what enclosures go with them, and what information needs to be noted on the list of names.

You will need to decide whether volunteers are to leave a message on an answering machine or simply hang up. If you're going to send out a "Sorry we missed you" letter, you can instruct people to leave a brief message to the effect that, "I wanted to talk with you about our work, but will send you some information instead. I hope you will be able to help us." Be sure the message you leave is brief, since people only like to listen to long messages from new lovers or old friends.

After the orientation, each volunteer or phone team goes to a desk. The committee that has planned the phone-a-thon begins making calls immediately to set the tone and the pace. When a few people are on the phone, shy volunteers will feel better about beginning to call. Try to avoid a situation where everyone in the room is listening to one person's phone call unless that person feels comfortable with that role.

A staff person or a phone-a-thon committee member acts as a "floater." He or she answers questions and fields difficult phone calls. The floater also continually tallies how much money has been pledged and updates the changing total on a large board visible to the group. The volunteers then change their scripts to reflect new totals. The floater can also prepare "Sorry we missed you" letters for bulk mailing if that will be used.

Each individual should be encouraged to take breaks as they need to, but the group as a whole does not take any breaks.

At 9:00 P.M. stop the phoning. The first step in wrapping up is to finish addressing all envelopes and to gather up the lists of people phoned. If a bulk mailing is being done with the "Sorry we missed you" letters, try to do that quickly or do it the next day at the latest. Gather up any leftover forms, envelopes, letters, and cards. Tally the final amount pledged and let the volunteers know how successful the evening has been. If the amount pledged is below your goal, explain that you set your goal too high. Do not let the volunteers leave feeling discouraged.

The callers should be able to leave by 9:30 P.M. leaving the planning committee to do any final cleanup.

AFTER THE PHONE-A-THON

Within two or three days, send all the volunteers a thank-you note for their participation. If you borrowed a space to conduct the phone-a-thon, write the owner/manager a thank-you note as well. Thank everyone for whatever they did to make the event a success.

During the next two weeks you should collect about 90% of the pledges made. As each one comes in, a thank-you note should go out. At the end of two weeks, go through your list and see who said, "Yes, I will give," but did not send their money.

Send them a gentle reminder, accompanied by a return envelope and a reply form. Most organizations do not find it worth the time and cost to remind people of their pledge more than once.

SAMPLE REMINDER LETTER

Dear _____ ,

      This is just a note to remind you of your pledge to Good Organization made on the night of _____. In case you misplaced our letter and return envelope we enclose another. Thanks again for your pledge of $ _____.

Sincerely,

Name of volunteer

Generally about 7% of people who pledge do not send money. (Some people's way of saying no is to say yes and not follow through.) If you have a higher loss than 7%, it may be that your volunteers noted someone as "yes" who only said she would think about it. Make sure volunteers understand how important it is to be accurate and that they need to hear what the prospect said, which may be different from what the caller wants to hear.

Tally up the final amounts received and write an evaluation of the event. The evaluation should note how many people were called, how many pledged, how many pledges were received, how many volunteers participated, where the phone-a-thon was held and who arranged for the space (if donated); include copies of all the letters and return forms used. File all this away so that the next time you do a phone-a-thon you won't have to start from scratch.

GETTING PUBLICITY FOR YOUR PHONE-A-THON

A phone-a-thon may be a good time to generate some publicity for your group. Publicity can make the community more aware of your group's work and can alert listeners or readers to the fact that many of them will be receiving phone calls from your organization on a specific day or evening. The organization's address and phone number can be included in all publicity so that people can call or send in their donation ahead of the phone-a-thon and avoid being called.

Unless you are on very good terms with press people, the phone-a-thon alone will not be a newsworthy event. While radio stations or local newspapers may run a short press release or a public service announcement (PSA) describing the phone-a-thon, an article or an interview is unlikely to come out of the phone-a-thon alone. It would be best, therefore, to use the occasion of the phone-a-thon to emphasize a new program, tell a human interest story, or have some other newsworthy reason to get press attention in which you mention the phone-a-thon.

All of your publicity should emphasize the need for community support. Stress that your organization relies on the community for the bulk of its support — or wants to rely on the community if you don't now. Talk about what a gift of $25, $35, or $50 will do for the group so that people have a sense that a small gift can make a difference.

Use a Public Figure

One way groups have interested the press is by having one or two famous people participating in their phone-a-thon. "Famous people" include not only national celebrities but also people only well known in your community, such as the mayor, city council members, a well-respected community activist, the president of the community college, or a major corporate executive. The novelty that someone "famous" would help your organization lends credibility to your group. Also, almost everyone is flattered to be called by someone famous. If you decide to ask public figures to participate, be sure that they are well liked by your constituency.

Public figures can simply come for the first half-hour of your phone-a-thon and make a few calls without making an enormous time commitment to the event. It is an easy way for both you and them to gain goodwill while they show their support of nonprofit organizations and of the work of your organization in particular.

Court the Media

If you can't get any publicity through your press contacts, simply send a letter to the editor of the local paper. Be sure to send it in time for publication (particularly if you are a rural group dealing with a weekly paper). Many groups have found that letters to the editor are an effective way to get publicity for many issues. Again, give the address and phone number of your organization and the date of the phone-a-thon.

If you do get any publicity (even a simple press mention or public service announcement aired), write or call press contacts with the results of the phone-a-thon and emphasize what a difference their publicity made. Include with your letter a press release or PSA announcing the success of the phone-a-thon, and a statement of thanks to the community for being supportive. A letter to the editor is also a good way to follow up publicity. It is important to sound successful even if your phone-a-thon was not as successful as you had hoped.

There are drawbacks to extensive publicity that should be taken into account before seeking it. Publicity for a direct service organization may generate more clients than donors. One organization, whose purpose was to help people with work-related injuries get the benefits they deserve, got a full-page interview about their work and their upcoming phone-a-thon in the local paper. The night of the phone-a-thon, volunteers were swamped with incoming calls from people needing the organization's help. The phone-a-thon was a financial failure; but the experience certainly demonstrated the need for this group's work.

A second disadvantage of publicity is that phone calls may keep coming in long after the phone-a-thon is over. If you have borrowed a space and the phone number you announced belongs to the business that owns the space, they will have to forward your calls. If you gave your office number, your staff or daytime volunteers will need to respond to those calls in addition to doing their regular work. While handling the calls is not too time-consuming, making sure the right information goes out and keeping track of pledges and so forth can be.

If you have taken all these contingencies into account, publicity may turn a good phone-a-thon into a giant fundraising success.

OTHER USES OF THE PHONE-A-THON

There are three more common uses of the phone-a-thon technique: using a phone-a-thon only to get prospects, following a mail appeal with a phone-a-thon, and using a phone-a-thon to renew lapsed donors.

Phoning for Prospects

This takeoff on a sales technique means phoning a large number of people, giving basic information about your organization, and asking if the person would like to know more. If the person says yes, he or she turns into a prospect. There is no attempt to solicit a gift at the time of the phone call. The purpose of the call is to create a "hot" list for later fundraising mail appeals.

During the telephone conversation the caller determines the degree of interest by asking the prospect some open-ended questions about what they know of the organization and whether they support its work. When interest is present, the prospect will be sent more information about the organization and a list of ways that they can help, including giving money. Some groups use this opportunity to seek new volunteers, get support for or against a piece of legislation, or ask for items that the program needs (for example, a shelter might ask for food or clothing). A return envelope is included in the mailing.

This strategy does not raise money per se. Instead it acquires donors. The costs of phoning and of any mail and follow-up may well be only slightly less than the total amount received as gifts. Nevertheless, the organization now has a group of new donors, many of whom will renew the following year, and may give in response to appeals during the current year.

This strategy is best for new groups that do not have an established constituency or for groups that have little name recognition even if they have existed for some time. It also works well for political organizations seeking to familiarize people with their candidate or their election issue.

This method differs from an ordinary phone-a-thon in the script and training volunteers for calling. The purpose of the call is only to determine interest and to get permission to send more information. Therefore, the script would be something like this:

> "Hello, I am Jane Smith, a volunteer with Shelter for the Homeless. I would like to talk to you for a minute, and I will not be asking you for money. Is this a good time?" (PAUSE) "Thank you. I'll try to be brief. Have you heard of our program?" (PAUSE; If the answer is "No" or "I don't know very much," continue:) "Shelter for the Homeless is a 30-bed facility for homeless single people and families. It also provides job counseling and referral, meals, and child care so that parents can look for work. Did you know that there are more than 2,000 homeless people in our community and more arriving every day?" (PAUSE) "We know that some people disagree with our approach or feel that some of the people using our services are freeloading while many other people find our program excellent. What do you think?"

Generally, the answers fall into three categories:

• People who are basically in favor of your work

• People who like your program generally but have a specific objection to something about it

• People who feel that everyone should help themselves and that your program is undermining the moral fabric of the country

For answers that fall in the first category the caller in this example might say:

> "I'm glad you feel that way. The shelter relies on community support for more than three-fourths of its budget, and it is good to know that members of the community like what we are doing. I wonder if I could send you a brochure and some other information about our services and about different ways that citizens can help us. There is no obligation, and no one will call you afterwards, but you may find the information interesting." (PAUSE for answer.)

If the answer is yes, then verify the name and address, thank the person for his or her time, and say good night.

If the answer falls in the second category, the specific objection in this case might be:

> "I support the ideals of your program, but the problem is that more people move to our community because you are here. We can't continue to absorb people this fast."

The caller needs to agree with the prospect in some way in order to acknowledge that the prospect's objection is valid. In this case, the caller could say:

> "It does seem that the more services that are provided the more people there are who need them, and that it's an endless cycle." (PAUSE.) "But in our case it is interesting to know that no more people are moving here now than before we opened the shelter."

Or,

> "Communities with no services for homeless people are also finding their homeless population is growing. In fact, sometimes people who are out of work call us from other states, and we are able to discourage them from moving here because our economy is so tight right now. Then they don't have to come and learn the hard way."

When a person's objection is acknowledged as valid and then corrected or new information is supplied, he or she generally becomes more receptive. If the person says something like "I didn't know that," or, "I am glad to hear that," ask if you can send him or her more information just as for prospects in the first category.

In case of answers in the last category, simply say (and mean it), "I appreciate your candidness. It helps us to know why people don't like our program. Thanks for your time. Good night."

Training volunteers for this type of phone work is much more detailed. Volunteers must be able to listen, deal with difficult questions, and know when to give up. Each call will take longer than calls in a fundraising phone-a-thon. Callers must be clear that they are only calling to determine interest, not to convert people.

Callers should practice handling difficult questions and responding in depth and familiarize themselves with many facts about the organization and the issues.

No list is needed for this phone-a-thon. The phone book can be used or you can do a random calling of any list of people. You can also use this strategy to determine the interest of people who give to an organization doing work in an entirely different arena from yours, but where there could be a connection. For example, an AIDS-related service organization called a list of donors from several arts organizations to determine their interest in the service organization. Because the arts community has been hard hit by the AIDS epidemic, they found a high level of interest and gained many new donors.

Phoning after a Mail Appeal

This method is quite straightforward. A mail appeal is sent to a list of prospects. After two weeks all the prospects who have not sent money are called. The purpose of this method is to increase the return from the mail appeal.

The script is the only part that is slightly different from a regular fundraising phone-a-thon, in that a sentence is added, such as "I am Joe Reilly from the Greenbelt Project. We recently sent you a letter about our work. Did you have a chance to read it?" Depending on the answer, the rest of the script is the same as that described in the first section of this chapter. If the person has read the letter and seems in favor of your goals, skip right to the question, "Will you be able to help us with a gift of $ ____?"

Generally, you will not indicate in the original letter that the prospects will be called. You want as many people as possible to send in their gift without being called. Some organizations have successfully tried a variation on this method, by telling prospects in a letter that they will be called unless the organization hears from them by a certain date prior to the phone-a-thon.

Phoning for Renewals

As I have said, in average organizations about one-third of all members do not renew their memberships from one year to the next. As a result, organizations spend most of their renewal budget trying to woo these recalcitrant members back into the fold. Usually an organization will send the member two or three renewal letters one month apart, each notice firmer than the one before. The third notice usually explains that the membership has or is about to lapse unless the member pays now. If there is still no response, the organization removes the member's name from its mailing list.

The phone-a-thon can be used in place of either the second or third renewal notices. Although it does not save the cost of printing and postage, it does provide a way to have much more personal contact with members than is generally possible.

Many organizations have renewal phone-a-thons twice a year. They find that, while the response to a second or third renewal letter is 2% to 5% and sometimes less, the response to phoning is at least 10% and can be as high as 30%. These organizations are cutting their member losses by 5% or more. This guarantees that the organization will have a 66% renewal rate, and not less, and they may be able to add another 5% onto that.

A renewal phone-a-thon is almost exactly like a regular fundraising phone-a-thon. First, identify from your mailing list all the people whose memberships have expired within the last 6 months, or, if your organization doesn't have members, those donors who have not given in 13 or more months, not including those who have had less than a month to renew. (Unless your organization is in a terrible financial bind and you really need the money, a person will feel harassed if you call too soon after your first renewal notice is sent.)

Next, prepare the letters to thank people for renewing and to contact people who weren't home when you called, as discussed in the first section of this chapter. Both of these letters are brief. The point is to remind the member of his or her commitment to give; there is no need to convince the person of the worthiness of your organization. Each letter is accompanied by a return envelope and a reply card.

When volunteers call the lapsed donors, they will generally hear the following reasons for not renewing: out of work, forgot about it, thought they had renewed, didn't receive the renewal letter, they were just about to renew and are glad you called.

It is important to believe whatever the member might say. A person who claims to have renewed although you have no record of receiving their renewal could be asked to produce a canceled check, but it is easier and more productive simply to take their word for it and reinstate them on the mailing list. Follow the adage, "The customer is always right."

When someone says that they no longer agree with the "course you are taking" or that they have a disagreement about a particular issue, ask them to explain. It may shed light on how the public perceives something you have done, or you may be able to clear up a misunderstanding.

At the end of the phone-a-thon, make sure you have carefully sorted all the names into categories: those who have renewed, those who requested to be taken off the mailing list, and those who were not home. Deal with complaints that same evening:

> Dear Mr. Upset,
>
> We are sorry you have not received your newsletter for the past two years. At your request, here are all the back copies you have missed. We will enter your name on our mailing list for the next year as a complimentary member. Your past support means a lot to us, and again, we apologize.

As you can see, grassroots organizations can take advantage of fundraising by telephone. In addition to raising money, finding prospects, increasing renewal rates, and allowing an organization to have more personal contact with its donors, fundraising by telephone has an added advantage of teaching volunteers how to ask for money. The skills volunteers learn through phone-a-thons can then be put to work in major donor campaigns.

nine

Personal Solicitation

Asking someone you know for money in person is the most effective way to raise funds. If you ask someone you know for a gift they could afford to a cause they like (a person fitting this description is called a "prospect") there is a 50% chance they will give something. Of the 50% that say yes to your request, half of them will give you the amount you ask for; the other half will give you less. This is a much higher response rate than you can get from any other kind of fundraising. (Compare the 1% to 3% you may get from direct mail or the 5% to 10% from phoning.) Further, the amounts you can ask for are much larger. It is ludicrous to ask for a $5,000 or $10,000 gift by direct mail or during a phone-a-thon, but it is appropriate to ask for such a sum in person if you know the prospect could make such a gift. People need more personal attention for large gifts because they have to give them more thought.

In studies in which people are asked why they gave the last donation they made, 80% will say, "Because someone asked me." Of course, millions of smaller fundraising requests are done in person — canvassing, Girl Scout cookie sales, raffle ticket sales, Salvation Army buckets, panhandling, and so on all have a strong element of personal asking. These forms of personal solicitation will not have the 50% rate of success unless the solicitor is known to each potential donor, but will have a higher rate of success than methods that don't use a face-to-face approach. More substantial gifts, major gifts programs, capital campaigns, and endowment drives all rely for success on personal solicitation.

Despite these facts, personal solicitation is one of the most difficult strategies to implement. It requires that people engage in an activity — asking for money — that most of us have been taught is rude, or worse, unthinkable. However, for organizations that are serious about fundraising, and particularly for organizations that would like to increase the number of people in their donor base who give at least $100 annually, learning how to ask for money in person is imperative.

WHY WE'RE AFRAID TO ASK FOR MONEY

If the idea of asking for money fills you with anxiety, disgust, dread, or some combination of these feelings, you are among the majority of people. If asking for money does not cause you any distress, you have either let go of your fear about it or you grew up in an unusually liberated household; or you may have come from a country that does not place talking about money in its list of taboos.

To identify the sources of our fears, we must look at both the role of money in American society and the attitudes about asking for anything that are the legacy of the strong puritan ethic that is our American heritage.

Most of us were taught that money, sex, religion, death, and politics are all taboo topics for discussion with anyone other than perhaps one's most intimate friends or family. Mental illness, age, race, and related topics are often added to this list of taboos and discomfort in talking about any one of them will be stronger in some parts of the country or among some generations.

The taboo on talking about money, however, is far stronger than any of the others. Many of us were taught to believe that inquiring about a person's salary or asking how much he or she paid for a house or a car is rude. Even today it is not unusual for one spouse not to know how much the other spouse earns, for children not to know how much their parents earn, or for close friends not to know each other's income. Further, few people really understand how the economy works. They don't know the meaning of things they hear and read about every day — the stock market, for example, including what the difference is between a bear and a bull market, or what the rising or falling of the various stock market indices mean. In the past 15 years, more and more social justice groups have recognized that economic literacy is a key component in community organizing, but it will take decades to reverse the general ignorance about how the economy works, and, more important, how it could work.

Many people, misquoting the Christian New Testament, say, "Money is the root of all evil." In fact, Paul's letter to the Philippians states, "The love of money is the root of all evil." Money in itself has no good or evil qualities. It is a substance made of paper or metal. It has no constant value, and it has no morality. It is simply a means of exchange.

People will also say, "Money doesn't buy happiness," as a way of minimizing the power of money and describing unhappy rich people they have known or read about, though most of them are secretly thinking that they would be happier if they had more money! Our taboos about money are changing also, giving us more mixed messages than ever. For example, starting in the 1990s, many young people in the computer industry felt they were failures if they hadn't made a million dollars by the time they were 30, but these same people have no idea what percent of the world's population lives in poverty or how many children starve to death every day. Large corporations are considered successful despite operating at a loss and being kept afloat by investor optimism. Sadly, our attitudes towards money change but do not get healthier.

Money is shrouded in mystery and tinged with fascination. Most people are curious about the salary levels of their friends, how much money their neighbors have inherited, and how the super-rich live. How much money you have and how long you have had it denotes class distinctions and helps each of us place ourselves in relation to others — while maintaining the American myth that our country is a classless meritocracy.

Consequently people speculate a great deal about the place of money in others' lives. Money is like sex and sexuality in this regard: It is kept in secrecy and therefore alluring. But just as much of what we learned as children and teenagers about sex turned out to be untrue, so it is with money. The comedian Kate Clinton says she was raised to think about sex like this: "Sex is dirty. Save it for someone you love." Most of us can relate to that, and can see much of what we learned about money in that same light. "Money is evil. Get a lot of it."

One major effect of money being a taboo topic is that only those willing to learn about it can control it. In America, an elite and fairly secret class controls most of the nation's wealth, either by earning it, having inherited it, or both. It serves the interest of this ruling class for the rest of us not to know about who controls money and how to gain control of it ourselves. As long as we do not understand basic economics, we will not be able to control the means of production, know what kind of tax structure to advocate, be able to finance our nonprofits adequately, or create a society in which wealth is more fairly and equally distributed, which is, after all, the main underlying goal of social justice movements.

Political activists and participants in social change must learn how to raise money effectively and ethically, how to manage it carefully, and how to spend it wisely. Activists who refuse to learn about money, including how to ask for it, wind up collaborating with the very system that the rest of their work is designed to change.

The idea of asking for money raises another set of hindering attitudes, which are largely the inheritance of a predominately Protestant culture. The puritan ethic that infuses our culture affects most Americans, including those who are not Protestants, and conveys a number of messages that guide our feelings and actions. For example, a strong puritan ethic implies that if you are a good person and you work hard you will get what you deserve. Further, most likely you have not worked hard enough and you probably don't deserve it. If you have to ask for something you are a weak person because strong people are self-sufficient (meaning they don't ask for anything).

Specific Fears

With these very strong taboos operating against asking for money, it is a wonder that anyone ever does it! Understanding the source of our discomfort is the first step toward overcoming it. By looking at the effects of the taboos against talking about and asking for money, we can decide to reject the assumptions on which these taboos are built — assumptions about what is rude, what is an invasion of privacy, and who is deserving and who is not — and change our own attitudes and actions.

The next step is to examine our fears of what will happen to us when we do ask for money. When people look at their fears rationally they often find that most disappear or at least become manageable.

Fears about asking for money fall into three categories:

- Those that will almost never happen ("The person will hit me." "I'll die of a heart attack during the solicitation.")

- Those that could be avoided by training and preparation ("I won't know what to say." "I won't know my facts and the person will think I am an idiot.")

- Those that definitely will happen sometimes, maybe as much as half the time ("The person will say no.")

In the last category—things that will happen—most people have three main fears.

1. "The person will say no." Rejection is the number one fear. Unfortunately, being told no will happen at least as often as being told yes. Therefore, it is important to get to the point where you don't feel upset when someone says no. You do this by realizing that when you ask someone for a gift, you are seeing them at a single moment in their lives. A thousand things have happened to the person prior to your request, none of which has anything to do with you, but many of which will affect the person's receptiveness to your request. For example, the person may have recently found out that one of their children needs braces, that the car needs new tires, or that a client is not able to pay a bill on time. This news may affect the prospect's perception of what size donation he or she can make. The person may wish your organization success, but may have already given away all the money they can at this time or determined other priorities for their giving this year. Events unrelated to money can also cause the prospect to say no: a divorce proceeding, a death in the family, a headache. As the solicitor, none of these things is your fault. Many of them you could not have known ahead of time and you may never learn them because the prospect keeps them private. By feeling personally rejected you misinterpret the prospect's response and flatter yourself that you had something to do with it.

As the asker, you have to remember that, above all, the person being asked has the right to say no to a request without offering a reason. Most of the time you will not know exactly why your request was turned down. Your job is not to worry about why this prospect said no, but to go on, undaunted, to the next prospect.

2. "Asking a friend for money will have a negative effect on our friendship." Many people feel that friendship is outside the realm of money. They feel that to bring money into a friendship is to complicate it and perhaps to ruin it. Friends are usually the best prospects, however, because they share our commitments and values. They are interested in our lives and wish us success and happiness. To many people's surprise, friends are more likely to be offended when they are *not* asked. They can't understand why you don't want to include them in your work.

Further, if it is truly acceptable to you for a person to say no to your request, your friend will never feel put on the spot. Your friend will not feel pressured by your request, as if your whole friendship hung on the answer. When asking friends then, make clear that yes is the answer you are hoping for, but no is also acceptable. Say something like "I don't know what your other commitments are, but I wanted to invite you to be part of this if you can."

3. "The person will say yes to my request, then turn around and ask me to give to their cause. I will be obligated to give whether I want to or not." This quid pro quo situation ("this for that") does happen from time to time, and happens frequently with some people. Giving money to a cause at the request of a friend so that you can ask them later for your own cause, or feeling you must give because your friend gave to your cause is not fundraising. It is simply trading money; it would be cheaper and easier to just give to your cause and let your friend give to theirs. Also, a person who gives out of obligation to a friend will not become a habitual donor. They will cease to give as soon as their friend is no longer involved.

If someone you ask for money gives to your organization, you are not obligated to that person, except to make sure that the organization uses the money wisely and for the purpose you solicited. The obligation is fulfilled if the organization is honest and does its work. The solicitor does not materially benefit from a solicitation. They present the cause and if the prospect is sympathetic, he or she agrees to help support it. The cause was furthered. Beyond a thank-you note and a gracious attitude, the solicitor owes the donor nothing. If the donor then asks you to support his or her cause, you consider the request without reference to your request. You may wish to support the person or the cause, but you are not obligated to do so. If you think that someone is going to attach any strings to a gift, don't ask that prospect. There are hundreds of prospects who will give freely.

Far from being a horrible thing to do, asking someone for money actually does them a favor. People who agree with your goals and respect the work of your group will want to be a part of it. Giving money is a simple and effective way to be involved, to be part of a cause larger than oneself.

Many volunteers find that it takes practice to overcome their fears about asking for money. To begin soliciting donations does not require being free of fear; it only requires having your fear under control. Ask yourself if what you believe in is bigger than what you are afraid of. An old fundraising saying is that if you are afraid to ask someone for a gift, "Kick yourself out of the way and let your cause do the talking." The point is this: If you are committed to an organization you will do what is required to keep that organization going, which includes asking for money.

PROSPECT IDENTIFICATION

Once people feel somewhat relieved of their anxieties about asking for money, they have two more questions: Who shall I ask? and, How shall I ask?

Focus on Prospects

Because personal solicitation is, by definition, done on a person-by-person basis, it takes more time than most strategies. For example, a direct mail appeal can reach dozens or hundreds or thousands of people with one letter, duplicated and stuffed into envelopes. With direct mail, there should be an attempt to ensure that the lists being used are those of people who are interested in a similar cause, but there is little attempt to go through the list name by name. The opposite is true in personal solicitation. It is done strictly name by name, person by person. As such, we are looking for people who are worth that much time.

In traditional fundraising, personal solicitation is generally used to ask for gifts of $500 or more. For smaller organizations, however, donors who could give a gift of $100 or more are worth the time for a personal solicitation, and defining a major gift as $100 or more opens the possibility of becoming a major donor to more people. The question that determines whether a person is a prospect could be phrased this way, "What evidence do I have that if I asked this person for 30 to 60 minutes of their time to meet with me, thus using up 30 to 60 minutes of my time also (plus preparation), this person would be likely to make a gift that is significantly bigger than one they might have made if approached through a less time-consuming strategy?"

Three broad qualifications determine if someone is a prospect:

- **A**bility to make a gift of the size you are looking for
- **B**elief in the cause or something similar
- **C**ontact with someone in the group who is either willing to ask this person or willing to allow their name to be used in the asking

When you have positive, verifiable evidence of A, B, and C, you have a prospect. If any one of the criteria is missing you have a potential prospect, usually called a "suspect." If you are only sure of one of the criteria, you have a virtual stranger. Let's look at each one of these in depth, beginning with the most important.

Contact

This is the most important of the three criteria and also the most overlooked. Do you know the prospect? Does anyone you know also know the prospect? Without contact, you cannot proceed with a personal solicitation because there is no link between your organization and this person.

There are three ways for a person to have contact with your organization:

1. A board member, staff, or volunteer knows the person.

2. A board member, staff, or volunteer knows someone who knows this person and who is either willing to let you use their name in the approach ("Mary Jones suggested I call...") **or, better yet, is willing to call on your behalf** ("Joe, this is Mary. I'm giving money to a really amazing group, and was hoping you would be willing to see a couple of their representatives, let them tell you about the group, and ask you to join.")

3. The person is currently a donor to your group, but no one close to the group knows the person. In that case, when you call you will say, "We don't know each other, but we share a commitment to _____ and I want to talk with you about an exciting project we are about to undertake."

Belief

In thinking through why someone who is not already a donor might believe in your organization, return to your case statement (see Chapter 4). What values does your group espouse? What organizations have similar values even if their goals are different? Be broad-minded and creative in assessing potential linkage. For example, people who give to children's organizations are often interested in environmental issues because they are concerned about the kind of world the children are growing up in and will inherit as adults. People giving to environmental groups are likely to be interested in health issues; people who give to libraries will often support literacy programs or creative educational projects that help people appreciate the value of reading.

In addition to looking for similar values, look for other things that might link a person to your group. Do you serve a neighborhood that the person's family comes from? If you have clients, do your clients patronize the prospect's business?

Try not to draw conclusions from facts about people that could lead you to assume they won't be sympathetic to your group. For example, many older people, particularly in the South, are Republicans because Abraham Lincoln was a Republican. Many American Catholics are pro-choice. Many donors to the arts also give to civil liberties organizations because of censorship issues.

In addition to reviewing your case statement, ask staff, volunteers, and board members to write down all the values they hold dear and what beliefs tie them in with your group. This should provide a broad list that you can use to help screen potential prospects.

Ability

Although first in the ABC order, ability is actually the least important factor in identifying prospects. An assumption can be made that if a person knows and respects someone in an organization and believes in the cause, they have the ability to make some kind of gift. The question is, how much should they be asked for?

One of the biggest mistakes fundraisers make is assuming that how much a person can give will be related to how much money they have. Obviously, how much money a person has influences how much they can give at one time, but sometimes people will give more than they could have at one time through pledges or credit cards. Many wealthy people could afford to give much more than they do, while many poor people give a high proportion of what little they have. Stockbrokers, bankers, and financial planners are interested in how much people have, because they are selling the idea that they can help them have more. Fundraisers are interested in how much people give, and giving is the behavior to focus on, not having.

In terms of identifying how much a person could give, the best indicator is how much they give elsewhere. To figure out if a person gives away money, you could ask the contact what else the prospect supports, you could look at lists of donors printed in other organizations' newsletters, annual reports, and programs. You can listen closely to what the person says. Do they complain about getting a lot of direct mail? ("I'm on everyone's list. Everyone writes to me.") This is probably a person who gives by mail. Do they complain about how many phone calls they receive? ("Just when we're sitting down to dinner, the phone rings, and it's the disabled, or the whales, or the rain forest. The needs never end!") These calls are rarely random — they are made to people who give by phone. Is the person very busy? With what? Board meetings at the legal aid society? Organizing a special event for International Women's Day? The PTA? Being a docent at the art museum? Working for a political candidate?

Here are some guidelines for how to determine the size of a possible gift. To determine whether a person could give $50 to $499, you need to know little more about their ability than that they are employed in a job that pays more than minimum wage, that they are not supporting very many other people (children, partner, elderly relative), and that they have given in that range to some other group.

To determine if a person could give in the $500 to $2,500 range will require knowing that the person has a well-paying job or some other source of income (inheritance, investment, retirement, royalties) or is married to or living with someone who has a good job or inherited wealth or a healthy retirement income and so is not the sole support of their household, that the household is not very large, and that the prospect is very committed to your group or to someone in your group.

To determine if a person could give more than $2,500 will require more research, and more important, will require that the person is already a donor to your group. No matter how wealthy and generous someone is, he or she will rarely start their giving to a small organization with such a large gift. (These larger gifts are discussed in Section Three, Strategies to Upgrade Donors.)

Ultimately you will not know with any certainty how much a person could give because you can't know all their circumstances and because their perception of what they can afford can change from day to day. You make your best guess and you ask. People are rarely insulted to be asked for more money than they can afford; it's flattering to have people think you are that successful financially.

Steps in Creating a Prospect List

The people who are going to be involved in the personal solicitation strategy seeking gifts of $100–$2,500 meet and create a Master Prospect List. This is to ensure that no one gets asked by more than one person and that the right person does the asking in each case. Also, in a group setting people get more excited about the process and come up with more names and more enthusiasm for asking than they would on their own. When more than one person in the group may know a prospect, more information can be collected.

The easiest way to create a Master Prospect List was developed by fundraising consultant Stephanie Roth and works as follows: Everyone at the meeting first creates their own personal list, set up as in the illustration below, of all the people they know or who would recognize them if they were to call. No one should censor themselves by saying, "He hates me," or, "She's a tightwad," or "I can't ask them!" They just make the list of their contacts, remembering that being the contact is not necessarily the same as being the solicitor. Who will solicit the gift will be decided once the prospects are identified.

PROSPECT IDENTIFICATION LIST

NAME OF PROSPECT	RELATIONSHIP TO YOU	BELIEVES IN CAUSE	GIVES AWAY MONEY	SHOULD BE ASKED FOR
				$
				$
				$
				$
				$
				$
				$
				$
				$

Beside each name the contact notes what their relationship to the prospect is, and then whether or not the potential prospect believes in the cause. If they don't know what the person believes in, they put a question mark. Next, they cross off all the people who they know don't believe. Next to the people whom they know and who believe in the cause, they make a note of whether they know for a fact that this person gives away money. If they don't know, they put a question mark. They cross off anyone they know for a fact does not give away money. Next to all the people whom they know, who they know believe in the cause, and who they know give away money, they put what amount between $100–$2,500 they think the prospect could give. If they don't know, they put a question mark. Each person then reads his or her list of firm prospects — that is, those people about whom they were able to answer affirmatively in all categories. Alternatively, write these names on a piece of butcher paper to construct a Master Prospect List. If anyone else knows the prospects, they can confirm the information or add other information.

MASTER PROSPECT LIST

NAME OF PROSPECT	ADDRESS	PHONE	CONTACT	SOLICITOR	AMOUNT TO BE SOLICITED	OTHER INFORMATION

Next, each person reads the names of people on their list with question marks concerning belief or whether they give money to see if someone else can be helpful. If no one else knows the person, he or she is not a prospect. If someone does know them, they are either moved to the Master Prospect List or crossed off based on the additional information.

Make a final master list of people whom someone knows, who believes in the cause and who could make this size of gift, and then decide who is going to ask each person. Each solicitor then ends up with their own Prospect List. From the Master Prospect List, a prospect record will be developed for each prospect containing more detailed information about that person.

The following is a generic form for gathering information on individual prospects. You will want to design a form that works for your group. Keep in mind that you need to know less about someone if you are asking for $100 than someone you will approach for $2,500.

PROSPECT RECORD

Name:_____ Date:_____

Address: (work) _____

Address: (home) _____

Phone: (work) _____ (home) _____

Fax: (work) _____ (home) _____

E-mail: _____

Contact(s): _____

Interest/involvement in nonprofits (be specific): _____

Donations to nonprofits: _____

Evidence of belief in our group: _____

Occupation: _____

Employer: _____ Matching gift possible? _____

Household composition: _____

Does this person have any other source of income besides his/her salary?
(for example, second income in the household, inheritance, investment, retirement, royalties):

_____

Other interests/hobbies: _____

Suggested gift range: _____

Suggested solicitor: _____

Relationship to solicitor: _____

Result: _____

It is imperative that one or two people take on the task of collecting this information and recording it systematically. This is the job of development staff. If your organization does not have staff, one or two people from the board should take on this task. The information must be accurate and confidential. Nothing should appear that is only known from gossip or that is not helpful in seeking a gift ("had an affair with the Methodist minister" may be interesting, but is not prospect information). Some kinds of information will be more useful to some groups than to others. A group working with prisoners may wish to know if anyone in the prospect's family or the prospect her or himself has spent time in prison. Otherwise, that would probably not be appropriate information. People working in historic preservation may want to know how long someone has lived in a community, whereas people working on animal welfare issues will not need to know that as much as whether the person has pets or livestock or likes animals.

The most helpful tip for putting together lists of prospects is to make your own gift first. In fundraising we say that the first time you ask someone for money in person, you should always get a yes, because the first person you ask should be yourself. Once you test the proposition that the group is worth supporting against your own bank account, you will have a much clearer sense of who else you know might give, and what amount they might consider.

HOW TO APPROACH THE PROSPECT

After the solicitor has made his or her financial commitment, the prospects have been thoroughly researched, and the best prospects have been identified, the solicitor begins the process of asking for the gift.

The most formal approach involves three steps:

1. A letter describing the organization or the specific need, including a sentence or two indicating that you wish to ask the prospect for a gift and requesting a meeting to discuss it further, followed by

2. A phone call to set up a meeting, and then

3. The meeting itself in which the gift is actually solicited.

Obviously, if you are approaching your spouse or your best friend you can skip the letter and perhaps even the phone call. In other cases, the letter will be enough and there will be no need for a phone call. In others, the letter and a phone call will be enough, and there will be no need for a meeting. Deciding whether a meeting or follow-up phone call is necessary will depend on your knowledge of the prospect and how much money you are requesting. Some people are very comfortable giving $250, $500, or even $1,000 in response to a phone call. If the prospect lives far away from the organization or the solicitor, they will be more willing to have a long phone call than to expect the solicitor to visit them. Regardless of how generous, easygoing, or committed a prospect is, he or she will almost always give more in a meeting than when asked over the phone. Because you are requesting a thoughtful gift — a gift that is big enough that the prospect needs to think about whether he or she can afford it, and whether he or she wishes to give your group a gift that big — you want sufficient time with the prospect to answer all questions and concerns. It takes about 30 minutes to have the conversation you need to have, and a 30-minute meeting seems a lot shorter than a 30-minute phone call.

The Letter

The letter should raise the prospect's interest, giving some information, but not enough for a truly informed decision. The letter should be brief, not more than one page. Its purpose is to get the prospect to be open to the phone call in which the solicitor requests a meeting. In other words, the letter introduces the fact that you will be asking for a large gift for your organization and that you want the prospect to be willing to give a short amount of time for you to explain why you want this gift and why you think this prospect will be interested. No commitment to give or to be involved in any way is asked for in the letter — only a request for the prospect to discuss the proposition of a gift with the solicitor. Here is a sample letter.

Ms. Connie Concerned Activist with Good-Paying Job
Professional Office Building
City, State, ZIP

Dear Connie,

For several years you have heard me talk about Downtown Free Clinic. As you know, I have recently been elected to serve on the board, which I am really excited about! At a recent meeting, we made a decision to launch a major gifts campaign, the main purpose of which is to help the clinic become financially self-sufficient. In the future, we want to depend on a broad base of donors rather than on foundations and government grants, which have proven most unreliable.

The goal of the campaign is $50,000 the first year. All of us on the board have made our own commitments, which total $15,000. We are now turning to people like you to raise the rest. We need some lead gifts in the $1,000 to $2000 range from people of high standing in the community, whose words and example carry weight. I am hoping you will consider being one of the leaders in the campaign because of your long-time activism in community health care.

(Include one more brief paragraph on the current programs of the organization.)

I know this is a big request, and I don't expect you to decide based on my letter alone, so I am hoping we can meet and talk. I am very excited about the direction Downtown Free Clinic is taking and I can't really do it justice in this letter.

I'll call you next week to set up a time. Hope you are well. Enjoyed seeing you and your family at the baseball game last week.

Best always,
Annie, Another Concerned Activist

The letter is straightforward. Connie knows what the request will be, including the amount. She knows what the money is for. If giving to this organization at all is out of the question, she can decide that now. If giving a lead gift is out of the question, it is implicit from the letter that a smaller gift is an option. Her importance to the campaign has been stated, which is flattering. Yet there is nothing she needs to do at this point except wait for the phone call. No action has been requested — in fact, she has specifically only been asked not to decide.

The Phone Call

If you are the solicitor and you say you are going to call, you must call. Rehearse the phone call beforehand to anticipate questions or objections the prospect may have. Be sure you know exactly what you are going to say from the very first hello. Many people find it useful to write down what they will say, in the same way that one writes a script for a phone-a-thon.

The phone call is the most difficult part of the solicitation. It is pivotal to getting the meeting, and without the meeting you will probably not get as large a gift as you might have and you might not get a gift at all, so there is a lot of pressure on this call. Also, you have no body language to help you decide what the prospect is thinking and feeling. You can't tell if he or she is frowning, smiling, in a hurry, or busy. You can't rely on how people sound on the phone. People who are easygoing may sound brusque or harried on the phone. Many people simply do not like to talk on the phone, and their dislike of being on the phone may come across to you as a dislike of talking to you or a reluctance to discuss their gift. Finally, a phone call is always an interruption, even if the prospect really likes you.

All of these things can make a solicitor very anxious; anxiety, unfortunately, makes for poor phone calls. Anxious people have a hard time listening to others because they are too absorbed in thinking about what they are going to say next. Practicing the phone call a few times with other people in your organization will help you be less anxious.

There are two things that can happen when you make this phone call: Either you won't reach the prospect, or you will.

You won't reach the prospect. In fact, 90% of the time you will get some kind of gatekeeper — an answering machine, voice mail, a secretary, someone else in the household. When this happens, leave a brief message that includes a good time to call you back and say that you will try again. Leave at least three such messages before you give up on this prospect. Messages are not reliable. Answering machines get erased accidentally, messages written on pieces of paper get lost, numbers get transposed, names are spelled so wrong that the prospect cannot recognize them, prospects try you back and get a busy signal or carry your message around with them meaning to call but never finding the time, etc. Many people are finding that leaving their e-mail address in addition to their phone number will at least result in the person getting back to you, as people answer their e-mail at all hours of the day and night. Again, don't assume that because you can't reach the prospect, the answer is no. However, your time is valuable also, and leaving more than three messages for one person is not as useful as moving on to the next prospect.

If you have made a serious effort to reach a prospect and have not succeeded, you may want to ask the contact for more information about the prospect. You may find out that the prospect is out of the country or is tending to a sick relative, or that you can make an appointment with the prospect through her secretary or even that the secretary is authorized to handle these kind of requests.

You will reach the prospect. To ensure that you have not caught the prospect at a bad time, ask if this is a good time to talk. Be sure not to read meaning into statements that can be taken at face value. For example, do not hear "I don't want to give" in a statement such as "I'm very busy this month," or, "I have to talk to my spouse before making any decision." Instead, in the first instance say, "I can understand that. How about if I call you next month, when things might have slowed down for you?" In the second instance say, "Would it be possible for me to see you both in that case?" Hear everything the prospect says as being literally true. If she says, "I've already given away all the money I am going to give this year," then ask if you can meet so that your group can be considered next year. If he says, "I need more information before I can meet," ask what information would be most helpful, tell him you will send it today, and then suggest penciling in a meeting for a later time after the prospect has had time to review the information.

Be clear about the purpose of the phone call, which is to ask for some time to discuss the possibility of the prospect making a gift — not to ask for the gift. The prospect does not need to decide about his or her gift until the meeting. If the prospect tries to put you off, do not assume that he or she is saying no. In fact, people who make a lot of big gifts will often use put-offs to determine whether you are serious about the organization and whether the organization can really do its work. This is particularly true for community organizing projects. It is hard to believe that a group will really face down corporate intimidation or stand up to political power if its members fold at the first sign of resistance from someone they have identified as a person who believes in their cause!

The Meeting

Once you have set up an appointment, you are ready to prepare for the face-to-face solicitation. This is not as frightening as it seems. First of all, the prospect knows from your letter or your phone call that you will be talking about making a contribution. Since he or she has agreed to see you the answer to your request is not an outright no. The prospect is considering saying yes. Your job is to move the prospect from consideration to commitment.

The purpose of the meeting is to get the gift. As the solicitor, you must appear poised, enthusiastic, and confident. If you are well prepared for the interview, this will not be too difficult. Board members and volunteers can go with each other or bring a staff person to such a meeting to provide any information the solicitor doesn't have. If you do go in pairs, be sure you know who is going to begin the meeting and who is going to actually ask for the gift.

The solicitor's job is to ask for the gift. The prospect's job is to give it, give less, need time to think about it, or say no. It is important that the solicitor does not get personally caught up in the prospect's response. You are not a good fundraiser if someone says yes, nor a poor fundraiser if someone says no. If you are asking enough people, a certain percentage will say no. In fact, a sign that you are not asking enough people is when you go for a few days without anyone saying no.

Meeting Etiquette

Regardless of how well you know this prospect, the subject of this meeting is business. You should begin the meeting with pleasantries, catch up on family and friends briefly, but avoid the temptation to have a long chat before getting down to the subject at hand. It is often helpful to say early in the meeting, "Well, you know why we are here, which is to ask you to consider making a gift to Important Group. Before we get to that, however, we want to tell you some of the exciting things we are doing." This moves everyone into the conversation about the group and its fundraising goals.

The more the prospect is encouraged to talk the more likely he or she is to give. No one likes to be talked at or lectured. Ask the prospect what they know about your group, how they keep up with the issues your group works on, and other open-ended questions. Share your own experience with the group and tell stories that illustrate facts rather than just giving a dry exposition of what the group does. Sentences that begin "I am most excited by…" or, "I got involved with Important Group because of my own situation/commitment/longstanding interest in…" are much more likely to be listened to than "We started in 1983 with funding from the Havelots Foundation."

In addition to asking questions, pause for a few seconds between every few sentences. Wait to see if the prospect wants to add anything or has any questions or objections. If the prospect says something you don't understand, ask for clarification or say, "Tell me more about that." If the prospect says something that offends you or you don't agree with, don't pretend to agree. Don't sacrifice your integrity for this gift, but see if you can find a way to counter what the prospect said without getting into an argument. You can use phrases like "I can see why you say that because that is the impression that the media gives, but in fact…" or, "We have discovered that fact-fact-fact, which is why we have designed the program the way we have." Said without rancor or defensiveness, statements like these can allow the prospect to change his mind without looking stupid.

Toward the end of the half-hour interview, or when the prospect seems satisfied with what you have said, you are ready to close — that is, to ask for the gift. Repeat the goal of the campaign and the importance of the work of the group in one or two sentences. Then, looking directly at the prospect, ask for a specific gift: "Will you help with $2,000?" or, "I'm hoping you can give a gift in the range of $500 to $1,500," or, "Do you think you could consider $2,500?" There are no magic words for the close — what is important is that you figure out a phrase that suits your personality and includes the range or the specific gift you want. Then be quiet. At this moment, you give up control of the interaction. At last, you are asking the prospect to make a decision. Wait for the prospect to speak, even if you have to wait what seems like several minutes. If you are anxious, time may seem to be passing very slowly. Keep looking at the prospect. You can breathe easy now, because you have said everything you need to say and you have put your best foot forward. Look relaxed and confident.

The Prospect's Response

At this point the prospect will say one of six things, or some variation on these themes:

1. "Yes, I'll help." Thank the prospect. Be grateful and pleased, but don't be overly effusive or you will give the impression you didn't think the prospect was really a generous person. Arrange for how the gift will be made (by check, by pledge, by stock transfer; now, later). The easiest way to do that is to ask, "How would you like to pay that?" Once those arrangements are made, thank the prospect again and leave.

2. "I'd like to help, but the figure you named is too high." This is a yes answer, but for a smaller gift. You can say, "Would you like to pledge that amount and contribute it in quarterly installments over a year's time?" Or you can say, "What would you feel comfortable giving?" or "What would you like to give?" Avoid the temptation to bargain with the prospect. Once the prospect has decided on an amount, follow the procedure in #1.

3. "That's a lot of money." This statement is generally a stall. The prospect feels he can give what you have asked, which is a big gift for him. He wants to be sure that your organization agrees that the gift is large. Your answer: "Yes, that would be a major donation. There are not many people we could ask for that amount." Or, "It is a lot of money. That's why I wanted to talk to you about it in person." Or, "It is a lot of money. It would be a big help." Then be quiet again and let the prospect decide.

4. "I need to think about it." Some people truly cannot make up their mind on the spot and if pushed for an answer will say no. Ask the prospect, "What else can I tell you that will help you in your thinking?" and answer any remaining questions. Then say, "May I call you in a few days to see what your decision is?" Set a time when the prospect will be finished thinking and will give you an answer.

5. "I need to talk to my spouse/partner/other party." This probably does mean the person needs to talk to someone else; however, it is surprising that the prospect didn't say that when you set up the meeting, so it probably also means the person needs more time. Often it means that the person has another question or objection, but is embarrassed to say it. This is called the "shadow question" and you need to surface what it is. You will do that by saying, "That makes sense. Is there anything your partner will want to know that I can tell you now?" The prospect may then tell you what's bothering him. "My partner will want to know why you spend so much on office space," or "My partner will want to know why you take money from Possibly Bad Corporation and will wonder if that affects your work." You can then answer these objections. You will end this solicitation by getting some agreement as to when the prospect can talk to the person they need to, and when you should get back to them.

6. "No, I can't help you." Although this is an unlikely response at this point, it should be treated with respect. Nod your head and wait silently for a longer explanation. Generally the prospect will expand to provide an explanation. "You know, I just don't really agree with your approach. I thought when I heard more about it I might understand and agree, but I don't." Or, "You know I just can't get past the fact that Person I Hate is the chair of your board." Don't join in trashing this person, but don't spend a lot of time defending them either, unless your defense is confined to discussing their work for your group. "He has done really good work for us, but I know he is controversial." If the prospect doesn't volunteer an explanation, ask for one. "Can you share with me why you are saying no?" If asked nondefensively, the prospect will answer. If the answer is a misunderstanding, clear it up and you may get a yes, or at least, "I'll think about it." Don't spend much time trying to change the prospect's mind, or you will seem disrespectful. Often, people who say no to a request like this later say yes as they learn more or have time to really think about what you have said. Try to end the meeting with a question the prospect can say yes to. "Would you like to stay on our mailing list?" Or, "When Person You Hate leaves the board, can I call you?" Or just, "What is the best way to get downtown from here?" Thank the prospect for their time and leave. Remember that you have a tacit agreement with everyone you ask for money that if they let you ask them, you will let them say no.

Immediately after the interview send a thank-you note regardless of the response you got at the meeting. Another thank-you note should come from the organization when the gift is received. Although it is anxiety-producing to ask someone for a large gift, it is also thrilling when a prospect says yes. Most people find that, with practice, asking for money becomes easier and easier. And most people are encouraged by being able to set aside their own discomfort about asking for money for the greater purpose of meeting the needs of the organization.

ten

The Thank-You Note

In 1977, a woman sent $25 to an advocacy group working on women's health issues. The organization was run collectively by 2 utterly overworked staff people and 40 volunteers. The group had won recognition for their work exposing the dangers of the Dalkon Shield IUD and championing reproductive rights issues. The donor did not receive a thank-you note for her gift, but she did receive the group's newsletter and she heard about the group from time to time.

A year after making her gift she received a letter requesting a renewal. She threw it away.

Some time later, she learned that a friend of hers was a member of the group. "That group sounds good," she told her friend, "but they don't even have it together enough to send thank-you notes for gifts. I can't imagine that they are really fiscally sound or that they use money properly."

Her friend defended the group: "They do really good work. Maybe they should take time to thank people, but saying they don't use money wisely is an unfair conclusion."

The one-time donor replied, "It is fair. It is my only contact with them. They claim to want a broad base of support, yet they show no regard for their supporters. But since you are in the group, I'll give them something." She sent $15.

During the year between this donor's $25 gift and her $15 one, the group had hired me to be their fundraiser. In response to her second gift, I sent her a scrawled three-line thank-you note: "Thanks for your gift of $15. It's a help financially and also a great morale boost. We'll keep in touch."

Two weeks later, this woman sent $100. Again, I scrawled a thank-you note. A few months later, she sent $1,500.

Valuing All Gifts

Although I had been drilled from childhood about the propriety of sending thank-you notes, I never really believed they were worth much one way or the other until that lesson. After I met this donor, she told me that she often sent relatively small gifts to groups to see what they would do. If she sent $100 or more (a lot of money in 1977) most groups would thank her. But that would not tell her how much regard they had for smaller donors. "Many grassroots groups talk a good line about not making class distinctions and everyone being welcomed," she said, "but the only people they really care about are the program officers of foundations and wealthy donors."

As it turned out, this woman was very wealthy, but she wanted to give money only to groups that had proven that they valued all gifts. I was flabbergasted that a sign of proof could be a sloppy three-line thank-you note, but for her it was better proof than a longer form letter with her name typed in, and certainly way better than no acknowledgment at all.

Since then I have seen over and over that a simple, handwritten note or typed thank-you letter with a personal note as a postscript can do more to build donor loyalty than almost any other form of recognition. Unfortunately, thank-you notes tend to be one thing that organizations are sloppy or even thoughtless about. They either don't send them, send them weeks late, or send form thank-yous with no personal note added. These practices are unjustifiable. Sending thank-you notes too easily falls far too low on people's work priority lists. They have to be placed at the top.

It is not clear to me why people like thank-you notes so much, particularly when there is usually very little content in the note. Probably reasons vary. Like our wealthy, testing donor, some see them as a sign that the group knows what it is doing. Others may just like the attention. While psychologists may be able to find out exactly why people like to be appreciated, for fundraisers it is enough to know that it is true. Doing what donors like — as long as we stay inside the mission and goals of the organization — builds donor loyalty. A loyal donor is a giving donor, giving more and more every year.

What about the donor who claims not to want a thank-you note, or the one who even more strongly states that thank-yous are a waste of time and money?

The first type of donor, who claims not to want a thank-you note, should get one anyway. These are usually people who are genuinely trying to save groups time. You will have greater loyalty if you send a thank-you note anyway. When these donors say, "You shouldn't have done that," or, "That's really not necessary," they often mean, "Thank you for taking the time. I can't believe someone would bother to notice me."

The second style of donor, who actually resents thank-you notes, probably should get a call thanking them for their gift. Even a brief message left on a phone machine will be appreciated. Sometimes donors don't know that gifts of more than $250 must be acknowledged in writing according to the FASB regulations. (The Financial Accounting Standards Board creates the regulations governing how non-profits have to report on monies given or spent, including pledges. These regulations change from time to time.) If the person is very close to your group — perhaps a volunteer or board member, or someone who used to work for the organization — you can combine your thank-you call with another function, such as to remind them of a meeting: "I called to thank you for your gift — we can really use it. By the way, don't forget about the meeting Wednesday at 7 P.M. at Marge's."

Overall, experience shows that, all else being equal, when you thank donors you keep them and when you don't you lose them.

Of course, there will be exceptions to this rule, but it is almost impossible to figure out who is really an exception and who is just pretending to be, so thank everyone and save yourself worrying about it.

When and How

How can you most efficiently thank your donors, and who should do it? Perhaps the most important rule about thanking donors is that no matter who is doing it — from the board chair to an office volunteer — gifts should be acknowledged *within 72 hours of receipt,* and no more than a week should go by in any circumstance. If possible, the person who knows the donor should sign the thank-you note.

If you are fundraising properly, you will have dozens of donations coming in from people you don't know. Volunteers and board members can send thank-yous to these. It is actually a good way to get board members who are resistant to fundraising to do some, because the thank-you note is part of fundraising.

Buy some nice notecards, or have some made with your logo on the front. There is only a small amount of space to fill on a note card so you can take up the whole space with a few short sentences. That is much better than a three-line thank-you on a full sheet of stationery.

People should come to the office to write the notes, and only the most loyal, trustworthy people should ever be allowed to write notes at home. It is just too tempting to put them aside at home. Also, information about a person's gift, while not secret, is also not something you want sitting around someone's living room.

The only equipment for handwritten thank-yous is legible handwriting. The format is simple:

> Thank you for your gift of $ _____. We will put it right to work on (name your program or most recent issue). Gifts like yours are critical to our success, and we thank you very much.
>> Sincerely,
>> (Your name), Board member

If you know the person, follow the same format, but add something more personal:

> Hope your cat, Fluffy, has recovered from her spaying.

It may be that handwriting thank-you notes or handwriting all of them is impossible, especially when you get a lot of contributions, such as at year-end, and volunteers aren't as available, or after a successful direct mail appeal when you are swamped for a few days with responses. Then you go to the next step, which is a word-processed letter. This should go on stationery and needs to be a little longer. Most databases can be programmed to generate a form thank-you note to which you can add a personal note.

Start the thank-you several lines down the page, and use wide margins.

> Dear Freda,
> Thank you so much for your gift of $100. We have put it right to work at our shelter. As it turned out, your gift came at a particularly crucial moment, as our boiler had just given its last gasp. We were able to buy a refitted, good-as-new boiler for cash (saving us $), which we wouldn't have been able to do without your gift.
> I am hoping you will be able to come to our art auction next month. We have the works of some well-known local artists and will be featuring paintings and sculptures by some of the residents of the shelter. I enclose two complimentary tickets.
> Again, thank you so much! I look forward to staying in touch.

You will notice that the letter refers to some very recent event (the boiler giving out). This gives a sense of immediacy to the gift. If the organization had not used the gift for the boiler, they could have still told the story, as follows:

> Your gift came the same day our boiler broke for the last time. I would have been really discouraged, but your contribution cheered me up. Fortunately, we were able to get a refitted, good-as-new boiler for much less than a new one would have cost.

The letter also invited the donor to an event. You do not need to provide free tickets, nor do you have to be having an event. The point is to refer to things happening in your office every day. Give your donors some sense of your daily work. Even things that seem routine to you can be made to sound interesting.

For example:

Dear Ricardo,

We got a pile of mail today — bills, flyers, newsletters, and then, your gift of $50! Thank you! $50 really goes a long way in this organization, and we are grateful for your support.

I just finished talking with a woman who used our educational flyer with her son. She said she had expected a miracle, and though of course that didn't happen, maybe something more lasting did. Her son called the Help Line. It's a start, and that's what we provide for people.

I hope you will feel free to drop by sometime. Though we are usually busy, we can always take a few minutes to say hello and show you around. I'll keep you posted on our progress.

Or:

Dear Annie Mae,

I just came in from an eviction hearing for one of our clients. I feel really good because we won, and we got some damages to boot! Then, going through the mail, I came to your gift of $25. Thanks! I feel like you are a part of this victory.

Or:

You wouldn't believe how many people came to our community meeting last night — more than 50! People are hopping mad about this incinerator proposal, and I am feeling confident that we may be able to defeat it and finally get the recycling bill passed. Your gift of $50 will go a long way in helping with flyers and phone calls. Thanks for thinking of us at this time. You don't know what a great morale boost it is to receive gifts from supporters like you.

If you have a matching campaign or a goal for an annual campaign, then include that:

Your gift of $100 will be matched dollar for dollar. Your gift brought us to just under $2,000 raised in just two months!

Or:

Your gift of $75 took us over the $1,000 mark in our goal of $3,000. Thanks!

If you are a volunteer, mention that in your thank-you:

Giving time to this organization is one of the high points of my week. I know we are making a difference, and I want you to know that your gift helps make that difference too.

The least effective option for thank-you notes, but one you sometimes have to resort to, is the form letter. If you use a form letter, acknowledge that it is impersonal, but give some sense of the excitement that would lead you to use such a method.

Thank you for your recent gift. Please excuse the impersonal nature of this thank-you — though we aren't able to write to each of our donors, we greet each gift with enthusiasm. The response to our call for help with sending medical supplies to Iraq was both gratifying and overwhelming. We will send you a full report about this effort in a few weeks. Right now, we are packing up boxes of supplies — supplies you helped pay for. Thanks again!

Who Gets Thanked

There are three common questions remaining about thank-yous. Don't waste a lot of time worrying about this. Having received many thank-yous that say, "Dear Mr. Klein," I know how offputting it can be, but it does not cause me to stop giving to the group. Anyone who will stop giving you money just because you (or anyone else) cannot tell from their name whether they are male or female, or whether they prefer to be called by their first name, last name, Mr., Ms., or Mrs. doesn't have much loyalty to your group.

The first question is, do all donors get a thank-you? The answer is always yes. You have no idea how much a gift of $25 or $5 or $500 means to someone. You need to act as though you would like to get that amount or more again. You also don't know how people use getting a thank-you note to judge whether to continue giving to your organization. Why take a chance?

The second question is, do all donors get the same thank-you? No, because the notes, if possible, are personalized. But people giving bigger gifts don't get bigger thank-yous. If you have thousands of donors, you will not be able to write to them all personally, so sort out the ones you know and write to them. But make sure each donor gets something.

The final question is, How do you address people you don't know? The choices are by first name only, by first and last names (Dear John Smith), or by title (Dear Mr. Smith). There is no clear right or wrong answer on this point, and no way to avoid possibly offending someone. In general, you will probably offend the least number of people by using titles, "Dear Mr." or "Dear Ms." Certainly, you could write to the person according to how they write to you. A letter signed, "Mrs. Alphonse Primavera" should be answered in kind. If there is ambiguity about whether the donor is a man or woman, write "Dear Friend." If you live in a fairly casual community, you can use a first name, "Dear Lynn."

Keep up with thank-you notes as gifts come in. Each thank-you is a link to the donor and you should see it as paving the way for the next gift.

Strategies to Upgrade Donors

The goal of any organization that gains the support of individual donors is to become the favorite organization of their donors. The financial payoff in building a base of donors is in being able to ask people who are giving donations regularly to consider giving bigger and bigger gifts. You want your donors to think, "That is the group to which I give the most money," or, "That is an organization I would do almost anything for." Building on that loyalty, you now invite your donors to give your organization the maximum amount of money they can afford. The strategies described in this section are used in that process.

The process of getting current donors to give more money is called "upgrading" and those donors who respond to these strategies have become the "thoughtful" donors described in Chapter 3, Matching Fundraising Strategies with Financial Needs.

It is highly unusual for a person to start their giving to an organization with a thoughtful gift, so almost all thoughtful donors will come out of the donor base that is built using the strategies described in Section Two. The only time someone's first gift might be the largest gift they can give is when they or someone close to them has been deeply affected by the issue the organization addresses or the service it provides.

Thoughtful gifts are most often gifts of more than $100; a thoughtful annual gift may be thousands of dollars, and a capital or endowment gift will be even higher. In this section, we will use $100 to describe the minimum thoughtful gift and then discuss much larger gifts. It is important to note, though, that if your organization's donor base includes low-income or poor people, there will be people giving less than $100 who are nevertheless giving your organization the biggest gift they can afford. On the other side are people giving a few thousand dollars who could give more if you asked them.

To the extent that you can identify them, thoughtful donors who are giving what are significant gifts for them, albeit small amounts of money, need to be treated with the same respect with which you treat thoughtful donors who give larger gifts.

In fundraising, we must spend large amounts of time working with people who can give large amounts of money. All donors expect that and would think it odd and not a good use of resources to do otherwise. But we don't overlook other kinds of giving and the significance of gifts to any donor, because it is the right thing to do. There is a practical angle, too: Someone who gives $10 a quarter through a pledge program may get a better job or a cheaper apartment and change their gift to $10 a month. When he or she gets promoted, the gift may increase to $50 a month. Or, a person may give a small amount for years and years, then die and leave their estate to the organization. In fact, research shows that long-time, loyal donors making small gifts are most often the ones that leave an organization a gift through a bequest.

Through the process of identifying prospects, described in Chapter 9, Personal Solicitation, and through careful and thorough recordkeeping, we can keep track of all our thoughtful donors, not just the ones who are able to give large amounts of money.

This section, like the last, is organized in order of the amount of personal asking that is required for each gift. The least-personal strategies are described first and the most personal — planned gifts — are described last. This also follows the order of their difficulty, from least to most difficult.

eleven

Major Gifts Programs

Grassroots organizations have three ways of including major gifts in their fundraising program. First, in every organization from the smallest to the largest, staff, board, and volunteers must feel comfortable asking people for money in person (see Chapter 9, Personal Solicitation). For many people, that comfort starts with being able to ask someone for $10 for a ticket to a benefit event such as a dance, or $35 to become a member.

Some people never move past that, but if an organization is to grow and thrive, a majority of board, volunteers, and staff must be able to ask for much larger gifts — $50, $100, $1,000, $10,000, and even more.

Let me note here that a person doesn't have to like asking for money to be able to do it. Some of the most successful fundraisers I have known have confessed that they always feel anxious when asking for money. But they do it anyway, and sometimes their nervousness makes them prepare thoroughly for the solicitation and feel even better about themselves and their group after they complete it.

Once an organization is in the habit of asking for large gifts, it quickly moves to needing a more systematic plan for soliciting such gifts. That system is a major gifts program and is discussed here. Some groups prefer to do their major donor fundraising in the form of a campaign; that type of major donor fundraising is discussed in Chapter 13.

Before beginning a major gifts program, your organization must define how much money it wishes to raise from large gifts, the minimum amount that will constitute a major gift (in this book it is $100), and how many gifts of what size are needed. You must decide what, if any, tangible benefits donors will receive for their gifts and what materials will be needed for the solicitors, and a core group of volunteers must be trained to ask for the gifts.

SETTING A GOAL

The first step in seeking major gifts is to decide how much money you want to raise from major donors. This amount will be related to the overall amount you want to raise from all your individual donors, and can be partly determined based on the following information. (For further information on goal setting, see Chapter 33, Creating a Fundraising Plan.)

Over the years fundraisers have observed a pattern of how gifts come into organizations. This is the established pattern:

- 60% of the income comes from 10% of the donors

- 20% of the income comes from 20% of the donors

- 20% of the income comes from 70% of the donors

In other words, the majority of your gifts will be small, but the majority of your income will be from a few large donations. Based on that pattern, it is possible to project for any fundraising goal how many gifts of each size you should seek and how many prospects you will need to ask to get each gift.

For example, if your organization must raise $50,000 from grassroots fundraising, plan to raise $30,000 (60%) from major gifts, mostly solicited personally; $10,000 from habitual donors, mostly solicited through mail and regular special events; and $10,000 from people giving for the first or second time, including from all other strategies, such as special events, product sales, canvassing, etc.

If you have 1,500 donors, then, expect that about 150 of them will be major donors, 300 to 400 of them will be habitual donors, and about 1,000 will be first- or second-time donors or donors who give small gifts every year, but for whom your organization is not a high priority. Your lowest major gift should be an amount that is higher than most give, but is a gift that most employed people can afford to give, especially if donors are allowed to pledge. Even many low-income people can afford $10 a month or $25 a quarter, which brings being a "major donor" into the realm of possibility for all people close to your group.

Some organizations try to avoid setting goals, saying they will raise "as much as they can from as many people as they can." This doesn't work because prospects are going to ask how much you need and will not be satisfied with the answer, "As much as we can get." If prospects think a group will simply spend whatever it has, they will give less than they can afford or nothing, because the organization doesn't seem very well run. Further, without a goal, there is no way to measure how well the organization is doing compared to its plans. Just as you can't build a house saying, "It will be as big as it needs to be," or, "It will be as big as we can afford," you can't build a donor base with vague or meaningless assertions either.

APPORTIONMENT OF GIFTS

It would be great if you could say, "Well, we need $40,000 from 10% of our donors, so that will mean 200 people giving $200." But 200 people will not behave the same way — some will give more, most will give less. So fundraisers have made a second observation: For the money needed annually from individual donors, you need one gift equal to 10% or more of the goal, two gifts equal to 10% (5% each) or more of the goal, and four to six gifts providing the next 10% or more of the goal. The remaining gifts needed are determined in decreasing sizes of gifts with increasing numbers of gifts. Using this formula, you can create a "Gift Range Chart" or a "Gift Pyramid."

Let's imagine an organization that needs to raise $100,000 from a wide variety of individual donor strategies. Using the pattern outlined above, $60,000 will be raised from major gifts. Their gift pyramid will look something like this:

GIFT RANGE CHART			
Goal: $100,000			
	NUMBER OF GIFTS	SIZE OF GIFTS	TOTAL
MAJOR GIFTS	1	$10,000	$10,000
	2	$5,000	$10,000
	5	$2,500	$12,500
	10	$1,000	$10,000
	15	$500	$7,500
	20	$250	$5,000
	50	$100	$5,000
TOTALS	103	$100–$10,000	$60,000
OTHER GIFTS	300–400	$25–$99	$20,000
	many	under $99	$20,000

The most important and useful part of the chart is the top part, which plots size and number of major gifts. It should not be seen as a blueprint. If an organization has one donor who can give 15% of the goal, then ask for that; you will need fewer gifts at the lower end of the chart. An organization in a rural community may not be able to generate the number of gifts needed, so it will have to get fewer gifts at larger sizes.

The chart serves as a guideline and also a reality check. For example, if your goal is to raise $100,000, but the biggest gift you can imagine getting is $500, then you will probably have to lower your goal. The chart is helpful for board members and other volunteer solicitors who may have difficulty imagining raising $100,000, but can imagine 50 people giving $100 each.

HOW MANY PEOPLE NEED TO BE ASKED

Every fundraising strategy, presuming it is done properly, has an expected rate of response. When major gifts are requested by someone who knows the potential donor, knows that he or she believes in the cause, and knows that he or she could give the amount of money being asked, there is about a 50% chance the prospect will say yes to making a gift. However, if the prospect does say yes, there is a further 50% chance that he or she will give less than what was requested.

So, minimally, for every gift you seek through personal solicitation, you will need four prospects — two will say no, one will say yes, and one will give a lesser amount. At the upper reaches of your chart, you should look for four prospects for every gift needed, but because the ones who give less fill in the number of gifts needed in the middle and bottom ranges of the chart, look for two to three prospects for every gift needed in those ranges. Overall, look for about three times as many prospects as gifts needed. For the $100,000 goal, then, the chart above would be amended to include numbers of prospects, and look like this:

GIFT RANGE CHART
Goal: $100,000

	NUMBER OF GIFTS	SIZE OF GIFTS	TOTAL	NUMBER OF PROSPECTS
MAJOR GIFTS	1	$10,000	$10,000	4
	2	$5,000	$10,000	(×4) 8
	5	$2,500	$12,500	(×4) 20
	10	$1,000	$10,000	(×4) 40
	15	$500	$7,500	(×4) 60
	20	$250	$5,000	(×3) 60
	50	$100	$5,000	(×2) 100
TOTALS	103	$100–$10,000	$60,000	288
OTHER GIFTS	300–400	$25–$99	$20,000	(×2) 600–800
	many	under $99	$20,000	(varies with strategy)

Overall, an organization needing about 100 major gifts will need to ask about 300 people. (For help identifying those 300 people, see Chapter 9, Personal Solicitation.)

MATERIALS NEEDED FOR MAJOR GIFTS SOLICITATION

In addition to the gift range chart and a list of prospects, three more elements need to be in place to be able to solicit major gifts: a benefits program, materials that describe your work and how to make donations, and people to solicit gifts.

Benefits

First, you need to decide what, if any, benefits people will receive for giving a major gift. While helping the organization is the main satisfaction for the donor, an added incentive such as a mug, an invitation to a special reception, or a T-shirt will show that you appreciate the extra effort the donor is making, and will remind the donor of their gift to your group.

There is no evidence that one kind of benefit works better than another (see also the discussion of benefits in Chapter 6, Using Direct Mail). Certainly, the benefit should not be very expensive. Under IRS law, any benefit that exceeds in value the vague definition of "token" must be subtracted from the gift before the gift can be used as a tax deduction. For example, if someone gives $500 to an organization and receives an etching worth $50, they can only deduct $450 of this gift because $50 is more than "token." If the same group gave a T-shirt or tote bag worth little or nothing on the open market, the donor could deduct the whole $500. The IRS is increasingly questioning fancy benefits for donors. (By and large, this will not affect readers of this book!)

The benefit should be easy to mail, which is why many groups use T-shirts or books as benefits. Because of the number of "things" people can get for their gifts to public television, libraries, or major national organizations, a small organization should probably offer something that is related to its programs. For example, an organization working for stricter controls on the commercial use of pesticides and for alternatives to pesticides sends its major donors a short booklet on alternatives to pesticides for home gardens and indoor plants. An after-school program for inner-city children aged 8 to 11 asked the teachers to save any drawings the children made that they didn't want to take home. The organization sent the best of those along with their thank-you notes to donors. This benefit is truly of "token" value, but is very popular with donors. Now the organization has one day on which the children are asked to make "thank-you" drawings.

A major donor program can be run successfully without giving any benefits beyond what are offered to all donors, such as the newsletter. This approach will work only if the donors are thanked personally and promptly and if the organization keeps in touch with them using the ways recommended in the section on renewing major gifts, below. Personal attention and information on what work the group was able to do will always work better in maintaining donors than any benefits.

Descriptive Materials

The second element needed is materials that describe your program. An organization should have a well-designed, easy-to-understand brochure. It does not have to be fancy or printed in several colors, but it should be professionally laid out, well written, and free of grammatical and typographical errors. This pamphlet will be used primarily in personal solicitation, so it should focus on ways to make thoughtful gifts. For example, if you have an electronic fund transfer program or a pledge program, or if you accept credit cards or you are seeking gifts of stocks and bonds, you can explain all that in the brochure. This brochure is a published version of your case statement. It also helps volunteer solicitors by giving them something to leave with a donor and to refer to if they forget some information they meant to impart. Return envelopes and return cards must be included with the brochure.

Solicitors

Finally, you need to have a core group of people willing to do the soliciting. Some of these people should be from the board of directors, but the board's work can be augmented by a group of volunteers and, in some cases, paid staff. These people should be trained in the process of asking for money (see Chapter 9, Personal Solicitation). They do not have to have previous experience, nor do they need to know many prospects themselves. But they must be donors, and ideally major donors themselves.

KEEPING IN TOUCH WITH MAJOR DONORS

One of the most frequent complaints from major donors is that organizations treat them like ATM machines — they punch in the amount they want and then walk away until they need money again. To keep donors interested in your group requires showing some interest in the donor, particularly some interest in why the donor is interested in your group. To give major donors this extra attention takes work, but it is worth it for several reasons: First, courtesy; second, because it brings donors closer to the work of your group, making them potential activists or advocates; and third, because it will bring in more money.

You should be in contact with your major donors two or three times a year in addition to the time when you ask the donors to renew their gifts. You will want to be in touch with some donors more often than that, depending in part on the size of their gift and mostly on their personality and expressed level of interest. Remember that major donors are a good source of feedback, advice, and volunteer energy, to say nothing of a source of other major donors.

There are several easy ways to keep in touch with major donors that make them feel personally appreciated and do not cost the organization much in time or money. You can choose from the suggestions below or develop your own system, but be sure to get a system in place.

1. Send major donors a holiday card during December. The card should wish the donor happy holidays and be signed by the chair of the board, a board member with a personal relationship to the donor, or a staff person. If possible, write a brief note on the card. The card goes alone — no return envelope, no appeal letter. (You may also send major donors a year-end appeal in a separate mailing.) Unless your organization is religiously identified, make sure the card has no religious overtones, including cultural Christian overtones such as Santa Claus, elves, or Christmas trees. The same applies to the postage stamp you choose.

2. Send all donors a copy of your annual report and attach a personal note to reports going to major donors. The note can be on a Post-it and does not have to be long. It says something like "Thought you'd be interested in seeing this since you have been so critical to our success," or, "I hope you are as proud of our work as we are — your gift helped make it possible." It doesn't matter if you don't know the donor at all — a personal note shows that they are appreciated. If you know that something in your report will be of particular interest, note that. "Paul, that program you asked about is featured on page five," or, "Fran, check out the photo on the back inside cover." Staff usually write these notes, but again, board members with relationships to these donors can write them as well.

3. Take advantage of things that happen during the year. If you have positive press coverage, if you win a victory in your organizing or litigation efforts, if you are commended by a community group, service club, or politician, take the opportunity to send a special letter to major donors telling them of the event. Send a copy of the article or commendation if possible. This letter does not have to be personalized.

4. When you know a donor's birthday, send a card. If you learn that someone graduated from college, or won an award, or had a baby, send a card. Don't spend a lot of time trying to learn all this, but pay attention and respond when the information comes your way.

5. Include brief personal notes with things major donors will be getting anyway, such as invitations to special events or announcements of meetings.

6. Generally, you will not send major donors all the requests for extra gifts that are sent to the rest of your donor base, but when a mail appeal is particularly timely or concerns a specific issue that will be interesting to them, include major donors in the mailing.

By keeping in touch with your major donors, you will lay the groundwork necessary to approach them for a renewal of their gift in the second year they give and a request to increase the size of their gift the third year of their giving. Even if no one in your organization has ever met this major donor and their gift came unsolicited, through personal notes and letters, you will begin to build a rapport that will make it easy to meet the person in the future.

RENEWING GIFTS OF MAJOR DONORS

The process for approaching major donors to renew their gifts will vary depending on the amount they have given.

Gifts of $100–$249

Near the anniversary of the donor's gift, send them a letter asking them to give again. The letter should be personalized, with a handwritten note added as a post-script. The letter should describe the highlights of the year just passed and attribute some of that success to the donor's gift. Wherever possible, use stories to illustrate your work rather than simply narrating one dry fact after another. One paragraph should be devoted to the needs of the coming year and then the letter asks the donor to renew their gift. The letter should ask for the same size gift as the donor gave the previous year, which both reminds the donor what their last gift was and shows that your organization keeps careful records. Include a reply card and stamped return envelope marked to the attention of the person signing the letter.

Gifts of $250–$499

Use the format above, but follow up your letter with a phone call. You can let the donor know you are going to call in the letter, or if you are worried that you won't be able to get to all the donors, then just call those donors who have not sent in a renewal after a week or ten days. Often the phone call will go something like this:

"May, this is June calling to follow up on my letter."

"Yes, June. It's lovely of you to call. I've already sent in my check and congratulations on your good work."

June can then thank May for renewing her gift and ask if she has any other questions or tell her something that wasn't in the letter (but be brief!). The whole interaction will take five minutes unless May has some questions.

Gifts of $500+

Send a much briefer letter telling the donor you would like to visit with him or her and that you will phone to set up a time. If you are simply asking for a renewal, the telephone request for a meeting will often go like this:

> "Frank, this is Earnest. Did you get my letter?"
>
> "Yes, it came yesterday."
>
> "Great. Can we get together sometime to talk about the possibility of you renewing your gift?"
>
> "You don't need to visit me for that. I'll be happy to renew."

In this exchange, even though he is planning to renew his gift, Frank may still feel pleased that he was given this attention and again, the interaction is very brief. If Frank does want to meet, he will be drawn even closer to the organization, and you will have a chance to see how your group appears to someone who thinks a lot about how much money to give you.

Many major donors, particularly those who live far away from the group, are willing and even prefer to conduct business by e-mail. You will still send a letter the old-fashioned way, and offer to call or call and meet, but you can add a note to your letter that says, "Feel free to e-mail me at Jim@goodgroup.org if that is easier for you." Be sure to print out copies of e-mail correspondence for the donor's file and note on the donor's record that he likes to use e-mail.

When to Ask for More

Two questions often arise: How many times should you ask donors to renew their gift at the same amount before asking for an upgrade? And similarly, once the gift is upgraded, how long is appropriate before asking for another upgrade? The answer is simple: Know your donor. The sooner you meet the donor and learn more about him or her, the sooner you will have a sense of whether they like to be visited, whether they are giving to their capacity and cannot give more right now, whether they would rather make up their own minds about when and how to increase their gift, and so on.

Of course, you can't know all your major donors right away and some you may never meet. When you don't know, follow this formula: Get the gift, the following year ask for a renewal, the third year ask for an upgrade. If you receive a larger gift, ask for a renewal, and then the year after the renewal, ask for a gift that is one-third again as much. Then repeat the cycle: For a couple of years ask for a renewal and then another upgrade, and so on. If the donor stays at the same level, keep asking for more unless you get information that the donor is giving as much as they can afford.

In addition to this formula, use common sense. If someone gives you $5,000, you may need to ask for a renewal for several years before asking for more. If someone gives you $100, then ask them to double their gift, but think twice before asking someone giving $10,000 to double. You can always add the phrase "or more" onto any request you make if you really don't know how much more to ask for.

Of course, your organization must be able to justify needing more money in order to ask for more, and that need must be expressed to the donor in a compelling way. This means putting it into programmatic terms. Hiring another staff person, for example, is not compelling; serving 20 more children (what the additional staff person is needed for) is compelling.

THE HARDEST YEAR

In planning to add a major gifts component to your fundraising, keep in mind that the first year of recruiting major donors may be the hardest. Do not set your goals too high; you don't want volunteers to be demoralized by failing to reach an unrealistic goal. Major gifts solicitation can be done in the form of a campaign — that is, with a formal beginning and ending time, specific materials, and special committee, as described in Chapter 13, Major Gifts Campaigns, or it can be an ongoing program, with different volunteers helping at different times.

The most important step to take in a major gifts program is to start it. Even if you have only one prospect, ask that prospect. If the largest gift you can imagine someone giving is $50, start by asking for $50. A major gifts program builds on itself; simply establishing the groundwork for the program will begin the process of getting major gifts.

twelve

Pledge Programs

Pledging is possibly the oldest form of thoughtful giving. It is found in almost every religious tradition in the practice of people "tithing" a certain amount of their income, usually 10%, to their house of worship. Since few can afford to give the entire 10% at once (if they could, they should be giving more), most donors give the amount promised over some period of time. In an annual giving program, they give it over the course of a year; in a capital campaign, a pledge may stretch over as many as five years.

A pledge is a legally binding contract in which a donor commits a certain amount of money and then fulfills the pledge with regular payments. While few organizations would sue a donor who did not fulfill her or his pledge, it is important for donors to understand that this is a serious commitment and under accounting law, the organization must count pledges as "accounts receivable."

There are two great advantages of a pledge program to an organization: 1) If payments are spread over a time period, any donor can give more than they could give all at once, and 2) a well-run pledge program means reliable monthly income.

There are also clear advantages for the donor. People who are committed to an organization can express that commitment with a bigger gift by pledging. Many working people who could not give $300 all at once could afford $25 a month. Further, people who give $100, $500, or even $1,000 in one-time gifts may be able to repeat that gift four times a year or even every month. Certainly, they can't make this kind of commitment to every group, but they can and will make it to their favorite organization if the mechanism is in place to ask them.

Pledging is the simplest strategy with which to start the upgrading process. You will have the pleasant surprise of seeing some people increase their giving by 400% — or even 1200% — as they go from giving $25 a year to giving that much every quarter or every month. Further, renewal rates for people who pledge are higher than for regular donors, particularly if those pledging are giving by electronic funds transfer (explained below). Finally, donors who pledge are more likely to include your organization in their will; in fact, introducing a pledge program is often the first step in introducing a planned giving program.

INTRODUCING A PLEDGE PROGRAM

Once an organization decides to institute a pledge program, it needs to introduce it in all its fundraising materials. First, send a special appeal to your current donors asking them to consider pledging. In the appeal letter, explain that the reader is a valuable supporter and your organization wants to give him or her an opportunity to give more without undue hardship. Explain how helpful it is to your organization to have a known amount of money coming in every month, and what kind of work you can do with these extra funds. Second, use a small amount of space in your newsletter to discuss the pledge program; and third, include pledging on all your return forms as one of the choices:

I want to give $ _____ per month/quarter (circle one). My first payment is enclosed/ here is my credit card number and expiration date: _____.

Put a "pledge" page on your Web site and, if you have a secured area for giving, let people sign up to pledge at the site. The idea of pledging sometimes takes a while to catch on, but when donors see this option in many different places and grow accustomed to it, more and more of them will take advantage of it.

Make it as easy as possible for people to pledge by allowing them to put their pledge on a credit card or give it through direct debit from their bank account via electronic funds transfer. Your organization will have 90%–95% collection with these methods and the amount pledged will often be higher than if the donor were billed.

Organizations sometimes find it helpful to provide incentives for pledging by creating a special category for people who pledge, such as a "Gift of the Month Club" or a "Sustainer Council." People who pledge can also be given a benefit not available to other donors, and can be listed in a special category in newsletters or annual reports.

COLLECTING PLEDGES

Many pledge programs have failed because the organization did not put time into collecting the pledged amounts or did not have a system in place to keep track of payments. I have pledged to more than a dozen organizations over the years to which I made one or two payments, then forgot about my pledge. Most of the groups have failed to remind me, or reminded me in such a sporadic way that my pledge was paid sporadically. In one case, after being asked to pledge and making payments for a few months, I received a letter asking if I could pay the rest of my pledge in one payment because the group "found the process of depositing so many checks every month too time consuming." Since the main point of making a pledge is to be able to pay more over time than one can afford at once, I thought their request reflected a lack of thought that I feared would be present throughout the group's work, so I stopped giving to the group altogether.

Systems for Keeping Track of Pledges

It is easy to keep track of pledges in your fundraising database. Most have fields built in to record pledges and to make sending reminders simple. Many have pledge collection modules specifically designed for managing a pledge program. If your database does not have this already, set up fields to record the pledge and the payment due dates. As payments are made, record them. Send the pledge reminder each month or quarter, so that it arrives right before the first of the month, when most people are paid. If your pledge reminder arrives by then, and if people are billed regularly, you will have the least number of dropouts. Send a form such as the one below and a stamped return envelope. The forms can come right out of the database, or can be filled in by hand. Make sure to note how much has been paid and how much is still owing.

SAMPLE PLEDGE REMINDER FORM

(sized to fit without being folded into a #6-3/4 return envelope)

Organization Name & Address

Date

Dear Donor Name,

Your monthly (quarterly) pledge of $_____ is now due.
Please use the enclosed envelope to return it. We are very grateful for your ongoing support and for your commitment to our work.

Sincerely,
Director or other staff name

Total amount pledged $_____   Total amount paid to date $_____

Make checks payable to: Your organization, address.

Your gift is tax deductible to the full extent of the law.

Although it is more laborious, you can keep track of this information on a paper system. Record the pledge information for each person on a 5"×7" card and keep all the pledges in a file box. Each 5"×7" card should contain the donor's name and address, the amount pledged, the date the pledge was made and how often payments will be made. Make a column noting the dates payments are due, and write beside each date when payments are made. A quick glance will tell you whether the donor is behind in payment. Once a month someone goes through the box, fills out preprinted pledge forms, and sends them with a stamped return envelope. Pledge collection is an excellent fundraising task for a careful and thorough board member or volunteer.

Most groups find that they collect 80%–85% of pledges that require the kind of billing described above. If a person has been reminded three times without paying, assume that he or she is not going to pay. Some groups have found it helpful to call the donor and see if there is a problem that the organization can rectify. Usually it has nothing to do with the group, but instead that the donor's financial situation has changed for the worse or that the donor didn't realize what a commitment their pledge was. Don't hound people for payment. Simply roll them back into the regular donor program.

At the end of the year send a personal letter with the final pledge note asking the donor to renew his or her pledge. Include a renewal form. The letter can be simple and straightforward, such as:

> Dear _____ ,
>
> This is the last payment on your pledge of $250. Your ongoing support has been tremendously important to us this past year. We have been able to use the extra funds provided by our Sustainer Council to do _____ and _____. I thank you very much for your commitment.
>
> I also hope that you will renew your pledge. We will continue to send you reminders, and you will receive _____, available only to people who pledge. I enclose a form for you to fill out. Thank you again for all your support.
>
> Sincerely,
> Director or Board Chair

Collecting Pledges by Electronic Funds Transfer or Credit Card

There are two systems for collecting money from donors that require little paperwork on the part of the donor and ensure immediate collection of the pledged amount of money: electronic funds transfer and credit cards.

Electronic Funds Transfer

Electronic funds transfer (EFT) allows the transfer of funds from one account to another via a computer network. EFT is in wider use in most developed countries than in the United States — for example, in Japan 95% of the population use it, and in Europe 85% of people use it — but EFT is rapidly becoming popular here. In fact, electronic banking is increasingly taking the place of check writing, with people authorizing their mortgage, phone bills, health club memberships, and other debts to be withdrawn from their bank account automatically; many people are also becoming used to paying a lot of their bills online.

The advantages of EFT to an organization are many. Pledge fulfillment is increased to nearly 95% because the funds are transferred from the donor's bank to the organization's bank. Donors must cancel the EFT in order to indicate that they are not renewing, which gives a renewal rate of 92%–98%. Organizations with established donor programs find that EFT is one-fifth as expensive as traditional pledge collection systems because there are no mail costs and fewer processing costs.

The main advantage for the donor is that EFT is very convenient — a one-time authorization takes the place of writing and sending a check each month or quarter. The donation is listed in the donor's monthly bank statement, so they are reminded of their gift.

Setting Up EFT

You can set up an EFT account with your bank or with an EFT service provider (see Bibliography for list of providers). Most organizations find that using an independent provider is preferable to a bank because EFT is the providers' only business, whereas it will be a very small part of a bank's business and may not get the attention it needs. You will need to investigate your EFT suppliers, get bids, and generally look for them with the same care you exercise in looking for good printers, adequate databases, technical support, and so on. EFT works best with a high volume of users. There is a set-up fee and a transaction fee for each transaction, which usually decreases the more transactions you have. Talk with other organizations that are using EFT to help determine what arrangement will work best for you.

When you first set up an EFT account, it may seem you are paying a lot to service a few donors, but the number of donors using it will grow exponentially if you keep advertising the service, and as the country as a whole becomes increasingly electronic in its financial dealings.

There are a few federal requirements for signing someone up for EFT in the United States, which mostly serve to ensure protection for the donor. The donor must sign a form that authorizes the transaction and the terms of the transaction must be clear. The terms must indicate that the donor is free to cancel at any time and how long the transaction is good for. Most organizations say that the transaction will go on until the donor requests it to stop. Finally, the donor must receive a photocopy of the transaction form.

There are no disadvantages to EFT, but an organization must have a solid donor base and excellent bookkeeping and accounting systems in place to work with the EFT vendor or bank and with the donors quickly and efficiently. Your system must be computerized, and you will want to be able to project at least 100 donors using EFT in some period of time, usually a year, for it to be truly cost effective for your organization.

SAMPLE AUTHORIZATION FORM
AND INCENTIVE OFFER FOR EFT PROGRAM

Join People for Cultural Preservation's Simple Gift Program...
and receive a cassette of early American hymns.

THE SIMPLE GIFT PROGRAM IS CONVENIENT:
Your gift is paid automatically each month by your bank, and you will never have to write us another check (unless you want to!). A record of your contribution will appear on your monthly bank statement. You can cancel at any time by writing us.

THE SIMPLE GIFT PROGRAM INCREASES THE VALUE OF YOUR GIFT:
The cost of processing your donation is reduced, so more of your money can go right to work in our preservation research and publication efforts.

HERE'S HOW TO JOIN:
1. Fill in your monthly gift amount, name, address, and telephone number on the attached form.
2. Initial the Inflation Guard line if you would like to increase your gift by 5% each year on the anniversary of your enrollment.
3. Sign and date the form.
4. Enclose your check payable to People for Cultural Preservation for this month's gift — transfers will begin in about six weeks.
5. Mail the form and your check in the enclosed return envelope.

TERMS OF AGREEMENT
My authorization to charge my account at my bank shall be the same as if I had personally signed a check to People for Cultural Preservation (PCP).

This authorization shall remain in effect until I notify PCP or my bank in writing that I wish to end this agreement and PCP or my bank has had a reasonable time to act on it; or until PCP or my bank has sent me ten days' written notice that they will end this agreement.

A record of my payment will be included in my regular bank statement and will serve as my receipt.

My initials on the Inflation Guard line authorize PCP to increase my monthly charge by 5% on each 12-month anniversary of the initial charge.

Monthly pledge $_____ Inflation Guard? ____Yes____No

Signed _____ Date _____

Credit Card Charges

Paying for goods or services with cash is becoming less and less common in the United States. Checks were the first item to replace cash, although they stand for actual cash. After checks came credit cards, which loan the consumer the money for each purchase until the consolidated credit card bill is presented; by allowing people to defer payments, credit cards also enable them to go into debt more easily, but they do provide a high level of convenience. Many credit cards come with incentives for using them — shopping points that create discounts on goods, frequent flier miles, free phone cards, and the like.

Hundreds of millions of people have credit cards and many have more than one credit card. Nonprofits that don't accept credit cards simply cost themselves money. Credit cards have become completely acceptable methods for making donations. Many nonprofit organizations, including grassroots groups, offer donors the option of giving with their credit card. Their reply device includes a space for the donor's credit card number and the amount of the gift. Groups that can handle gifts on credit cards report strong donor acceptance and often report an increase in giving. In the same way that people will spend more with credit cards than with cash, so will they give more.

Setting Up Credit Card Use

If you decide to use a credit card option, set it up through your bank. The bank will run a credit check on your organization to see how many checks you have bounced, whether you pay your rent and other bills on time, and what your assets are. If your organization uses credit cards for its own purchasing, your credit rating will be a help (or hindrance if you don't pay your bills on time). Someone from the bank will also visit your organization, mainly to verify that the organization exists and seems to be what it claims.

Sometimes board members, in their capacity as trustees, will be asked to supervise the maintenance of a credit card program and to attest that, to the best of their knowledge, the organization is sound enough to undertake such a program. (Such management is part of board liability and is not an extra duty for board members.) The bank may also run a credit check on those individuals. (Such investigation is not part of board duty.)

Many organizations have not arranged to take credit cards because of the costs involved. Although there are several costs, remember that most people will give more on a credit card than by check, which more than covers the extra cost. Some people won't give at all unless they can give by credit card. With them, you can actually lose not only money, but donors.

The bank has a nominal set-up charge, a monthly fee whether or not anyone uses the service, and a transaction fee of 2%–5% depending on your volume. You have to decide how to handle authorization and you have to factor in a very small number of bad cards. Unlike EFT, you also have to contact the donor directly to ask them to renew their pledge because your authorization to debit their card only lasts until the expiration date on that card.

Credit cards can be used to make one-time donations or to fulfill pledges. The donor's credit card is charged every month with the amount of the pledge. (See Bibliography for an excellent book called *Hidden Gold* by Harvey McKinnon, which has a number of tips on using EFT and credit cards and some recommendations for EFT providers.)

THREE DON'TS OF THE PLEDGE PROGRAM

Organizations are sometimes tempted to try cost-cutting measures on their pledge programs. They may, for example, try to save the cost of mailing to remind donors of their pledges and instead send a donor who has pledged $10 a month 12 envelopes at one time, expecting the person to return one envelope containing a payment each month. People cannot be expected to remember to pay their pledges or to keep track of envelopes for an entire year. Even though churches give congregants a box of envelopes for an entire year, they have the advantage of reminding people weekly about their pledges. Further, for people who don't come to church regularly, the church may send a letter reminding the congregant to pay, and the minister or the chair of the Finance Committee may call.

Other organizations send the envelope to collect each payment, but leave the stamp off it, reasoning that if the donor can afford and is committed enough to pledge, he or she can afford a stamp. The purpose of the stamp is not to save donors money. It is to make it as easy as possible for them to pay their pledge in a timely fashion, and to show respect for the commitment they have made. Do not set up a pledge program only to undermine it with these types of penny-pinching measures.

And finally, don't set up any pledge program unless you are confident that your recordkeeping and accounting systems are adequate to handle it. This is particularly important for EFT and credit card collections, which involve banks, institutions that have long and unforgiving memories.

Start by having board members and volunteers pledge while you work out any glitches in your system, then move on to your donor base. Next, move your donors into EFT and/or credit cards. Organizations often find that they upgrade their own infrastructure as they upgrade their donors, which not only means they raise more money but also that they run more efficiently and effectively overall.

thirteen

Major Gifts Campaigns

Once an organization has mastered the process of identifying prospects and asking them for money and has a working major gifts program, it is ready to consider moving to a more formal major gifts campaign. The main differences between an ongoing major gifts program and a major gifts campaign are that a campaign is time-limited — it begins and ends on specific dates; the goal of the campaign is made public; and markers toward achieving the goal are announced frequently, as in thermometers showing how far the group has come toward its goal, announcements in the newsletter, etc. Reaching or surpassing the goal in the time frame that is set becomes part of the excitement. Although a major gifts *program* has a goal that is part of the overall fundraising plan, the program is in place all year and the goal is not necessarily public. You have a full fiscal year to reach the goal and achieving it feels more like meeting your budget than an accomplishment in itself. Because a major gifts *campaign,* on the other hand, is time-limited and public, you can use it to generate publicity about the overall needs of the organization.

During the time of the major gifts campaign, a few volunteers devote themselves intensively to meeting a specific financial goal, giving amounts of time and effort to the campaign that would be difficult to maintain beyond a short commitment.

THE STEPS OF A MAJOR GIFTS CAMPAIGN

A major gifts campaign requires nine steps, some of which are the same as for any major gifts program. The steps are listed below, then discussed in detail.

1. **Decide on the length of the campaign and set a goal for the amount to be raised.**

2. **Prepare supporting materials.**

3. **Identify and train solicitors.**

4. **Identify prospects.**

5. **Assign prospects and solicit gifts.**

6. **Kick off the campaign with a special event** (optional, though it can attract media attention and recognize donors).

7. **Hold regular reporting meetings to discuss progress and boost morale of campaign volunteers.**

8. **Celebrate the end of a successful campaign with a special event** (also optional, though it can attract media and recognize donors).

9. **Thank donors, record gifts, and incorporate new donors into ongoing fundraising efforts.**

The Steps in Detail

1. Set a goal

The first step in a major gifts campaign is to decide how long the campaign will last and how much money will be raised. For small organizations, a campaign of 6 to 12 weeks is ideal because volunteers and overworked staff can maintain momentum and excitement for that much time fairly easily and a lot of money can be raised in this short period of time.

To determine a fundraising goal, first calculate how many prospects could be asked in that length of time. Generally a volunteer can ask about one to three people a week for 8 to 12 weeks without undue strain. A committee of five volunteers, then, could ask between 60 and 180 people during a 12-week campaign. Assuming the usual 50% rate of success, your group would have anywhere from 30 to 90 new major gifts after such a campaign.

If you have a shortage of volunteers, ask each volunteer to solicit more people per week, but only expect full-time volunteers to be able to ask more than ten people in one month, and then only if they are very well connected, comfortable and familiar with asking for money, and can get a number of the gifts with just a phone call.

Knowing how many gifts you can get, now plot how many gifts of specific amounts you will need to reach your goal as follows: Select the lowest amount that will be solicited in face-to-face meetings. Most groups choose $250 as the minimum request for which they will seek a meeting; others start in-person solicitations for gifts of $100. Rarely would it be worth the time to make face-to-face solicitations for less than $100. Next, determine what your largest gift will be, which is usually 10% of the total goal. With the largest and smallest gifts decided on, you can now chart what size gifts you will need and how many of each to meet the goal. (See Chapter 11 for how to create a Gift Range Chart.) A campaign for $25,000 might look like this:

GIFT RANGE CHART
Goal: $25,000

GIFT SIZE	NUMBER OF GIFTS NEEDED	TOTAL	NUMBER OF PROSPECTS
$2,500	1	$2,500	
$1,250	2	$2,500	
$1,000	5	$5,000	
$500	10	$5,000	
$250	20	$5,000	
$100	50	$5,000	
TOTAL	88	$25,00	

Complete your gift range chart by figuring out how many people need to be asked for each gift size to be received, and filling in the Number of Prospects column. Assuming a 50% rate of success, and factoring in that half of those who say yes give less than what was asked for, you would need to ask three times as many prospects as number of gifts needed in each gift size category. In this example, a total of 264 people would need to be asked to get 88 gifts. To accomplish this $25,000 campaign, then, you would need approximately 24 people soliciting 1 person per week for 11 weeks, or 8 people soliciting 3 people a week for the same amount of time.

When you make your chart, don't get bogged down. There is no scientific way to do it. Basically, the chart is a triangle with fewer people at the top and more people at the bottom. The point of the chart is to recognize that not everyone will give the same amount and to set a limit on the number of people needing to be solicited. Share this chart with prospects and donors; it lets them know that the group has planned the campaign and where they might fit into it.

If you are doing a major donor campaign for the first time, set your overall goal lower than you think is reasonable, so that you are almost bound to make it. This will give an early sense of accomplishment and provide momentum to future campaigns.

2. Prepare supporting materials

A campaign needs a number of materials for solicitors to use, some of which will already exist in your organization and some of which will need to be created for the campaign. The supporting materials are of two types: a) materials that solicitors will give to donors; and b) materials that are for the solicitors' use only, or that relate to the campaign committee.

For the solicitor to use with donors you will need:

• **A campaign case statement.** This can be in the form of a report or a brochure. It should be simple and inexpensively produced — a high-quality or laser printer and a photocopy machine can turn out something quite adequate. The case statement spells out the goal of the campaign, the gifts that are needed, what the money will be used for, and a brief history of the organization. It invites donors to a celebration at the end of the campaign (if you are having one) and tells them what special benefits they get for their money (if anything). A book, their name on a plaque at the organization, or a specially created artwork are all very nice benefits. The benefit should not cost more than $5 per donor. While not imperative to give, special benefits have an appeal to many donors. Some donors will give more to get the benefit, some will give the same amount regardless of a benefit offer, and a few will tell you that the money could be better spent and will refuse the benefit. Whether to go to the trouble of having a special benefit will depend on your organizational culture, what benefits you have access to, and how the solicitors feel about the need for them.

• **A pledge card.** This is a small card on which the solicitor notes the donor's name, what he or she has agreed to give and the method of payment. Once the solicitation is complete and the card filled out, it is returned to the office and kept as part of the permanent record on the donor.

• **Stationery, envelopes, and return envelopes.** Have enough printed for all the prospects and extras for mistakes. These are used for both initial letters and thank-you notes. It is not necessary or useful to create special stationery or envelopes for a major donor campaign.

For the solicitors or committee use only:

• **A timeline of the campaign steps**

• **A complete description of the campaign and some soliciting tips**

• **The organization's overall budget**

• **A list of difficult and commonly asked questions about the organization and possible answers**

• **A list of the other solicitors and whom to call for more information**

All of these materials should be put together in a "Campaigner's Notebook," which can be as simple as a manila folder, but looks nice, has the name of the campaigner on it, and seems official. At the training meeting, each person is given a copy of the materials and all the materials are reviewed. In addition, each person will be given a copy of the master prospect list and the cards with more personal information about each of their prospects.

3. Identify and train solicitors

Invite people to be on the campaign committee as solicitors, assembling the number of people you need to meet your goals. Committee members should fulfill two simple commitments, with a third commitment optional. First, each member should themselves be giving a gift that is significant to them; the number of committee members and total of their gifts are used against the goal and are a nice way to begin the campaign. Second, each member must agree to solicit a certain number of prospects each week for a certain number of weeks. Third, and optional, members of the committee can provide names of prospects for the master list. If your committee does not provide these names, you will need another way to get them.

Some organizations have found that getting people to agree to be on the major gifts committee is the biggest hurdle. People are afraid they won't be good at asking for money or they don't know anyone to ask or they don't have time or any number of other objections. To get people to agree to serve on the committee, first ask them to come to a training session where they will learn what is involved and what their commitment would be. Tell them (and mean it) that there is no obligation to serve on the committee after the training, but that you are simply asking them to be open-minded. If the training is fun, the food is good, and the other people who might be on the committee are friendly, generally you will have no trouble getting the majority of people to agree to serve. Reassure them that they will not be asked to do more than their time allows, and that if they don't know anyone they feel comfortable asking, they will be provided with names of prospects. Be sure to emphasize that what is required for successful major donor work is commitment to the mission of the organization.

After the training, ask who wants to be on the committee and either have them stay longer at the meeting, and continue with the steps below, or set another meeting to divide up prospects.

Once enough people have agreed to serve on the committee, set a meeting for them to be briefed about the campaign and taught how to ask for money. The meeting should last about three hours, with the following agenda:

- An overview of the campaign and the organization's need for money (step 1) (20 minutes)

- Training in how to ask for money, including practice solicitation (step 3) (2 hours)

- Distribution of prospect names (step 4) and supporting materials (step 2) (15 minutes)

- Assigning some prospects (step 5) and discussing a system for getting more prospects. People only need enough prospects to get them through their first week or two. At their check-in meetings, or even over the phone individually, they can be given new prospects as they finish asking the prospects on their current list. (15 minutes)

- Responding to final questions and setting the next meeting time (10 minutes)

The staff or fundraising committee of the board should conduct the meeting, but many groups find it helpful to have an outside trainer lead the training in how to ask for money (see also Chapter 9, Personal Solicitation). It is imperative that every person on the committee be at this training even if they have participated in fundraising solicitations before. The experience of people who know how to do it will be of great benefit to those who are feeling unsure. This initial meeting helps the committee develop a sense of itself as a team and should encourage a strong camaraderie from the very beginning.

4. Identify prospects

Review Chapter 9, Personal Solicitation, for the basics on prospect identification. Ask members of the committee for names of people they know, and review your list of current donors to identify people who have given a major gift, those who have the ability to give a major gift, or those who should be asked to give more this year. For example, anyone on your list who has given the same large donation for two or more years ought to be asked to increase their gift, and this campaign provides an excellent way for this to happen. Unlike an informal, ongoing major gifts program, in a campaign all the prospects must be identified before the campaign can begin. Now prepare a master list of all the prospects as in the following example.

MASTER TRACKING FORM

PROSPECT NAME	AMOUNT ASKED FOR	SOLICITOR	OUTCOME	THANK-YOU SENT

Everyone on the committee will receive a copy of the Master Tracking Form. No one should be solicited who is not on this master list to ensure that no one is asked by two people. All of this information is highly confidential and solicitors must be people who have a clear sense of discretion and can be trusted. On your database, keep the address, phone number, and other information needed for each prospect. Personal information will only be given to the person soliciting the prospect and will not be available to the rest of the committee.

If you have trouble identifying the number of prospects you need, you may wish to lower the goal of your campaign, or to continue your regular major gifts program for a while longer before moving into a campaign.

5. Assign prospects and solicit gifts

At the meeting, after the solicitors are trained and familiar with the materials and the campaign, they are each given a master prospect list and asked to read through it and choose which prospects they will solicit. They should write down the prospects they would be willing to solicit, then each person reads his or her list out loud. Everyone else listens for duplication. Should two solicitors have the same person on their lists, they briefly discuss and decide right there which of them will take the prospect (they also have the option of going together to see the prospect). As the names are read aloud and assigned, the group should decide how much each prospect will be asked for. At the end it should be clear that everyone has different prospects and no one prospect will be solicited twice. Having everyone read their lists out loud also helps to ensure that prospects are being asked for the right amount and that the right person is doing the asking. Solicitation can now begin.

6. Kick off campaign with special event (optional)

A kick-off event is not a gala affair, but the press might be invited, as well as all the prospects and all the solicitors. Wine, soft drinks, and hors d'oeuvres can be served. Someone from the committee should give an impassioned, enthusiastic, and articulate but brief speech about the campaign, including its goals, the need for the organization, and what donors will receive for their gifts (if you have benefits, hold them up for everyone to see). The event also provides a time for people to see who else is involved and who is giving — this peer identification adds an important element to the desire to give. The speech ends with "We will be contacting all of you individually in the next few weeks to see what questions you have and whether you can help in this important endeavor."

For campaigns covering large geographic areas, such as whole states or large rural areas, a series of small events would be appropriate.

7. Hold regular reporting meetings to discuss progress and boost morale of campaign volunteers

These meetings should take place at least once every two weeks and preferably weekly during the campaign. The meetings need only last 30 to 45 minutes; many groups hold them over breakfast at 7:30 A.M. so people can attend them before work. The purpose of the meetings is to give everyone a chance to report their progress, which forces everyone to have made some progress between meetings. They can share frustrations, fears, and successes. A report on the progress toward the goal should be made (possibly using an illustration, like a thermometer or some other measure). Any additional materials (brochures, return envelopes, extra stationery) can be given out then as well. Again, if a group covers a large area, meetings may not be possible, but phone check-ins become imperative.

8. Celebrate the end of the campaign with a special event

Though optional, this is an excellent way to recognize and reward the committee as well as the donors. A simple reception offering wine, soft drinks, fruit, and cheese from 5:00 to 7:00 in the evening, with a speech announcing the successful conclusion of the campaign, is fine. Some groups have formal dinners — or, in the case of capital campaigns, ground-breaking ceremonies — but it is not necessary to be elaborate, simply gracious, warm, and rewarding to volunteers.

9. Recognize donors and incorporate them into ongoing fundraising efforts

Aside from raising money, a major donor campaign strengthens donor loyalty, brings in new donors, and upgrades current donors. You need to be in regular touch with all these donors through a newsletter and occasional personal correspondence. Because major donors do not get the regular mail appeals that other donors get, they must be kept abreast of the organization's work in other ways. Like all donors, major donors must be thanked promptly, and there has to be a method by which the solicitor knows which of her or his prospects has sent in money. All donors to the campaign should receive another thank-you note at the successful end of the campaign, telling them the organization was able to reach its goal, and stressing again the work you will be able to do with this money. Major gifts campaigns must be done right to succeed. Don't try to take shortcuts or launch the campaign without proper preparation. A major gifts campaign should be both fun and lucrative, and its success will be a reward for good planning and good organizing.

fourteen

Capital Campaigns

A capital campaign is a time-specific effort to raise money for a project that presents a one-time need over and above the annual budget. Capital campaigns are traditionally used to finance buying, building, or refurbishing a building; more and more frequently they are being used to begin an endowment. The financial goal of a capital campaign is often at least as large as the organization's annual budget and more often many times larger. Most capital campaigns last two to three years; some go on as long as five years. They allow donors to pledge a large amount and take as many as five years (and for very large pledges, ten years) to pay it off. Donors are asked to give to the capital campaign in addition to their regular annual donations, and are explicitly asked not to decrease their annual gift in order to make a capital gift. Capital gifts are usually so large that the donor cannot finance the gift from their income and must donate cash from savings or other assets (stocks, property, art).

There are no rules for capital campaigns. The conventional capital campaign described above is not the only way to conduct a capital campaign. In fact, some grassroots groups have conducted "capital campaigns" to buy new computers or send staff to fundraising workshops, which meant their goal was $5,000 or less, their time frame was a few weeks, and people were simply asked to put in a few extra dollars. However, capital campaigns are best used to seek gifts of assets from a wide pool of people and institutions and not just to seek "something extra" from the annual incomes of current donors. Capital campaigns should be aimed at people in your donor base who may own property or securities, and at people who would not help you every year, but might give you a big gift once in a while.

The smallest gift one generally seeks for a capital campaign is $1,000. (As in all fundraising, every gift is welcomed and helpful, but people who can afford and are committed to giving to capital campaigns should be able to give at least $1,000, particularly if they spread their payments over three to five years.)

While your most loyal annual donors will also give to a capital campaign if they can, there are many other kinds of people who give to capital campaigns who are not regular annual donors. For example, a local attorney helped a small community organization in Alabama file a lawsuit against their city. The attorney admired the group's feistiness and their willingness to take risks. She was impressed that the sole staff person would work for such a low salary and that the volunteers put in many hours at the organization beyond their own jobs elsewhere. She did not charge for her assistance with the lawsuit and she donated $50 once after that. However, she did not wish to become a regular donor to this group, so she did not respond to their annual appeals. When, a few years later, the group decided to buy a building to house their organization, they asked her to be one of the largest givers to their capital campaign with a gift of $20,000. The work she had done pro bono on the lawsuit had been worth about that much, and the group figured she still admired them. She did, and she admired their boldness in asking her. She gave $10,000 outright and pledged an additional $10,000 as a challenge to be met by other lawyers. She told the group only to ask her for special projects and not to ask her every year.

Universities and private schools often have the experience of receiving a one-time gift from an alumnus or alumna who had been a minimal donor prior to the campaign. Some people like the idea of contributing to something as substantial as a building.

To ask donors to stretch their own giving and to seek donations outside of the immediate "donor family" means having a goal that implies stretching will be required to meet it. It must seem to a prospect — including a corporation, government agency, foundation, or religious institution that might not support your annual program work — that the group cannot get this money simply by asking a few people or writing a single grant proposal. For this to be true, your capital campaign goal needs to be at least $100,000. If you need to raise less than $100,000, structure your campaign as a major gifts campaign as described in Chapter 13 and run the campaign for a short time during one year, or seek two or three foundation or corporate grants to meet the goal, and don't run a campaign at all.

BEGINNING A CAPITAL CAMPAIGN

The first step is for the organization to identify a large one-time need. The board of directors must fully concur that this is a need and must support the idea of conducting a capital campaign, which is a lot of extra work for everyone and may require an initial outlay of money to hire extra staff and develop materials.

Key volunteers who are not on the board and long-time major donors should also be consulted about doing a capital campaign. Everyone who is important to an organization should have an opportunity to voice their concerns and feel part of the decision. If they aren't given this opportunity, their negative opinions will come out later on in refusing to support the capital campaign and spreading negative comments about it in the community. In other instances, campaigns have had to be called off halfway through because so many volunteers and donors had left the organization to protest doing the campaign in the first place. A capital campaign is a very visible enterprise; it needs widespread support within the organization.

Estimating Costs

After all the parties have been consulted and there is general agreement on the need, a price tag needs to be set. Similar to the understanding that in a fancy restaurant the true cost of the meal will be double the entrée (with drinks, dessert, and tip), the true cost of a campaign is far more than the cost of the project itself. One group learned this the hard way. They needed larger office space and decided that buying a building would, in the long run, be less expensive than continually paying rent. They found a building that suited them for $250,000. The group launched their campaign for $250,000, forgetting that the price of the building is only part of the cost. The true cost of the building rose to $310,000 with closing costs, insurance, furnishings, campaign costs, and so on. The organization spent two years climbing out of a $60,000 deficit caused by their lack of planning.

The following items need to be added in to the actual cost of buying or constructing a building or starting an endowment:

Fundraising materials: These include a case statement, brochures, pledge cards, background information for solicitors, pictures, architect's renderings, special newsletters to capital campaign donors to keep them informed of progress, and a prospectus (see page 215).

Cost of staff time: Someone has to coordinate (and sometimes conduct) the tasks, handle pledges, write thank-you notes, report to the board, work with the contractor, decide who has to approve paint color or carpet choices, know what to do when someone donates stocks, and handle emergencies.

Recordkeeping: A process needs to be set up to keep the campaign's income and expenses separate from the annual budget, and to collect pledges (which may extend well past the end of the campaign). If you plan to use current staff to do that, then someone will have to do some of their regular work. In a multi-year campaign, it is unlikely that a group could get by without hiring any extra staff.

Office extras: You may need to put in an extra phone line or buy an additional computer. If you hire staff, that person will need to sit somewhere, so you may need another desk and chair.

For the building project itself: Someone with expertise in this area will need to help you list costs related to the building, such as insurance, building permits, design costs, earthquake/hurricane/tornado preparedness, fire extinguishers, landscaping, and wiring. They will also need to help you determine how much to estimate for cost overruns or unforeseen delays.

Furnishings for the building: What are you going to bring from your current office and what else will you need? What will these items cost?

Debt service on a bridge loan: You will probably have to pay bills before pledges are fully paid and may have to borrow money to cover the gap between pledged income and received income. The interest on that debt needs to be factored into the goal of the campaign. Banks will lend money with pledges as collateral, but then you have to pay interest on the loan.

Add 15% for people who pledge but cannot finish paying, or decide not to pay.

Add an additional 5%–10% onto the grand total and you can feel reasonably safe that this will be the cost of the campaign.

In any fundraising endeavor, but particularly campaigns with big-ticket items such as buildings, follow the adage: Plan expenses high and income low.

PREPARING A CASE STATEMENT

Once the need is established and the costs are known and provisionally approved by the board, the next step is to write up a case statement for the campaign. This case statement is separate from the organization's overall case statement, although certainly it borrows from it. The capital campaign case statement focuses solely on the goal of the campaign and shows how this goal will help the organization meet all its other goals. The case statement implies or overtly states that the work of the group will be greatly enhanced by the addition of whatever the campaign is proposing and will be significantly slowed down or impaired by the lack of whatever is being proposed. The final page of the case statement is the financial goal displayed as a gift range chart.

The Gift Range Chart

The pyramid that is constructed by a capital campaign gift range chart is much shorter and narrower than that of an annual major gifts campaign (see page 181). In a capital campaign, the lead gift equals 15%–20% of the total goal, and 80% of the money comes from about 10% of the donors.

The chart follows this pattern:

1 gift = 15%–20% or more of goal

2 gifts = 10% each or more

4 to 5 gifts = 5% each or more

So, 50% to 70% of the goal will come from about seven or eight gifts.

After these largest gifts, increase the number of gifts and decrease the gift size as makes sense for your group and number of prospects until the goal is reached.

Here is an example:

GIFT RANGE CHART
Goal: $1,000,000

NUMBER OF GIFTS	GIFT SIZE	CUMULATIVE TOTAL
1	$150,000	$ 150,000
2	$100,000	$ 350,000
4	$50,000	$ 550,000
8	$25,000	$ 750,000
10	$10,000	$ 850,000
15	$5,000	$ 925,000
20	$2,500	$ 975,000
25	$1,000	$1,000,000

In this example, 85 gifts will be required. Whereas in an annual campaign, we assume that three prospects will be needed for every gift that is given, with a capital campaign we look for four times as many prospects as donors in order to give the group a little padding for those people who give less than $1,000. In this example, then, the group will need to identify 340 prospects (85 × 4). All of these people will have to be asked in person, and some of them may have to be visited more than once. If any of these gift amounts come from foundations or corporations, proposals will have to be written.

Sometimes grassroots organizations feel that seeking only gifts of $1,000 or more will exclude too many people who may want to be part of the campaign. However, when they realize how many people it will take to reach their goal and how many people will have to be asked, they usually see the logic of aiming the capital campaign largely at people who can give big gifts.

Timing

The final decision the organization must make is about timing of the campaign. You need to find out which other organizations will be having capital or intensive fundraising campaigns during the time you wish to run your campaign and assess whether any of your prospects will be key prospects for those groups. You need to launch your campaign during years when you expect your annual campaign to be doing well, and you need to make sure you do not anticipate any shortfalls in annual income. Since during the capital campaign your annual income will not be able to rise, you must not plan major new programs outside of the capital project.

FINAL APPROVAL

Once you have prepared the case statement, with costs, gift range chart, and timing included, bring the whole package back to the board, key volunteers, and staff for re-approval. While people may have approved the concept of the campaign, when faced with the realities of the money and time involved, they may wish to change their minds. Without full board and staff ownership, the campaign will fail. Taking the time to make sure that everyone understands the implications of the campaign is imperative because once the campaign is launched publicly, it must be seen through to the end.

FOUR STAGES OF THE CAMPAIGN

A capital campaign is conducted in four stages. The first stage is the "pre-campaign" stage and starts when the case statement is ready and approved. The second stage is the "launching" stage, when the campaign is publicly announced and begins to seek support beyond the inner circle of donors. The third stage is the longest, and is usually referred to by what it is — "intensive." This is the stage where solicitors are out visiting prospects and gathering commitments. When the campaign has reached between 85% and 95% of its goal, the "wind-up" stage (sometimes called the "topping off" stage) begins.

The Pre-campaign Stage

Have you ever noticed how people announce capital campaigns by saying, "We are proud to launch our $2 million building campaign today, and are pleased to report that we already have $1.3 million pledged"? Do you wonder how could they have raised all that money in just one day? Of course, that money was not raised in a day — in fact, it may have been raised over a period of months or even years. The purpose of the pre-campaign is two-fold. The first purpose is to test the concept of the campaign on people who could actually pay for it. Everyone can feel good about the case and the need for this campaign, but the true test is whether people feel good enough about it to give a big gift. Some campaigns have to be abandoned or seriously rethought at this phase, but no real harm is done because the campaign has not been made public. The second purpose is to give a feeling of momentum at the public launching of the campaign. "Wow, that's great they have so much money already. My gift can move them forward," is the response one wants from the people at the launching.

The goal of the pre-campaign is to get 30% to 50% of the campaign's total from the top three to five donors. Most fundraisers feel that if you can get the largest gifts first you will be able to find all the remaining gifts needed. (The largest gifts are called the "lead" gifts, though they may not truly be first gifts, which should come from board members.) The power of the lead gifts may sound like a superstition, but there is much anecdotal evidence to support it. Lead gifts provide momentum, instill confidence in the campaign, and inspire other big donors. Smaller gifts seem more helpful when they are put toward a goal already partly reached.

Conversely, starting a capital campaign without lead gifts is dangerous because the momentum lags. Furthermore, if a group doesn't know possible lead donors at the beginning of the campaign, where does it think it will meet them later? It is worth postponing a campaign for months or even years in order to ensure that the first gifts given are also the largest. At the risk of redundancy, let me repeat: An organization does not need to know all of its prospects ahead of time, but it must know the ones capable of making the lead gifts, and it must have a sense that it could know about as many donors as it needs for the whole campaign.

The Lead Gifts

The lead donor must not only be able to give a big gift, he or she must also be a person who likes to set the pace, to set an example, and to take a leadership role. These first large gifts come from people who will gamble with you that the campaign will succeed and actually pride themselves on being risk-takers. Obviously, they must care very much about your cause and be committed to the capital project. Frequently (and ideally) the lead gifts come from a few people who were involved in the planning and approval of the campaign. If those people are not able to give the biggest gifts, they need to know people or institutions that can.

Approaching the Lead Prospects

The process of approaching these people is the same as approaching any major donor — a letter, followed by phone call and request to meet, followed by a meeting at which the gift is requested — with one slight change. With requests for capital gifts, an answer almost never comes at the meeting, and often the prospect wants more information that must be sent or brought to a subsequent meeting.

When prospects seem to be stalling or wanting more information, see it as a good sign. In fact, many fundraisers believe that if a person says, "I need to think about it," in response to a request for a large gift, they have been asked for just the right amount. The amount was not one they could give easily at the meeting, nor was it an amount that was patently out of their range, but it was an amount they could give, albeit not very often. A person who says yes to a request for $10,000 in one meeting may be someone who has thought a great deal about the campaign and made their decision, but it also may be someone for whom $10,000 is not a stretch gift. Don't be discouraged by prospects wanting more information or needing additional meetings; making a capital gift is a big decision. Even very wealthy people can't afford to give capital gifts very often and they want to make sure their gift will be well used.

These gifts should be solicited by teams of two people — usually a board member and a staff person, or two board members. The board members must be giving what is a stretch gift for them and should be willing to share information about their gift with the prospect. For example, the board member might say, "I am giving ten times my annual gift to this campaign and paying my pledge over five years." Or, "My partner and I decided this endeavor was as important as our car, so we are giving the same amount as our car payment over the next two years." If the solicitor feels comfortable, he or she may also share how much their gift is. The point to make clear to the prospect is that the people asking are giving as much as they can possibly afford and their gift has been made after a lot of thought. They are hoping the prospect will make a similar commitment.

The case statement can be shared with the lead donors and, once they have agreed to a gift, they should be asked if they would be willing to help solicit other gifts. Others find it flattering and sometimes emotionally moving to be asked for a gift by someone who has given the biggest gift.

Once the very top of the pyramid has been filled in with donors, the group is ready to move to the second stage.

The Launching Stage

The launch of a capital campaign should be marked with a special event. The press, donors, volunteers, and foundation and corporate staff should be invited. The press should receive a press release ahead of time or at the event, giving them background information. The invitation to the launch should look very nice because it is the first impression most prospects will have of your capital campaign. The event itself doesn't need to last very long. If you want to make it into a regular special event, you can add a dance or speaker, but this is not necessary. Large graphics on display should describe the overall goal of the campaign and show how much money has been raised and the gift range chart. A board member should describe to the gathered crowd how important the campaign is and invite everyone to celebrate what has been raised so far. Champagne, soft drinks, and hors d'oeuvres may be served.

The Prospectus

For the launch, you will need to design a document called the "prospectus," which is a brochure, booklet, or folder using information from the case statement, but shorter and more artistic. The prospectus will be given to all prospects and it must look good. This document shows the prospect that you know what you are doing and that your group is able to handle these large amounts of money and manage this large capital project.

The Intensive Stage

Immediately after the launch begins the intensive stage. Here teams of two people visit prospects with as much speed as that process will allow. Most prospects are visited at least once during this stage, which is the longest of the four stages. As each gift is received, the total still needed is revised and publicized at least to staff, board, and solicitors, so there is a constant sense of movement toward the goal. During this stage, the two most important elements are good recordkeeping and keeping in touch with volunteer solicitors. Thank-you notes must go out promptly. When people pledge to pay over several years, they must sign a pledge agreement. It can be very simple:

SAMPLE PLEDGE AGREEMENT

I, (name) , pledge the sum of $_____ (amount) to be paid in monthly/quarterly installments of $_____ for the next _____ years.

This is a legally binding pledge, and I know that plans are being made and money is being spent based on the expectation that I will pay this pledge in the way I have described. A copy of this pledge agreement has been placed with my will.

Signed: _____

The system for collecting pledges (as described in Chapter 12) must be in place.

Solicitors must be notified of new gifts and must meet regularly (at least every three weeks) to report on their progress. The problems they run into must be dealt with promptly. One such problem is conditional gifts. Often prospects will offer to make a gift on certain conditions ("I'll give if three other people match my gift," or, "I'll give if the conference room can be named for my mother," or, "I'll give if I can have a seat on the board.") Conditional gifts, regardless of how benign the condition proposed, must go through an approval process, preferably at the board level. Solicitors can say to prospects, "That's a very kind offer. Let me see what we can do about it. I don't have the authority to make those promises." Then the group decides if they wish to accept the condition or not. A group should never take money on conditions that it doesn't wish to meet. People should not be able to "buy" board seats, for example.

The Wind-Up Stage

When more than four-fifths of the money has been pledged, the group goes into the wind-up stage. Here you look for one or two people who can put the goal over the top: "Mr. Jones, we are $10,000 short of our goal — would you finish this campaign with your gift?" To find people who will do that, go back to your original prospect list for lead gifts and see if any of these people were not asked because solicitors felt that they would not take a risk on being the lead gift, or see if any of them said, "Come back to me when you are further along." The wind-up stage is also a good time to ask for a lot of small gifts, because at this stage gifts of $1,000 are clearly helping to move the group toward its goal. The end of the wind-up stage is a large celebratory special event. If you are purchasing or constructing a building, this is often an event involving a ribbon-cutting or ceremonial ground-breaking (if that hasn't happened already).

THE POST-CAMPAIGN

Volunteer solicitors should be given their own party, such as dinner at a fancy restaurant, and should be presented with gifts of appreciation. These are often plaques. Though nice, the gifts should not be expensive. Staff should also be rewarded at this party, possibly with a weekend at a bed-and-breakfast, or a gift certificate to a store they would like.

Staff and solicitors should review all records about donors to make sure they are accurate and that all documentation needed is in place. A special report should be sent to all donors and funders describing the successful conclusion of the campaign and reiterating what wonderful work the group will be able to do in its new building.

Very soon after the end of the capital campaign, you will need to increase the amount of money you are raising annually, since you will not have had an increase in two or three years. A good capital campaign usually has the effect of helping increase annual income, as donors feel closer to the organization and realize they can afford to give more than they thought.

As you can see, a capital campaign is a time-consuming and very detailed project. Only organizations with a strong working board of directors, a loyal donor base, and a well-designed major gifts program should undertake such a campaign.

fifteen

Planned Giving

Aplanned gift is any donation that requires a lot of thought on the part of the donor. However, we mostly use the term "planned giving" to refer to arrangements made for a group to receive contributions from the estate of a donor after the donor has died. These gifts are generally made by long-time, loyal donors who believe in the need of the group to exist after their own life is over and, more important, who have faith that the organization will continue to do a good job for years and years to come. These are not necessarily major donors; many bequests come from donors who have given small amounts to a group for a long time. When I look around at board meetings I attend, I often reflect that in 50 years (which is really very little time), people who aren't even born yet will be running the organization. I will probably be deceased. What will I need to know about the group to trust that people who don't exist yet will continue to do a good job? That information and that confidence form the basis for donors making planned gifts.

Some organizations use planned gifts for annual expenses, but since the gift is not repeatable, this is unwise. Others use planned gifts for capital improvements; most use them to build endowments. An endowment is a permanently restricted fund invested to generate interest. The principal, or corpus, is never spent but is added to as more planned gifts come in. The interest income can be used as the organization wishes unless the gift has been restricted by the terms of the donor. Interest income is usually used to offset general operating costs since these are the most difficult to raise money for.

GETTING READY FOR A PLANNED GIVING PROGRAM

Many organizations think that getting ready for a planned giving program involves going to seminars and memorizing complicated financial planning language, then identifying the organization's oldest donors, explaining what you have learned to them, and watching them sign on the dotted line. Many people have told me that they imagine that getting money from people after they are dead is easier than getting it during their lifetime! One woman was chagrined when I pointed out to her that the donor makes these arrangements during his or her life and, as yet, we have no mechanism for getting gifts from donors after their death.

In fact, before anyone in the organization begins the process of learning what a remainder trust is or the many different ways to word a bequest, a number of things have to be in place.

First, your organization has to decide that it needs to exist decades into the future. For many social change organizations, this is an admission of failure, at least in the short term. To be endowed is to say, "We will always be needed." Do we really want to say this about anti-death penalty groups, homeless shelters, or environmental advocacy organizations? The answer is different for libraries, theaters, parks, and the like, and even free legal services, consumer information programs, or leadership training programs that we will want to see continue in perpetuity. Nevertheless, social change organizations can have a mission that theoretically could be accomplished and still have an endowment. For example, a domestic violence program that started an endowment talks about it this way:

> We work always toward the goal of ending domestic violence and we can imagine a society in which domestic violence would be a part of the historical record but not the present reality. However, we cannot imagine that society in our lifetime and we feel an obligation to make our programs easier to fund by ensuring some kind of financial stability. We have opened an endowment fund to help ensure that we will be around as long as we need to be, and when we are no longer needed, we will give our endowment to our local women's foundation to help them address the needs of the women of future generations.

It is critical that your organization discuss and agree on the need to exist far into the future, and come to grips with what that means for your overall mission.

Second, in addition to deciding how far into the future your group may want to exist, it's important to look at whether people trust you to do your work now and understand your need for funds. Does your group have a good reputation — not just for work accomplished, but for stewardship of resources, handling money responsibly, and raising money with integrity? While many grassroots organizations could answer yes to all these questions, they may be surprised at the extent to which their donors have no sense of how their group deals with money. If you don't put out an annual financial report, if you don't publish the names of your donors from time to time, and if you don't regularly talk about how you raise money, your donors may have never thought much about your long-term financial needs. For example, if someone were to ask where the local college or symphony orchestra gets their money, many people would answer that they get a lot of money from individuals and a lot of money from bequests. Because of that, as someone makes their will, they think of their local college or arts group. You can start a planned giving program without people being aware of how your organization raises and spends money, but it will not go very far until that information is more commonly known.

Third, which is closely related to the previous point, does your donor base include people who have given your group money for several years and who think of your organization as a group that they will support as long as they can? Many groups need to develop their donor base before they begin a planned giving program — not just in terms of numbers of donors, but also in terms of donor loyalty.

If one or more of these elements are not in place, skip this chapter and re-read the preceding chapters. Do what is recommended in those and you will be ready to come back to this chapter in a year or two.

PREPARING TO TALK ABOUT PLANNED GIVING

Many organizations that have the donor base in place to start a planned giving program hesitate to do so because of the almost universal taboo about talking about death: People feel awkward talking to anyone about their money and their death at the same time. It may seem in bad taste or intrusive. However, it is important to remember that in the United States bequests, which are the most common form of planned giving, account for between 5% and 8% of all the money given to non-profits. In fact, the money given from bequests in most years is equal to the money given by foundations and always surpasses the money given by corporations. (An old joke in fundraising is that dead people give away more money than corporations, which is used to illustrate how minimal corporate giving is relative to the publicity they receive for it.) Other forms of planned giving, such as charitable remainder trusts, pooled income funds, lead trusts, and so on (explained later in this chapter) account for millions more. People who make planned gifts can make your organization a beneficiary or they may make some other group a beneficiary, but if they are inclined to remember a charity in their will, they will do so. If you ask them, they may remember you. If you don't, they may not. If you would like them to think of you as they make their will, you must ask them in one way or another.

When you ask someone for a bequest or another type of planned gift, you are not asking them to die. You are instead making a statement about your organization and its need, complimenting the donor on their loyalty and commitment to your cause, and giving them another opportunity to act on that commitment.

THE IMPORTANCE OF A WILL

The vast majority of planned gifts, regardless of size, are bequests. Fully four out of five planned gifts are made this way, so for most grassroots organizations, establishing a solid bequest program is as far into planned giving as they will ever need to go. Further, the terms of almost all planned gifts, even very complicated ones, are laid out in a will.

Everyone should have a will because no one knows when they are going to die and because everything you own during your lifetime you also own after your death. You have the authority to direct what happens to your property after you have died, but if you choose not to make a will, the state makes that direction for you. Surprisingly, seven out of ten people do not have a will, and of the 30% who do have a will, half leave their entire estate to their spouse. Introducing your donors to planned giving is a service to them because it causes them to think about making or updating their wills. Your nonprofit may get some money as a result, but the main service is that making a will protects the donor's family and other interests.

If you die without a will (called "dying intestate"), the law specifies who will receive your estate, as follows:

- If you are survived by a spouse and not survived by a child or parent, your spouse receives all your property.
- If you are survived by a spouse and a parent and not a child, your spouse and your parent share your property.
- If you are survived by a spouse, child, and a parent, your spouse and your child share your property, and your parent receives nothing.
- If you are not survived by a spouse or a child or a parent, your brothers and sisters and the children of your deceased brothers and sisters share your property.

MOTIVATING DONORS TO MAKE A WILL

In most grassroots organizations that have middle-class, working-class, and low-income donors, the first step in a planned giving program is motivating your donors to make wills. The second step will then be to encourage them to name your organization as one of their beneficiaries. A few case studies about what happens to people who don't have wills motivates most donors to create one. Names have been changed in the three examples that follow, but they are true stories.

Mary Springhill, aged 50, died of breast cancer. She had no children and her parents were deceased. She was separated but not divorced from her husband. Mary was a fairly successful artist and her estate, including a house, a new car, and some savings, was worth a little over $400,000. Mary had never gotten around to writing a will. Then, during the time she had cancer, she was too sick to think about preparing one. Mary had left her husband three years prior to her death, after enduring his physical and emotional abuse for 15 years. Now, as the surviving spouse and sole heir, he is the beneficiary of her entire estate.

Alice Williams, pro-choice activist, age 33, was killed in a car accident. She and her parents had clashed about her pro-choice views as well as her progressive attitude toward many issues. Her parents were active in their fundamentalist church and had told their daughter on a number of occasions that she was "going to hell." Although they were all on speaking terms and Alice spent some holidays with her parents, their relationship was very strained. Alice believed she was too young to need a will and that her estate did not warrant the cost of going to an attorney to draw one up. (Like many people, Alice erroneously believed that only attorneys can make legally binding wills.) At 21, Alice had inherited $100,000 from an aunt. She had never spent the money, although she often used the interest it generated to augment her meager salary. Without a spouse or children, Alice's estate of $100,000 went to her parents. Alice may not have objected; however, in the belief that the money could, as they put it, "nullify some of the evil work poor Alice had done," her parents gave it all to a variety of anti-abortion organizations.

Fay and Marianna were lovers for five years. Fay had inherited an apartment building in New York plus a handsome stock portfolio. She and Marianna lived in a house that Fay had bought before they knew each other. They were planning to add Marianna's name to the title of the house, as well as create wills, when Fay was killed by a drunk driver. Her parents had never approved of her relationship with Marianna but, since Fay had no will, they became Fay's legal heirs. They are in the process of evicting Marianna from her house and have told her that she can have nothing from Fay's estate.

Other classic cases involve daughters caring for an aging parent until the parent's death, then learning that the estate is to be shared equally with a brother or sister who had no part in their parent's care or the expenses for it; people dying with seemingly no heirs having been cared for by neighbors and friends, then seeing a previously unknown relative walk away with the estate, and so on.

Most people underestimate the worth of their estate and overestimate the time or cost involved in setting up a will. They do not realize that when there is no will, whoever is dealing with someone's estate can be in for a tremendous amount of work. Finally, besides the distribution of property, a will can carry wishes about how the person wants to be buried, whom they want looking after children or pets, and any other legal or other obligations the deceased wishes heirs to assume.

A Warning before Proceeding Further

Nonprofits cannot be involved in the creation of someone's will. They can encourage people to create a will, offer workshops about wills led by attorneys or estate planners, and discuss what they know about wills with donors and in written materials, but they must not get involved in giving legal advice or in helping people write their wills. The only advice anyone in a nonprofit should give current or potential donors about the best planned giving instrument for them is to consult their own attorney or financial planner. No one from your organization should ever negotiate a legal arrangement with a donor without the donor's attorney, financial planner, and children being present or at least being knowledgeable about the agreement the donor is making.

The reason for all these cautions is that people who work for nonprofits are subject to being accused of "exerting undue influence," thus opening the way to legal challenge of a will. The way to avoid that accusation is to know only enough about planned giving instruments to give general information to a donor. Your organization will want to have access to its own legal advice before accepting any complicated arrangement or certain kinds of property that may not be in the best interest of the organization.

THE BEQUEST

The simplest form of planned giving and the most common is the bequest. A person notes in their will what property they wish your organization to have — cash, stocks, bonds, art — anything of value. People who already have wills and don't want to change them substantially can add a "codicil" or amendment to their will to specify gifts to your organization.

One of the most famous and oldest bequests was given by Ben Franklin in 1790. He left the equivalent of $4,000 to be divided between the people of the state of Pennsylvania (76%) and the city of Philadelphia (24%) on the condition that it not be touched for 200 years. (Franklin had great faith in the future of his state and city!) In 1990, the 200 years were up; Franklin's bequest was worth $2.3 million. A group of Franklin scholars given authority to recommend the best use of the money decided that the city's money should be kept in a permanent endowment at the Philadelphia Foundation and the state's money should be shared between the Franklin Institute and a consortium of community foundations around the state.

HOW SOMEONE MAKES A BEQUEST

Anyone can make a bequest. All that is required is that they are alive and of sound mind when they make their will, and that they own something they can't take with them. Many people think bequests are only for wealthy people, but in fact, if all someone owns is a 1990 Toyota Corolla, they can leave that car to a nonprofit, which keeps whatever amount they can sell it for.

All bequests are revocable during the life of the donor — a will can be changed any number of times. Your organization may be included in one will and left out of a later version. Thus, unrealized bequests (bequests promised to you by donors who are still alive) cannot ethically be counted toward a fundraising goal.

Wording of Bequests

Although you will not be directing people in the wording included in their wills, you should know the accurate wording for various types of bequests that may come to you. In addition, people may occasionally ask you for the proper wording of a bequest when including your group in their wills.

The General Bequest

This is the simplest bequest, where a donor gives a stated amount to the nonprofit group without attaching any conditions. The bequest reads as follows:

> I give and bequeath to (exact name and address of organization) the sum of $ _____
> (or a specific piece of property) to be used as the board of directors determines.

To be absolutely certain there is no confusion about which nonprofit organization the donor meant, it is a good idea to include the address of the group.

Similar to the general bequest in language and intent are the following:

Bequest of a Percentage

> I give and bequeath ____ percent (name a specific percentage) of the total value of
> my estate to (exact name and address of organization) to be used as the board of
> directors determines.

Bequest of Residue

A bequest of residue is a provision that all wills should have, which leaves the remainder of one's estate to an organization or a person after all other bequests are fulfilled.

> The rest, residue and remainder of my estate, both real and personal, wherever situated,
> I give and bequeath to (name and address of organization) to be used as the board of
> directors directs.

The remaining three types of bequests have more strings attached or only come into play under certain circumstances.

Contingent Bequest

This leaves a bequest to the nonprofit if any of the other beneficiaries are unable to receive their bequests because of death or other circumstances. Everyone should have a contingent bequest in their will in case the will is quite dated and circumstances have changed since it was drawn up.

> Should (name of heir) predecease me, the portion of my estate going to (name of heir) I give and bequeath to (name and address of organization).

Income Only to Be Used

> I give and bequeath to (name and address of organization) the sum of $ _____ to be invested or reinvested so that the income only may be used as the board of directors directs.

Designated Bequest

This provides a sum of money for a specific or designated project or program.

> I give and bequeath to (name and address of organization) the sum of $ _____ (or the property or percentage) to be used for (specific description of program, scholarship, building, etc.).

Ideally, a designated bequest has some kind of contingency, such as, "Should this program no longer be needed, or be fully funded from another source, the bequest may be used as the board of directors directs."

The most flexible bequests are those that are best for the nonprofit and it is the wording of those that you will wish to advertise.

The fact that bequests are revocable works in favor of nonprofits as well as donors and should not be seen as a disadvantage. A donor might change their will over time to make your organization more of a direct beneficiary. Some donors start with a contingent bequest, which is basically saying that if one or more unlikely things happen, your group will benefit. They may move to a residue bequest — anything they have forgotten about is yours. Then they may move to a percentage or an actual amount for your group.

OTHER KINDS OF PLANNED GIFTS

Besides the bequest, there are a number of other giving instruments your organization should know about.

To understand any of these strategies, it is necessary to understand certain principles concerning the value of any investment, including property. First, remember that most of the income of the government is from taxes. A tax is a fee assessed on the transfer of something of material value from one entity to another. Income tax, sales tax, capital gains tax (tax on the difference between what someone paid for something and what they sold it for), and estate tax are familiar terms to most of us. These various taxes help to fill the government's coffers (whether local, state, or federal governmental entities). One of the few things of value that can be moved from one place to another without any tax being imposed is a gift to charity. For donors committed to a nonprofit, an added incentive to make large gifts to that organization is that they will lower their income tax and they may lower or avoid capital gains and estate taxes.

A second principle is that everything a person owns (their assets) has three values:

• What they paid for it (called "cost basis")

• What a willing buyer would pay for it (called "fair market value")

• What it will be worth at some designated point in the future, such as at their death (called "future value")

The difference between the cost basis and the fair market value, if the fair market value is more, is called capital gains. Selling something for a profit can trigger capital gains tax but giving it away avoids that tax. Further, the donor gets to deduct from their taxable assets the fair market value of the item; so, with highly appreciated securities (that is, investments that have made a lot of money), a donor will save some money by giving away the security. For example, if John Smith buys stock for $1,000 and sells it for $10,000, he must pay capital gains on $9,000 (the gain). If he gives an organization the $10,000 he sold the stock for, he will be able to deduct from his taxable income that $10,000. Let's say his tax bracket is 31%. In that case, his tax deduction is worth $3,100. On the other hand, if he did not give the money away, he would owe $1,800 in capital gains tax ($9,000 × 20% capital gains tax), so he actually makes $300 by giving this money away ($3,100−$1,800 = $1,300, minus $1,000 cost basis = $300). If instead of giving a nonprofit the money he makes by selling the stock he gives them the stock and they sell it, Smith makes even more money by both avoiding capital gains tax and getting to deduct the fair market value ($3,100−$1,000 cost basis = $2,100). Of course, this is not as much as he would make if he had simply sold the stock and kept the money ($10,000−$1,800 capital gains = $8,200, minus $1,000 cost basis = $7,200 profit), so he has to have a charitable motive. But for donors who have highly appreciated stock and who want to make large gifts, donating the stock can make that wish possible. (A person's actual tax situation is subject to a number of variables not discussed here, so actual savings and cost will vary from person to person.)

Moving to using these three values — cost basis, fair market value, and future value — for planned giving requires understanding that a donor can give away one of the values, but keep the others. I can give the current value (our example above), or I can give the future value by putting the stock in my will as a bequest, or I can split the value, giving some and keeping some. For example, I can give an organization the stock (the fair market or current value) on the condition that I am paid interest from the investment for the rest of my life. By giving away one value, what I keep (the interest) may have more value to me, in part because I have saved myself paying taxes on the larger value, which is the stock itself.

The split values present in planned giving instruments allow people to meet their charitable needs, which must be foremost for anyone to make a planned gift, but also to give themselves some financial security (fear of financial insecurity will prevent many people from making big contributions). There are four financial problems all people may face and plan for:

- Having an emergency without enough savings or insurance to carry them through

- Dying prematurely without having been able to accumulate enough assets to take care of dependents

- Becoming unable to work and not having enough assets to support themselves or their family

- Outliving their savings and not having an adequate income at the very end of their life

One of the goals of planned giving is to allow a donor to have economic security while also expressing their charitable values. Here are a few examples to give you a general sense of what may be possible. Again, each person's situation will depend on many variables, which require whole books to explain.

Charitable Gift Annuity

A charitable gift annuity is a contract between a donor and your organization in which your organization agrees to pay the donor a fixed amount of income annually (called the "annuity") during the life of the donor in exchange for money or assets transferred to your organization. The amount of the annuity, which you set, is determined by the value of the gift and the life expectancy of the person(s) who will receive the annual income. Once the amount of the annuity, or annual payment, is fixed, it does not alter regardless of the value of the asset. This benefits the organization when the asset is able to increase in value and generate more income than the organization is paying out; however it can be hard on a group if the value falls. Your organization is legally obligated to continue paying the amount you contracted for regardless of the subsequent value of the asset. The donor has traded the possible increase in value of their asset for security and peace of mind.

Here's an example. A husband and wife, both 68, wish to make a large gift to their favorite cause, which is their church, without decreasing their retirement income. To do so, they give $30,000 to their church, which promises to pay them $2,000 in annual income for as long as either of them lives — a return of 6.7% per year on the $30,000. The couple is allowed an income-tax deduction on the $30,000 gift and may be able to deduct some of the income they receive if the church derives some of the income by investing the money in tax-exempt securities. The church invests the $30,000 in a mutual fund that grows by 10% per year, which generates more than enough money to make the annuity payment and pay administrative costs. When both donors have died, the church will have the $30,000 plus any interest they have saved beyond the annuity payments to the donors. The donors could have gotten more money from a commercial annuity, but they would not have had the tax deduction and they would not have helped their church.

Deferred Payment Gift Annuity

This annuity is like the charitable gift annuity, except the payments are deferred until the donor reaches a certain age. This can be an attractive option for younger donors.

For example, a 45-year-old donor wants to make a significant gift and guarantee some retirement income. She has a high income now, so the tax deduction is attractive, but she does not need annuity income. In fact, she wants to defer the income from the annuity until after retirement, when her lower income will mean lower taxes. The calculations for this type of annuity should be done by a professional, as they depend on the actuarial tables of the age at which the donor wants the payments to begin and the age of the donor at the time of the gift.

Trusts

There are a wide variety of trusts, but the following four are the most commonly used for charitable purposes.

Pooled Income Fund

A pooled income fund is similar to a mutual fund. The "pool" is made up of contributions from many donors (although it can start out with just one). The contributions are commingled to minimize investment risk and maximize income. Your organization, or more often, an investment firm you designate and oversee, manages the funds. The donors are paid an annual amount based on the number of shares they own and the amount of money the fund has earned. This can vary from year to year. All of the income from this type of fund is taxable because a pooled income fund cannot invest in tax-exempt securities. When any particular donor dies, the amount of his or her original investment is removed from the pool and belongs to the charity.

For both charities and donors, the pooled income fund is best for smaller gifts. Where any of the other instruments require at least $2,000 from any one donor and often more to be worth setting up, a contribution to a pooled income fund could be as little as $500 and still be worthwhile for the charity, while giving the donor earning potential from a much greater amount of money. (In other words, interest on $500 invested in a pool worth $1,000,000 will be greater than any interest the $500 could earn on its own.) The cost of managing the investment is spread over all the shares in the pool, so only small administrative costs need to be passed on to each donor.

Charitable Remainder Annuity Trust

Like an annuity, the annuity trust pays a fixed amount of income for the life of the donor or beneficiary, or for a specific period of time, which cannot exceed 20 years. By law, the annuity cannot be less than 5% of the initial fair market value of the donated asset. The donor can choose how frequently to be paid, but it must be at least once a year.

The goal of an annuity trust is maximum income. If the asset makes more than the amount you are paying the donor, you have realized some extra income for your organization. However, if the asset makes less than your required payment, you have to fund the payments out of income accumulated by the trust previously or out of the principal of the trust. From the point of view of the organization, an annuity trust is preferable to an annuity because once you have exhausted the trust principal to maintain your agreed-upon payments, the trust collapses and your payment obligations to the donor cease. Of course, you no longer have the asset either.

With an annuity, on the other hand, you always owe the donor the amount you contracted for, even if the amount they gave is used up.

Let's look at the tax advantages of a charitable remainder annuity trust. Marga Lopez and her husband, Will Firestein, both aged 70, own appreciated stocks that are now 20 times as valuable as when they bought them. They have not received any dividends to date. They want to increase their retirement income and make a gift to their favorite nonprofit when they die. They place the stock in a charitable remainder annuity trust with the nonprofit, that agrees to pay 7% of the net fair market value of the stock annually. On Marga and Will's deaths, the remaining principal of the stock will revert to the nonprofit. This way, they are able to make a gift to the charity on their death, avoid capital-gains tax now, receive an income-tax deduction for the present value of the charitable remainder interest, and create an income stream for themselves from an asset that was not producing income.

Charitable Remainder Unitrust

A unitrust is similar to an annuity trust, except the payout rate (minimum 5%) is based on a fixed percentage of the total value of the trust, determined annually. Growth of the principal or corpus, rather than maximum income, is the investment goal here. Income to the donor can go up in this arrangement because it is based on the changing value of the fund.

Lead Trusts

The other type of trust you may have read or heard about is the lead trust. The amounts of money involved in setting up a lead trust are beyond the scope of most organizations using this book. The main difference between the remainder trusts described above and a lead trust is understood again in the split value principle. In any kind of remainder trust, the donor gives the asset and keeps what the asset produces (sometimes called "giving the tree and keeping the fruit"). The organization has whatever remains of the asset at the death of the donor, which is usually a more valuable asset than the donor originally gave. In a lead trust, the donor keeps the asset and gives away the interest for a specific period of time (called "giving the fruit and keeping the tree"). If someone wants to set up a lead trust with your organization as a beneficiary, call a lawyer or estate planner for details.

Gifts from Insurance and Retirement Funds

Any time a person owns an asset and is asked to name a beneficiary, they can name a nonprofit, or they can name an heir and then a nonprofit in the case that the heir dies first. Here are a couple of common examples:

Existing Life Insurance Policies

People generally buy life insurance to protect their survivors if sufficient assets have not been accumulated. The value of the life insurance policy may cover mortgage debt or protect a business. As a person gets older, they may not need that protection and can change the beneficiary of their insurance to a charity of their choice. The older the life insurance policy, the more cash value it has built up and that can be given outright during the policyholder's lifetime. The "Life Insurance Fact Book" (a real page-turner) estimates that there are some 400 million (400,000,000) life insurance policies in existence in the United States.

Buying Life Insurance to Fund a Gift

For people wanting to make a gift to an organization that is far greater than they imagine they would ever be able to give from accumulated assets, buying a life insurance policy and making the charity a beneficiary may be a way to go. The premiums on such a policy may be tax deductible. From an organizational viewpoint, this kind of insurance is problematic because it means the donor is paying out money to help your organization, but you will not see the results of this money until the death of the donor, which hopefully will be far into the future. If the donor stops paying his or her premiums, the nonprofit has neither the insurance nor the donor.

IRAs or Other Retirement Plans

Most Americans are eligible to participate in some kind of tax-deferred retirement plan. You can encourage your donors to make your organization the primary, secondary, or final beneficiary of their plan or to name your organization as a recipient of a percent of the proceeds. This money may come to you if the person dies before retirement or if their retirement plan is overfunded (that is, they do not use up all the money in the plan after they retire but before they die).

WHAT DOES ALL THIS MEAN FOR YOUR ORGANIZATION?

If you have read this far, you have probably thought, as I often have, "I can't understand this, and even if I could, I don't how I would bring it up with anyone, and even if I did, they couldn't understand it, or if they did, somebody else probably asked them already and I am too late."

These feelings and all others of inadequacy are totally normal. However, once you put your mind to learning what you need to know, allowing yourself to not understand all of it, and finding a lawyer or estate planner who does understand more of it, you will realize that what your organization needs to know about planned giving is not that difficult to learn. The obfuscation of planned giving terms and ideas has been part of the structure that keeps small groups small and impermanent.

I have known donors who had a favorite grassroots organization to which they made significant donations and for which they volunteered, only to make planned gifts to their university or another much larger institution. They made this decision because they could not be sure the grassroots group would last long enough to benefit from a bequest or they did not trust that the organization could handle a remainder trust. This is a vicious circle, and those of us in fundraising roles in small organizations need to break it by learning as much as we can and convincing some of our bolder donors to take the leap with us. Once a few do it, others will follow.

INTRODUCING YOUR PLANNED GIVING PROGRAM

The best way to introduce a planned giving program is also the easiest and most low-key: Use the letters and newsletters you already mail to donors. In them, add a description of the various kinds of bequests and an invitation to make your organization a beneficiary of a donor's will.

Start with the newsletter. Once or twice a year, include an article that focuses on the need for your organization to exist for a long time, and therefore to have an endowment, and the need for each donor to have a will that expresses their commitments. Use real-life stories and give examples of language they can use to create a codicil (amendment) to their current will.

Once a year, send a mailing specifically focused on wills to your whole donor list, or, if you want to segment, to donors who have given three or more years in a row. You may wish to develop a brochure explaining bequests and send it with the mailing and to anyone else who requests one. If you develop the capacity to work with other planned giving instruments, describe those as well. There are many planned giving professionals who will, for a small fee, provide you with a generic brochure that you customize for your own organization, so there is no need to start from scratch on this.

Many people are happy to answer questionnaires, so one way to introduce your planned giving program is to include a questionnaire in a mailing or newsletter with the following questions:

REVIEWING YOUR PLANS

Do you have a will? .... ☐ Yes ☐ No

If the answer is no, would you like more information about how to create one? ..... ☐ Yes ☐ No

If you have a will, have you reviewed it in the last three years? .... ☐ Yes ☐ No

Have you experienced significant changes since you last reviewed your will
(such as moved to another state, had a child, bought a house)? .... ☐ Yes ☐ No

Have you included the organization you care about in your will? .... ☐ Yes ☐ No

After the questionnaire has gone out, follow up with another article in the newsletter or with a letter giving some of the answers to commonly asked questions about preparing wills and leaving money to charity. Offer to meet with anyone who would like to discuss your organization's need for an endowment and how they might help.

In every newsletter, include a notice (like a classified ad) that your organization is receiving bequests and ask people making up their wills to remember you. Here is sample language for such ads:

> As you are making out your will, remember us with a bequest. Our full legal name and address is (name and address of group). For more information about bequest language, call or write: (phone number and address).

Or:

> If you have provided for (name of your group) in your estate plans, please let us know. If not, please let us show you how you can. Call or write: (Group's name and address).

Givers can also be reminded that they can name your organization as the first, second, or final beneficiary for part or all of the proceeds from IRAs, insurance policies, wills, or any other estate planning documents.

Present this information frequently and people will begin to notice. Once they begin to notice, when someone is making out their will, they will remember your organization. It generally takes about five years for a planned giving program to begin to produce results (meaning either that you actually begin receiving bequests, or that you know that some of your donors have provided for your organization in their wills) so it is certainly not a quick fix to an immediate financial crisis.

Create a Planned Giving Mailing List

As you do more mailings about planned giving and as people contact you for more information, you will develop a list of people who have identified themselves as wanting information about planned giving. This list includes some serious prospects who want to help your organization and may consider doing so with a planned gift. It also includes fundraisers for other groups who want to see your material, people who love to get mail and write away for everything, and people who thought planned giving meant you planned to give them something. You will have to sort out the serious prospects from the others in order to focus any personal attention you want to give to genuine planned giving prospects.

To do so, in your mailings to this list, describe your organization's planned giving options in more detail, using examples and possibly providing more worksheets. Topics for these special mailings would be any planned giving instrument you are set up to handle — remainder trusts, pooled income funds, gifts of highly appreciated securities. Include a detailed return coupon with these mailings so you can identify true prospects. This coupon is action-oriented and might look like this:

Please send me more information on:

☐ Making a gift of appreciated securities   ☐ Generating income from my gift

☐ Wording of bequests   ☐ Giving life insurance policies

Date of birth _____

Type of asset I am considering _____ Value (if known)_____

Name_____

Address _____

_____

Phone _____   Best time to call _____

People who fill out these forms want to be called; call them. Of course, there are still hot prospects who don't fill out these forms and there are other strategies to identify them.

Hold a Seminar

A good community service that can also generate some planned gifts is a seminar on estate planning. Invite people who have indicated an interest in planned giving and announce your seminar to the broader community, if you like. Have an estate planner there and plenty of materials both about your group and about estate planning strategies. If you can, have someone there who will discuss how they made up their estate plans to include your organization.

The purpose of the seminar is to help people think through what they are going to do with their estates, so you don't want to spend a lot of time talking about your organization. However, you will need to mention yourselves a few times to drive the point home that if a person includes a charity in their will, you hope it will be yours.

A seminar lets you meet people, making follow-up easier. One follow-up technique is to form groups of people who want to discuss estate planning or planned giving options with the help of an expert. Each month or so, the group meets to discuss one topic in depth. The group can also discuss more difficult personal questions, such as when children should have access to their inheritance, the kindest thing to do with pets at the death of an owner, living wills, and so on.

Work Collaboratively

Many groups have found success in co-sponsoring seminars such as described above. More people attend and it is clear that no one charity is being pushed.

Some organizations have had good luck working with their local community foundation to hold and manage trusts and pooled-income funds. Since community foundations are set up to handle complicated giving arrangements, they have the language and the knowledge as part of their program. A foundation may also impart to a donor a sense of solidity and stability that reassures them that their investment will be well managed. Your organization receives the interest, just as you would if you were managing the asset, but without any of the headache.

The Most Mutually Beneficial Gift

Once you are able to move past your anxiety and awkwardness about talking about planned giving, you will see that a planned gift is probably the most mutually beneficial gift a donor can make. In any gift, the organization benefits from the donation and the donor benefits by knowing that work he or she believes needs to be done will be done. The bigger the gift, the more assurance the donor needs to have that this is true. An organization expresses its gratitude to donors for moving the work forward through thank-you notes, special events, and other kinds of attention. With a planned gift, the donor may actually be thanked with income earned as well as taxes lowered.

Robert Sharpe, Sr., one of the leading planned giving experts today says that fundraising is not really the appropriate description for people who work in planned giving. In *Planned Giving Simplified* he writes, "[Those who work in planned giving]…are fund gatherers, or those who harvest. They reap what others have sown." (See resources). I think this is a useful insight — planned giving is the final expression of commitment from a donor to a group and the final opportunity the group offers the donor to help. It is the ultimate exchange. It does not and cannot take place outside of a relationship that the person has with the cause and the mission of the organization, even if this person has never met anyone in the group.

An organization that wants a working planned giving program will have in place everything that a group that wants a working fundraising program has: a desire to work with donors, capacity to keep records, people willing to ask, plans and goals, and a belief in the enduring value of the work.

sixteen

Using Donor Analysis

To build a broad base of donors, an organization must periodically analyze the makeup of its current donor population and assess what kinds of people give to the organization, what attracted them to it, and how it can attract more of them. Doing this may also reveal the characteristics of people the organization would expect to be among its donors, but who are not there. The results of the analysis provide directions for recruiting new members and for keeping and upgrading current donors.

There are six steps in doing this analysis and using its outcomes:

1. Learn who your donors are demographically (objective characteristics such as age, sex, zip code) and psychographically (subjective characteristics such as beliefs and values).

2. Based on the demographic study, identify who your prospects are and, using the strategies that invited your current donors to give, invite those prospects to give.

3. Use information from the psychographic survey to find new donors and to provide all donors with opportunities to give more often.

4. Use public education, media, house parties, conferences, and so forth to turn segments of the population you haven't reached before, but who you think you should be reaching, into prospects.

5. Use new fundraising strategies to turn those prospects into donors.

6. Go back to step one.

The first three are steps discussed in detail in this chapter.

1. LEARN WHO YOUR DONORS ARE

There are three tasks to completing this step:

- **Know exactly why your organization exists, what your goals are, and how you intend to accomplish them.** Go back to the beginning of this book and review Chapter 4, Making a Case for Your Organization. If you feel that your organization is clear on its mission, goals, and objectives, then you are ready to consider whom you would expect to support your organization and to conduct a demographic survey of donors to see who actually does support you.

- **Before surveying your donors demographically, think about the characteristics you would logically expect them to share.**

- **Determine the values and commitments of your donors through a psychographic survey.** This survey tests donor loyalty and indicates how to make donors more loyal.

The Demographic Survey

A committee of two or three people who will conduct the surveys first predicts who they would expect to be donors by answering a series of questions to help determine what to look for in the actual survey of donors. The answers provide a baseline from which to notice significant differences between the group's self-perception and the perceptions of its donors. These are the questions the survey committee answers for itself:

- With regard to the issues we work on, what ideas and values would we expect our donors to have?

- How would they get those ideas and values, and how are these ideas and values reinforced or challenged in the culture?

- What types of people have these values and beliefs?

- How does our group convey our values in our work?

- How have we recruited donors up to now? (Mail appeals, special events, canvassing, etc.)

- Who do we think our most typical donors are in terms of demographics?

Next, board and staff complete a demographic survey (see Sample Demographic Survey on page 247), developing a composite profile of the group's average donor. The sample demographic survey includes questions that may only be relevant to certain types of organizations. Choose the items most relevant to your donor population, and change the questions to best serve your organization.

Once the leadership of the organization has answered these questions, the committee can administer the demographic survey to the organization's donors. The survey should be accompanied by a letter explaining the reasons for seeking the information and that answers are to be given anonymously. (A demographic survey only asks about and analyzes actual facts about people — it does not generally address issues of values. The psychographic survey will do that.)

As a point of comparison, the committee should learn what it can about the demographics of its town or city. (To find local or regional demographics, consult the federal Census Bureau Web site, your local Chamber of Commerce, and other groups that have done similar surveys. A national group would need to get comparable demographics; a reference librarian can help with this.) Comparing the profile you get from your demographic survey with that of your city or town lets you see whether and how the makeup of your group differs from that of your population base.

Eliminate from the demographic survey board members, volunteers, staff, and anyone very close to the organization who is also a donor. Because this survey is used primarily to help you acquire new donors, which you will do mostly by mail, survey those people who give mostly by mail, and who are for the most part personally unknown to the majority of the leadership. Thoughtful donors can be surveyed, but their questionnaires should be coded and the results of their survey tallied separately, since they (presumably) have more access to information about the organization from people in it as well as from newsletters and other printed materials.

While you need a certain percentage of response to have an accurate perception of your donors, much depends on how many donors you have to begin with. If you have 200 donors, you will need at least a 20% response to have a significant body of information to go on. On the other hand, a group with 200,000 donors will be unlikely to get a 20% response and would have enough information from a much smaller sample.

Your response tells you what the demographics are of those donors who respond to surveys sent in the mail. To round out the picture, you will need to phone some of your donors. Again, how many you phone will depend somewhat on the size of your donor pool and the response to your survey. If you have a small response to your survey, you will need to phone more people, partly to see why so few people responded to the written survey. Generally, 20 to 50 phone responses should give you the information you need. You can simply ask those you phone if they have seen the survey and if they have responded. If they have not seen it or responded, ask if you can take the information now. Reassure the donor that you are a surveyer and will not be recording their name or any identifying data. Many groups use students in marketing classes or student interns to conduct these surveys to ensure maximum confidentiality and have minimal bias in interpreting answers.

Compare the results of your survey with your predictions. Note gaps, surprises, populations that are under-represented, or types of people you didn't expect. Here is an example to show what this part of the process can teach an organization.

AN ENVIRONMENTAL JUSTICE ORGANIZATION'S SURVEY

An environmental justice organization in a Northwestern town of 100,000 people conducted a survey such as the one in the sample. Their internal survey came out as follows:

Beliefs and values our donors tend to have:
• Poor communities and communities of color are disproportionately exposed to toxic chemicals, whether in water, air, or in the ground.

• No one should be exposed to toxic chemicals and toxic waste.

• Communities can be mobilized to fight dangerous environmental practices of corporate polluters and can win.

• Protection of the environment and protection of human health are interrelated.

• The environmental movement has generally not addressed the relationship of race and class to environmental degradation, but can and must be persuaded to do so. Similarly, community organizing and labor groups need to include threats to the environment in their organizing agenda.

How they would get these values:
• Personal experience with the environmentally caused illnesses of neighbors or family members, especially asthma and lead poisoning

• Reading literature from other environmental justice organizations they belong to

• Being active in local groups doing community organizing on other issues related to poor communities of color, such as police brutality, predatory lending or redlining, lack of access to affordable health care

How these ideas would be supported or challenged by the culture:
Generally, these ideas are unknown in the broader culture; however, on hearing them, people tend to agree with them. Corporations, some parts of local government, and the media will dispute the evidence of a relationship between pollution and illness, or low-income neighborhoods and toxic exposure, creating misinformation in the culture at large. Community people who work for corporate polluters may feel that our organizing efforts threaten their jobs, and environmentalists often neglect to respond to urban problems, preferring to focus on conservation of wilderness.

What types of people have values and beliefs that would cause them to give to our environmental justice group?
• Teachers, particularly those working in schools with problems with lead paint

• People living in the neighborhoods we serve

• People who belong to other environmental justice organizations

• People who belong to other community organizing efforts in other parts of town

• Public interest attorneys and public health professionals

How does our group convey our values and our work?

Through direct action, including demonstrations and speaking at city council meetings; through printed materials, including direct mail, brochures, and a quarterly newsletter; and through attempts to reach the media, with press releases and appearances on some radio talk shows.

How have we recruited donors up to now?

About 40% have been recruited through a door-to-door canvass, services and referrals provided to families or neighborhood block associations, direct mail to donors of like-minded organizations, word of mouth, and board member efforts. We don't have information about the source of donation for the rest of our donors.

What will the demographics of our donor population be?

Most donors will be white, but at least one-third will be African American or Latino, earn between $30,000 and $50,000, be married and have children, and as many will be men as women. Half our donors will be college educated but very few will have graduate degrees. More than half will be active in a church or other religious institution. (This profile also conformed to the profile of the town's population, except in the area of race, as the population of the town included only 10% African Americans and Latinos.)

The results:

Of 1,000 donors surveyed, 200 completed the demographic survey, and an additional 50 responses were taken by phone.

The donors had various racial backgrounds: 70% were white and the remaining 30% were people of color, of which 5% were Asian. Unexpectedly, 75% of the donors were women, and the most common profession was working for the schools: as teachers, administrators, counselors, or janitors. About 25% of the donors were self-employed as landscapers, housecleaners, therapists, acupuncturists, and printers. About 80% were not married and only half of the donors had children. Ten percent were retired. All the respondents had completed high school, and almost 70% had attended college; more than 15% had graduate degrees. More than half attended a church regularly.

The income range was broader than predicted, with most donors in the $30,000 to $50,000 range as expected, but about 33% earning "over $75,000."

Twenty-five percent had joined the organization because of a mail appeal and 15% had joined because, they said, "a friend gave me the newsletter." About 10% had become donors from the door-to-door canvass. A majority of donors (55%) did not live in the neighborhoods primarily targeted by this group.

The organization was not that far off in predicting who would belong from who did belong. However, it is clear that this group needs to do more donor recruitment in the neighborhoods where they organize and evaluate whether their canvass is an effective fundraising tool. (They may choose to keep it as a useful organizing tool.) They were pleased to learn that they have a much broader appeal than they might have thought, particularly among self-employed people.

The Psychographic Survey

Describing people based on their lifestyles, values, and attitudes is called "psychographics." Together, demographic and psychographic data give an overall profile of donors and prospects, allowing you to focus your fundraising and education efforts on the needs, wants, and desires of your donor population, and to find prospects who share the commitments and ideals of your organization.

Once the group has completed and analyzed the demographic survey, it is ready to conduct a psychographic survey. This is a more in-depth personal survey, and is generally given to fewer people. (See sample survey on pages 248–249.)

The psychographic survey helps you know why people give to your organization, why they are loyal to it, and what makes them more (or less) loyal. With this information, you can maintain and strengthen existing commitment and gain new donors with strong loyalty. This process may seem lengthy, but by completing it you will gain important information that will ultimately save you time and money in recruiting new donors.

The first step in conducting a psychographic study is to divide your donors into categories. First, identify people among your donors who qualify in one or more of the following ways:

1. People who give or pledge large gifts ($100 or more) at least once a year
2. People who give any size of gift three or more times a year (assuming that your group asks your donors for money at least three times a year)
3. People who have given for three years or more

People who pledge fall into category 1, even if their total pledge amount is less than $100; however, if they give in addition to their pledge payments, they belong in both categories 1 and 2.

Now, sort these donors into further categories as follows:

A. People who belong to categories 1, 2, and 3.

B. People who belong to categories 2 and 3.

C. People who belong to categories 1 and 3.

You will probably not have more than a few dozen (if that) people in category A. If you do, however, then take a random sample of 50 or so for this survey.

You are now ready to conduct the survey. What you will do is this:

1. Interview in person as many people in category A as possible.
2. Interview by telephone as many people in category B as possible.
3. Send written surveys to people in category C, with phone interviews of a random small number of these people.

Each group will be asked the same set of questions. The personal interviews, which can be done one at a time or in informal settings of several donors and an interviewer, will yield the most wide-ranging opinions. The telephone and written surveys will be easier to analyze because the answers will be more fixed, but will not yield the kinds of additional comments you can expect from the personal interviews. All questions should be tested on a small group of people to make sure they are sensitive, necessary, and not ambiguous. (See box, On Asking Questions.)

It may not be possible for small organizations to get what statisticians would consider "significant" numbers. Obviously, the more people you survey, the more accurate your response, if all other variables are the same. Small organizations, however, do not have a huge donor base to survey and do not have the money to conduct extensive research. Generally speaking, a well-worded survey administered to 100 or more people will be accurate within a 4% margin of error. Smaller numbers, particularly small numbers of personal interviews (in-depth interviews of five key donors), will nevertheless yield information that is useful and can be tested on new prospects.

ON ASKING QUESTIONS

Only seek information necessary to your group. A group working on housing issues or pollution control might find it useful to know what percentage of their donors use mass transit and how often. However, a hospice does not need this information unless it is related to care.

Don't ask questions that assume a behavior. For example, asking the question, "Our last newsletter critiqued welfare-to-work programs. Did you agree with our position?" assumes that the person both read the newsletter and remembers what position your group took.

Remember that you may be asking questions that some donors find embarrassing or sensitive. Be sure you give people multiple choices in your written surveys and that you do not ask socially unacceptable questions in your telephone or personal interviews. For example, do not ask, "What is your income?" but instead offer a series of ranges for people to choose from. In a written survey you can ask for a person's sexual orientation because the survey is clearly anonymous; however in a phone call that would generally be too personal a question.

Don't bias your questions. For example, do not ask a question such as "Our board of directors feels that more prison construction is wrong. How do you feel?" Instead ask, "What is your opinion of more prison construction?" followed by "If our organization were to work against it, would you support us financially in that particular endeavor?"

People generally prefer to mark a category than give a specific answer, so as much as possible include categories rather than asking for a specific answer, for example,

Age: ___ Under 21 ___ 22–30 ___ 31–40 ___41–50, etc.

rather than "What is your age?"

Keep in mind that surveys of donors have serious limitations. For example, you probably will not be able to determine the value of listing donors' names in your newsletter, or giving them plaques, membership cards, and so on through a donor survey, because so few donors will admit the importance of those benefits to their giving. Also, most people aspire to be more idealistic and high-minded than they really are, so they will check options that reflect their ideal of themselves rather than their true behavior. However, it is important to know what ideals you do strike in people so you can aim your fundraising efforts at those.

What Have You Learned?

When you have completed your survey, compile all your data. You now have a profile of your donor base by sex, age, race, income, occupation, source of knowledge about the organization, and other demographic data from the demographic survey, and by commitments, priorities, self-image, and commitment to your group from the psychographic survey. Sit down with your committee and discuss what you have learned. What are the surprises? How do your donors' broad perceptions of your organization differ from those of board members and volunteers, or from your mission statement? What are the most important programs to your donors compared with the priorities of board and staff?

A diversity of values and opinions among your donors shows you have broad appeal. By careful approaches to different populations, you have the potential to expand your donor base among many types of people.

2. IDENTIFY YOUR PROSPECTS

To use the results of your demographic and psychographic surveys to find new donors, first list all the strategies that you currently use for getting donors. (If you are doing this in a group, write all the strategies on a piece of butcher paper or on a blackboard where everyone can see it.) Your list will probably include direct mail, phone-a-thons, special events, products for sale, fees for service, foundation and corporate grant proposals, and major gift solicitation.

Now, list your survey results, and note what fundraising strategy would be best for finding donors similar to the ones you already have. To illustrate, let's look at the surveys point by point and how you can use their information.

The results of the demographic surveys have given you the age, income bracket, occupation, education, religious, and political identifications, etc., of your donors. Ask yourself: Where are more people like that? How can we find them?

For example, a group discovered that 25% of their donors live in a particular neighborhood of the city. Those same donors generally have incomes between $30,000 and $70,000. They are upwardly mobile career-oriented individuals, mostly without children. They are a market with a good deal of disposable income. Also, according to the survey, most of them are Democrats, and for the most part, they have no religious affiliation.

Using this data, the organization identified from all its possible fundraising strategies one that would allow it to focus on that neighborhood. They decided to ask donors who had given $100 or more for two or more years to host a house party for the group and to invite their neighbors. At each party, the guests were educated about the work of the group and asked to participate by donating to the group, holding a house party of their own, and voting a particular way on certain issues at an upcoming local election.

From their data, the group knows that most of the people would be voting the way they recommend anyway, so the only new behaviors they are asking for are a donation and a house party. They set a goal of five house parties hosted by current donors, and ten more hosted by people recruited by donors. This turned out to be a very effective strategy to reach an upper-income group in a relaxed setting and bring them in as major donors.

The same group also decided that because so many of their donors were in an upper-income range, the group could provide information that would be useful to others with similar income. In conjunction with several other nonprofits, they hosted a seminar on socially responsible investing. They advertised widely in the neighborhoods where they already had many donors and attracted many new people to their seminar. The focus of the seminar was not on the organization, but during the seminar, the organization was able to give a pitch for itself.

3. FIND MORE DONORS AND KEEP ALL DONORS GIVING

One organization compiled the names of all the magazines people mentioned in their psychographic survey responses. The three magazines that were mentioned most often are only available by subscription and are published by nonprofits that solicit money from their subscribers to help underwrite the magazines. The organization decided to rent lists of those people who are both subscribers and donors to those publications for the geographic area the group served (where available) and use direct mail to reach those people. They reasoned that the readers of those magazines, in addition to their political beliefs, also have in common that they buy and give by mail.

To back up their mail appeals, the group placed classified ads in these magazines during the two months that they were sending mail appeals. The ads offered a publication for sale that the group had produced, but the real purpose of the ads was to increase the group's name recognition in order to increase response to the mail appeals. Although it is impossible to tell exactly what results this dual strategy produced, it seemed to work. The organization expected a 1% response to its mail appeal of 5,000 pieces, and received just over 2.5%. In addition, they received some orders for the publication advertised.

Another group saw that more than half of their donors indicated in the psychographic survey that they talked about the organization to their friends and co-workers. Some respondents even wrote that they always shared the organization's newsletters with friends or brought them to work. Using that information, this organization launched an "each one reach one" campaign. They sent a special appeal to current donors asking that each donor ask one person to join the organization. They included a copy of their newsletter, a fact sheet on the organization's latest work, and a return card and envelope. (They also sent a card for donors to request more recruitment materials if they wanted to ask more than one person.) The donor was asked to sign his or her name on the return card before giving it to the prospective donor. Everyone who brought in a new donor was sent a small gift. Some people recruited 10 donors, some only 1, and one person recruited 25 donors!

Many organizations discover from a psychographic survey that their donors do not have any set formula for determining how much to give to nonprofits, and that they either don't know what their annual charitable giving is or that it is less than 2% of their disposable income (1.8% of disposable income is the national giving average).

Some of these groups are launching educational efforts to teach people to be better donors. Their newsletters contain stories from thoughtful donors; their appeals compare the cost of hamburgers or movies with the amount of a donation. These strategies help make the point that social change needs to be a priority — not something done after all other needs and wants are taken care of. One peace organization did an appeal on this theme: "Most people spend several hundred dollars a year to insure their homes and cars against theft, fire, flood, or other destruction. Our world needs this insurance. Please calculate how much you spend on insurance, and then send us a check keeping in mind that peace is our only insurance against nuclear destruction."

Each aspect of your survey should be used as a brainstorming point to determine the implications of the information you have learned. How can we take advantage of this information in recruiting new donors? What strategy will be most effective in reaching similar people?

Groups that thrive into the future will be those that think carefully about their donors: who they are, what they respond to, and where there are more of them. Knowing the donors will be the key to success.

SAMPLE DEMOGRAPHIC SURVEY

Please answer the following questions. If you do not know something, write DK; if the question is not applicable, write NA.

1. Zip code or neighborhood where you live: _____

2. How long have you lived there? _____

3. Do you live in a ☐ house ☐ apartment ☐ duplex ☐ other_____?
   How many people live with you? _____

4. Your age: ☐ under 18 ☐ 19–25 ☐ 26–35 ☐ 36–45 ☐ 46–60 ☐ over 60

5. Your sex: ☐ Female ☐ Male

6. Your race: _____

7. Your ethnic identity: _____

8. Do you have children? ☐ Yes ☐ No If yes, how many? _____ What are their ages?_____
   Do they live with you ☐ all the time ☐ part of the time (what part _____)
   ☐ none of the time?

9. Are you ☐ Married ☐ Divorced ☐ Single ☐ Widowed ☐ Lesbian/Gay (☐ with ☐ without partner)?

10. Your income level:
    ☐ under $10,000 ☐ $10,000–$20,000 ☐ $21,000–$30,000 ☐ $31,000–$40,000
    ☐ $41,000–$50,000 ☐ over $50,000 ☐ over $100,000 ☐ over $250,000

11. Your education:
    ☐ High school graduate ☐ College graduate ☐ Attended graduate school ☐ Postgraduate training
    What academic degrees do you have? _____

12. Your occupation: _____

13. Do you attend a ☐ church ☐ synagogue ☐ another religious institution? _____

14. Are you registered with a political party? ☐ Yes ☐ No
    If yes, which one? _____ Are you active? ☐ Yes ☐ No

15. How long have you belonged to our group? _____

16. How did you join? ☐ Mail appeal ☐ Phone appeal ☐ Friend ☐ Special event
    ☐ Other: _____

SAMPLE PSYCHOGRAPHIC SURVEY

Your group will need to make up a survey that gives you appropriate information. It should ask the following kinds of questions (the specifics here are meant as examples only).

1. How long have you belonged to our organization?
   ☐ 1 year ☐ 2 years ☐ 3 years ☐ 5 years ☐ Longer (specify) _____

2. Why did you join? _____

3. What other nonprofit organizations do you give to? _____
   _____

4. What is the largest gift you make to any group?
   ☐ $15–$25 ☐ $26–$50 ☐ $51–$150 ☐ $151–$250 ☐ $251–$500 ☐ $501–$1,000
   ☐ $1,001–$2,500 ☐ More than $2,500

5. What is your total annual giving to charity?
   ☐ $100 ☐ $500 ☐ $1,000 ☐ Other:_____ ☐ Don't know

6. How do you determine your giving to charity?
   ☐ As a percentage of income ☐ As a set amount each year ☐ No set formula ☐ Other_____

7. Which, if any, of the following words describe you, and to what extent?

Feminist	☐ Yes	☐ Sort of	☐ Not really	☐ Not at all	☐ Don't understand
Environmentalist	☐ Yes	☐ Sort of	☐ Not really	☐ Not at all	☐ Don't understand
Christian	☐ Yes	☐ Sort of	☐ Not really	☐ Not at all	☐ Don't understand
Democrat	☐ Yes	☐ Sort of	☐ Not really	☐ Not at all	☐ Don't understand
Civic-minded	☐ Yes	☐ Sort of	☐ Not really	☐ Not at all	☐ Don't understand
Family-oriented	☐ Yes	☐ Sort of	☐ Not really	☐ Not at all	☐ Don't understand
Activist	☐ Yes	☐ Sort of	☐ Not really	☐ Not at all	☐ Don't understand
Radical	☐ Yes	☐ Sort of	☐ Not really	☐ Not at all	☐ Don't understand
Liberal	☐ Yes	☐ Sort of	☐ Not really	☐ Not at all	☐ Don't understand

8. If you had to cut back on your giving, when would you eliminate our group?
   ☐ Immediately ☐ Soon ☐ Not until I had to ☐ Never

9. If your income were to increase dramatically, would you:
   (a) Give more money to charity? ☐ Yes ☐ No ☐ Maybe
   (b) Give more money to our group? ☐ Yes ☐ No ☐ Maybe

10. What is the most important issue we address? (List your issues): _____

11. In describing our group to a friend who had never heard of us, what would you say? _____
    _____

12. Do you talk about our group to:

Your friends   ☐ Sometimes   ☐ Rarely   ☐ Never

Your colleagues at work   ☐ Sometimes   ☐ Rarely   ☐ Never

Your family   ☐ Sometimes   ☐ Rarely   ☐ Never

Other (specify): _____

_____

13. If you talk about our group to anyone, do you think most people you talk to have heard of our work?

☐ Most   ☐ Some   ☐ Very few   ☐ Almost none   ☐ None

14. If our organization keeps doing work of the current quality, do you foresee continuing to support us?

☐ Yes   ☐ No   ☐ Maybe   ☐ If possible   ☐ Probably not

15. If probably not, or no, please say why: _____

16. Where do you get news about world affairs or current events?

☐ Television   ☐ Radio   ☐ Newspaper   ☐ Friends   ☐ Don't keep up

17. What magazines do you subscribe to? _____

_____

Other Methods of Fundraising

The more appropriate title for this section would be "Some Other Methods of Fundraising," because an entire book could be devoted to ways of raising money that are not mentioned in this book. However, the following six chapters outline the most common methods that grassroots organizations use. Two of them—fees for service and setting up a business — suggest creating income streams outside of charitable giving altogether; payroll deduction programs describe a collaborative, if complicated, approach to fundraising; the chapter on canvassing looks at a strategy that combines community organizing with fundraising; the chapter on approaching religious institutions, service clubs, and small businesses points out that there are other institutional sources of funds (including some significant funds) besides corporations and foundations; and the chapter on using the Internet for fundraising introduces some of the techniques for and pros and cons of this new tool.

All the methods described in this section incorporate the most important aspects of any fundraising solicitation: researching the prospects, creating a clear plan to approach them, and asking for money.

In all the other sections of this book, there is enough information for you to begin the strategy without needing to read further (although I encourage you to read further and talk to more people). In this section, there are basic definitions and some preliminary how-to's, but more in-depth reading and research are required before you can add these methods to your fundraising plan.

seventeen

Voluntary Fees for Service

The director of a program serving seniors in a small industrial city in Michigan described his experience in starting a fee-for-service income stream. His organization provides a wide range of services to people 65 and older, including Meals on Wheels; transportation to medical appointments; help with doing taxes or dealing with Social Security, Medicare, and private insurance; leisure activities in a community center as well as field trips; and help with aging parents. All of these services had been free. The agency's $300,000 budget was mostly provided by the United Way and the city, with a few other government sources. The program is run inexpensively because 75 active volunteers do much of the work.

Three years ago, the city entered into a state of decline, with high unemployment and a low priority on senior services. At that point, the city began cutting the senior program's funding and now has withdrawn all funding for the program. The United Way also cut their contributions, by 50%, with further cuts expected. Reluctantly, the senior service program director created a free-will donation system to encourage those who used the service to contribute toward its cost. He posted a big sign in the community center that read:

THE COST OF PROVIDING SERVICES IS AS FOLLOWS:

One delivery of a meal (Meals on Wheels) $5
One trip to and from a medical appointment $3
Lunch at the community center $3
Field trips per person per day $10
Magazine subscriptions (average) $15

Any amount you can pay toward these services is gratefully accepted, and will be put right to work.

Thank you.

This same announcement appears in the program's newsletter and on a sign in their van. No one actually asks for money. To donate, one has to be able to read the sign, then put money in a box or hand it to the person in charge.

Over the past two years, this director reports, there has been a 300% increase in the number of people using the various services the center provides. Puzzled, he has investigated. Are there 300% more seniors in town? No. Are 300% more seniors falling into need for these services? No. Finally, he surveyed center users about what brought them to the center, how they found out about it, and what they liked about it. Among other things, he learned that people liked being able to pay for the service. Several people made comments to that effect:

> "I never used this place before because I don't like taking things for free. I am not so poor to need free service. I can pay my own way."
>
> "I can take care of myself pretty good and I don't need handouts. I've worked hard all my life. I like coming to the center and seeing people, and the prices are affordable. Sometimes I put in a little extra for someone who isn't as well off."

The experience of this organization is repeated over and over again as organizations, forced to start suggesting donations to their clients, discover that the clients prefer to pay. More and more organizations are realizing that giving services away to people perpetuates a patronizing and condescending system where some people are seen as needy and others as those who meet needs. Further, when clients pay what they can, they feel empowered to demand better services or to ask questions of their service provider. This strengthens the organization providing the service as they begin to get accurate feedback on their work. From strictly a fundraising viewpoint, fees can also provide the income stream that keeps an organization afloat.

Many nonprofit organizations have mandatory fees. They charge well below the "market rate" for their service, but in order to get the service, one has to pay a fixed price or a fee determined by some criteria such as income or reimbursement from insurance. Health clubs, counseling services, job training and placement, public swimming pools and recreation areas, national and state parks — all often have mandatory fees.

This chapter discusses how to determine fees and how to collect them for organizations that have traditionally provided free services to clients and now wish to charge voluntary fees.

WHAT IS A VOLUNTARY FEE?

You can charge voluntary fees in one of two ways: You can still provide the service for free but request money to help cover the cost; or you can ask that people pay something for the service, but whatever they pay is acceptable.

Which system you use depends on the nature of your clients. Organizations serving the homeless will probably not require a contribution. Cultural organizations, groups serving the working poor, mental health providers, and so on may opt to require some payment.

Or you can mix the two methods. For example, one homeless shelter provides shelter, showers, and clothing for free and does not attempt to charge. But they have a suggested voluntary donation of $.50 for meals and a mandatory processing fee of $10 for job placement (collected after the person has received their first paycheck). This agency now receives donations from clients for almost 70% of their meals served, with many people giving $1.00, and a collection rate of 80% on their job fee. Another shelter provides free meals, but charges $.50 for second helpings, and $.10 for coffee or tea. Water and juice are free.

STAYING LEGAL

Charging fees is not illegal, but if you are asking for donations rather than fees, they must be perceived as voluntary by the client for you to stay within your non-profit status. No coercive measures can be used to collect voluntary fees. A coercive action would be one that makes a person feel the service was not really free or that he or she was the only one asking for free service, or some other method of seeming to intimidate a person into paying or paying more than they want to. Behavior that is coercive can be a matter of perception, but more obviously coercive actions need to be avoided.

For example, one free meal program separated those who had given a donation from those who had not, with those who contributed placed at tables with table-cloths and given dessert. In another instance, admission to a class on how to prepare for job interviews was free, but the person registering people loudly announced each donation so that someone sitting across from her could record it. Although thoughtless and probably unintentional, this practice caused some who had intended to take the course for free or even for a low price to pay more than they had wanted to; others simply left before reaching the registration table.

People tend to be embarrassed by any practice that makes them feel as though they don't have enough money. Any system that can embarrass someone may cause them to feel pressured to pay more than they want to or can afford, and the voluntary fee is no longer truly voluntary. (Ironically, this same embarrassment can arise from an agency insisting on providing a service for free, which can also keep people from seeking services they need.)

The second legal obligation is that your fee, whether voluntary or mandatory, be well below what a for-profit business would charge for the same or a similar service.

SETTING THE FEES

There are several ways to set your fees. The least effective, judged by the amount of money raised, but least intrusive is to post a sign near a collection box that simply reads, "Donations," or, "Donations welcome," or, "Your gift ensures that we can continue to provide this service to others. Thank you." You will tend to get only people's spare change; however, you will never be accused of forcing someone to give, and this can be a good way to introduce the idea of giving to your clients.

If all your services cost about the same amount, you may want to suggest a range for the voluntary contribution. You could post a sign that says, "The cost of providing our services ranges from $10 to $25. Any amount you can pay will ensure that we can continue to provide these services to all who need them. Thank you." If you want, you can add an explanation: "The budget for the services you are receiving was previously provided by the government/United Way/foundations, but these funds have been cut back. To make sure that we can continue to help people, we are asking all our clients to give what they can. Thank you."

The most effective system is one similar to that used by the senior center discussed in the beginning of this chapter. A wide range of costs was established, and people could donate toward only the service they had used. Just as when fundraising from individuals, asking for a specific amount rather than leaving the amount up to the prospect will result in more people giving something, so suggesting specific amounts for services rendered will bring more donations overall and will show that you are serious about raising money and you know what you are doing.

Most service providers have someone who staffs a desk by the front door. This person should be trained to ask for money, particularly if any of your clients cannot read a posted sign. The front-desk person adds to whatever they would normally tell people, "The service is free, but we ask you to give a donation if you can. The donation box is over there." Many clients will ask if there is a charge, which makes it easier to explain. For clients accustomed to getting the service for free, explain that you are still providing it for free, but that you are asking people who can help to do so. If you hand out literature to your clients, include a card explaining your need and a return envelope. They can drop the envelope in the box or send it later.

INTRODUCING THE PROCESS OF COLLECTING FEES

At first, volunteers and staff are often uncomfortable with the process of asking clients for money, regardless of what process you use. In discussing the move to asking for money, validate everybody's feelings: Yes, it is difficult to ask for money, and it may be more difficult to ask people who have very little. It would be a much better world if people did not have to pay for things to which they are entitled: housing, health care, education, or food, and did not have to feel embarrassed about receiving these things. Next, place the new policy in context: Your organization has to keep on providing services, and your costs are going up while your ability to get government (and possibly other) grants is probably going down. Your clients would much rather you exist than watch you go out of business. They will help if they can and will feel good about helping.

Once everyone has a few experiences of asking for money and seeing people feel good about giving, their initial discomfort will go away.

WHEN SERVICE IS PROVIDED BY PHONE

So far, we have concentrated on organizations that can collect fees at the door or at the time of service. But what if your way of providing a service is by telephone or by mailing information? Your organization has a harder task. Certainly, you cannot ask someone calling a crisis hotline for a donation once they have calmed down. Voluntary contribution for a service will not be possible in those cases. However, if you are providing non-crisis information, after you are finished giving it, ask if you can send more information about your organization and how it is supported. If the caller gives you their name and address, immediately send them a fundraising letter.

If your service includes mailing information to people, include a card and return envelope. The card should tell how your group is supported and ask the person to return the envelope with a donation as soon as possible. A card is more effective than a letter because the letter may get put aside while the person is looking at the other information you sent. However, they will be inclined to put the card with the envelope, and respond once they have determined that your information is useful. You may also wish to use a "wallet flap" envelope where the outside flap serves as the "card" (see the section in Chapter 6 on reply devices).

Setting up a voluntary system for collecting money from clients will create a steady income for you, and it may be larger than you think. Further, the system may inspire people who are not clients to give. Many times volunteers are just as uninformed about how your organization is supported as are clients. Once educated, volunteers often give regularly. Finally, you may even get more clients, which will serve your broader mission.

eighteen

Payroll Deduction Programs

Using payroll deduction programs has proven to be one of the most efficient and effective methods of raising money for some organizations. Donating through payroll deduction has been in use since Henry Ford introduced the concept to his employees in 1940. For the past decade, more than $3.5 billion has been pledged through payroll deductions every year. The pioneer agency for this type of fundraising is, of course, the United Way, with affiliates in almost every town of more than 25,000 people in the United States. 90% of the money raised through payroll deduction giving goes to the United Way, with the rest going to a wide and growing variety of alternative federations of groups focused on arts, service, health, environment, women's, and other issues.

A payroll deduction plan is a cross between a pledge program and an electronic funds transfer program. Employees specify how much money they want to donate each pay period and the amount is deducted from their paycheck by their employer. On a quarterly basis the employer sends the collected money to the federation, which keeps a percentage to cover its own costs and distributes the rest to its members.

There are several ways smaller nonprofits can benefit from payroll deduction programs, including becoming a beneficiary of the United Way or of one of the other federated funds in your area. Even if your group isn't affiliated with a federation, it may be able to receive money from any of the funds through what is known as a Donor Option Plan (described below).

Because the United Way is the oldest, largest, and most powerful federated fund, health and human service groups should start by applying to it for funding before pursuing any alternative workplace solicitation program. If you are turned down by the United Way, you have a strong case with the other federated funds or a case for starting your own fund. If you are accepted, you need go no further.

UNITED WAY

The United Way of America is actually a federation of United Ways around the country. While United Ways have many things in common, each has a great deal of autonomy. Direct service nonprofits will have to approach the United Way in their community. A service agency in one community may be accepted by its local United Way, while another local United Way may turn down an agency providing the same service in another community. The United Way does not support arts or environmental groups unless the work of the group involves health issues or provides health education.

Application forms and details of the application process can be obtained from your local United Way. The process, which can be long and tedious, involves an extensive written application, site visits, and reviews by various United Way committees. The bulk of United Way funding has customarily gone to a variety of "mainstream" direct service organizations, such as Boy Scouts, Red Cross, Salvation Army, and YMCA. Traditionally, the United Way has not funded women's or minority organizations, groups with advocacy programs, or groups working for social change. Both nationally and in many local communities, the United Way has been severely criticized for its lack of responsiveness to social change and social justice concerns, and it has responded by making significant changes in funding policies. In some cities a progressive United Way leadership has funded shelters for battered women, groups working with the disabled, gay/lesbian health clinics, AIDS organizations, and some advocacy programs. Further, the United Way in many communities has chosen to work with other federated funds, which has benefited everyone.

To find out what types of organizations the United Way funds in your community, talk to groups that receive United Way funding and to those that have been turned down by them. If possible, meet some United Way officials and discuss your organization's needs with them. If it seems from this research that your group falls within United Way guidelines, and that the amount of money you might receive would be worth the restrictions that the United Way might impose, then proceed to apply.

Pros and Cons

There are obvious advantages to getting United Way funding. Most inviting, United Way membership will usually provide a sizable amount of money that can be counted on from year to year. Even though groups must reapply each year and allocations do change, once an agency is accepted by United Way it will usually continue to receive grants for many years.

However, for organizations truly interested in building self-sufficiency and in diversifying their funding sources, there are many disadvantages to United Way funding. First, organizations receiving United Way funding are not allowed to do their own fundraising from September to November. This so-called "black-out" period is when the United Way conducts its payroll solicitation campaign. To lose three of the best months of the fundraising year is a serious drawback. Unless the allocation from the United Way is significantly larger than what your organization could raise in that time, it is not worth submitting to this structure.

Second, because many people think that agencies supported by the United Way need no other funds, they will not give to organizations receiving money from the United Way. Third, many Americans simply do not like the United Way. They do not like being pressured to give at their workplace and they see the United Way as wasteful of funds and bureaucratic in structure. While this perception is false for many United Ways, the reputation of your local United Way will affect your organization's own reputation for better or worse.

Because most organizations, especially those doing work related to health or human service, will be asked by individual donors, foundations, and corporations whether they have applied for funds from the United Way and if not why not, groups need to explore the possibility of becoming a member even if such exploration leads to the conclusion that such a move would be impossible (you don't qualify) or unwise (your grant from the United Way is not enough to put up with the rules). Then the group can present its reasons for not being involved. This will help donors realize that your organization is responsible and knowledgeable.

The Donor Option Plan

Groups can receive United Way funding through the Donor Option Plan. This plan is not available in every community, but when it is available it allows employees donating through the United Way to designate the agency they wish to receive their contribution. Even if your organization does not qualify to be a United Way–funded agency, you can still receive donations through the Donor Option Plan. Generally, local United Ways do not promote the Donor Option Plan and some try to discourage employees from using it. The United Way sometimes complains that the Donor Option program is expensive for them and complicated to manage. They will ask local groups not to advertise it and not to solicit gifts through Donor Option. Some United Ways have imposed minimums that must be given before an employee can select an organization to receive their United Way pledge. In spite of all this, almost 20% of United Way donations are designated for charities that are not United Way members.

Nevertheless, there is nothing the United Way can do if you do advertise Donor Option Plans to your donors. Ask your donors to notify you if they have given to you through Donor Option, so that you can check up on the pledge if the United Way fails to notify you. Find out from someone in the United Way or from a workplace that gives to United Way how someone can designate your group (this process varies widely) and let your donors know exactly what they should do to designate their payroll deduction for your group.

ALTERNATIVE FUNDS

If your organization cannot or does not wish to receive United Way funding but still wishes to pursue funding through a payroll deduction plan, you will want to explore alternative funds. First, find out if there are any in your community and what their grantmaking capabilities are. Most alternative funds belong to an organization called the Alliance for Choice in Giving, headquartered in Portland, Maine. You can contact them for more information about what federations your organization might be qualified to join, as well as information about starting your own fund (NACG, P.O. Box 4572, Portland, ME 04112-4572; 207/761–1110; www.nacg.org.) Also see the Bibliography for other sources of information on alternative funds.

The alternative fund movement has grown dramatically; as of 1997, there were 130 federated funds serving every state and raising just under $350 million. Some of the newer funds may not yet be able to make large grants but have excellent technical assistance programs. Others are giving away money but may not yet have gained access to many employers and must raise money in ways other than payroll deduction.

There are also several national federations that raise money for national organizations. Examples of those are Earth Share, which fundraises for national and international environmental organizations; Children's Charities of America, which funds teaching, feeding, and protection programs for children nationally and abroad; and the National Black United Federation of Charities and the Black United Fund, both of which promote organizations working towards the betterment and advancement of the African-American community.

Starting an Alternative Fund

If there is no alternative fund in your community, you can start one. This is a major undertaking and, like a small business, takes several years before it will pay off. However, it can eventually be lucrative if you have the time and the skills required. Setting up an alternative payroll deduction plan is simple in theory. Your organization calls together organizations similar to yours either in size or issues addressed or with a broad agenda in common to form a federation. This entails the same work as forming any nonprofit. The federation acts an as umbrella for the member groups and other groups that may apply. The federation seeks employers' permission to solicit donations from employees and distributes the money to member groups, first taking out their own operating expenses from the collected funds. The overall fundraising costs are much lower than if each group were to try to do this type of fundraising on its own.

There are many decisions to be made in forming a federation. Who is a member? How does the federation choose new members? What will the application process be? How will the money be distributed? Will it be divided evenly among all the members, given out according to each agency's need, given out in accordance with the wishes of the donor, or a combination of these three approaches? Fortunately, there are so many federated funds now that you can save yourself a lot of time by learning from their mistakes.

Once the federation has made these decisions, which can take many meetings and many months of negotiation and discussion, it must gain access to the workplace to solicit the funds. Since the United Way has dominated employee giving since 1946, it is understandably reluctant to share the stage with alternative funds. Employers may find it easier to limit access to the United Way only. Interestingly enough, however, studies show that when employees have several choices of funds to give to, and when they have Donor Option programs, total giving goes up. Some United Ways have discovered to their surprise that they did better when other funds were also allowed to solicit. This will not be a surprise to anyone who understands one of the basic premises of marketing, which is that customers buy more when they have more choices of products to buy.

Finally, because a great deal of money can be involved and because the politics of the organizations forming an alternative federation are often in clear conflict with those of the United Way and individual employers, groups may find themselves embroiled in legal battles to protect their right to free speech in soliciting employees.

Ultimately, as the nature of work changes — with fewer factories and assembly line jobs and more and more jobs in the technology sector; as a younger workforce, which has always experienced choices besides the United Way, comes into management; and as the United Way itself seeks to shake off its old image — workplace fundraising will continue to evolve. Since it is one of the most lucrative fundraising strategies, it is worth the effort of social change groups to be the leaders in the nature of that evolution.

nineteen

Door-to-Door Canvassing

Canvassing is a technique that involves a team of people from your organization going door-to-door requesting contributions for your group's work. The canvassing technique is used primarily by local groups and by local chapters of state or national organizations. Canvassing is primarily an organizing strategy; no organization should undertake a canvass simply to raise money. Canvasses work best when the organization is doing work that directly affects the people being canvassed. Canvassing is often used to get out the vote or to drum up support for a candidate or issue. Used in the context of organizing, canvassing can be an excellent acquisition strategy; by returning to neighborhoods, it can also be used for retaining donors.

While part-time or temporary canvasses can be run with volunteers, most canvassing is a full-time operation involving salaried or commissioned employees who work 40 hours a week and solicit in neighborhoods on a regular, revolving basis. Well-run canvasses can bring in from $50,000 to $500,000 or more in gross income. However, they are labor-intensive, generating high overhead that absorbs 60%–80% of the gross earnings of most canvasses.

ADVANTAGES AND DISADVANTAGES OF CANVASSING

There are three main advantages to canvassing as a fundraising strategy: First, an established, well-run canvass can provide a reliable, and sometimes substantial, source of income for your organization. Second, the volume of personal interaction from face-to-face contact with dozens of people each evening can bring in more new members than almost any other strategy. Third, canvassers bring back to the organization the public's opinions and perceptions of what your organization is doing.

There are also disadvantages to a canvass. If it is done on a full-time basis, it requires separate staff and office space as well as extensive bookkeeping and supervision. As with a small business, canvass income can be unreliable if the top canvass staff is disorganized or incompetent or if too many canvasses are operating in an area. The canvassers themselves can give the organization a bad reputation if they are unkempt, rude, or unpleasant to the people being canvassed. More and more, people are frightened by a stranger coming to their door and may not even answer. A final disadvantage is that many donors do not like to give to organizations that use canvassing because of the high overhead costs. While the amount of gross income can be impressive, these donors know that much of their donation is lost to overhead expenses.

ELEMENTS NEEDED TO RUN A CANVASS

Four elements must be present for an organization to operate an effective canvass. First, and most important, the organization must work on local issues. People give at the door when they perceive that an issue affects them and their neighborhood. The work of your organization can have national impact and your organization might be a branch of a national group, but in door-to-door canvassing, you must explain how this issue affects the resident directly.

Second, people must feel that even a small donation will make a difference. Most people make a cash donation to a canvass, and even a check will rarely be for more than $50. People must feel that their small donation is needed and will be well used.

Third, people must feel confident about your organization. Their confidence will be inspired by your organization's accomplishments, which must be clear and easy to discuss. Newspaper articles about your work are a major boon to canvassing. A specific plan of action that can be explained simply and quickly and that sounds effective is essential. The work of some organizations lends itself to canvassing, if it is on issues of general importance and interest to the majority of people, such as health care for all, lower utility rates, fixing up public parks. Citing litigation can work if the suit is easy to understand, and if there is a clear "good guy" (your group) and "bad guy." Complex regulatory reform and issues requiring historical background, legal knowledge, or patience in listening to a long explanation do not lend themselves to canvassing.

Finally, you must be able to distinguish your organization from any other organization doing similar work without implying any disrespect for the other organization. In some communities where there are not only two or more groups working on similar issues but also several groups canvassing, potential donors get confused and then angry that they are being solicited so often for issues that seem interrelated. People will explain to your canvassers that they just gave to your group last week, that someone from your organization was just there. No amount of protest from you will change their minds. The only thing that will help is to clearly distinguish your group from any other.

All these requirements for a successful canvass, except the focus on local work, are also necessary for many other fundraising strategies, particularly mail appeals and phone-a-thons, where the object is to get the donor's attention quickly and hold it long enough to get the gift.

SETTING UP A CANVASS

First, check state and local laws and ordinances concerning canvassing. If canvassing is heavily regulated in your community, it may not be worth the time involved to comply with the regulations. Some communities have tried to stop canvassing operations altogether by enacting ordinances governing what you can say when soliciting door-to-door and establishing strict qualifications for canvassers, including expensive licensing. If your canvass violates even a minor sub-regulation, it could be forced by the city or state to cease operation and may bring bad press for your organization. Many of these ordinances have been challenged in court and found unconstitutional, but most organizations have too much work to do to also take on costly and lengthy legal battles in this area.

You can find out about state laws governing canvassing from the attorney general's office, which generally monitors all rules related to charitable solicitation. Many states publish handbooks on canvassing regulations.

Local ordinances are sometimes more difficult to discover, since several city departments may have jurisdiction over different parts of the canvassing operation. Contact the police department and ask for notification and application procedures for a canvass. Be sure to write down whatever the person tells you, and get his or her name so that if you get a different story from another police official you can refer to this phone call.

Contact the city attorney's office for information regarding solicitation of money for charity. Sometimes the mayor's office has some jurisdiction over these matters. In general, informing as many people as possible about your canvassing operation will ensure the least amount of interference later.

Study the Demographics

After making sure that you can comply with the law, you must determine if your community is a good candidate for a canvass. Gather demographic data on your area: For various neighborhoods, find out the population density, the property values, how many of the people are homeowners, what type of work most people do, what the income levels are, and so forth. This information is available from various sources, including local people, items in the newspaper, volunteers and board members who have lived in the area, the Chamber of Commerce, and from developing your own sense from driving around the neighborhoods.

Remember one important point in assessing demographic data: A canvass rarely does well in an affluent neighborhood, and canvassers sometimes conclude that "rich people" are unfeeling tightwads. In fact, affluent people generally do not make contributions at the door. Their charitable giving is usually done through major gift solicitation, personal mail appeals, or special events. Canvassing operations do best in middle- and lower-income neighborhoods, where giving at the door is more common.

Another demographic item you need to evaluate is whether the population is dense enough per square mile to make it worthwhile to canvass. Canvassers need to be able to reach 80 to 100 homes per night (assuming a high number of people are not home). This means that there must be enough people in the area and that the terrain must be flat enough to allow canvassers to walk quickly from house to house. It is much harder to run a successful canvass in a rural area simply because of the distance between houses and because of the lack of people.

Finally, you need to evaluate whether the area is safe for canvassers. A good canvasser may be carrying $500 or more by the end of the evening, much of that in cash. Canvasses in high-crime areas (which still can be successful) sometimes send their canvassers in pairs, but this doubles the labor cost. Others have a roving car to check in on canvassers and to pick up their cash.

Hire Staff

If you determine that your area can support a canvass, you are ready to hire canvass staff and prepare materials for them.

The staff of a canvass varies from place to place but generally includes several individuals with the following roles:

Canvass director. This person supervises the entire canvass operation, including hiring and firing canvassers, researching areas to be canvassed and mapping out the revolving canvass for the area over the course of a year, keeping the organization in compliance with the law, keeping up-to-date on new laws, and planning and updating materials.

Field manager(s). Each of these staff people transports and supervises a team of five to seven canvassers. Each field manager assigns their team to various parts of the neighborhood, collects the money at the end of the evening, and trains new canvassers on the team. This person also participates as a canvasser.

Secretary/receptionist/bookkeeper/office manager. This support person manages the office, including keeping records of money earned by each canvasser, replacing canvass materials as needed, scheduling interviews with prospective canvassers for the canvass director, answering the phone, and generally acting as back-up person for the canvass operation. This person does not canvass.

Canvassers. These are the people actually carrying out the canvass. Canvassers work from 2 P.M. to 10 P.M. five days a week. They usually have a quota, that is, an amount of money they must raise every day or every week. Their pay is either a percentage of what they raise (commission), a straight salary, or, most commonly, a base salary plus commission.

Canvassers must represent the organization accurately and be respectable ambassadors for it. The individual canvasser is often the only person from the organization whom donors will see and may well be the only face they will ever associate with your group.

Because the pay is low and the hours long and arduous, there is a high turnover in canvass staff. In the summer, college students help expand canvassing staff. In the winter months, recruiting canvassers is more difficult, and in places where there is low unemployment, recruiting canvass staff can be almost impossible.

Materials

Canvassers must be equipped with various materials. These include any identification badges or licenses required by the city or state, newspaper clippings about the work of the group, a receipt book, and clipboards to carry the materials to be given away, which include brochures about the organization and return envelopes.

Many canvassers use a petition to get the attention of the person being canvassed. The canvasser will ask, "Would you sign a petition for..." and briefly explains the cause. While the person is signing, the canvasser will ask for a donation as well.

Canvassers should try to get the gift right at the door. However, for people who need to think about it or discuss it with a roommate or spouse, the canvasser can leave a brochure and a return envelope. A brochure should also be given to people making a donation, because on reading it, some of them will send an additional donation. Do not assume when people say they need to think about your request that they mean they are not going to give. This is a common mistake. Leave the materials and act as if you believe the person. Many people do not make any decision on the spur of the moment, and people who need to think about what their gift will be to your group may well become major donors.

All of the information is carried on a clipboard, which makes it easy to display and lends a degree of authority to the canvasser. People are more likely to open their doors to someone who looks like he or she has a good reason to be there.

The Canvasser's Workday

At the beginning of the canvassers' workday, their field manager describes the neighborhood they will be canvassing and relates any new information or special emphasis on issues that they should present to this neighborhood. The crew has a late lunch or early dinner and the field manager drives them to the canvass site. They begin canvassing around 4 P.M. and end at 9 P.M., when they are picked up by their field manager and taken back to the office. They turn in their money, make their reports, and finish around 10 P.M.

Because canvassing is hard work, essentially involving daily face-to-face solicitation with a "cold" list, it is critical that the rest of the organization's staff and its board members see the canvass staff as colleagues and as integral to the total operation of the organization. To help build this support, many organizations require non-canvass staff to canvass for an evening every couple of months.

Second only to quality of canvass staff in ensuring the success of a canvass is an efficient recordkeeping system. After each neighborhood is canvassed, an evaluation of the neighborhood should be filed along with the demographic data on that neighborhood that led to its being chosen as a canvass site. These data can then be reevaluated in the light of the canvassers' experience. Any special considerations, such as "no street lights," can also be noted in the evaluation.

Many people worry that theft by the canvassers will be a problem. Theft occurs no more often by canvass workers than by any others. Careless bookkeeping, however, can cost money and can give the impression that money has disappeared. At the end of the evening, both the canvasser and the field manager should count each canvasser's money brought in. The field manager enters the amounts under each canvasser's name on a "Daily Summary Sheet." The money and the summary sheet are then placed in a locked safe, and the secretary/bookkeeper will count the total again in the morning and make a daily deposit to the bank. At the end of the week the bookkeeper tallies the total receipt of each canvasser and prepares the payroll sheet.

Canvassers who fail to bring in their quota for more than a week must be retrained or fired. Strict discipline is important in a successful canvass, and keeping performance records will help to maintain a good canvass team.

Canvassing is an excellent strategy for some groups, and if done properly it can be a good way to mobilize members and make money. However, there are many pitfalls, and it is neither a simple nor a low-cost strategy. Canvassing changes the nature of the organization. It doubles or triples staff size and requires office space and additional equipment. Only groups that have thoroughly researched the pros and cons of canvassing should consider using this fundraising method.

twenty

Setting Up a Small Business

The idea of a nonprofit starting a small business seems sound at first: Sell something people want to buy and use the profits to finance your organization. For many years, nonprofit organizations have run small businesses — thrift stores, gift shops, concessions. More recently, a number of nonprofits have moved into the world of e-commerce and sell things online. Some nonprofit organizations have well-known multimillion-dollar businesses, such as the Girl Scouts' cookies, the Salvation Army's secondhand stores, and UNICEF's gift shops.

Despite these glowing examples of success, the unfortunate fact is that most nonprofits that have started small businesses have failed in this endeavor. Their failures were caused by the same factors that cause nine out of ten small businesses to fail: undercapitalization, poor management, inability to respond to market conditions, and underpricing of goods.

In addition to the problems that come with starting any small business, nonprofit organizations have several other problems. First, the staff and board members are often not business people themselves. In fact, they may have a distaste for business and capitalist ventures and feel uncertain about the politics of adding a commercial component to their work. Further, staff and board members are usually already putting in a great deal of time. Almost any staff person knows the feeling of being constantly behind in their work, always barely catching up, conscious of tasks that never get done. Board members, squeezing in time for the organization between jobs, families, and other commitments, know this feeling also. To expect board and staff to help establish and supervise a business on top of these time commitments is often unrealistic.

To start a small business an organization must be financially sound. A successful small business takes three to five years to show a profit and should not be seen as a "quick fix" to financial difficulties. Even after three to five years of development a small business will provide, at the most, 10% of an organization's budget. The main problem in thinking of a small business as an income stream for an organization is the sheer cost of doing business. Even though some industries are more profitable than others, a 5% net profit is a conservative but realistic amount to estimate you draw from the business on yearly basis. If you wanted the business to contribute $10,000 to your organization's income, the business would have to gross $200,000. Certainly this is not impossible, but it would require an enormous commitment on the part of the group to create the business, keep it going until it shows a profit, and then continue to keep it profitable.

In figuring out the profit margin from a business, groups must keep in mind that not all the profit can be given to the organization's work. Some money must be reserved for business slumps and to reinvest in the business to ensure its long-term growth. Of course, if you are able to run your business using volunteers instead of paid staff, or by providing certain kinds of training your paid staff expenses are subsidized by government grants, you may be able to show a higher profit because your staff costs do not need to be covered by income from the business.

This chapter details the types of businesses nonprofits are allowed to engage in, their tax consequences, and the risks and benefits of a small business for a nonprofit.

TYPES OF SMALL BUSINESSES FOR NONPROFITS

There are two broad categories of business that a nonprofit may engage in under existing tax law. One is called a "related" business. In a related business the profits from the business are exempt from income tax. To qualify, the business activities must "contribute importantly" to the accomplishment of the organization's mission. While there is no limit on how much can be earned from a related business, salaries cannot exceed general market levels for comparable work. Many organizations that run related businesses use them to help promote program work. For example, several domestic violence programs have thrift stores where survivors of domestic violence learn business skills of various sorts, from sales to bookkeeping, and where people who have had to leave home with only what they could carry can buy what they need to start a new home or new life.

The other broad category is an "unrelated business": that is, the product or services sold do not advance the mission of the group. In that case the organization must pay tax on the business's income at a corporate rate. A serious problem with an unrelated business is that if the business activity is "substantial" compared to the nonprofit activity, the nonprofit may lose its tax-exempt status. This happens in cases where the business becomes so consuming that the purpose of the organization seems to be to run the business rather than to run the organization.

There are a few circumstances under which income tax is not collected even from unrelated businesses, including the following:

- The bulk of the work is done by unpaid volunteers

- The products sold have been donated to the nonprofit

- The revenue comes from the rental of property for which little or no property management services are provided

- Revenue comes from interest, dividends, investments, or royalty income

The key element the Internal Revenue Service uses to evaluate the continuation of the organization's tax-exempt status in the case of a business component is whether the nonprofit organization has an unfair advantage over a profit-making business and is thus engaging in "unfair competition." Because a nonprofit organization's related business does not pay income tax, it can reinvest that money to expand the business faster than a for-profit concern. Under pressure from the Small Business Administration, small business owners, and sometimes the general public, the IRS is being more and more strict about what kinds of taxes nonprofits can avoid. Because the livelihood of so many small businesses are imperiled by large chain stores, by the high cost of borrowing money, and by high labor costs, they watch closely the benefits that nonprofits are granted in starting and running businesses and insist that these businesses be closely related to the nonprofits' work. To avoid the accusation of unfair competition and to avoid losing your tax-exempt status, your group can opt to incorporate the business as an entirely separate entity and pay "unrelated business income tax" (UBIT). The business then donates its profit to your organization.

Remember: The laws governing businesses are complicated and somewhat vague. Groups should always consult an attorney and a business advisor about their situation before proceeding with a business.

ARE YOU READY FOR A SMALL BUSINESS?

Several elements must be present before an organization is ready to start a small business. First, the organization should have a strong donor base, regular special events, and an ongoing program of recruiting new donors. In other words, the organization should not need the money from the small business. A small business is a further strategy for diversifying sources of income for a group that already has diverse sources from the more traditional fundraising strategies and is looking ahead five years or more to other strategies.

An organization must also have people who are very committed to the idea of the nonprofit starting a small business, and it would be best if many of these people own or have owned successful small businesses of their own. These people can constitute a planning group to do the research necessary to decide if and what kind of a small business is appropriate. An organization with all of these elements in place can then consider starting a business.

The organization must have or borrow the start-up capital to open the business. Starting a business almost always takes more money than is planned and that money almost always takes longer to recoup than is anticipated. Small nonprofit organizations, which often live from month to month, are obviously not going to have the financial reserves to risk on starting a business. Even for groups that are financially sound and have some financial reserves, deciding to risk them on the gamble of a business is a difficult decision. Borrowing the money does not solve your problem because the money must be paid back. With borrowed money, the board of directors, some of whom will sign for the loan and may even put up collateral for it, are personally liable for the loan.

The Risks

An organization must reflect on several major risks in undertaking a business venture. The most obvious risk is that the business will fail. If the business goes bankrupt, the nonprofit corporation and its board of directors may be liable for any debts the business has incurred. If the business was begun with a loan secured by the board of directors, some of their personal assets may be vulnerable. If the product is faulty, the staff unfriendly, the price too high, the place dirty, and so forth, there is the danger that the business will give the organization a bad reputation. A bad business reputation attached to your organization will not only affect the success of your business, it will also hamper your fundraising and organizing endeavors.

A second risk is that the business will not fail but will be so marginal that it becomes a financial and emotional drain to the organization. Any profits the business makes will have to be reinvested into the business or, if it operates at a loss, the organization will have to decide whether to invest more money in it. This is a drain in many ways, not the least of which is the stress involved in deciding whether to persevere, hoping that time will make the difference and the business will become successful, or to cut your losses and bail out. If you decide to persevere, how long do you keep the business going? What will progress look like? All the fancy business plans in the world cannot ease the anxieties involved in running a business.

A further risk, as discussed above, is that the organization will lose its tax-exempt status.

The Gains

The advantages of a successful business are tremendous. First, of course, the organization can count on a reasonable amount of income from the business on a regular basis. Second, the skills acquired in learning how to run the small business are useful in all aspects of fundraising and financial management for the entire organization. Many organizations that have small business ventures have discovered that the management of the overall organization is greatly strengthened. When an organization is strong and well managed it is more attractive to donors and more money can be raised.

Third, just as an excellent and repeating fundraising event increases visibility for a group on an annual basis, a business does so on a daily basis. A good business draws people in who may never have heard of your organization. Some of these people may become more involved with your group as donors and volunteers, and others will simply patronize your business because they like what you sell even if they don't care about the goals of your group.

For direct service organizations a business can sometimes provide valuable training and job experience for clients.

STARTING A SMALL BUSINESS

The planning phase prior to starting a small business can be years long. The shortest time frame will probably be a year if you do a proper job of getting board and volunteer ownership of the idea, thoroughly investigating the law, and developing a formal business plan. The beginning of your process should be an examination of other nonprofits that have businesses in your community. Interview the director or manager of the business. Is it successful? How long did it take to show a profit? How did they decide on their product or service? Patronize their business. What does it feel like to be a customer? Read a few books about starting small businesses. The Small Business Administration has a wide variety of free periodicals and your local library will probably have a shelf full of "how-to" books about starting and running various businesses.

Above all, think about what else you want from a business besides money. There are many faster ways for an organization to raise money than starting and running a business. Other goals must be paramount in pursuing this idea, such as wanting an income stream outside of charitable sources altogether, seeing the business as a good opportunity to promote visibility, using the business to pursue program goals such as job training, and seeing the customer base of the business as possible donors.

You may want to test the idea of a small business by offering products for sale through your group, such as T-shirts, mugs, books, or tote bags. Note the ease or difficulty with which you distribute these items and the kind of profit you are able to make. If your organization is good at selling products and you seem to have a natural constituency of buyers and/or entrepreneurs among board and staff, then proceed. You will always learn valuable skills from the process of planning a small business venture, so even if you don't open the business, your time will not be wasted.

twenty-one

Religious Institutions, Service Clubs, and Small Businesses

eople familiar with raising money from religious institutions, service clubs, and small businesses will rightly state that each of these could use a chapter of their own or even a short book. Because they are not technically in the taxonomy of raising money from individual donors, however, I am not going to give them that kind of attention. Nevertheless, I believe that grassroots organizations should know that these sources may be useful to them and have at least a cursory understanding of how they work. The purpose of this chapter is to provide an overview of these sources.

Religious groups, service clubs, and small businesses often provide some funding to community groups, neighborhood projects, and projects with low budgets. With rare exceptions, national organizations will not get money from these sources, as they tend to concentrate their giving on local projects. All three of these sources can be asked to support specific projects with financial contributions or to give specific in-kind items such as office supplies, raffle prizes, or the use of space. These groups should also be approached as audiences for speaking engagements to broaden your visibility. Once you have received money or services from any of these sources you have a good chance of having the gift repeated. Few groups, however, will find any of these to be sources of major funding.

RELIGIOUS INSTITUTIONS

In Chapter 1, Philanthropy in America, I noted that religious institutions receive about half of the money given away by the private sector in America. Religious institutions use most of the money they raise to pay for their own programs: maintaining buildings, paying staff, providing dues to their national offices, offering scholarships for seminary students, and supporting various mission programs in America and abroad. However, organized religion is also a major source of funds for other, secular nonprofit organizations. We don't know exactly how much is given away by religious institutions; because of the separation of church and state they are not required to report their giving. However, reliable studies show that organized religion's philanthropic giving to nonreligious activities exceeds that of foundations and corporations combined, putting churches right behind individuals as the largest source of charitable giving.

Most grants from religious sources are in the range of $500 to $10,000. Some large sources, such as the Catholic Campaign for Human Development, the Unitarian Universalist Veatch Program, or the Episcopalian United Thank Offering, give $30,000 to $75,000 in multi-year grants to some of their grantees. Within local houses of worship, the Women's Guild or the Altar Society may give donations of anywhere from $50 to $1,000 to a few local groups.

Each religious body has lines of accountability (some more, some less) flowing from the local house of worship through regional structures to national offices. Not all religious institutions have national offices, but most that give money do. In churches, the regional structures are called "judicatories" and you will need to be familiar with how they are organized in each denomination to understand the giving process of most churches. If you want to understand the structure of any Christian denomination, the *Yearbook of American and Canadian Churches* (check your library) is an excellent resource for seeing the whole picture. In some religious bodies, there are also regional or national programs that make contributions, or there may be ecumenical efforts in one community focused on one population or set of issues. The best known of these are the Catholic Campaign for Human Development, the United Church of Christ's Board of Homeland Ministries, the United Methodist Voluntary Service, the Jewish Fund for Justice, the American Friends Service Committee (Quaker), the Unitarian Universalist Service Committee, and the ecumenical Commission on Religion in Appalachia (CORA). Many orders of nuns and priests provide funding to local groups as well. To learn more about formal giving programs such as these, research them as you would foundations and approach them in much the same way.

All faith-based communities can give contributions if they choose. The best guide to which local religious institutions are in your area is the Yellow Pages. Find out who in your group is affiliated with any of the major religious institutions listed. In most cases, in order to seek a gift from a religious institution, your group will need to have a relationship with the clergy or a leading layperson. Then, there are several avenues for obtaining local funding:

- A clergyperson can give a group money (generally up to $1,000) from a discretionary fund that he or she has authority over.

- In churches that take up a collection, the minister or laypeople can call for a "second collection." In that case, after the collection for the church has been taken at Sunday service, the minister or representative from your group will describe your work to the congregation and the collection plate will be passed again. The proceeds from this second collection go to your group. Some organizations have formalized this into a "Second-Collection Sunday," on which churches all over a town will take up a second collection for an organization. Many domestic violence programs do Second-Collection Sundays during Domestic Violence Awareness Month.

- Within most congregations, there are various guilds and clubs, each of which does its own fundraising and many of which distribute the money as they wish. Generally, any house of worship will have at least one women's guild, several mission programs (the money from which can be used for "domestic" missions), and youth projects.

- Houses of worship often make their facilities available free or for a nominal charge. These can include meeting rooms, office space, use of a photocopy machine, limited use of a computer, telephone, or fax machine, and so forth. For groups just getting started, these services can be invaluable, as the facility can also serve as your mailing address and staff may agree to receive phone messages for you until you are established.

Remember that certain denominations take stands on specific issues. One obvious example is the Catholic Church's stand against freedom of choice in abortion and birth control. Many churches have reaffirmed their position that homosexuality is incompatible with Christian life. Almost all religious institutions place a strong emphasis on the integrity of the family, the importance of marriage, and other traditional values.

When I was first in fundraising, I was in charge of raising money from churches and synagogues for a shelter for battered women. I went to a minister who was very sympathetic but told me the only fund he could draw from for our program was the flower fund. It seemed that someone had died and left the church a very large bequest, the interest from which was to be used for flowers. He said, "I can write you a check today for $500 to be used for flowers for your shelter." Not wanting to turn down money, but also not really wanting $500 worth of flowers, I said, "That's a lot of flowers." He said, "Buy a few flowers every month or plant some flowers — whatever you wish. We realize that we cannot visit the shelter and so we will never be able to see our flowers, and that's OK." He was smiling broadly. I, being a little slow to catch on, said, "Would you like me to send you pictures of the flowers we buy?" With some impatience in his tone he said, "No pictures! What if someone recognized the house from the pictures or you accidentally photographed one of your residents? No pictures. We will trust your taste in flowers." Finally the light dawned that he was giving us $500. I quickly thanked him and left with the check.

SERVICE CLUBS

Every city, town, and village in America has service clubs whose members are active in civic and community affairs and often raise funds for various community causes. The most common service clubs are Rotary, Kiwanis, Lions, Oddfellows, Shriners, Moose, Elk, Ruritan, Soroptomist, Zonta, and the Junior League. Some of these clubs restrict membership to one sex, but increasingly these clubs welcome both men and women.

Sometimes service clubs simply adopt an organization or a program for which they then sponsor an annual fundraising event. Organizations adopted for such support are usually Boys' and Girls' Clubs, camps, scholarship funds, school programs, or vocation-specific programs, such as a trip to Washington, D.C., for young people wanting to go into politics, specially equipped vans for disabled people needing to get to college classes, and so forth. Service clubs will also give funds to buy equipment and will occasionally give to capital campaigns.

A group can approach a service club in one of two ways. If you have contact with someone in the club who knows the club's fundraising program, ask if that person will advocate with the club for a donation to your group. If you don't know anyone in a service club, write or call the club for the name of the volunteer in charge of the program for monthly meetings, and then write or call him or her and volunteer a speaker from your group. Most groups will gratefully accept your offer.

Clubs' politics, commitment, and size and level of activity vary greatly from community to community. Therefore, research the clubs in your town to find out what, if anything, they can do for you.

SMALL BUSINESSES

Groups seeking money from corporations and large businesses are often surprised by the generosity of owners of small stores and sole proprietors of businesses compared with the frequent lack of response from bigger operations with more money.

Small businesses are best approached for in-kind rather than cash donations. Businesses can give raffle prizes, buy ads in an adbook, give your group items at wholesale cost (or at discounts for volume purchasing), underwrite special events, and buy tables at your luncheons or dinners. The key element in securing a business donation is to show the business person that his or her business will materially benefit from supporting your group. For example, in soliciting a raffle prize, stress how many people will see the raffle ticket with the business's name on it and how many will read the listing of supporting businesses in your newsletter. One raffle prize is a small investment for all that advertising.

Businesses that sell supplies that your group uses, such as office supplies or paper products, sometimes find that they need to discontinue a product line that isn't selling or to reduce inventory. Be sure you let them know that you will be glad to receive donations of such products.

Businesses can also extend credit to your group, enabling you to buy needed items and to pay when your cash flow is better. As long as you are trustworthy and keep in touch with them, businesses may be willing to carry a debt for quite some time.

Most business people belong to one or more business associations that meet regularly and need speakers. By being invited to one of these meetings, you can meet many business people at once. Use the same procedures as for getting a speaking engagement with a service club.

The economic conditions of your community and the health of small businesses generally will affect your ability to raise funds or services from them. If you show, however, that it is in their self-interest to help you, you will be able to expand your fundraising to these areas.

One of the main advantages of raising money from any of these sources is that it leads you to a new group of individual donors and helps you to broaden your base. With proper follow-up, all of these sources can be valuable additions to your fundraising plans.

twenty-two

The Internet

The most significant change in fundraising since the last edition of this book, written in 1994, is the increasing use of the Internet for fundraising. E-mail, Web sites, charity portals, e-commerce — all terms that have become common in the last few years — are very new in the lexicon of fundraising, and the effect of the Internet on fundraising is still in its infancy. That it will easily change fundraising at least as dramatically as direct mail did in the 1970s and 1980s, or even as workplace fundraising did when it began in the 1940s, is not in debate. How that will happen and what the pros and cons of these changes will be remain to be seen.

Right now, there are three types of reactions to the idea of using the Internet to raise money: unbridled enthusiasm, particularly on the part of people who love new things and on the part of those for-profits that see a lot of profit in it for themselves; a curious but cautious "Let's-not-jump-in-the-deep-end" approach from people who have seen a lot of new things come and go; and the increasingly rare reaction, "What is the Internet?" from those on the other side of the digital divide.

This chapter describes some of the ways small nonprofits can take advantage of the Internet and encourages readers to keep exploring but not to take anyone's word (including mine) for granted.

The advantages of the Internet, especially in the United States, are clear. More than 50 million Americans use the Internet every week, and millions more have daily access to it at their workplace or use it from time to time at their local library. The government, often in partnership with corporations in the computer and technology business, places increasing emphasis on the need to close that part of the digital divide created by class, and to make sure that all schoolchildren have access to computers and learn how to use them. Given the exponential rate at which

Internet access and familiarity with it is growing, it is clear that in ten years anyone in the United States who wants to will probably be able to "log on," either from home or from some public facility set up for that purpose. For many nonprofits, organizing and fundraising via the Internet and a site on World Wide Web is tailor-made for a culture that increasingly expects everything to be available all the time. The Web is a 24/7 (another new phrase) proposition that allows your organization to be "open" across time zones and international boundaries, even when your office is not.

Of course, the shadow side of all this availability is built into its success — massive competition, lots of sites with junk, enormous amounts of junk e-mail (spam), viruses introduced by hackers that can shut down computer systems around the world, secured areas accessed by hackers out to steal credit card numbers of donors and customers (who are only gradually becoming comfortable committing them to cyberspace), misinformation, lies, and propaganda as common as useful information, and a public that may eventually tire of this new toy, probably decreasing the response to it. Further, any time a person spends online is time they are not spending with other people. The Internet has exponentially added to the isolation of many people, who confuse chat rooms with community.

Despite its drawbacks, there are effective ways your small organization can take advantage of all that is good about the Internet without losing a lot of time in pursuits that may not be so useful and without spending a lot of money that you don't have.

USING E-MAIL

The vast majority of even tiny nonprofits now have e-mail, and if you don't have it, you need to get it. In a few years, and in some highly cyber-connected communities, not having e-mail will put you at the same disadvantage as not having a telephone.

The first step in using the Internet for fundraising is to gather as many e-mail addresses of donors as you can and send them an e-mail newsletter once a month or once a quarter. Your e-mail newsletter can have much the same content as your paper newsletter (some groups simply post their newsletter online and no longer mail it), and will be read by people who don't read your paper newsletter. Ideally, your e-mail newsletter will also have different information and will be shorter than your paper newsletter. You may even wish to give donors a choice of getting the newsletter online or in the mail, and, depending on the demographics of your donor base, you will find that many people prefer the online newsletter. For you, that can be good news. Posting your newsletter online rather than through the mail saves paper and postage, so is a cost saver for your group. Further, people often forward these newsletters over the Internet when they would not take the time to do the same with a paper newsletter. Some organizations, particularly those dealing with environmental issues, have ceased to send a regular paper newsletter altogether and have gone to an e-mail-only format. E-mail is especially effective for posting information "alerts" or "calls to action" — anything that requires an instant response.

Some organizations have an e-mail newsletter that is different from, and in addition to, their paper newsletter. They build a list of subscribers to the e-mail newsletter, and try to convince some of them to receive the paper newsletter, which will be longer or have more articles and more opportunities to showcase the organization's work and ask for donations. You can also ask your e-mail subscribers for money, giving them a form to download to go with a check, or providing a way to donate online by credit card (see "Creating a Secured Area," later in this chapter).

You can also use e-mail to correspond with donors (although do not use it for thank-you notes). When you call a donor who uses e-mail, if you have to leave a message, leave your phone number and your e-mail address. I've heard a number of stories of donors engaging in conversations and eventually making a gift by e-mail.

E-mail is an excellent way to keep board members and volunteers posted on internal happenings that would be interesting to them but would not go in a general newsletter. Many groups use e-mail to encourage board member efforts in fundraising with notes like this: "Update on Major Donor Campaign. Eric Johnson just concluded a request for $1,000 and the donor is sending it today. He is following up with three other prospects. Martha was finally able to set up a meeting with the two donors who may give us $10,000 on Tuesday. Keep your fingers crossed. Earlyse is the leader in number of gifts so far — five @ $50 and four @ $100! Good work, everyone!"

Some organizations have created an internal e-mail list of board and staff members, enabling any of them to post information to the group. Some organizations have a member listserv, where any member can ask a question or give advice or announce upcoming events. This is particularly useful in coalitions or associations of several organizations. Generally someone will need to moderate the listserv to make sure that one or two people don't dominate or that the content stays focused.

DEVELOPING AND USING A WEB SITE

In the same way that every group should have and use e-mail, any organization that serves a wide geographic area or that has appeal outside of its immediate geographic boundaries should probably have a Web site. I say "probably" because the verb "have" does not really describe what a group has to do with a Web site. The notion of "having" a Web site has led many groups down a garden path to invest money (sometimes a lot of money) into building an attractive site, but they then have no more money or staff time to maintain the site, drive traffic to the site, or create links to the site. The group is then disappointed with the technology of the Web.

If you are going to have a Web site, you need to have someone (a Webmaster) who maintains and updates the site, and you need to constantly advertise the site in various ways. Your Web site should have an icon on every page that says something like "Click here to donate," or, "You can help." Clicking on that icon then brings people to a page that tells them how to donate. You can also ask for money right on every content page of your site and, of course, on your home page. This allows you to give the reader a different reason to donate on every page.

Links are key to driving traffic to your site. You should certainly have a link and be linked to any organization similar to yours. With some organizations, vendors and board members link to the group's site, so that, for example, someone looking at an office supply site can go to the office supply site's favorite nonprofit clients. Sometimes business sites and Internet sites will donate banner ads on their sites calling attention to your nonprofit, which also increases traffic.

Advertising the existence of your Web site in all your written materials, including business cards, newsletters, direct mail appeals, thank-you notes, and so on, is also critical. Your Web site address should be on your letterhead, the sign on your door, and even on your answering machine.

The second most important element to driving traffic to your site is to register with all the major search engines. You need to think of all keywords related to your work and register those with as many search engines as you can. This is a laborious and ongoing process, but it is well worth it.

Of course, all of this means that when the people you have successfully advertised your site to actually visit it, they must have a good experience and want to come back. If you have used your site to advertise your Annual General Meeting, for example, and to allow people to register for the meeting online, then three weeks after the meeting is over, you don't want that advertisement still there (in fact, not even three days later). In addition, your work plan for the Annual General Meeting now needs to include posting reports on your Web site at the end of each day of the meeting of what happened that day, then posting a full report and possibly a few pictures within two or three days of the end of the meeting.

As with beginning a direct mail program, an organization shouldn't enter the World Wide Web unless they are able to really work with it. Some may disagree (they can write their own books), but I strongly believe that having no site is better than having a bad site.

Creating a Secured Area

Organizations that already have the capacity to accept credit cards and electronic funds transfers, and who have items they can sell, or expect to receive a number of donations through their Web site, will want to get a "secured area" — a place that people can key in their credit card number to donate or buy right online with the assurance that their transaction is safe. Many organizations have found receiving donations or making sales this way to be extremely lucrative, but it is also an added layer of work. Someone has to download the orders and fill them. The site has to be programmed to send an instant message acknowledging the order or donation. Credit card numbers have to be processed. All of this will be worth it as the site gets more traffic and more donations come in, but there is an initial investment that will take a few months to a year to pay off (see Bibliography for information about setting up secured areas).

Costs

Web sites can cost anywhere from a few thousand dollars to $100,000 to design and maintain; higher costs do not necessarily mean better sites. Some organizations have been able to get the design of their site donated by a Web site designer just getting started who wants to have something to show clients, from a class of students learning Web site design, or even from an established designer willing to do pro bono work. Spending a lot of time trying to get your Web site designed and set up for free, however, is not as good a use of time as trying to get someone to maintain your site for free or to train staff people in how to maintain it, because the cost of a Web site is ongoing. Dropping unprofitable fundraising strategies and freeing up the money to focus on your Web site is one way to pay for it. Many groups have found the money for their site simply by dropping people from their mailing list who have never donated or haven't made a gift in several years. One organization with a mailing list of 10,000 and a donor base of 2,000 dropped 5,000 names from their list after they figured out that it was costing them $2 per person per year to keep them on the list. They invested the $10,000 they saved into creating and maintaining what is now a very successful Web site. Other ways to find funding are to see if you have donors who work in e-commerce whose firms may have money earmarked for this purpose, and to investigate foundations that are beginning to help groups with Internet infrastructure.

CHARITY PORTALS

Many for-profits and a few nonprofits are offering to list a variety of charities on a site, with a description of each charity and a way to donate to each one. Such sites are called "charity portals." The theory is that there are people wanting to give money who do not have a way to find groups that meet their values. These people would go to a charity portal, look under "children" or "environment" or whatever they care most about, and find names and descriptions of groups they can give to. When they donate, the sponsor of the portal takes a small percentage of the donation and sends the rest to the specified charity. Some portals are designed to let people buy products, then donate a percent of the sale to a charity.

If you decide to register with a portal, try to choose one that is itself a nonprofit. Make sure you know what you get from being registered and what the costs are. Also make sure you will get the name and address of the donor and not just the money the donor sent. Some donors have been disgruntled to learn that the charity they chose never knew who they were, but their name was sold to other Internet companies or catalog companies wanting to expand their pool of potential customers.

Remember that, above all, you want people coming to your Web site, and anything you do, including being listed on another site, needs to lead to that end.

NO MIRACLE, BUT ANOTHER STRATEGY TO EXPLORE

The Internet is neither a miracle cure to your fundraising problems nor something to be suspicious of. It is simply another strategy. It appeals to a younger crowd, generally well educated and possibly affluent. It appeals to people who feel that they have little or no time. Through search engines, it allows people to find out about your group without having to know the name of your organization or without having to actually talk to someone about it. The Internet can be used to build a certain kind of community and feeling of belonging on the part of people who may never make it to your office or to an event. The use of the Internet is something that is growing exponentially and will not go away any time soon.

Using the Internet effectively requires an ongoing investment of time and money. For groups that make that investment and don't try to short-circuit the process, it can be worth the effort.

Fundraising Management

Fundraising for low-budget organizations generally falls apart because of one of the following three difficulties:

- Strategies are not used properly and so are rendered ineffective.

- The organization doesn't have a clear case, or loses sight of its mission and goals in its search for funding.

- Fundraising is not managed properly — there are bad recordkeeping systems, the fundraising staff have more than their own jobs to do, and the organization cannot keep to its plans.

This section is meant to help organizations forestall the last difficulty. Starting with the office and basic working conditions, and covering finding staff, consultants, and volunteers for fundraising, this section explains what has to be in place for effective fundraising to happen.

twenty-three

The Fundraising Office

Few offices of low-budget organizations are adequate in size, equipment, or support staff. Buying state-of-the-art computer equipment and hiring more and more administrators and secretaries are not options, but there are basic requirements for fundraising staff to carry out an effective program. The same requirements hold true whether your fundraising program is run by volunteers or by paid staff. Some of the requirements detailed here cost money; but they will pay for themselves and these costs should be seen as front money. Other requirements cost time, which also must be seen as a front-end cost.

SPACE AND MATERIALS

There must be a separate space in the office for fundraising staff, files, and materials — preferably a room or at least a partitioned area. This space must be quiet and include a desk of adequate size with drawers, a chair, a filing cabinet with at least three drawers, and a telephone. (Some of this equipment can be obtained for free from corporations.) A bookshelf and other storage space, such as a closet, are also important. The space must have proper lighting and ventilation, and it should not be used by people other than fundraising staff and volunteers — too much of the information here is confidential. Moreover, files, mailing lists, reports, letters, and the like need to be kept in order and should not be touched by anyone who is not dealing with them. Fundraising staff should have access to a good computer with a word processing program and database for donor records. Preferably, one computer should be dedicated to fundraising.

The organization must take the fundraising process seriously. Both paid and volunteer fundraising staff should be seen as professionals, needing certain tools to carry out their job. A computer, desk, filing cabinet, phone, and separate space are the tools of a fundraiser in the same way, and with the same importance, as hammers, saws, levels, and the like are the tools of a carpenter. Just as you can't build a building without construction equipment, you can't build a donor base without fundraising equipment.

In addition to an adequate office set-up, a fundraiser should have a basic library of fundraising books, as well as a dictionary, thesaurus, and style manual to aid in writing and planning. (See Bibliography for a recommended basic library.)

Obviously, fundraising staff should not have nicer office space or fancier equipment than everyone else in the office. The whole organization should examine its working conditions from time to time and make it a priority to improve them if needed. It is ironic that many social change or social service groups will work in conditions that include too much noise, dim light, inadequate equipment, and so on when they would be outraged to read about such conditions for other workers. Good working conditions cost time and money, but poor working conditions cost more: lower productivity, stress, burn-out, loss of creativity, loss of information, and, finally, loss of income to keep the organization going.

twenty-four

Managing Information

A major part of fundraising is information — about people, about sources of money, about timing, about strategies. But fundraising is not just knowing things. The creativity to make fundraising successful is in putting things together: asking the right person at the right time for the right amount; scheduling the right event and inviting the people most likely to be interested to attend; using volunteers to the best of their abilities.

In order to use all the information available in the most effective ways, a fundraiser must know how to manage the information in his or her office. Often when you visit the office of a fundraising staff person, you notice piles of papers on the floor, on the table, and on the windowsill, unlabeled computer disks, multiple phone books and foundation guides, a desk strewn with notes, Post-its stuck to every surface, and a telephone perched precariously atop the overflowing in-basket.

Too often we mistake the message of such an office — the inability to handle paper — with overcommitment on the part of the staff person. Since overcommitment is often a major component of many fundraisers' workstyles, one compounds the other. A fundraiser confided to me recently that she was secretly relieved when her office flooded and many of her papers as well as her computer were destroyed. She now had an excuse for not getting work done she wouldn't have gotten to anyway.

What has been called for the past two decades the "information age" is rapidly turning into the information glut. Not only are there increasing numbers of books, magazines, newsletters, and newspapers related to fundraising, but in addition to these traditional sources of information there is the seemingly endless number of sources of information to be gained or used by computer: dozens of search engines and millions of Web sites, computer programs to help you gather and sort information in ways you never thought of, CD-ROMs, and thousands of toll-free numbers to help you access even more information. For information to be useful at all, it does not have to be gathered so much as filtered and sorted. There is more to know about everything than any human can process, plus there are mountains of disinformation.

People in fundraising must always be clear about what they need to do and what they don't. This chapter will help you deal with the overload of information.

INFORMATION YOU NEED FOR FUNDRAISING

In order to know what to keep, what to throw out, what to delete, what to order, and what to file, you must make a list of priorities about your job. What information do you need to be on top of, what do you need to have access to from time to time, and what doesn't matter at all? While the answers to these questions will vary from person to person, most fundraisers must keep track of the following information, which is the most important to their work:

- Information pertaining to current donors

- Information pertaining to prospects

- Information about the organization that will be used to get more donors and prospects

- Reference materials and records about past fundraising activities

To keep track of this information, set up three filing cabinet drawers and three main directories on your computer that reflect these priorities: current donors, prospects, and information that will attract donors. Any papers that come across your desk that pertain to anything else should go into the recycling box. Among other items that will get tossed are newsletters from other groups unrelated to your group, advertisements for seminars and classes, catalogs, annual reports of foundations your group will not be applying to and old annual reports of prospective foundations, old to-do lists, and reports on all causes unrelated to your group. Similarly, delete from your computer any information you downloaded from the Web or that was sent to you in an e-mail or that you have in a file on your computer that is not related to the three main directories you have established. In your physical filing cabinet, use the bottom file drawer for reference material from your group. In it, put one copy of each of your past newsletters, one copy of proposals funded, evaluations of direct mail appeals, reports on special events, board minutes and reports, and financial statements.

Every piece of paper and every byte in your computer should be held up to this test: Will this help me get money from someone? If yes, who? How? Put it in the prospect's file, or in the reference drawer if it might be needed for reference (such as board finance reports). If the answer for any piece of paper or computer file is no, throw it out or delete it or pass on it to another staff person whose work it will help.

Simple Rules

Once you learn a few simple rules about what to keep and what to save, keeping track of information will actually not be that difficult.

First, review the basics. What is your job? What do you have to know? What would people reasonably expect you to be able to lay your hands on quickly? Even if you are the only paid staff person, you still have a limit to your job.

- You must have records of official meetings of the organization, and reports offered to the board, the public, or the IRS about the organization. Keep one (at most two) copies of minutes, audits, 990 forms, newsletters, direct mail appeals, annual reports, etc.

- You must have records on the donors: their names, addresses, and gift history, as well as information that would help you or someone else ask them for more money or for some other type of involvement.

There are other items you probably should have if you are a one-person shop — you decide. But do you really need copies of newsletters from organizations you are not interested in? Dozens of samples of invitations? (Pick the best ten and throw the rest away.) The latest reports from the most prolific think tanks on every subject from the ozone to police brutality, campaign reform to the role of women in rural Hindu communities? No. What is your group? Read only what pertains to you.

Having set priorities on what kind of information you need — and limiting yourself to five priorities at the most — sort all your papers into those categories and throw away anything that doesn't fall into them. Especially throw away the volumes of information you now keep that you feel you "should" read. The stuff that you bring home but never quite get to, and take on business trips but always manage to find something else to read. If you feel like you "should" read it, you won't. Get off your own case and lighten up. It's all right not to read everything, or even not to read most things.

The final guideline about what to throw out is that if you haven't looked at it in six months, and it is not needed for the IRS or as an archive copy, throw it out.

KEEPING TRACK

Setting up filing systems now involves not only dealing with the masses of paper that arrive at your desk, but with virtual files as well.

The Physical Files

Think through your filing system. Many people simply put their files into alphabetical order and call it a day. I was in an office recently where the personnel policies were filed right behind a donor named "Alice Pershing," followed a few files later by one called "Policies." I asked the staff person how she decided what to file under "Personnel" and what under "Policies." She had no answer.

Create broad categories, then file within those categories. Categories might include board, donors, prospects, foundations, finances, programs, personnel, and publications. Inside some of those categories, you may want subcategories. For example, the board section might have the following subcategories: board members — current, past, potential; board reimbursements; board minutes; staff reports to the board. Some of these categories will then contain alphabetical files, but some will be easier to find if you file them chronologically. For example, board minutes and reports to the board should be filed chronologically.

To test your filing system, ask a friend or another staff person to come into your office and start naming things for you to find. You should be able to lay your hands on any piece of paper you are in charge of in 30 seconds. If you can't do that, reassess your system. Once your system passes this test, see how well it works for someone else. Suppose you were hit by a train, how transparent is your information set-up? If it takes someone else more than five minutes to figure out where something is, your system is too mysterious.

The Electronic Files

Finally, there is the subject of files in your computer. This is more beguiling because you don't often notice how much room these are taking up — the "clutter" is invisible, so it is easy to let hard disks get overloaded and chaotic. I have watched people scroll through their directories and subdirectories with the same intensity and frustration with which they previously tried to sort through their papers.

The same standards apply to computer files as to paper files: Will you need it again? What category and subcategory should it be listed under?

When you save something on your computer, think about what you name it. There are people who name their files after their lover of the moment, or the day of the week, or even some abbreviation of something in the file, but all of this makes the files obscure even to the one who named them. Again, apply the standard, "If I were hit by a train, could someone else find this?" Give it a name that makes some sense.

STICKING WITH IT

To help you stay on top of your papers and computer files once you get organized, post a 3" × 5" card with the one, two, or three things that will most help you keep clear on what to keep. One person has this on his card:

> Is it a donor?
> Is it a prospect?
> Could it lead to a donor or a prospect?

Another has this:

> When in doubt, throw it out.
> After all, what is the worst thing that can happen?

Another's says:

> If this were my last day at work, and I was sorting through my stuff, would I give it to the person succeeding me?

In our business, information is like food: We eat it, we serve it to others, we save it for a few days, but we don't keep it permanently. It is useful for what it does for us, but is not really useful beyond being converted to energy and/or enjoyment, or, in this case, donors. Seeing information in that light will let you be in control of it, so that you can use it to do your work.

twenty-five

Managing Time

Effective time management often marks the difference between a good fundraiser and someone who is never going to make it in this field. First, remember that the fundraising job is never done and you are never caught up. In this case, Murphy's Law says that expenses rise to meet income. The more successful the fundraising plans are, the more plans the organization will make to spend that money. Consequently, no amount of money raised is ever enough. Fundraising staff (paid and unpaid) must set their own limits, because no matter how supportive the organization may be of your work, it is still relentless in its need for more money.

GUIDELINES

Here are some guidelines for using your time to the best advantage.

Every Day:

Reserve at least one (and sometimes two or three) hours during which you cannot be interrupted by phone calls. Either get someone else to answer the phone or let an answering machine do so. Use that time for research and writing.

Spend 15 to 30 minutes at the end of the day writing up a to-do list for the next day. At the beginning of the day review your to-do list. Unless something comes up that really can't wait, do only those tasks already on your to-do list. Put new things on tomorrow's list.

Make sure thank-you notes are getting written — ideally a board member or volunteer is coming into the office to write them, or the executive director is adding a personal note to a thank-you note generated by your database program, but you have to stay on top of that.

Every Week:

> **Update your donor records.**
>
> **Go over your fundraising plan for the month and make sure you are on target.** Don't put off tasks such as getting a letter to the printer, calling a foundation, setting up meetings of the major gifts committee or the special events committee. Do these tasks on time.
>
> **Watch for time sinks.** How many times have all of us looked up at the clock and in total disbelief said, "How could it be 4 o'clock?" or, "Where did the day go?" Sometimes this is a sign that we have been very absorbed in important work, but sometimes it is a sign that we have used up our time on a lot of stuff that seems important, but isn't, or is important but could have been handled in a fraction of the time. These are the most common time sinks:
>
> - *The telephone:* Limit the length of your calls by standing up while you are on the phone. If you know the telephone is a big temptation for you, move it off your desk so that you actually have to move to answer it or to make a phone call.
>
> - *E-mail:* What could have been a great timesaving device has become the greatest time sink ever. Get off of listservs that you don't find useful or that are unrelated to your work. Delete (without reading) anything that has been forwarded to you that you know is simply a list of jokes or a petition. Don't feel obligated to answer every e-mail, particularly if you get e-mail from people who are not and are never going to be important to your group, or who would never have paid the money to call you. Limit yourself to looking at your e-mail once a day.
>
> - *Chatty co-workers:* Learn to sort out what kind of conversations are important for maintaining morale and being interested in other people, and what is simply you or your co-worker procrastinating in doing work.
>
> - *People who drop by:* If someone comes by whom you don't need to talk with, and you don't have time to talk, you can tell them that you will call them later or set a lunch date right then, or you can stand up and remain standing while talking to them (they will probably not sit down if you are standing). Another tactic is, while YOU are talking to them, look at your watch or your calendar. This will remind your visitor of time passing without your being rude. You never need to act hurried or rushed with spontaneous visitors as long as you don't get panicked about how you are going to get rid of them.

DEADLINES

Understanding that information is time-related is integral to running an efficient office. Once you have organized your office, paper, computer files, and desk in a way that allows you nearly instant access to the information you need and provides a sensible system that someone else can follow, assign a time by which you will have used or acted on the information you are keeping track of so effectively. There are two principal methods: calendars and action plans.

Calendars

Buy or make three calendars:

1. A "Year-At-A-Glance" wall calendar. This calendar shows all 12 months at once, with each month divided into 1" × 1" boxes for the days.

2. A "Month-At-A-Glance" calendar. Some people get these calendars as desktop blotters. You can also buy a smaller desktop calendar from a worthy group so you have uplifting stories or fabulous nature photos to look at. Just be sure that the box for each day has enough room to write a few lines.

3. An appointment calendar to carry with you in your purse or briefcase. This is a simple daily calendar, with all the days of the year laid out two or so to a page spread.

While you can certainly invest lots of money in fancy calendar systems that have places to record your expenses, birthdays, car mileage, meeting notes, priority to-do lists, meeting agenda items, tax information, and the like, I have yet to meet anyone who actually used all those systems. Further (and this is not a judgment of these calendars, simply an observation of people who use them), in my experience the fancier the calendar, the less reliable the person. I always know when someone pulls out the ten-pound, multi-colored and tabbed calendar, and turns to the special section for "commitments made" to write something they just said they would do that it will probably never happen. On the other hand, when someone takes the free calendar they got from their insurance agent or an inexpensive one bought at an office supply store and writes what they have committed to on the day they made the commitment, I am reasonably certain it will get done. In terms of calendars, then, the simpler the system, the more workable it is likely to be.

Now, take your "Year-At-A-Glance" wall calendar and put Xs through the following:

- Major holidays, and one or two days before and after those holidays

- Your vacation

- Your birthday (Don't work on your birthday.)

- The day (or two, if you wish) after any work meeting or conference that you know will be grueling or that you have to travel a long distance to attend.

What you have left is close to the true number of days you could get work done.

Now put a large dot on the dates of board meetings, the annual meeting, special events, proposal deadlines, newsletter deadlines, and any other meetings or deadlines that you can anticipate. Take a fine-line marker and draw a line from each deadline back as many days as you think it will take you to prepare for it, and if work will be generated by the event, then extend your line for one or two days after the event. Whatever workdays don't have lines, dots, or Xs are days you can do the rest of your work.

You now have a clear visual picture that allows you to assess quickly, "Can I take on this commitment?" "Does it make sense for me to attend this conference when I will be exhausted from our annual retreat?" "Should we conduct our major donor campaign during our audit?"

Remember also that some of the days of the year will be used up by illness (yours, your partner's, your children's, etc.), by goofing off or not working efficiently, and by other emergencies that take precedence.

Now take your "Month-At-A-Glance" desk calendar and write down the major task areas that have to be taken care of each day in order to keep on schedule, such as thank-you notes, the tasks related to a special event, newsletter production, etc. This calendar does not take the place of a "to-do" list. However, most people do not keep the relationship of their "to-do" list and their calendar clear enough. For example, someone calls you and asks for an appointment. You look at your calendar and, seeing a clear day, make the appointment, only to realize later that the day was kept clear because of the approaching deadlines covered by the to-do list. Whenever possible, set your meetings, appointments, lunch dates, and so on by referring to your yearly or monthly calendar. A day does not stand alone. Do you really want to have a 7 A.M. breakfast meeting with a major donor the morning after a board meeting that will run until 10 P.M.?

Use the daily calendar that you carry with you for appointments, addresses, phone numbers, making future meetings and appointments when you are not in your office, notes from meetings, etc. However, every two or three days (some people do this at the end of every day), move all relevant information from your daily calendar onto the monthly one or onto a to-do list. Note in your daily calendar deadlines and days that are filled with writing work or preparation, including all that you have already noted on your yearly calendar. Make appointments with yourself also. One man named Bill who had a hard time saying no to anything would make up names of people and then assign meeting times to them in his calendar. He does this because of the obnoxious habit some people have of looking at other people's calendars to find open space. Often at meetings, he says, someone will say,

"How's Wednesday at 2:00?" Leaning over to peer at his calendar, the person will say, "Bill, looks like you have an open afternoon." So when Bill knows he has a hard day of work, even though it involves no appointments, he writes in fake appointments and puts the letters "hh" beside these, which stands for "ha-ha." These fake appointments jar him into not saying yes. He can say, "I have a meeting," which for him, like most people, is easier than saying, "I have to write the campaign brochure." It also spares him the agony of having to respond to someone saying, "This will only take 20 minutes — it will be good for you to have a break from your writing."

Some people like putting their monthly and daily calendars onto handheld computers such as "Palm Pilots." If that technology works for you and makes you more efficient, use it. If it is a toy, something to chat with others about, or something that you never really learn to use, go back to a paper system.

Things to Avoid about Calendars

1. Avoid having a home calendar and a work calendar. People who do that almost always miss their Monday morning appointments and are constantly trying to recall whether they can make an evening meeting on Thursday, because they think that's the night of their daughter's soccer match, or is that Wednesday? Your daily calendar shows your whole day, from home to work and back home. Put your important home-life appointments and activities in your single daily calendar.

2. Avoid saying to yourself or others, "I am so busy," or, "I don't know how I'll get everything done." Both these statements could be true, but they also become self-fulfilling and they don't accomplish anything except to use up time. Most people are busy and few people get everything done. Tell yourself instead, "I can get this done. I have enough time."

3. Skip meetings or conferences that you do not need to attend. Conferences, training, workshops, seminars, and classes are the order of the day. They are both expensive and time-consuming and rarely worth it. Choose those events where you will really learn something or see people you truly want to see. Then go, and be there. Too often we decide to attend a conference half-heartedly and spend most of the plenaries and workshops making notes or to-do lists for when we get back. A sign that a conference is not worth it for you is when you have to phone your office more than once a day while you're gone.

4. Avoid too many meetings. While we have work to do in meetings and admittedly a certain amount of the work we do at meetings is socializing and building camaraderie, many meetings are not essential, and almost every meeting lasts too long. Question every meeting: Is it necessary? If it is, do I need to be there? Can I be there for part of it and not all of it? If you have any say in the meeting, make sure there is an agenda with times beside each item. People tend to talk for the amount of time that is listed. People can negotiate the need for extra time as it comes up.

Action Plans

One of the hard things about working with individual donors is that this work has no externally determined deadlines, so you have to create your own. Once you have your calendars set up, you are ready for the next step in organizing your fundraising office: creating action plans.

Whenever you work with a donor or a prospect, make a note in their record of what you intend to do next. This is called your "action plan." It can be recorded in a separate field in your computer database or a separate entry on a donor information card. An "action plan" is brief, such as "Invite to house party," or, "Call with outcome of organizing effort in Roane County," or, "Send report on toxic waste dumping as soon as available." Then add a date to the action you plan to take. Now take this date and put it in your "Month-At-A-Glance" calendar. Note the donor's last name or some identifying phrase that will remind you to check what you were going to do on that date.

If you are systematic about your donors, each donor or prospect will have a date on which you are going to work with them and move the process of building their relationship with the organization along. By spreading these dates out over the year, you can give more personal attention to donors and not get jammed with unrelated donor meetings during a campaign or at the end of the year. If you have thousands of donors, obviously you will have to decide which ones you want to work with personally, but the action plan concept can be used for group activity also, such as "Oct. 1: all $50–$100 donors receive news alert mail appeal."

A fundraiser's job is often compared to that of the circus performer who balances plates on sticks by keeping the plates twirling and runs from stick to stick to keep the spinning going. If she misses, the plate falls and may break. The calendar is the stick, and the action plans are the plates. This is how you keep your plates spinning and not falling. The overall idea is to have as little to remember as possible. You shouldn't have things in your memory that you could write down or enter in your computer. This frees you to use your mind to be creative or to learn new details about new people, and write those down later.

The wide variety of tasks involved in fundraising is both exciting and one of the many difficulties of the job. You can minimize some of the difficulties by relatively simple procedures to keep your office running efficiently. A calendar and action plan system allows you to use the information you accumulate to raise maximum dollars for your work.

twenty-six

Recordkeeping

Accurate, up-to-date, and thorough records that are easy to access are the most basic necessity for an ongoing fundraising program. Without such records, you have little capability to ask donors for more money, target projects to specific donor interests, track response to appeals, set goals or evaluate your progress against your plan, or any of the other requirements for maintaining and increasing your base of individual donors.

DATABASE PROGRAMS

Obviously, the most important thing to keep track of is information about your donors. The vast majority of even the tiniest organizations do this on a computerized database program. If you are on a paper system, you still need to keep good records; most of this information will be the same for a paper system as for a computerized one. (At the risk of revealing myself to be a Luddite, I need to say that a paper system that works is preferable to a database that doesn't. People raised billions of dollars before there were even memory typewriters, let alone computers. However, a database that works well for you gives you a lot more options than any paper system, and allows you to sort information in many useful ways, so I recommend getting one if you don't have one now.)

Your database needs to be able to do at least the following five things:

- Hold a lot of names (preferably an infinite number)
- Hold a lot of information in many fields about each name
- Sort by those fields quickly and easily
- Produce reports by compiling information, such as total number of gifts from the summer appeal, amount pledged vs. amount received, difference between this year's direct mail costs and income and last year's
- Merge with a word processing program for individualized letters, and format labels of different sizes for mailings.

PURCHASING A DATABASE PROGRAM

Although some off-the-shelf database programs can be customized to meet all of the requirements I've listed and more, I strongly recommend getting a program designed for fundraising. All computer programs will have bugs that have to be fixed, and all people using computer programs will run up against their own ability to understand a function and the inability of the manual to explain it. If you have a program designed for fundraising, there should be a technical support person you can call. If you have a customized database program, you have to hope that the person who customized it is available. Just in the last year, people have told me the following sad stories about using their customized database programs: "We can't get that database to do a mail merge for our major donor campaign and John, who designed it, is in Nepal for six months." "The database has freaked out! It won't sort anything and it freezes every five minutes. Mary, who customized it for us, is mad at us and won't help." "Fred, the guy who put this program together, is in Switzerland for a sex-change operation, and meantime the database seems to have lost all current information. I know it's in there, but I can't figure out how to restore it."

Your database should be as useful as having another staff person. If it takes a staff person to handle it, something is probably wrong.

A big mythology of fundraising database programs is that they are all terribly expensive. You can pay a lot if you want, but there are some very effective ones for well under $2,000, and now there are some free ones that can be downloaded from the Web. Several commercial databases will also let you pay over time with low or no interest, and several have versions you can "grow into" — that is, you buy a program that has fewer functions or holds fewer names, and as you grow and need more sophistication, you apply the cost of your previous program to an upgrade that serves you better. The final reason to buy a database program designed for fundraising is that you will get upgrades to the program, usually for free.

If you are thinking of buying a fundraising database program, ask for a "demo disk." This preview will show you what the program can do and give you a sense of how "user friendly" it is. Before buying anything, be sure all your questions have been answered and that you understand the answers. Don't be afraid to ask elementary questions and don't let salespeople make you feel stupid or old-fashioned. Finally, find out what kind of support the company provides once you purchase their program — is there a toll-free telephone number? Can you call as often as you need to? How difficult is it to get through to a tech support person? How are charges for this support figured? What kinds of training programs to help you understand the program does the company have, where are they held, and what do they cost?

Many organizations have a bought either a fundraising or a database program they had to customize that they did not fully understand, but could not afford the extra cost of a support package, and so did not use the program. There is a marked difference between the number of nonprofits that have computers and the number that actually use them to their full advantage.

Think through the information you will want to gather and keep up-to-date, so that you have consistent information on each donor. You don't need to know as much about someone who gives you $25 as someone who gives $2,500. You will want to know more about someone who has given you money several times a year for ten years than about someone who gave one gift and then didn't give again.

For all donors you need to know the following information:

Name and address. Get this off of the photocopy of their check, if they give using a check. Information on people's checks is generally accurate, particularly the spelling of their names. People are offended when their name is misspelled, and they don't take into account that their handwriting made their name impossible to read.

Phone number, if it appears on the check, or if they wrote it on their reply device.

Form of salutation (i.e., "Dear Mr.," "Dear Joe," "Dear Anna and Mary," "Dear Rev. Lloyd," etc.). If you don't know, use a formal salutation that is not sexist: "Dear Ms. Smith" is preferable to "Dear Mrs. Smith." For couples, try "Dear Friends."

Gift history. Date of gift, size of gift, and what the gift was in response to (i.e., board member request, direct mail, canvass, etc.).

Renewal date. In many cases this will be in the "Gift History."

Correspondence record. Note "thank-you note sent" with the date and any other correspondence you have. Actual copies of the letters will probably be in a paper file or in another file in your computer.

Other information. This category (or "field" as it will be called on your computerized database) may remain empty if you have no other information, but it can be used to note anything you know about this person that is pertinent to him or her being a donor or a prospect for a bigger gift. For example, "Sister of board president" would go here. Or, suppose a gift of $30 comes in from Joe Cumberland, but his check says, "Joe Cumberland; Janice Ruark, MD." First, you can check to see if Janice Ruark is also a donor. If she is not, just make a note: "Check in his name and Janice Ruark, MD." This may be useful, or it may never lead anywhere. Sometimes a reply card will carry the name of a person, such as "Lydia S. Turner," but the check says, "Sampson Family Foundation." Make a note of that. Probably the "S" in Lydia's name is for Sampson. In the "action plan" field for this donor (see previous chapter), make a note to look up the Sampson Family Foundation at the Foundation Center Library.

If you trade lists with other groups and you have given donors the chance to check a box on your reply device asking not to have their names traded, this information would be coded in another field so their names are suppressed when you trade names. People who indicate they only want to be asked once a year, or never want to be phoned, will have that information coded on their database record.

This is all the information you keep on people who have given only once so far, or who have given less than $100 for less than three years and whom you don't know anything else about. For people who give more than $100, or have given some amount for more than three years, or who give several times a year, or whose gift does not reflect how much they could give considering how much they seem to care about your cause, start keeping the information outlined in Chapter 9 on "prospect identification."

Your database will have categories to help you think through what you need to keep track of, and you will be able to add fields for your particular situation. There are two useful categories that can be easily added: "Missing Information" and "Next Step." It often happens that you know some details about a donor but not enough to include them in the upper ranges of your gift range chart, for example, or to ask them to give an extra gift for a capital improvement. It is very helpful to focus on what you would need to know to feel comfortable asking them for more money or extra money. Possibly you need to know more about their friendship with a board member. Are they very close, or simply acquaintances? Perhaps you need to know what other charitable commitments the donor has made. Maybe you need to know more about what the donor thinks about a particular issue that your group is working on. Or maybe it is something simpler, such as their phone number. Make a note of whatever it is under "Missing Information." Once every month or so, sort your records so as to find any with notes in the "Missing Information" category. The result will give you a complete list of what you need to do to get your donor records in better order.

The other useful category is "Next Step." Obviously, a logical next step may be to find the "missing information," but this category can be used more proactively. Often the next step is not to ask for more money, but to be sure to send some article of interest that you promised the donor. Maybe Sally, your board member who lives down the road from this donor, needs to invite the donor to a house party or a meeting. Maybe this donor has a lot of contacts and you want to ask her to give you a list of them right before the spring major donor drive. Note what the next step is and a date by which it should be done. Then you can sort by dates and give yourself a to-do list for "next steps" with donors.

THE IMPORTANCE OF DONOR RECORDS

People sometimes feel that gathering this information so systematically, and writing it all down or entering it on a computer, is an invasion of the donor's privacy, and feel nosy and manipulative. They fear becoming people who only see other people in terms of money. To gain some perspective on the reasons for keeping donor records, remember the following three facts:

1. If you don't record this information, you will forget it, and you will not be able to raise money effectively. Many people have "birthday books" where they write down all the dates of the birthdays they want to remember. No one thinks this is an invasion of privacy — in fact, they are pleased to get a card on their birthday. You are trying to use donor resources to the best advantage, which is what donors want and deserve. There is no point in asking someone for more money who only gives once a year, but it is a waste not to ask someone who likes your organization and would gladly give more often if asked. Further, how will the organization know that your long-time loyal donor, Tania Lopez, hates to be called at work if someone doesn't record it? Or that Steve who owns the deli said he would cater your annual meeting for free if you get back to him by March? Finally, you are obligated by law to keep a record of gifts received so that if a donor is audited by the IRS, you can provide verification that they gave the amount they said they had given to your group.

2. You don't record anything that you don't need to know. Your goal is to get every donor to be as loyal to your group as possible and to give you as much money as they can afford because of their loyalty. Everything you record about a donor should be information that helps you toward that goal. So, no matter how interesting it might be that Max was once lovers with Fred, don't record it. If a donor who is also a friend confides to you that she spent time in prison and is having trouble with the parole board, don't write it down. Think of this: If a donor asked to see his or her record, would you be embarrassed to show it? Why? What's in there that shouldn't be? You are recording information that is easily obtainable, or that people would not object to your knowing, such as how many children they have, or where they work.

3. This information is highly confidential. Only a few people, such as the executive director, the development director, the treasurer of the board, and some-times the bookkeeper or administrator, should have access to all the information. (A good database will include some kind of password system. One password allows access to the fields for name, address, and phone; a second password accesses the gift history field; a third password allows one to see all the information. Only a few people should have all three passwords.) Donor records, such a paper files, back-up disks, correspondence, and so on should be kept in a locked file cabinet with limited access. People who can see this information must understand its delicate nature and use the same discretion in revealing it as is used in recording it. Even though this information is not secret, it is not to be shared carelessly.

KEEPING YOUR LIST IN SHAPE

Update your donor records on a regular basis. Don't let more than ten names go unrecorded or you will get careless with numbers and spelling. Many small, understaffed groups put off updating their records until the night before they need their mailing list for the newsletter mailing. Then a staff member and a volunteer frantically try to get everything in order. That kind of list is inevitably full of errors.

Watch for duplicate entries, particularly when you are going to use the list for a mailing. Donors dislike getting more than one copy of your newsletter. A database program will not know that J.P. Miller and John Miller are the same person, or that Sally Jones doesn't live at 22 South St. anymore, but is now Sally Moondaughter on 44 North St. Every so often, you will have to print out your whole mailing list and go through it looking for duplicates, spelling errors, incomplete addresses, and so on.

Don't keep people on your mailing list who have never given and whom no one knows. I have known many organizations that have mailing lists of 4,000 but donor lists of 700. When I ask what the other 3,300 people are doing on their list, they will say, "This is our outreach program." When I ask what evidence they have that these people gain from this outreach, or even if they have evidence that all of these people are alive, they say nothing. Considering it costs at least $2 or $3 per entry every year to keep someone on a mailing list — presuming you send at least two newsletters and at least one appeal, you could be spending hundreds or even thousands of dollars keeping people on your mailing list that you know nothing about. That same money could be invested in a true "outreach" or direct mail program, or invested in driving traffic to your Web site and using an electronic newsletter for outreach.

You can get address corrections from the post office by putting "Address Correction Requested" on all your bulk mail. You pay a certain amount per piece to get it returned, but it keeps your list clean. You should do that at least once a year.

SAFETY FIRST

You need to save your work constantly as you go along, and you need to back up your hard drive at the end of each day. At least once a week, you need to take a back-up disk to another location, such as a safety-deposit box at a bank or to the home of a board member or staff person. In addition, you should keep copies of legal documents and any records that it would be difficult to replace in a location away from your office. You need to think through what would happen if your hard disk crashed or your building burned, or if there was a flood, vandalism, earthquake, hurricane, or any number of other disasters that have ruined nonprofits' offices the same way they have ruined residences and businesses.

For many fundraisers, recordkeeping is the bane of their existence. But keeping records takes less time if you do it regularly so that you don't get far behind than if you wait until the last minute and do it badly and then have to spend time cleaning up your mess. Recordkeeping needs to be seen as being as necessary and habitual as brushing your teeth.

You the Fundraiser

The National Society of Fund Raising Executives (NSFRE), which is the trade association for development directors and other fundraising professionals, has noted in several studies that development directors leave their jobs every 18 months. Most of these people move to other development jobs, but sadly many also leave the profession. The cost of replacing an employee and training a new employee is estimated to be at least $5,000, so the cost to nonprofits of this kind of turnover is exorbitant.

One of the reasons for this high turnover is a lack of understanding on the parts of all parties involved as to exactly what the job of a development director is. Many grassroots groups have hired enthusiastic but inexperienced first-time development directors and neither the group nor the person has a clear idea of what the job involves. Soon, both parties are disappointed, and the employee leaves. This section reviews the job of a development director, a consultant, and the field of development as a career, as well as the two things most likely to drive someone from development — anxiety and the executive director. When everyone knows what they can expect, we will see less turnover and more successful organizations, as well as many more people making social justice fundraising their career.

twenty-seven

Hiring a Development Director

As small organizations grow, they grapple with the ongoing need to raise more and more money. Inevitably, they must consider hiring someone to take charge of the fundraising function. This is a difficult decision. A group is gambling that the investment of salary — money they often barely have — is going to generate much more money than they are currently raising. The gamble will pay off if the person they hire is effective, the board already accepts its role in fundraising, and the organization has its basic infrastructure in place — that is, adequate record-keeping systems and a fundraising plan with clear goals and objectives. However, there is little margin for error. What if the person isn't skilled enough or isn't a good worker? What if everything is in place, but the fundraising program takes longer than planned to bring in the needed funds? How will the organization support itself in the meantime?

To avoid these problems, before your organization decides to hire a staff person to manage fundraising, clarify the following three issues:

1. The role of a fundraiser or development director. It is most important to understand that the person whose primary responsibility is overseeing fundraising does not run around bringing in money. With the input of the board or fundraising committee, the development director plans for fundraising, developing yearlong plans that spell out each strategy and set income goals. She or he maintains or supervises fundraising records and the mailing list; sends out thank-you notes; reports to foundations or large donors on specific projects; does prospect research; writes and sends mail appeals, renewals, and other fundraising letters; helps write the annual report; and goes on major donor visits as needed. She or he works closely with the board, helping them make and then fulfill their fundraising commitments. The development director may also research the grantmaking programs of foundations and corporations and write grant proposals, if that is a part of the organization's plan, and there may be other fundraising strategies that he or she must oversee or implement. The development director primarily works behind the scenes, establishing a structure for effective fundraising by volunteers.

Many board members and paid staff imagine that hiring a development director will save them from further fundraising tasks. "Let's pay someone to do this so we can do the real work" is a common and potentially fatal suggestion. First of all, fundraising is "real work" and should be integrated into the day-to-day functioning of your program and organizing work. Second, while the paid fundraising staff obviously relieves the load of other staff and may relieve the board of some tasks, everyone's consciousness of fundraising and involvement in it must stay the same or increase for the expanded fundraising program to be successful.

2. What you want this person to do for your organization. Many people wonder why the task of fundraising has so many different job titles attached to it, such as "fundraiser," "fundraising coordinator," "development director," or "resource developer." In many social change organizations, the person is called the fundraising coordinator in a straightforward way. In other, usually larger organizations, this position is called the director of development. Sometimes small groups think this title is a sign of elitism or an attempt to disguise the crassness of raising money, similar to saying "your support" rather than "your money" in fundraising appeals and letters. However, there are actually important differences between fundraising and development.

Fundraising is the process of bringing in the amount of money an organization needs in order to carry out its programs from year to year. Development, in addition to raising the funds for operations, includes most of the following activities:

- Creating a strategic plan and updating it on a yearly basis (augmenting the case statement)
- Instituting a planned public relations program
- Maintaining a planned and frequently evaluated process for bringing on new board members
- Providing fundraising training for board, staff, and volunteers
- Planning and evaluating the financial needs and fundraising plans for the organization's future

- Developing the group's capability to conduct capital campaigns and start planned giving programs

One development director characterized the difference between fundraising and development this way: "In fundraising, you make do with what you have. You keep the organization going and out of debt. In development, you start with what you have and you help it grow."

3. Whether hiring a development director will actually solve the problems you have. Analysis of your situation will show whether your problems lie in fundraising or elsewhere. To begin this analysis, answer the following questions:

- Is your board active in fundraising? Does every board member participate in fundraising in some way, whether organizing special events, getting mail appeals out, or asking for money face-to-face?

- Does it sometimes seem that the board and perhaps the staff spend more time planning for fundraising than actually raising money?

- Do board members and other volunteers involved in fundraising seem to suffer from a lack of knowledge of what to do rather than a lack of enthusiasm?

- Is the executive director or other staff constantly pulled away from program development and organizing to do fundraising? Does she or he feel torn about setting priorities for use of their time?

- Is your budget more than $200,000, or do you need to raise more than $100,000 from sources other than government or foundations?

If your organization answers yes to three or more of these questions, you should seriously consider hiring a development director. This person would direct and kindle the fundraising energies of the board, plan for fundraising, train others in fundraising tasks, and enable program staff to get on with program work.

If, on the other hand, you need a better and more involved board, then you should strengthen your board and provide some motivational training for them before you hire a development director.

If what you need is help with data entry, writing the annual report, compiling financial reports, answering the phone, dealing with the mail, handling checks, sending thank-you notes, and the like, then you should consider hiring support staff, such as a secretary or office manager.

If what you want is someone to help you plan and carry out a time-limited fundraising project, such as a direct mail or major gifts campaign, consider hiring a consultant.

PAYING THE DEVELOPMENT DIRECTOR

Imagine this scenario: An organization is debating whether to hire a development director. They have little front money, and they worry about both finding the right person and meeting a salary. As if in answer to a prayer, a handsome stranger shows up and offers to raise $150,000 (their budget) for a 20% commission. He will only take his commission from money he raises, and if he raises nothing, he explains, they pay nothing; however, they pay him 20% of any money he raises. He says he can do it in six months, which means he will earn $30,000.

There are several reasons that no organization should accept such a deal (whether the stranger is handsome or not). First, no one else in the organization is paid on commission. People are paid a salary in recognition that their work is part of a process; they may be very good at their job without showing a lot of immediate progress toward ending racism, stopping pollution, or whatever the group is working on.

Second, a commission tends to distort salaries. In this case, this fundraiser would be paid the equivalent of $60,000 a year, a third again more than the director, who makes $40,000.

Third, this person will not bring his own list of contacts. He will be working with the organization's donors. He says he has some contacts from previous jobs, but are they appropriate for your work? And do you want him taking your donor information to his next job? Further, his whole livelihood depends on donors saying yes to his requests. Even a totally honest fundraiser working under these conditions would be tempted to distort information, seeing his rent check in the eyes of each prospect. Also, many big gifts take cultivation, which can mean several visits with a donor. This fundraiser may be willing to settle for a smaller gift in order to get it quickly rather than take the time to carry out proper cultivation.

Fourth, what will the donors think if and when they find out that 20% of their gift went to this temporary staff person? Few things make donors angrier than learning that a significant part of their gift was used for inappropriate fundraising expenses.

Fifth, as was stressed earlier, one person should not be in charge of actually raising money for an entire campaign. Suppose he is both honest and successful. When he leaves, the group is $150,000 richer, to be sure, but no wiser in regard to fundraising.

Finally, the person coordinating the fundraising should absolutely believe in the cause and be a part of the team of people putting the campaign together.

For these reasons, paying on commission is highly frowned on in fundraising. All the trade associations for fundraisers, including the National Society of Fundraising Executives, the National Association of Hospital Developers, and the Council for the Advancement and Support of Education, have issued statements decrying the practice of commission-based fundraising.

The development director's salary should be based on other staff salaries. If you have a collective salary structure, then it is the same as everyone else's. If there are pay differentials, then the development director's salary is less than the executive director's, but more than the office manager's. In a hierarchical structure, the development director is a management staff person, usually reporting directly to the executive director.

Many times you hear that you have to pay "a lot" to get a capable development person. This is not true. A good person for your group is someone who, first and foremost, believes in your group and wants to be part of it. This person will express his or her belief through fundraising, just as someone else is expressing their belief by doing direct service, organizing, or policy development. If someone who meets the criteria of believing strongly in your work has fundraising skills but can't afford to work at the salary you are offering, you may need to reevaluate everyone's salary. Chances are you are losing out on good staff people for other positions as well.

HOW TO FIND A CAPABLE DEVELOPMENT DIRECTOR

Once you have decided that you need a development director, you need to create a fair and accurate job description and begin the hiring process. Many job descriptions fail to attract candidates because the job has been structured to encompass too many responsibilities. Avoid the temptation to add components to the job that are not related to fundraising or public relations. It is fair to ask the development director to edit and oversee the publication of the newsletter; it is unwise to ask that person to also be the accountant.

You should be able to describe the job in one page (see the example on the next page). Think about what skills are essential as opposed to those that are desirable but not imperative. Ask applicants to send a writing sample, since writing will be a large part of almost any fundraiser's job.

Advertise in publications geared to nonprofits. Unless you are in a small town, avoid advertising in the newspaper — you will receive a lot of resumes from unqualified people. Post your job description at the Foundation Center Collection nearest to you (see listing on page 395–398) and in places where social change activists hang out or shop, such as coffeehouses, independent bookstores, health food stores, progressive churches and synagogues, meditation centers, or retreats. Send the announcement to other nonprofits and call directors and development directors you know and tell them the job is available.

SAMPLE JOB DESCRIPTION

Position Available: Development Director

Starting Date: June 1 — Application Deadline: April 1

Harry and Jane's House serves the homeless population of Buckminster County. Formed in 1983 after itinerant day laborers Harry and Jane Smith were found frozen to death on the steps of the Methodist Church, Harry and Jane's has sheltered 400 people every year. In addition to shelter, we provide job counseling, access to medical care, and a school program for children. The shelter's budget is $500,000, with $200,000 provided by city and state funding. Harry and Jane's House seeks its first development director to help ensure stable funding so we can expand the range of services we provide.

Major Responsibilities: The Development Director will be responsible for expanding the shelter's development program. The program currently raises income through major gifts, direct mail, special events, and foundation grants in addition to government funding. Under the supervision of the Executive Director and in partnership with the rest of the staff, the Development Director will expand the shelter's fundraising program in the following areas:

1. Seeking major gift donations in the $250–$10,000 range
2. Expanding the direct mail program
3. Working with a consultant to set up and maintain a Web site with a secured area for accepting donations
4. Expanding the amount of money raised through the Combined Federal Campaign
5. Expanding the board of directors' role in fundraising, particularly in soliciting new and upgraded gifts

The chosen candidate will also take primary responsibility for written materials, special events, and foundation proposals. Prospect research and identification will be a shared responsibility with the Executive Director and fundraising committee of the board.

Qualifications: At least two years of experience as a volunteer or paid staff, preferably in the areas of housing and homelessness; at least two years of fundraising experience, including major gift planning and solicitation; good writing and communication skills; and experience working with a board of directors.

Demonstrated ability to work well with a diverse constituency, be self-motivated, work well under pressure, and be able to handle several projects at one time. Must be computer literate and familiar with how databases work. Familiarity with Buckminster County is highly desirable.

Salary and Benefits: Commensurate with experience and with existing pay and benefits scales at the shelter.

To Apply: Please send cover letter summarizing what you would bring to this position and why you want to work for Harry and Jane's House, along with your resume, two writing samples, and three references. Women and people of color are encouraged to apply. Harry and Jane's House is proud to be an equal opportunity employer.

Send application to: Search Committee, Address
Please do not fax your application.
E-mail inquiries: Sharon@Hjhouse.org

Don't be stuck on hiring someone with all the "right" qualifications and experience. If you find such a person, hire them immediately. But if you don't find such a person, look for other sorts of qualifications that are evidence of skills related to fundraising, such as running a small business, teaching, or managing personnel. Any job that required that a person be a self-starter and called for planning, working with diverse groups of people, and good organizational skills is a good background for fundraising.

Look closely at volunteer experience, and encourage applicants to describe their work as volunteers. Many people know more than they realize about fundraising from having volunteered. People with little or no volunteer experience are not good candidates because they will have little idea of how to work with volunteers.

In addition to broadening your criteria in hiring someone, be willing to hire a consultant for a few days to help your new staff person get a running start on their job, or send the new development director to some of the many classes and courses that are offered on fundraising. The theories and how-to's of fundraising are not particularly difficult to understand, even though they take a lot of work to implement. Getting someone who is underqualified but bright, committed, and eager to do a good job is almost as good as getting an experienced person with the same attributes.

twenty-eight

Hiring a Consultant

There are times in the life of almost every group when a fundraising consultant or trainer can be very helpful. These times are characterized by one or more of the following situations:

1. Your organization needs advice as to how to improve its overall fundraising or some particular aspect of fundraising. You need someone with skill and knowledge who cares about the issues your organization is concerned with, but is far enough removed to be able to "see the forest."

2. You need help deciding on a course of action: Can you really launch a capital campaign now? Would a monthly donor program be a good strategy to explore?

3. You need someone to do a time-limited piece of work: run a special event, train the board in fundraising, plan a major gifts campaign, design a Web site, write a proposal.

4. You need someone to help design the fundraising staff's work plan, provide guidance, and answer questions. Working one day a week or month, a consultant can help bring a bright, energetic, but inexperienced staff person up to speed.

5. You need someone to run the development function of your organization temporarily, until staff can be replaced.

Consulting assistance is characterized by being time-limited (lasting either a few hours a week or a few days a month, or being based on a contract for a specific number of months), uninvolved in day-to-day operations, and generating advice and guidance more than actual doing any of the fundraising work.

It is partially because of the latter aspect that the concept of employing a consultant carries a negative meaning for many people. The jokes, "A consultant borrows your watch to tell you the time," or, "A consultant gives free advice for a price," are said only half in jest.

The problem is compounded by the sheer number of consultants working in the United States. There are sleazy and unreliable consultants in the fundraising profession, but a more common problem with consultants is that many have little knowledge of their professed subject. Sometimes people ask me how they should go about becoming a consultant. When I ask what experience they have, they respond with a list of the books they have read and the trainings they have attended. They think consulting would be exciting because one travels a great deal and can charge a lot of money. They are also excited because consultants do not carry the ultimate responsibility of the fundraising success or failure of any organization.

What my inquirers fail to see, however, is that consultants carry a different level of responsibility: The advice we give must be correct. If implemented, it must work. Further, consultants must trust others to carry out plans that the consultant designed. This means the plan must be communicated very clearly and be appropriate to the level of skills and resources the people carrying it out have, or have access to.

Consultants must know what can be learned by teaching, guiding, and giving advice, and what can only be learned from experience. They must know what they can do for an organization, and what an organization can only do for itself. Here is a list of the kinds of activities fundraising consultants can and cannot do:

Consultants can:

- Train and motivate people in all aspects of fundraising
- Create fundraising plans and help implement and evaluate those plans
- Research prospective donors (individuals, corporations, foundations, religious sources), and write proposals if needed
- Set up a database for keeping track of donor information
- Conduct feasibility studies
- Conduct direct mail campaigns, including list acquisition, package design, tracking of results, and sometimes thank-you notes
- Help board members understand their responsibilities, and help organizations recruit and train good board members
- Study and recommend structural changes in an organization to improve functioning and fundraising efficiency
- Help hire fundraising staff, including writing job descriptions and advertising for and interviewing candidates

- Organize special events

- Set up any other fundraising strategy that an organization has decided to use

- Manage mailing lists and donor information. This can include sending out pledge reminders, thank-you notes, and renewal letters, but generally, this is not cost effective for small organizations.

Consultants cannot:

- Actually solicit money from individuals, unless they go as part of a team with someone from the organization

- Use their personal contacts to raise money. Consultants often know a great deal about wealthy givers in the community and, with discretion, can share that knowledge in prospect research. However, consultants do not go from job to job with their own list of prospects.

- Actually raise money. If a consultant offers to do all your fundraising for you, run the other way. This is not an effective solution because, at best, it postpones the necessity of getting the board, staff, and volunteers involved in fundraising.

- Guarantee their work. There are no absolutes in fundraising. There is a body of fundraising knowledge, largely based on common sense, and there are many applications of this knowledge. No strategy will work every time for every group.

HOW TO CHOOSE A CONSULTANT

Once you have decided that your particular situation may be helped by a consultant, what do you look for in that person?

1. Track record. Ask how much fundraising he or she has done, and with what success. Has the person worked with organizations similar to yours in both purpose and strategy, and in similar locales? A successful consultant for social change groups in Manhattan may be less useful for rural advocacy groups in North Dakota than someone familiar with rural fundraising. Superb consultants for large institutions may not be good with all-volunteer operations with budgets of less than $25,000. If questions of gender, sexual orientation, race, class, or disability are very important in your organization, ask the consultant what experience they have working on these issues or with diverse groups of people.

2. Recommendations. If you don't know the person by reputation, ask for the last three groups she or he has worked with. Then call those groups and ask about the consultant. Was the person helpful? Did the consultant listen well and really understand the situation? Would this group hire this consultant again? You can also check references, but you may get a more candid evaluation from non-reference groups.

3. Compatibility. If you envision a relationship with the consultant involving more than a one- or two-day training, you may wish to meet the person. This meeting, which should take about half an hour, should be free. You get to see if you like the person and would feel good taking his or her advice. It sometimes happens that an excellent fundraising consultant is not the right person for your group because the personalities will not mesh. If the organization dislikes the consultant, both their advice and your money are wasted.

4. Confidence. Ask what the consultant will do for you, or what they recommend. Avoid asking for long written plans. Elaborate "work plans" or proposals are often standardized; each one is essentially the same as the next, with the name of your organization substituted for the name of the previous organization. You can ask for a resume, if you find that helpful. By the time of the first meeting, you are not looking so much for proof of fundraising knowledge as for ability to put that knowledge across. Ask yourself, "Is this person believable?" "Does she or he convey confidence, enthusiasm, and goodwill?" "Will the people who have to work with this person like him or her?"

5. Belief. Finally, the consultant must be able to articulate the mission of your organization and believe that your group should exist. The consultant does not have to be a donor to your group, and does not have to think that your group is the greatest idea since sliced bread, but he or she needs to care about what you stand for and want to help you out of conviction as well as needing a job. This belief is particularly important if your group is controversial or has a "troublemaker" image with those who would protect the status quo. Avoid consultants who advise you to "tone down" your message or broaden your goals "to make everyone feel included." A fundraising consultant's job is to help your group raise money — not to water down the group's message or philosophy and then help a newer, lightweight group raise money.

PAYING CONSULTANTS

There are no standards or guidelines for how much to pay a consultant. A high price does not necessarily mean better performance or more accountability, but a price that is too good to be true probably is. By hiring a consultant, you are investing in the present so you will have more money in the future.

Most consultants charge by the day or the hour, but some charge by the job. A person's daily rate will work out to be less per hour than their hourly rate; several days' work will average out to less per day than just a one-day job. Consultants also charge for all their expenses: hotels, meals, telephone, photocopy, and travel are the most common. You can cut some of these costs by offering to house the consultant in someone's home and providing their meals, but if you do that, make sure the consultant is comfortable and can get a good night's sleep. I have often agreed to stay with someone only to discover that I was sleeping on a fold-out couch in the living room, which would be invaded by small children wanting to watch the cartoon channel on TV beginning at 6 A.M. When you cut costs on comfort, you decrease the consultant's ability to be helpful by increasing their exhaustion.

Establish clearly just what you are paying for. For example, you pay for the consultant's time. But when does that time start? In some cases, the time starts when the consultant reaches the office of the client or the training site. Even if it takes a day to get there, they do not charge until they are there. Other consultants start charging the minute they leave their house or office. Find out if the consultant charges for phone calls, and at what rate.

If you are hiring a consultant for several days or months of work, build in evaluation points. For example, you might say, "At the end of one month, we will evaluate progress and decide whether or not to continue, or whether the plan needs to be modified." This is best for the consultant also, who may need to re-estimate the time involved, or may have run into some unforeseen obstacles. It is important to have a written statement spelling out your understanding of the consultant's role, fees, and expenses, which you both sign.

For the same reasons listed in the Chapter 27, Hiring a Development Director, do not pay the consultant on a contingency or commission basis.

CONSULTANTS ARE NOT MIRACLE WORKERS OR MAGICIANS

Consultants play an increasingly important role in helping organizations increase their fundraising ability, in solving problems, and in getting board members and volunteers to understand all the ways they can help raise money and why they should be involved in fundraising. However, like the results generally reported from personal psychotherapy, it seems that one-third of the groups get better, one-third get worse, and one-third stay about the same. Consultants cannot create motivation and cannot force people to change bad habits. Timing is key: Is the group willing to change? Willing to try something new? Or is the group at the point where it wants to be willing to change, but isn't really quite ready to do that? Does the group only want to hear what it wants to hear, or is it willing to hear what the consultant has to say?

During the first meeting with your group, a good consultant should be able to help you figure out if consulting is what you need. If you do need a consultant, they can also help you determine what the best use of their time would be. But for a consultant's time to be truly useful, your organization has to be willing to hear what the consultant has to say.

twenty-nine

Making Fundraising Your Career

What would you say if you could have a career that paid you a salary from $10,000 to $150,000? Gave you work with fairly measurable outcomes? Where talking about your values and writing about what you believe is part of the job? Where all the people you work with agree that what you do is really important?

Sounds like a great career, doesn't it? It is: It's a career in fundraising.

I have had many goals in my life, but my new goal is to have more people make fundraising their career. I have three major reasons for wanting to expand the number of fundraisers:

1. I have too much work, much more than I can handle. In another ten or fifteen years, I want to retire knowing that there are many other people able to do the work I was doing.

2. I want fewer phone calls from headhunters, desperate executive directors, friends who sit on boards, all saying, "Do you know anyone who can take our development job? We've looked everywhere. We've extended the deadline for applications indefinitely."

3. I want to see good organizations succeed in their fundraising, and one thing many groups need in order to succeed is someone who is paid to coordinate the organization's fundraising efforts.

Of course, my goal is more specific than simply bringing new people into fundraising. What I really want is to bring a new generation into fundraising for progressive social change, which is at the lower end of the salary scale I mentioned earlier.

"But fundraising isn't a cool career," I hear you say. "Not like actually doing advocacy or service, or maybe even being a public interest attorney — being on the front lines of changing society."

A woman I once worked with recently wrote to tell me that she had left her fundraising position to take a job as an advocate in an agency serving homeless mentally ill adults. "I'm glad to have had this fundraising experience," she wrote, "but it will be good to be out on the front lines again." Her letter came on the same day as a phone call from another colleague who said, "I just have to get back into doing the real work. I can't do this fundraising anymore."

I know that we need organizers and attorneys and social workers. But none of these positions needs to be exempt from fundraising, and someone needs to be the main person in charge of that fundraising.

Before you dismiss a fundraising career as for nerds only, consider these facts:

- Fundraising allows you — in fact, requires you — to talk to people whom you would probably never otherwise meet about what you believe in and the difference their money will make in implementing those beliefs.

- Fundraising gives you the chance to experiment with strategies. Will this letter work? Can you raise money on the Internet? Would people pay to come to this kind of event? While some strategies are formulaic — you follow a recipe and you can predict the result (comforting, but often boring) — others are a combination of good luck, timing, and creativity.

Of course, fundraising does have its drawbacks. As with any difficult job, you have to be able to handle lots of tasks at the same time. In most organizations the fundraising staff has a lot of responsibility with very little authority. People tend to blame the fundraising department for everything that goes wrong in the organization. People who have no knowledge of fundraising have unrealistic ideas of how much money can be raised in short periods of time. And worse, they tend to believe that all the organization's problems can be solved by finding previously unknown but very large foundations to get grants from, or by meeting lonely, generous, and previously unsolicited rich people.

WHY FUNDRAISING IS COOL

Now I'm going to tell you why people think fundraising isn't cool, and why they're wrong. Let's admit it, fundraisers are regarded with the same mixture of admiration, loathing, suspicion, and awe with which we in America regard money itself. And this explains some of the problems in attracting people to fundraising positions. Money is one of the great taboos of our culture. We are taught not to talk about it or ask about it, except to a very limited number of people in a very limited number of circumstances. As with the subjects of sex, death, mental illness, religion, politics, and other taboos, people say little about their experiences with money. If people are so carefully taught that it is rude to talk about money, it's certainly not going to be easy to ask for it.

Yet, as George Pillsbury points out, "Although money cannot buy social change, no significant change can happen without it." Organizations cannot do their work without money. An organization that does not have enough money to accomplish its goals winds up wasting the time of its volunteers and staff, and possibly hurting the constituency it claims to be working for.

When I decided to make fundraising my career more than 20 years ago, it was not because I liked fundraising. In fact, like most people drawn to working for social change, I had wanted to do advocacy work. But I found that the advocacy work was not going to happen unless someone brought in money, and if I wanted to do work that was important and useful in the groups and movements that I cared about, fundraising, I learned, was one of the most useful things I could do.

I also chose fundraising because it meant that I would have to talk about money, which, in a small way, could begin to break down the taboo that surrounds it. This taboo, I believe, helps promote both racism and sexism: If you can't ask others at your workplace what they are earning, you will never know if minorities there are being paid less than whites, or women less than men. That way, management has no fear that you will seek more equitable salaries. And the taboo supports the class structure in other ways as well: If only a tiny handful of ruling-class people understand how the stock market or other forms of investing work, they will fear no threats to the economic system they control.

In fact, put more strongly, people who cannot talk about money, who will not learn to ask for it and deal with it, actually collaborate with a system that the rest of social change work seeks to dismantle. That alone makes fundraising not only a cool profession, but also a dangerous one.

Here are some other reasons fundraising is exciting, sexy, and cool.

1. Fundraising brings you face-to-face with the good, the bad, and the ugly about money. If you are serious about addressing class issues, this will be a good thing.

2. Although there are technical aspects to fundraising, it does not require years of education. In fact, the three main requirements for success in fundraising can be found in people of all educational backgrounds: common sense, a basic affection for other people, and a passionate belief in a cause.

3. At the same time, fundraising requires you to learn new things all the time, while perfecting the set of basic skills you bring.

4. Fundraising connects donors to an organization. Many donors have little relationship to the organizations they support aside from giving money. They don't have time to volunteer, or they are not part of the constituency. A fundraiser helps them continue to feel connected and useful, so that they will want to continue to give.

5. Fundraising is organizing. Good fundraisers organize teams of volunteers to help with fundraising, and they should be teaching organizers how to ask for money, too. Organizers usually ask people only for time — go to a meeting, plan a strategy, come to a demonstration. Good fundraisers teach people skills and increase their confidence that they actually can raise money. By combining fundraising and organizing, people are asked for time and money — as much of either or both as they can give. A much wider range of gifts and talents and abilities can be brought out in our constituents by adding fundraising strategies to the mix.

6. Fundraising will allow you, perhaps even force you, to confront basic issues of class in yourself, in your organization, and in the people you raise money for and from.

BECOMING A FUNDRAISER

You can enter the field of fundraising in a variety of ways. One of the best ways to learn fundraising is to volunteer, and fundraising is one of the few jobs for which volunteer experience qualifies you. Being on the fundraising committee of a board of directors or helping put on a special event has launched many a fundraising career. Interning at an organization is another form of volunteering that can be very instructive.

You can also learn about fundraising in college classes and courses, but they only have merit if you have a way to apply what you have learned in a real-life setting. Working in a large organization as an assistant to the development director will give you a range of experience without requiring you to take on a lot of responsibility.

If you are serious about fundraising as a career, find a mentor. Many development directors enjoy mentoring people new to the field, and they can help you find your way through the difficult times.

Don't hesitate to jump in at the deep end. Take a job that you are not totally qualified for, then read, take classes, use your mentor, and wing it. I have often encouraged organizations seeking a staff fundraiser to stop looking for the person with perfect skills who may not exist and instead to find a bright, hardworking, quick learner. Give that person a solid team of volunteers to work with and watch what happens. With enough support and a little latitude, this person is likely to be successful.

JOIN THE FRONT LINES

As you can see, when I say I want people to make fundraising their career, what I really mean is that I want people to say, "My role in working for social justice will be to help generate money." Fundraising cannot be separated from its context. It is a necessary and central part of developing an organization and fulfilling its mission. It is real work, and though it takes place on a slightly different set of front lines, they are front lines all the same. The more fundraising is integrated into the rest of the organization, the more successful it will be, and the more fundraisers we can hope to have in the future. The sooner that happens, the sooner I can retire.

thirty

Dealing with Anxiety

During the 24 years I have been in fundraising, I have observed that the greatest factor causing people to leave fundraising, or to "burn out," is not the work itself, or even the challenge of having to ask for money. It is the constant, gnawing anxiety that the money won't come in, and the knowledge that once you have raised money for one month or one quarter you must simply turn around and begin raising it for the next period of time. There is never a rest, success is short-lived, and lack of success shows up immediately. Fundraising can also be an isolating job, with the burden of producing money too often placed on one or two people.

Many paid fundraising staff have told me that they wake up in the middle of the night worrying, that they never feel really free to take a weekend off, let alone a vacation. Fundraising staff often watch their self-esteem eaten away by the constant pressure of a job that by its nature can never be finished.

There are five ways to deal with this anxiety besides psychotherapy or quitting one's job.

1. Recruit volunteers and delegate. Saul Alinsky, one of the most important figures in community organizing, had an iron rule for organizing that also applies to fundraising: "Never do for someone what they can do for themselves." When you are doing something that a reasonable, intelligent person could do with minimal training, find such a person and get them involved. This will decrease your isolation and increase your productivity. Having volunteers help you will not save time, as the time you save by having them do the task is used in recruiting, training, supervising, and then thanking them, but the goal of having the work spread over a wide variety of people is accomplished, and the feeling that it is all up to you is diminished.

2. Remember that if you do your job, the money will come in. Of course some mail appeals will fail, some donors won't give, and some grant proposals will be turned down. But your job is to generate enough requests for money that even when only a small portion are successful you will have the money you need. Fundraising is basically a numbers game — get the word out in as many ways and to as many people as you can. If you ask enough people for money, you will raise the money you need.

3. If your primary responsibility is to raise money, then every day that you come to work set your priorities around that goal. Ask yourself, "Of all the tasks that I have to do today, which one will raise the most money over the longest period of time?" Do that task first, then do the task that will raise the next most money, and so on. This will call for some judgment on your part. For example, if you have the choice of writing a grant proposal for $10,000 or approaching a major donor for an additional gift of $1,000, you may decide to go to the donor because she is more likely to give year after year than the foundation. Or, if you follow the advice in #1, you will try to get a board member to go to the prospective donor, freeing yourself up to write the grant proposal. Just remember that no one ever gets their whole job done. Make sure that the things you don't get done are things not related to fundraising.

In one organization, the director was the only staff person. Feeling responsible for everything, she did those things she knew how to do and that she could finish. She kept accurate and excellent books, paid bills on time, got out minutes and agendas for meetings, and wrote, edited, and produced the newsletter. The board did a lot of program work under her direction. Soon, the group had little money and was in danger of going out of business. This director quickly learned to change her priorities; now she works on fundraising at least four hours every day. If she has time, she does the books. Board meeting minutes and agendas are handled by the board secretary. At each board meeting, the director brings a fundraising to-do list for the board. While some board members object that they want to do program work and do not want to do fundraising, the director is teaching them that without money there is no program and no group. The primary responsibility of the board and staff of any organization is to keep the group going, and this usually means active, ongoing participation in fundraising.

4. Detach from the results of your work. A request turned down or an unsuccessful mailing does not mean that you are a failure as a person or as a fundraiser. Not being able to do everything is not a condemnation of your worth as a person. If you make a mistake, it doesn't mean you are a mistake. Ask yourself whether it will be important in ten years whether you got the newsletter out today or next week. One person can only do so much. Do what you can do in the time allotted, and let the rest go. Too often, groups have fundraising goals that no one could reach. Instead of trying to live up to impossible expectations, evaluate your goal setting.

Some people have found it helpful to form support groups with others doing similar types of work — either informal gatherings over happy hour, or more formal, structured meetings at a specific time and place. If you do use a support group, make sure it supports your work and helps with strategies. Do not use it as a gripe session to compare notes on how awful everyone's job is. That will only make you more dejected.

5. Take care of yourself. Don't always work overtime. Take vacations. Ask for help. Delegate tasks. The overall work of social justice is the creation of a humane and just society, where, among other things, work and leisure are balanced. If the culture of your workplace does not encourage balance, it is unlikely that your organization can have a positive role in creating social change.

Consider these words from the great religious thinker and activist, Thomas Merton:

There is a pervasive form of contemporary violence to which the idealist fighting for peace by nonviolent methods most easily succumbs: activism and overwork. The rush and pressure of modern life are a form, perhaps the most common form, of its innate violence. To allow oneself to be carried away by a multitude of conflicting concerns, to surrender to too many projects, to want to help everyone in everything is to succumb to violence. More than that, it is cooperation in violence. The frenzy of the activist neutralizes one's work for peace. It destroys the fruitfulness of one's work, because it kills the root of inner wisdom which makes work fruitful.

thirty-one

Working with the Executive Director

For many people reading this book, this chapter could be called "Working with Yourself," because the title "executive director" describes you, as does the all-encompassing title of "staff." You are the only paid person. However, if your group is at the stage where it has hired a development director, it probably has other staff as well, such as organizers or other program people.

If you are the development director and you have an executive director, this chapter is for you. If you are the executive director, this chapter is for you also, to help you not make any of the mistakes described here.

When you are the development director, the executive director (ED) can be your greatest ally or your biggest challenge, but rarely anything in between. The job of the development director is an odd one in the sense that you report to and are accountable to the ED, yet your job includes organizing the ED's time efficiently with regard to fundraising — which means telling your boss what to do. To work effectively with an ED requires discussing early on in your tenure how the ED wants you to present the fundraising tasks that he or she is to carry out, and how the ED intends to be accountable to that work.

The ideal working relationship between an ED and a development director (DD) looks something like this:

At the beginning of the year, the ED and the DD create a fundraising plan. Perhaps the DD does most of the work on the plan and then brings it to the ED to discuss, but the ED is very familiar with it and believes it is the appropriate plan for the year. These two staff go over the plan in great detail with the fundraising committee of the board or with board leadership and make any necessary revisions. They present the plan to the full board and receive enthusiastic buy-in (or at least willingness to do the job). The DD feels supported by the ED in all her efforts to work with the board and with the ED. The ED sees the DD as a partner in the financial future of the organization — a junior partner to be sure, but still someone she turns to for advice and whose counsel and instincts she trusts. The DD, in turn, sees the ED as someone she learns a lot from and likes and respects a great deal. If not friends, at least these two see themselves as strong colleagues, interested in each other's opinions on a wide variety of topics related to running the organization.

Some co-workers develop this relationship naturally. They are usually people who are competent, not competitive and not controlling, more committed to the mission of the group than to their own ambition, able to delegate tasks and share information. These people are not without their struggles or disagreements, but they are able to be straightforward in conversation and listen to each other, and they are willing to take the time to work things out.

Other people are able to have this relationship if they work at it a bit. These are usually people who are competent but can be controlling, committed to the mission of the group but wanting some personal recognition, overwhelmed with work so not as able to sort out what can be delegated and what cannot, and who keep information to themselves more out of sheer inability to find the time to share it than any real intent to conceal. Again, honesty in communication will let this be a working relationship.

Unfortunately, there are way too many situations in which the relationship between the ED and DD does not work. Although some of these may be primarily the fault of the DD, the majority have their roots in the work style of the ED. Here are the most common reasons a productive relationship between ED and DD fails to occur:

1. The ED is initially very good at her job, but the organization grows past her ability to run it. Rather than admit this, the ED becomes more and more controlling and may actually shrink the organization back down to a size she can manage.

2. The ED has been at the organization too long. She feels tired and has lost enthusiasm for the work, but stays in the job because she can't imagine what to do next. Mediocrity becomes the standard of work.

3. The ED is sensitive to criticism, even defensive. She creates a work environment in which only total loyalty to her is acceptable and any questioning

of her decisions or directions is perceived as insubordination. Creativity is squelched.

4. The ED is afraid to ask for money and will not help with fundraising from individual donors. Often this fear is disguised as, "I can't deal with a bunch of little gifts. Let's just get a foundation grant."

5. The ED believes that the DD's job is to get the money. She wants the DD to bring in the cash, no questions asked.

6. The ED doesn't trust the board members or want them to have any power, so does not share decision making with them. Few boards (none that I ever met) will actively engage in fundraising if they are not involved in policy making and other board activities, so the board is of no use in fundraising.

7. The ED is threatened by the DD's knowledge of fundraising and feels that her own lack of knowledge will be perceived as incompetence. She constantly belittles the DD's ideas or ignores them altogether.

8. The ED has too big a job. He or she works 60 to 70 hours every week, is often at the office on weekends, rarely takes a vacation, and expects the same effort from the other employees. Such people do not realize that they simply disguise the cost of doing business and they wonder why they have high employee turnover.

There are many other variations on these themes, but these are the most common. If you are already working for someone who has some or all of the characteristics described in the above list, it is possible to make a change in the staff dynamic, but more likely you will need to find another job. To guarantee that you don't take a job where these are the dynamics, make sure that you know what you have the right to expect from an organization and an ED and what they have the right to expect from you.

BEING CLEAR ABOUT YOUR JOB

Your job is to coordinate the fundraising function of the organization. You are to make sure that all fundraising tasks are completed, one of which is to help the ED complete his or her tasks. You lead by pushing others into doing the work, and your job is to get as many people involved in fundraising as possible so that you can raise as much money as you need from as many sources as you can manage. Given that these are your responsibilities, the ED should expect that you and she would work closely together to create the ED's fundraising task list, and that you would have the authority to make sure she was able to move through her tasks. She, in turn, would expect you to provide any support she needed, such as materials, thank-you notes, reports, and so on.

Your job is to coordinate the fundraising efforts of the board of directors. You should have access to all board members and, most important, be actively supported by the ED in your efforts with the board. Both of you should work closely with board members, particularly on personal face-to-face solicitation.

Sometimes the ED will know a lot more about fundraising than the DD. In that case, the ED should mentor the DD. More traditionally, the DD knows more about fundraising than the ED. The ED should welcome this, recognizing that an organization hires staff partly because the ED doesn't have time to do the whole job, but also because she doesn't have every skill.

Both parties should know how the other likes to work. The DD needs to know the answer to questions such as, Are interruptions OK? How about editing each other's writing? (The ED needs to feel good about everything that comes out of the office, so she or he gets to edit a lot.) How about being nagged about getting a task done? How do each of you deal with conflict? What is the best way for you to hear criticism? And so on.

The ED is the front person for the organization. Many donors will prefer to meet with that person rather than anyone else in the organization. The DD has to appreciate that the ED balances many tasks, of which fundraising is only one — even if it is very important.

The way to have a good working relationship between the DD and ED is to be clear from the beginning what each of you thinks the ED and DD jobs are and are not — and agree on that. Work as much as possible as partners in fundraising and see the board as an asset to be developed. Be mission-driven and know that your main loyalty has to be to the good of the organization. Know that you are not always going to see eye-to-eye and that final decisions do rest with the ED. Above all, be honest and demand honesty in return. Your relationship needs to mirror the kind of relationships we want to see in the world — respectful, caring, nurturing, genuinely interested in the other, joined in a mutual belief in something bigger than yourselves.

Budgeting & Planning

Lily Tomlin once said, "I always wanted to be somebody. I guess I should have been more specific." I think of this quote whenever I think of planning. All non-profits want to have enough money to do their work, but few can name what amount that would be. They certainly want to use the time and money of volunteers and donors wisely and make progress in accomplishing their goals, but the work of defining exactly what that would mean often doesn't get done. When a group does not take the time to talk it through, write it down, and get everyone in the group to own it, the budgeting process might proceed as follows: "We need money — whatever we can get. We'll spend what we have, but it won't be enough." The fundraising plan consists of "Help! Write a grant, quick! Let's do an event — what's fast? Does anybody know anybody they can ask?" If you thrive on this chaotic crisis approach to budgeting and planning, then don't read the following chapters. But if you think, "There has to be a better way," you are right.

Because time is our most precious non-renewable resource, all efforts that use time respectfully, efficiently, enjoyably, and with the greatest results for the time put in ought to be our life's top priorities. Developing a financial plan — a budget and a fundraising plan — will let you use your time to maximum effectiveness.

thirty-two

Developing a Budget

The first step in developing a fundraising plan is to develop a working budget. In its most simple form, a budget is a list of items on which you plan to spend money (expenses) and a list of sources from which you plan to receive money (income). A budget is balanced when the expenses and income are equal; an ideal budget projects more income than expenses. Budgets are usually prepared from year to year. There are many ways to prepare a budget and as groups grow they may change the way they prepare their budget a number of times before finding one that gives them the most accurate projections.

There is a simple, two-step process for preparing a budget that most small non-profit organizations can use effectively. The process takes into account the largest number of variables without having to do extensive research or prepare elaborate spreadsheets. In some organizations a single staff member prepares the entire budget and presents it for board approval, but this is a large burden for one person. Therefore, the method presented here assumes that a small committee will undertake the budget-setting process. This committee can be a standing "finance" committee of the board, which would then be in charge of monitoring the budget, or it can be an ad-hoc committee of two or three board members and a staff person. Many grassroots organizations lack expertise in developing budgets, and so recruit someone onto their budget committee to help them create it. This is particularly helpful if you are switching systems or fiscal years, or if you want to plan for more than one year at a time.

If you work with a committee, it should not be more than five or six people. Each should have some knowledge of the organization and be willing to put in the time it will take to do the job as thoroughly as possible.

STEP ONE: ESTIMATE EXPENSES AND INCOME SEPARATELY

The budget committee should first divide into two subgroups: one to estimate expenses, the other to project income. When these tasks are completed, the subgroups will reconvene to mesh their work in Step Two.

Estimating Expenses

The group working on the expense side of the budget should prepare three columns of numbers representing "survival," "reasonable," and "maximum" expense figures (see example, next page). The "survival" column spells out the amount of money the organization needs simply to stay open. If you are not able to raise this amount of money, you would have to shut your doors. Items here generally include office space, minimum staff requirements, postage, printing, and telephone. This column does not include the cost of new work, salary increases, additional staff, new equipment, or other improvements.

Next, the group prepares the "maximum" column: how much money the group would need to operate at maximum effectiveness. This is not a dream budget, but a true estimate of the amount of funding required for optimum functioning. Finally, the committee prepares the "reasonable" column: how much money the group needs to do more than survive but still not meet all its goals. These figures should not be conceived of as simply the middle of the other two columns. For example, an organization may feel that in order to accomplish any good work, the office needs to be larger, or in order to maintain staff morale, the organization must raise salaries. Because higher rent and increased salaries aren't necessary to a group's survival, they will not be included in the group's "survival" budget; however, they are important enough to the organization's work to be included in the "reasonable" budget.

The "survival," "reasonable," and "maximum" columns give the range of finances required to run the organization at various levels of functioning. If you have a year or two of financial history, you can use those numbers and those line items to help you in creating your budget.

The process of figuring expenses and income must be done with great thoroughness and attention to detail. For example, to estimate how much you will spend on printing, think through all the items you print and how many of each you will need. A simple mail appeal has at least three printed components — the letter, the return envelope, and the envelope the appeal is sent in. The budget for creating a Web site will need to include keeping it up-to-date, a marketing plan for driving traffic to the site, and the staff time required to respond to e-mail generated by the site. When you don't know how much something costs, do not guess. Take the time while creating the budget to find out.

To assure completeness and accuracy in budget-setting, many organizations have found it helpful to send board and staff members to training sessions on financial planning.

SAMPLE EXPENSE PROJECTIONS

ITEM	SURVIVAL	REASONABLE	MAXIMUM
Salaries			
Director			
Fundraising Coordinator			
Support staff			
Program Coordinator			
Benefits and taxes			
TOTAL PERSONNEL			
Travel			
Office rent			
Office equipment			
Lease photocopier			
Computers (desktop and laptop)			
Other (specify)			
Office supplies			
Telephone			
Handsets			
Office lines			
Fax line			
Internet Service Provider			
Photocopy			
Design			
Printing			
Brochures			
Annual report			
Mail appeals			
Newsletters			
Stationery			
Other			
TOTAL OTHER OPERATING			
Postage			
First-class mail			
Bulk mail			
Bulk mail permit			
Other (specify)			
TOTAL POSTAGE			
Bookkeeping contract			
Training for board and staff			
Other (specify)			
Miscellaneous			
TOTAL OTHER FUNDRAISING			
GRAND TOTAL			

Projecting Income

At the same time that the expense side of the budget is being prepared, the other half of the committee is preparing the income side. Crucial to this process is a knowledge of what fundraising strategies the organization can carry out and how much money these can be expected to generate. Much of this information will come from records kept in previous years. The income side is also estimated in three columns, representing "worst," "likely," and "ideal." (See example on the next page.)

To calculate the income projection labeled "worst," take last year's income sources and assume that with the same amount of effort the group will at least be able to raise this amount again, unless you know that the effort expended was more than can be expected in future years, or that you were given some one-time-only gifts. In the case of foundation, corporation, or government grants it may be wise to write "zero" as the worst projection, unless you have been promised or strongly led to believe that your grant will be renewed.

Draw up the "ideal" income projections next. These figures reflect what would happen if all the organization's fundraising strategies were successful and all grant proposals were funded. Again, this is not a dream budget. It does not assume events that will probably not occur, such as someone giving your group a gift of a million dollars. The ideal budget must be one that would be met if everything went absolutely right.

The "likely" column is a compromise. It estimates the income the organization can expect to generate with reasonable growth, hard work, most people keeping their promises, expanding old fundraising strategies and having success with some new strategies, yet with some things going wrong.

All income categories are figured on the basis of their gross: that is, the amounts you expect to earn from each strategy before expenses are subtracted. The expenses must then be included in the expense side of the budget. Be sure that the committee developing the expenses side of the budget includes expenses for fundraising in the total expenses of the organization.

Both the income and expense sides of the budget are presented in columns of numbers, but each subcommittee should also include a narrative that explains some of the rationale behind the numbers and outlines goals other than money that some fundraising strategies will be seeking to accomplish.

SAMPLE INCOME PROJECTIONS

SOURCE	WORST	LIKELY	IDEAL
Major gifts			
New and upgraded			
Renewals			
Monthly donors			
Membership			
New			
Renewals			
Special appeals			
Sale of products			
T-shirts			
Booklets			
Special events			
House parties			
Dance			
Conference			
Board donations			
Fees for service			
Foundations (specify)			
Other (specify)			
TOTAL INCOME			

STEP TWO: MEET, COMPARE, NEGOTIATE

Once income and expense projections have been completed, the two halves of the committee can share results. When the income and expense sides of the budget have been figured separately in this way, there is less chance of giving in to the temptation to manipulate the figures to make them balance. The committee should follow the old fundraising adage, "Plan expenses high and income low." If you do follow this advice and your numbers are wrong (that is, if your expenses are lower or your income higher than projected), you will be pleasantly surprised. If you do what many groups do, which is to boost income estimates to make the budget balance, you will soon be in financial trouble.

When the entire committee reconvenes, you hope to find that the amount in the "reasonable" expense column and the "likely" income column are close to the same. In that happy circumstance those figures can be adopted as the budget with no more fuss. Occasionally groups are pleasantly surprised to discover that their "likely" income projections come close to their "maximum" expense projections. However, compromises usually need to be made; most of the time the expenses need to be adjusted to meet realistic income potential, not the other way around.

When no two sets of numbers are anywhere near alike, the committee will have to find solutions. There is no right or wrong way to negotiate at this point. If each committee has really done its job properly, there will be no need to review each item to see if it is accurate. However, with more research, each subcommittee may discover other ways to delete expenses or add income.

NINE POSSIBLE WAYS
INCOME AND EXPENSE PROJECTIONS CAN MATCH UP

EXPENSES	INCOME
Survival	Worst
Reasonable	Likely
Maximum	Ideal

EXPENSES	INCOME
Survival	Worst
Reasonable	Likely
Maximum	Ideal

EXPENSES	INCOME
Survival	Worst
Reasonable	Likely
Maximum	Ideal

Once the budget is developed and adopted, it must be monitored. There are many inexpensive accounting software programs that can help you do this, or you can do it by hand. Every month, you note what you have spent or raised in each category of your budget. Every quarter, you note what your expenses and income are for the quarter, and what they should be if your cash flow was exactly even. (In other words, you divide your budget into fourths, and each quarter you compare how much your real expenses and income correlate to your planned ones.) Many software programs will figure this out for you, including giving you a percentage of the total budget to show where you are compared to where you should be. You can then make adjustments as needed and catch problems fairly quickly. Unless your budget projections are totally wrong, do not change your budget — use it as a learning tool. Adjustments that you need to make will be noted as such, so that, as you create budgets year after year, you will know where you tend to be accurate and where you tend to go wrong in making budget projections. Compare what you projected would happen with what did happen and discuss the differences. This way, as the years pass you will be able to create more and more accurate budgets.

Two case studies that illustrate different ways of reaching a workable budget using compromise and research are discussed below.

THE MAKING OF A BUDGET: TWO CASE STUDIES

Neighborhood Advocacy

Neighborhood Advocacy was founded ten years ago. For the past five years, they have received a federal grant of $30,000 annually. Last year, however, they were informed that federal money was no longer available. Of their total budget of $73,700, this shortfall represented more than 40%. Their budget committee developed the following estimates:

EXPENSES		INCOME	
Survival	$ 56,500	Worst	$43,720
Reasonable	$ 73,700	Likely	$45,000
Maximum	$103,000	Ideal	$50,000

All of their income projections were below the amount they needed in order to survive. Furthermore, their reasonable budget was their actual budget from the past five years, and their survival budget represented significant cutbacks in service. After much discussion among the board and staff the group decided that they wanted to continue operating at the current level to avoid undermining morale completely and curtailing the program. Therefore, the board asked the budget committee to develop a budget that would be between the existing "survival" and "reasonable" options and to research further some expanded fundraising programs, including getting a loan.

The expense half of the committee then created a budget called "Survival Two" which called for renting part of their office to another group and reducing a clerical position. The income half of the committee investigated hiring a consulting firm to help implement a large membership recruitment drive using telephone and direct mail. The strategy would pay for itself the first year and begin making money the second year. The front money required for this whole package was $10,000. The budget committee returned to the board with these figures:

EXPENSES		INCOME	
Survival One	$56,500	Likely	$45,000
Survival Two	$60,000	Ideal	$50,000
Loan	$10,000	Loan	$10,000

When the full board met they first adopted the "Ideal" income projection and the "Survival Two" expense budget. This involved risk, and board members all realized and agreed that their level of involvement in fundraising had to increase over that of previous years. They then committed themselves to the loan: a move of considerable risk, foresight, and courage. They reasoned that the worst that could happen was that they would have to cut their budget drastically and extend the loan payments. But with some luck and a lot of hard work, Neighborhood Advocacy would never be as dependent on one source of money again. Two board members agreed to co-sign for the loan, meaning that they would have to pay it back if Neighborhood Advocacy defaulted. This raised the stakes a good deal for all the board members.

Their final decision was to adopt their Survival Two and Ideal income projections along with taking out the loan. They planned to pay the loan back in the second year, when the strategy began to make more money. They realized they either had to grow dramatically in their ability to raise money or they might as well fold, because the program allowed by their "survival" budget just wasn't worth it.

North Fork Watershed Protection

North Fork Watershed Protection had been functioning for only two years. The first year the program was run entirely by volunteers, most of them residents living near the watershed area. In the second year, in conjunction with the group incorporating as a nonprofit, some volunteers agreed to form a board of directors. They were able to raise enough money to hire a staff biologist. With this person's expertise, the organization was able to document the sources of the pollution entering their watershed, to get a good deal of publicity, and to attract the attention of the public health department. To keep the pressure on, and to ensure that appropriate steps are taken to mitigate this pollution, this staff member now needed a half-time assistant to help with fundraising, administration, and dealing with the press. While the board had been successful in fundraising, and a few people made significant financial contributions, no one was certain that these gifts would be repeated. It was also difficult for them to make fundraising projections based on past experience because they had so little to go on. A budget committee estimated these figures:

EXPENSES		INCOME	
Survival	$ 38,000	Worst	$40,000
Reasonable	$ 50,000	Likely	$50,000
Maximum	$100,000	Ideal	$63,000

The only difference between the "Survival" and "Reasonable" expenses was the cost of an assistant. Even though the "Likely" income could cover the "Reasonable" budget, the board elected to adopt the "Survival" budget for the first six months, along with the "Likely" income. They reasoned that although their track record for fundraising was good, their fundraising program was not well enough established for them to draw conclusions about the future.

Because the program had grown rapidly, the board felt that taking on another staff person was ill-advised until they were sure of meeting their income goals. They decided that at a six-month income review they would hire the assistant if they had raised at least half of their "Likely" goals. This gave the board some "breathing time" and assured the staff person that the issue of her workload was being addressed and could be solved in a short time. In the meantime, board and volunteers committed themselves to helping out in the office and handling more of the media calls.

These case studies illustrate that budgets are designed to be flexible, to serve as measurements of progress, and to provide structures for the way money is spent and raised. Using a budget this way makes it a helpful document rather than a club hanging over your head. Small organizations cannot know exactly how much money they will raise or spend beyond certain fixed costs such as rent or salaries, but they need the parameters that a budget can provide.

thirty-three

Creating a Fundraising Plan

Veteran fundraiser and organizer Gary Delgado says that there are four steps to successful fundraising:

1. Plan   2. Plan   3. Plan   4. Work your plan

Because there is so much truth to this formula, it may surprise readers that this planning chapter is relatively short. That's because planning for fundraising is not difficult to explain, nor is it difficult to do. Not only is planning fully three-fourths of what makes fundraising successful, is it also true that one hour of planning can save three hours of work. But the final and most important truth is that planning does not take the place of doing.

Given that an organization is going to have to work its plan in order to raise money, how can a workable plan be created? There are five steps:

1. Set a goal. This will come from your budget, which you can create using the principles outlined in Chapter 32 on budgeting. Setting accurate goals requires also analyzing your fundraising experiences over the last two years.

2. For each income strategy (including strategies not related to individual donors), think through the following details:

- Tasks required to complete the strategy
- Due date for each task
- Who is in charge of each task
- How much the strategy is going to cost and how much it is going to raise

You can put these pieces of information on a spreadsheet or write them up as a narrative with a budget attached.

Now put the plan on a "Year-At-A-Glance" type of calendar so you can make sure that you have spread the work out over the course of the year as evenly as possible and that you have not made unrealistic plans.

3. Plot out your plans for raising money from individuals. From the amount of money the budget shows you must raise, subtract any that will be raised from strategies not involving individual donors, such as product sales, foundations, government, fees for service, and interest income. The amount that remains will form the basis of your individual donor fundraising plan. The other methods you have for generating income will be added on to your plan during the last step. For this step, analyze the types of gifts the money will need to come from and the types of donors you have now. This will help you develop a clearer sense of what strategies you need to focus on to meet your financial goals.

a. Given the amount of money that must be raised from individuals, determine how much will be raised from each group of donors, as discussed in Chapter 3, Matching Fundraising Strategies with Financial Needs. Following that formula, figure that 60% of the money will come from 10% of your donors, 20% of the money will come from 20% of your donors, and the remaining 20% of the money will come from 70% of your donors. The first number is your goal for major gifts; the second number is your goal for habitual donors responding to retention strategies, particularly from those donors giving several times a year; the last number is your goal from first-time donors giving through acquisition strategies.

b. Analyze your current donor base using the following questions:
• How many donors do you have now in each of those three categories?
• What is your renewal rate? (It should be around 66%.)
• What are the organization's strengths in working with donors?
  – Do you do a good job of acquiring donors, but have a higher-than-normal attrition rate? Or, do you have a strong base of very loyal habitual donors, with a lower-than-normal attrition rate? (This would indicate a weakness in use of acquisition strategies.)
  – Do you do a good job of identifying the top 10% of donors and regularly seek upgraded gifts and major gifts from them?
  – Has the number of donors to your organization grown, decreased, or stayed the same in the last three years? (If it has decreased, you are not doing enough acquisition and may also have a problem with retention of donors. If the number of donors has stayed the same, you are either doing a good job with retention or acquisition, but not both because otherwise you would see an increase.)

4. Decide how many donors you need to meet your goals, and match them with the strategies that work best for reaching those donors.

5. Put the plan onto a timeline and fill out the tasks.

On the next page is a sample fundraising plan for an organization seeking $213,500.

FUNDRAISING PLAN/ 2000

STRATEGY	ACTION STEPS	WHO	WHEN	EXPENSES
BOARD FUNDRAISING Goal: $20,000	1. Proposed ID process & asking 2. Board members make own gifts	Staff/BD comm BD	June–Nov by Nov	$100

NEW MEMBER ACQUISITION
Goal: 250 new members
$12,500
	1. Four mailings to 1,000
	  prospects each (50 new members)
	2. Each board member recruits
	  three members (60 new members)
	3. Events (50 new members)
	4. General public relations (20 new members)
	5. House parties (70 new members)
		Staff
		
		BD
		
		Committee/Staff
		Committees/Vols/ Staff
		BD
			quarterly
			
			May–Dec
			
			May–Dec
			ongoing
			Feb–Dec
				$2,000
				
				no cost
				
				see below
				no cost
				see below

RENEWALS Goal: 330 renewals (66% of 500 members) $20,000	1. Four mailings	Staff	quarterly	$1,000
SPECIAL APPEALS Goal: $5,000	1. Spring appeal 2. Year-end appeal	FRC/Staff/ Vols FRC/Staff/ Vols	by Feb 1 by Nov 1	$250 $250
SPECIAL EVENTS Goal: $6,000	1. Auction ($5,000) 2. Dinner-dance ($1,000)	BD/Vols BD/Vols	Feb Sept	$2,500 $200
MAJOR DONORS Goal: $50,000	1. Finalize MD plan 2000 2. Implement plan 3. Plan and host gatherng	Staff/FRC Staff/FRC Staff/BD/FRC	Jan Jan–Dec June	no cost $1,000 $200
HOUSE PARTIES Goal: $10,000	1. Finalize dates for 10 gatherings 2. Hold gatherings 3. Follow-up letters/calls	FRC/BD/Staff Hosts/BD Hosts/FRC/Staff	Feb 15 Apr–Oct each gathering	$1,200 no cost
BUSINESSES Goal: $10,000	1. Design and implement plan 2. Mail solicitations (3 mailings) 3. Business breakfast	Staff/FRC/BD Staff/FRC/Vols FRC/Staff	Feb–Dec Mar/June/Oct May	$200 $500
FOUNDATIONS Goals: $80,000	1. Evaluate '99 grant program 2. Prepare grant strategy 2000 3. Prepare 1 more capacity-building grant 4. Prepare program grant	Staff Staff Staff Staff	Jan Feb Mar May	$200 $100
PLANNED GIFTS Goal: future income	1. PG seminar 2. Request in every newsltr 3. Set up accounts in all local stock brokerage firms 4. Design/print PG brochure	Staff Staff Staff Staff Staff/PGC	Oct 3 ×/year by Mar 1 June 1 Sept 1	$150 no cost $50 $100 $3,500

TOTAL INCOME: $213,500   **TOTAL EXPENSES: $13,500***

Key: BD=Board members   FRC=Fundraising Committee   PGC= Planned Gifts Committee
* Does not include Development Director's salary

FUNDRAISING PLANNING AT WORK: TWO CASE STUDIES

Artworks

Artworks is a community theater serving a town of 250,000 people. The theater performs works of local playwrights and works aimed at raising consciousness about, or demonstrating the talents of, children, seniors, and disabled people. It has a budget of $150,000 a year and two paid staff people — an artistic director and an administrator. The administrator is also in charge of coordinating fundraising. The group also has an active board of directors of 13 people.

This year Artworks plans to raise $75,000 from ticket sales, small government grants, and fees from their acting classes. They will raise the remaining $75,000 from community donations, which they have been able to do for the past three years because of a private foundation grant of $10,000. This grant is not being renewed, so next year they must raise at least $10,000 more than they have in the past.

Using the formula in Step 3a, the group sees that they will need to raise $45,000 from major gifts, $15,000 from habitual donors, and the remaining $15,000 from their current fundraising program of three special events and direct mail.

The group is highly visible in their community. Currently they have 1,000 donors, 600 of whom give about $25, and 200 of whom give between $50 and $100. Many of these gifts are given at the end of performances, when a board member comes out to the stage and asks people to make a gift above the cost of their ticket. Fifty of their donors give $100 or more. The biggest gifts are $1,500 from a board member, two gifts of $1,000 each from past board members, and two gifts of $750 each from sisters who support all the arts programs in this community.

The group's donor attrition rate is more than 50%. For the past three years, they have steadily lost donors, going from 1,500 to 1,250 and now to 1,000. Some board members have blamed this decline on the artistic director's choice of productions. In the last two years, the group has put on a disability rights play that some people complained was too strident, two avant-garde plays that some people found too obscure, and a play about an aging priest and his struggle with and eventual expulsion from the Catholic Church because of his views on sexuality, which some found anti-Catholic, others found anti-gay, and others found too pro-gay. Because the director mixes these productions with works appropriate for families to attend and plays written and largely produced by children, other board members feel that the range of works is appropriate and suits the variety of people in the community. They also feel that since their mission is to raise consciousness, the plays that are chosen will necessarily raise hackles as well.

The board and staff have spent countless hours discussing these plays and audience reaction to them, and by and large have found these conversations helpful. However, fundraising has lagged. Now, they have decided to focus on fundraising and then determine whether the plays they are producing are the cause of the decline in their donor base, since there has been no decline in their audience numbers.

Applying the formula to their donor base of 1,000 donors, they come up with the following figures:

• 100 donors should give $100 or more, for a total of $45,000
• 200 donors should give $50 to $100, for a total of $15,000
• 700 donors should give under $50, for a total of $15,000

Projecting a normal attrition rate of 33%, they will need to acquire 300 new donors just to maintain their base of 1,000 donors.

Moving to Step 4, they draw up this outline:

Goal 1: Double the number of major donors from 50 to 100 people.

Goal 2: Maintain the number of people giving $50 to $100 at 200 people.

Goal 3: Attract 300 first-time givers and strengthen their retention strategies to ensure that 700 donors renew (some of these will become major donors). This way they will maintain their base of 1,000 donors and not experience any more shrinkage.

To accomplish these goals, they will conduct two major donor campaigns, one in the spring and one in the fall. They will create a gift range chart for major donors and seek 400 prospects who could give gifts in the range of $100–$2,500 (projecting a 50% refusal rate, and that 50% of the positive responses will give less than what was requested). Fifty of these will be requests for renewals from current major donors, 150 will be prospects identified from current donors who give less than $100, and the remaining 200 prospects will be from the community at large through board and staff contacts.

To retain donors, they will write to current donors three times during the year, describing different projects and aspects of their work. They will introduce a pledge program and have a fundraising column in their newsletter.

Finally, they will continue to ask for donations at the end of their theater shows, and will continue their three special events because they have had good luck acquiring donors this way.

Moving to Step 5, they are ready to put their plan on a timeline. On a master calendar, they mark off when their plays are running. They note when their government grants are due to be submitted, when their special events are scheduled, and when their quarterly newsletter goes out. Next, they schedule their extra appeals so that they go out just after the first three plays, but at least three weeks before or after each special event. Finally, they schedule their major gifts campaign in two small remaining windows of "down" time: January 15 to February 15, and November 1 through Thanksgiving.

With this plan approved, Artworks' board divides itself into three committees: acquisition, retention, and major donors/upgrades. With the help of the organization's administrator, each committee prepares a task list and divides up the work.

By using these steps, the planning process can be both simple and accurate. Once a plan is developed, working the plan should bring in the money you need.

The Children's Museum

The Children's Museum is located in another town of 250,000 people. Started two years ago, the museum is based on the now-popular model of encouraging children to touch and interact with the exhibits. The museum has a board of 40 committed people from all walks of life. Most have children. About half volunteer with other arts organizations in the community. All agree that board members should both give and help raise money.

Before understanding the larger issues in fundraising and learning the fundraising strategies discussed in this book, the fundraising committee of five board members and a staff person presented monthly fundraising plans, consisting mostly of special events, at board meetings. They never planned more than two or three months in advance. In one year they had the following activities:

January–February: A sushi benefit at a Japanese restaurant. Tickets were $10 each. Board members were expected to sell five tickets each, which they did. Net: $1,950.

March: A yacht trip on a nearby lake donated by an expert schooner sailor. The museum provided food and drink. Board members were expected to sell two tickets each at $25. Most board members bought one ticket and sold the other to their spouses. Net: $1,800.

April: A pancake breakfast held in cooperation with five other arts organizations. The breakfast was widely advertised, but each organization had to guarantee to bring in 100 participants. No requirements were set, but most of the board members came with their families and a few friends. Cost: $4 for adults, $2 for children. Overall net: $2,000; Children's Museum: $400.

April–June: Membership campaign. Board members came to one extra meeting that month in order to help send out 4,000 invitations to join the museum. In addition, each board member was expected to enroll 15 new members at $25 each, for a total of 600 new members. All board members enrolled at least 3 new members and some got their full complement of 15. Total new members from all efforts: 200. Gross: $5,000. Cost of mailings: $1,500. Net income: $3,500.

July: Traveling fair benefit, in which a traveling fair agreed to set up its Ferris wheels and other rides and booths and give a percentage of income from the Fourth of July weekend to the museum. Museum board members and volunteers staffed booths for drinks, hot dogs, cotton candy, and so on; proceeds from those sales went to the museum. In addition, 10% of the proceeds from admissions and rides went to the museum. Admission was $2, with an additional charge for each ride. Anyone who worked at a booth could bring his or her family in free, plus each child of a volunteer worker got three free rides. Fifty volunteers in all worked at the fair during the weekend. Net: $7,500.

August: A well-deserved breather, except for the fundraising committee that planned the September event. No board meeting.

September: An art auction, with paintings and sculpture by local artists. The museum paid the rental fee for the auction gallery and the publicity expenses. The artists paid for the auctioneer and split the price of each item sold with the museum. Board members were each given 50 posters announcing the auction to display around town. For this task, the fundraising committee assigned each person several square blocks near their home or work. Further, board members were to help stuff invitations. These had to be mailed first class because, as the committee explained, "This all came together very fast." Front costs were high. Because the museum did not have the money to front, each board member was asked for an interest-free, one-month loan of $100. Net: $2,000.

October: Restaurant opening benefit and flower-selling project. When these two opportunities arose, the fundraising committee did not want to pass them up. First, a fancy restaurant donated its opening to benefit the museum. Everything would be donated, that is, if the museum could keep the restaurant full all night. Capacity of the restaurant was 200. The event was free for board members, $20 for others. No children were allowed. Each board member was encouraged to bring at least five friends. The museum succeeded in its bargain. Net: $3,500. The other opportunity was selling bouquets of flowers at a shopping mall on three consecutive Saturdays, one of which was also the night of the restaurant opening. The museum would buy bunches of flowers at $1 and sell them for $2.50 to $5.00. Two volunteers for two-hour shifts were needed for three shifts each Saturday, or six volunteers per Saturday. The board dutifully signed up. Net: $400.

December: The board evaluated their fundraising efforts. Every event had been successful. A total of $20,250 had been raised, plus the museum had acquired more than 600 new members and massively increased its visibility.

Not surprisingly, however, in spite of their success, 36 board members resigned at the end of the year, including 3 members of the fundraising committee. All cited overwork and too much fundraising as their primary reasons for leaving the board.

Almost miraculously, the museum recruited 36 more board members of the same high caliber, largely from their volunteer pool. With the help of a consultant, the museum board evaluated its fundraising plans and decided to change them considerably. First, they looked at the special events themselves. While all the events were appropriate, not all enhanced the image of the museum. Therefore, the new fundraising committee scrapped those events that did not include children, except the art auction, which promoted the museum in other ways. They scrapped the sushi benefit, the sailing adventure, and the restaurant opening (an unrepeatable event in any case). The pancake breakfast, which had raised the least amount of money, was repeated with two changes: 1) As much as possible, the advertising was designed to attract new people, and 2) every family or adult attending would later be sent a fundraising appeal offering membership in all five arts organizations at a cost slightly higher than that of joining any two of them. Although this event would still not be a giant moneymaker, it would bring in many new members and increase visibility for all five organizations. Further, it promoted the sense that all the arts organizations were working in harmony. The flower-selling was also repeated. Although labor intensive, the chance for volunteers to discuss the museum with so many people brought a notable rise in museum attendance in the weeks during and after the sale. Each bouquet was accompanied by a 3" × 5" card that briefly described the museum and listed its hours.

Board members joined one of three committees, each of which helped the fundraising committee in different ways. The membership committee worked all year to increase membership through mail and phone solicitation. The major gifts committee solicited major gifts from current donors.

The events committee worked on the special events, with no board member working on more than three events. An auxiliary of volunteers is now being formed to help plan and staff these events.

The entire fundraising calendar was prepared a year in advance, with projected income. It looked like this:

January–December: Ongoing membership recruitment. New members: 1,000. Net income: $12,000.

April: Pancake breakfast, with mail appeal follow-up. Net income: $1,000.

July: Fair with food booths. Net income: $9,500.

September: Art auction. Net income: $6,000.

September–November: Major gifts campaign. Net income: $25,000.

October–November: Three weekends of flower sales. Net income: $600.

Total projected income: $54,100. Total projected new members: 1,200.

At the end of the first year of the new fundraising plan, only five board members resigned, none of them for other than personal reasons.

thirty-four

What to Do in Case of Financial Trouble

First, don't panic. Like most people, organizations get into difficult financial straits from time to time. Panicking, searching for who is to blame, and whining will not solve your problem. What you must do first is carefully analyze the nature of the financial problem and how you got into it. This will help create a strategy for getting out of it.

There are several kinds of financial troubles, ranging from simple cash-flow problems to serious mismanagement or even embezzlement of funds. I will discuss each of these major types of financial problems below. However, it is important to recognize that financial problems are usually symptomatic of deeper management difficulties. These difficulties usually show up first, and often most seriously, in the areas of fundraising and spending. The root cause may be the failure of the board of directors to plan the year thoroughly and thus anticipate the financial crisis; or it could be the reluctance of a staff person to discuss the finances of the organization honestly and fully with the board, leading them to approve an unrealistic budget. Sometimes the deeper problem is that fundraising projections are inaccurate because not enough research was done to make reasonable estimates of income or because of overdependence on foundations, which sometimes string groups along for a long time before rejecting them. Whatever the problem turns out to be, it must be addressed and solved. If only the financial problem is solved and the underlying organizational issues remain unaddressed, the financial problems will recur, each time with increasing severity.

There are four main types of financial problems: cash-flow problems, deficit spending, serious accounting errors or mismanagement of funds, and embezzlement of funds.

CASH-FLOW PROBLEMS

A cash-flow problem occurs when anticipated income is not coming in fast enough, creating a temporary lag in income in relation to spending. A cash-flow problem has an end in sight. You know that when a certain major donation or grant comes in, or a reimbursement from the city, county, or state is received, you will be able to pay your bills and say goodbye to your problem. Until that time, however, the organization has to draw on its reserves; once the organization exhausts any savings it might have, then it is in a bind.

You have several choices at that point. You can try to put a freeze on spending and even up your income and expenses by ceasing to incur expenses. You can attempt to stall your creditors by paying bills in installments and by postponing paying as many bills as possible. In that case, call creditors and explain your situation, giving them a date by which you will pay the bill. Many times creditors will allow you to postpone payment if they believe you will have the money soon. Another option is to borrow money to cover your expenses and repay the loan when your cash flow improves. Depending on the size of the loan, you may be able to borrow the money from a loyal board member or major donor who will charge little or no interest and create no publicity. Foundations and corporations in some communities have "emergency loan funds" to help groups through cash-flow difficulties when those problems are not the organization's fault. A final option is to set up a line of credit at a bank and draw on that to cover expenses. Depending on interest rates, however, this could be an expensive move.

A cash-flow problem is largely a logistical one and often can be solved by setting aside money in a reserve in anticipation of times such as these.

DEFICIT SPENDING

A deficit is a chronic cash-flow problem, or more accurately, a situation in which you are spending more than you are raising with no end in sight for this discrepancy. Irresponsible or short-sighted organizations finance their deficit with money from their savings, if they have any, or with money earmarked for special programs, which then is problematic for the special program and may cause distress to the person or grantmaking source for the program. At some point, however, the organization will run out of money and no longer be able to finance the deficit.

There is only one solution to deficit spending: Create an ongoing way to raise more money or permanently cut down on spending. Examine where you are over-spending and put a freeze on those areas. Designate one staff person or board member to authorize all expenditures of more than $25. In a low-budget organization, careful attention to money spent on photocopying, postage, and office supplies can make a big difference.

Obviously, the organization's fundraising plan and income reports will have to be carefully examined and strengthened. Raising more money, however, is a long-term solution; deficits require immediate attention because the longer they continue, the worse they get. Once you are out of the deficit, avoid the situation in the future by spending only as much money as you raise.

SERIOUS ACCOUNTING ERRORS, MISMANAGEMENT OF FUNDS, OR EMBEZZLEMENT

In these cases, the entire board must be notified immediately and the people responsible for the error or crime must be dealt with swiftly. In the case of crime, the person must be fired. In the case of serious error, some mitigating circumstances may be taken into account, such as if the person had never made an error before, the person admitted it immediately and took steps to remedy it, or the error was clearly a mistake and not indicative of carelessness or deception. Nevertheless, the person should probably be suspended until the situation is resolved. In the case of fraud or theft, the board will have to decide whether to take legal action against the person or people responsible.

Board members should prepare a brief statement on what happened and what the organization is doing about it. This statement can be sent to funding sources and used should the story get into the newspapers or other media. Honesty and swift action are the best ways to ensure the fewest repercussions.

The more difficult problem to solve is how to make up the loss of money that this error or crime has caused. Asking close major donors for extra gifts, seeking loans, instituting spending freezes, vacation without pay, or pay deferments for staff are some options. In the last resort, staff layoff may be necessary.

If the financial situation cannot be improved by any of these means, the organization should consider closing. An organizational development consultant or a facilitator will be helpful in leading the board to a proper decision.

The most serious problem in this third case is the morale of all the people involved. Very little work goes on when everyone in the organization is depressed and shocked. Morale will be boosted when the staff and board have decided on a course of action. If the organization is to stay alive, this must be decided quickly and the plan implemented immediately. A crisis of this magnitude can pull people together and strengthen the organization as long as those who stay with it agree that keeping the organization going is of the utmost importance.

Special Challenges

If I had a dime for every time I have been told, "You don't know what it's like to raise money for _____ ," followed by a description of the place where the group works, or the issue they work on, or the people they encounter, or some other variable, I could endow every group I ever cared about. Of course, it is true I don't know what it is like, but I can ask questions and learn, and that is usually why an organization is paying me to be there. What people mean when they tell me that I don't know what it is like is that I don't know how hard it is. No one says, "You don't know what it's like to have an easy time raising lots of money."

People in nonprofits often imagine that it would be easier to raise money for a different group than the one they are in. People in the arts think social service fundraising is a cinch, people in advocacy imagine that providing free legal services would really loosen the purse strings, environmentalists covet the fundraising jobs of labor rights activists, and so on. For the most part, people kid themselves that fundraising would be much easier in another setting, but occasionally special circumstances make fundraising more difficult for certain kinds of organizations or at certain times in an organization's life. An accurate analysis of your fundraising situation is essential for planning long-term fundraising.

Here are some ways groups mistake what their real fundraising problems are:

- A group that feels it can't raise money because its board is inadequate in fundraising may in fact be hampered because their executive director is not well respected.

- A group may feel that they can't raise money because no one agrees with their program, when in fact they have failed to articulate a clear case as to why they deserve support.

External factors can play a much bigger role than groups realize:

- The local economy may be really bad.

- A scandal in a large well-known nonprofit can cause distrust of all nonprofits and decrease revenues temporarily.

- A large natural disaster takes attention and sometimes funding away from the day-in and day-out work of service agencies.

- Issues come into style and go out of style, and long after it has ceased to be popular to fund solutions to a particular problem, the problem will still be there.

I have chosen five of the more common special challenges that a group may face, from being in a rural area to deciding the thorny question of clean and dirty money. An entire book could be devoted to special challenges, but these five should give you a sense of how to think through special challenges of your own and make fundraising plans that overcome the adversity of the circumstances.

thirty-five

Raising Money in Rural Areas

Just as cities and towns vary greatly one from another, making fundraising in each somewhat particular, so do rural areas. However, as with cities and towns, there are some things many rural areas have in common. The following six factors must be taken into account in doing nonprofit work in a rural community.

1. Everything takes longer. This applies not only to the obvious time involved in getting from one place to another when vast distances separate homes or towns, but also to rural hospitality, which tends to be much more deliberate than that of city dwellers. For example, suppose you decide to visit a major donor on his or her ranch. You make an appointment, then drive one to three hours to the ranch. Once there, you do not chat briefly, ask for the gift, and leave in 45 minutes, as you might in a city. The graciousness often customary in rural areas may lead your host or hostess to give you a tour of the ranch, invite you to stay for lunch or dinner, and perhaps encourage you to spend the night. This graciousness is wonderful but time-consuming, and you disregard it at the cost of the relationship with the donor.

2. The necessities of ranch or farm life can create obstacles. Depending on the main economy of the area, there may be times — such as planting, harvesting, lambing, or calving — when contact with donors will be limited because people are working almost around the clock. Then, when none of those things are going on, the weather may make driving conditions so hazardous that volunteers cannot get to meetings, people cannot attend special events, and prospects cannot be visited. In an agricultural community, you have fewer months to raise your money.

3. Fundraising costs may be higher. The city person's idyllic notion that everything is inexpensive or free in a rural area is false. Almost all supplies and equipment have to be shipped in, adding freight to their cost. Consultants to help repair your computer or handle your bookkeeping needs may be few and far between, and thus more expensive. Lack of competition among businesses can also create high prices for goods and services. While office space may be less expensive, there may not be any available. The distances between people and places make driving costs high, the price of gasoline may be higher per gallon, and there is rarely adequate public transportation.

4. Logistics are complicated. If you wish to print a newsletter, mail appeal, or flyer, you may have to send it to the nearest city. If you need something sent or received quickly, there may be no overnight mail service from or to your community. Fax machines and e-mail have helped to solve this problem to some extent, and the world of virtual communication is changing rural life a lot. However, in communities where electricity goes out often during storms or where steady phone service is unreliable, these twenty-first-century conveniences may not always solve the problem.

If your rural community or your constituency is made up of low-income families or individuals, logistical details can take on nightmarish proportions. For example, a small organization covering 20 counties in a southern state held an annual meeting. The meeting was timed perfectly between planting season and the onset of unbearably hot weather, and the organization offered to pay transportation costs for their low-income members. Five members decided to drive to the meeting together; none of them, however, had a car that could be trusted for the eight-hour trip. After the organization encouraged them to rent a car, they drove two hours to the nearest rental-car facility, only to be told that they must present a credit card, which none of them had. The organization called in a credit card number to the rental car agency and the group made it to the meeting.

5. Relationships are often complicated. When organizing and fundraising in a rural community, one must keep in mind that people often have known each other for many years; sometimes families have known each other for generations. A person in an organization may well be related to someone who is opposed to the organization. People depend on each other for help in hard times or for assistance in emergencies. Thus, rural people are cautious about doing anything that might cause offense. If you live down the road from someone who is dumping effluent into your water source, you will think twice about publicly confronting this person when you know that if you have a medical emergency in the middle of winter and can't get your car started you may need to call on them.

This reluctance to challenge other people's actions often includes a hesitation to fundraise assertively or ask people for money directly. Fundraisers and organizers mistakenly interpret this reluctance on the part of volunteers as a sign that they are either conservative (wishing to maintain the status quo) or passive (willing to sit by while land is destroyed or people's rights are violated). In fact, this reluctance may be a survival mechanism; it must be respected and taken into account. Because of these and other factors, change comes more slowly in rural communities.

6. Not everyone has equal loyalty to the area. One often thinks of residents of rural communities as people who have lived in the same place all their lives and make their living from farming or ranching. This is a common situation, and these people usually have deep and abiding loyalty to their area. However, other circumstances often bring people to rural communities who do not develop such loyalty. For example, some rural areas are retirement communities; many of the people living in these communities are not from the region and have little loyalty to it. Some of them do have money and, being retired, they may also have time to volunteer. Other rural communities, such as those within a few hours of major cities such as San Francisco, Washington, D.C., Boston, and others, are bedroom communities for commuters who work in those cities. For other people, the increasingly common use of computers and modems for business enables them to live in rural communities hours from their workplace and still carry on their business, going to a city only as needed. Their loyalty to their local community may depend on whether they are raising a family there and how strongly they wish to be accepted and involved. "Back-to-the-land" small farmers, vintners in boutique wineries, owners of bed-and-breakfast inns, and the staff of retreat centers are some of the many types of people that can make up or contribute to rural communities. The finances and values of these people are extremely varied.

There are also many rural communities where people make their living from mining or timbering (many of these people are now unemployed), or as workers on other people's farms or ranches, in some instances as sharecroppers. Increasingly, there are rural communities where the majority of the population are non-English-speaking immigrants or refugees from Mexico, Latin America, Cambodia, and other countries. All of this adds layers of complexity to any rural fundraising efforts.

STRATEGIES FOR RAISING MONEY

For groups in communities located near cities with populations of 10,000 or more, focus attention on raising money in those towns and cities where the financial base is strongest. Form support groups with people living in the town or city. Hold special events there and use direct mail to locate donors there.

Focus on finding a few people locally who can give larger gifts. Every community has generous people and a few of those will be able to give major gifts, if asked. Whenever possible, ask current donors for the names of other people who could give as well. People tend to be friends with people who share their values, but also who are in a similar economic situation. Someone who gives your group $100 will know two or three other people who could give $100 and one or two people who could give $250. They in turn will know people who could give $500. Here are two examples.

There are a number of communities called "colonias" that span the borders between Texas, New Mexico, and Mexico. These communities often lack running water or electricity. Their community facilities — schools, roads, or local government — are poor or nonexistent. The people in these communities tend to work in factories or farms near the colonias. Many people have lived in these communities for years. Raising money for nonprofit work is not easy in a place where so many people have so little, but some organizations have done well. In addition to setting up food booths and collecting small amounts of money from residents, they have identified a few people who care about the community and who can afford to give more. In one instance, a staff person of an organization working with teenagers identified a small farmer who they thought could give $100. When they asked him for that amount, he misunderstood the question. "Yes, I can give that every month," he said. He has been helpful in identifying other people who can also give substantial monthly or yearly contributions. Further, illustrating the relationship between fundraising and organizing, he has helped several community groups petition for roads, sewage systems, and public schools. He has helped people understand that since they pay taxes, they have the right to services that taxes are meant to provide.

In the second example, a town of 600 people in northern California decided to expand their library. They needed to raise $35,000. Everyone involved in the nonprofit part of the community agreed that such an amount would drain the community and make other large fundraising drives impossible. Nonetheless, they decided to proceed because the library would be so well used. Soon after they raised the $35,000, the community center in town decided they desperately needed a new space and set out to raise $50,000 to build a new community hall. They raised it, but now the common wisdom of the community was that there certainly was no more capital money in the community. Two years went by; then the health clinic needed to modernize and expand and had no choice but to launch a capital campaign. This fundraising effort was also successful.

The lesson here is that in any community, but more obviously in a rural community, fundraising is not a zero-sum game. There is always more money and it is not diminished or used up by big campaigns. Organizations in rural communities will want to time their campaigns — to run two capital campaigns at the same time will rarely be as successful as running them sequentially. The need has to be well established and the community has to agree with the goal of the campaign, but it must be remembered that, money grows back and produces more money. In addition to raising money in the nearest population center and from major donors, try to discover ways to raise money from people who pass through the community, particularly tourists and visitors. Some communities mount events just to attract tourists. For example, many communities have county fairs or various kinds of festivals, such as the Garlic Festival in California, the Ramp Festival in Georgia, and the Storyteller's Convention in North Carolina. These attract tourists.

If you live in a place where tourists come to see the natural beauty or to vacation (such as along the coasts, or near national parks or monuments), consider developing products that tourists will buy. Local crafts and homemade jellies and jams are always appealing. Photography books, guides to the local sights, and collections of stories of people who live in the community have all proved to be steady income streams for rural organizations.

If you live near a freeway or a frequently traveled road, set up a rest stop where truckers and tired drivers can buy coffee and doughnuts or other treats. This can be very lucrative in the cold winter months, particularly at night. It is also a community service that helps keep people from falling asleep at the wheel.

You can raise money from your local community as well. It is important to note that even in the poorest and most rural areas, churches, volunteer fire departments, rescue squads, service clubs, and the like are supported by local residents. Even the smallest, poorest towns in the Bible Belt, for example, support at least two churches. Even if they do not have paid clergy, the people manage to support a building.

Money can be raised locally through special events. This helps counter the reluctance rural people have for asking for money directly by providing a way to give something in return. Events such as raffles, auctions, and bake sales can be good moneymakers. Many times people from rural community groups simply stand with buckets at busy crossroads and ask drivers to drop in spare change. Three hours at a crossroad on a shopping day can bring in $300 to $500. Flea markets are also popular. It is often easier for rural people to donate items rather than cash, and people always seem willing to buy each other's castoffs. In Sitka, Alaska, there is a thrift shop run by volunteers called the "White Elephant." The store shows $100,000 profit every year, which they donate to a variety of other nonprofits on the island. Often a prom dress or fancy suit will be sold and redonated to the store several times before it must be converted to rags.

All of these are labor-intensive activities and make fundraising in rural communities even harder than it is elsewhere. We must face the fact that an organization located in a low-income, rural area doing work related to social justice issues (tax or land reform, appropriate economic development, peace and disarmament work, or opposing such things as hazardous waste dumping, clearcutting, or wildcat strip mining) will need to seek funding from foundations and from outside their immediate region. Unless the organization has a very low budget and no paid staff, it is unlikely that it will be able to become entirely self-sufficient. However, your community will support you and your work will be more successful if community members have bought into it with a donation.

thirty-six

Fundraising in a Coalition

There are hundreds of organizations whose board members are representatives of other nonprofits that have joined together for the benefits that a coalition of groups can bring. For example, in most federated funds, members of the federation hold the majority of seats on the board. Almost every state has a Coalition Against Domestic Violence, for which directors of local battered women's programs serve as board members. Most regional associations and national organizations operate the same way, with most of those on the board of directors drawn from the member organizations.

There are obvious advantages to this type of board. A regional or national organization whose mission is to strengthen local groups and to raise overall visibility for an issue will be best governed by those most affected and involved in the decisions made. Sharing resources, working collaboratively, developing joint projects, and seeking to expand the reach of the work will all be done best by a coalition made up of people with power at their local level. A board or staff member of a local chapter will be in the best position to represent the concerns of the local organization to a regional or national group. This person will also well understand the need for a regional or national umbrella, engendering a commitment to the coalition as well. Ideally this person will be the best qualified to make policy and help plan for the umbrella group and to translate the work of the umbrella group to the people at the local level.

From a fundraising point of view, however, this arrangement is difficult for the umbrella group because its executive director or development director is working with board members whose primary loyalty and main fundraising commitments lie with the organization they are representing. Sometimes these people are appointed to a coalition board by their organization and have not actually chosen to serve. It may be a part of their job description. Getting such a board to raise money requires patience, perseverance, and a degree of maneuvering. However, if you are the person in charge of that fundraising, keep in mind that it can be done.

EXAMINE THE PROBLEM

The first step is to examine the problem. Evaluate the excuses coalition board members offer for not being able to raise money. Most will say they can't participate in fundraising because they have to raise money for their local group. They can't ask the same people to give money to the umbrella as to the local group. Next they will point out that strategies other than face-to-face fundraising are difficult for a consortium to carry out. Special events, for example, require a local presence to generate interest in the event. Direct mail is not a good way to sell an umbrella group because the service is too complicated and local representatives are reluctant to provide names of possible donors.

On the surface these excuses make sense. However, a closer examination of the people who complain most about how difficult it is to raise money for an umbrella organization reveals that these people are often not effective at raising money at the local level either. Ironically, people who are very effective at their local level, with active fundraising committees and well-executed fundraising campaigns for their local organization, often make the best fundraisers at a regional or national level.

The reality of fundraising is that some people, foundations, or corporations prefer to give locally; others have no preference and will give locally, regionally, and nationally; and still others would rather be part of a national picture.

Local organizations are in the best position to identify sources of funding based in their communities but committed to regional or national work. Those sources should be solicited for the umbrella group, provided that the sources are also committed to the issues. Further, some donors will give to both the local group and the larger coalition, understanding the importance of both organizations.

Another common excuse from local people is that they don't have time to raise money in addition to all their responsibilities for the umbrella board and their local group. This is a legitimate problem; however, these same people will spend hours debating personnel issues, discussing policy and program problems, and poring over the budget to see what can be cut. By shaving a few minutes off of each of those tasks, they would have some time for fundraising.

To be frank, you will fight an uphill and pointless battle if you spend all your time trying to get executive directors or very active board members of local groups to raise money for the umbrella group. It is better to spend time recruiting and developing other board members who will raise money for your umbrella group.

SOME SOLUTIONS

First, every board of an umbrella group should have at least three slots reserved for "at-large" members — people who are not associated with a local group. These can be former staff, former board members of local groups, or simply people committed to the cause who don't happen to work for a local version of the cause. Their primary loyalty should be to your umbrella group, and their primary task should be fundraising. They should be recruited for this purpose.

Second, umbrella groups usually call for a "representative" of each local group to be on the umbrella board. If someone who is neither on the staff at the local level nor an active board member there is recruited to represent a local group, they will have more time to devote to the umbrella board. A person can represent their local organization who has previously been a staff person or a board member or who is a key volunteer but not on the board.

One federated fund requests that member groups send as their representative someone who "does not have major responsibility for the health and well-being of the local organization." Their board is very active in fundraising and they do not have the problem of divided loyalties. Board members are clear that they represent their local group, yet their primary task is to promote the umbrella organization. Further, they understand that they work best for their local group by being part of a strong umbrella organization.

Finally, it is critical to look closely at fundraising strategies and give all your board members tasks they can do. When people say, "I can't fundraise," ask what they mean. Do they mean they can't make coffee? Or take tickets at a special event? or stuff envelopes? Or ask individuals for money? Usually it is the latter. If that is the case, find out which individuals they can't ask. Friends? Donors to their local groups? Strangers? Anyone? If they can't ask anyone, send them to a fundraising training so they can get over their fear and in the meantime give them a fundraising task that does not involve direct solicitation. Fundraising is a series of at least a thousand tasks and there is no one who cannot do something.

Working closely with individual board members, lobbying with member groups for the most appropriate people to be nominated, and creating an "organizational culture" where everyone participates in fundraising will enable an umbrella organization to get maximum use of its board for fundraising.

thirty-seven

When Everyone
Is a Volunteer

Thousands of very successful organizations are run entirely by volunteers. Service clubs, volunteer fire departments, PTAs, and most neighborhood organizations have no paid staff. Many of these organizations have run successfully for years. They are designed by volunteers and designed to be run by volunteers. Other organizations may prefer to have paid staff but cannot afford them, so they, too, run on the energy of volunteers. If you are such a group, here are six pointers to help you function smoothly and effectively.

1. Volunteers should think of themselves as unpaid staff. Staff people have jobs and tasks for which they are accountable. Volunteers have the same obligation as paid staff to do what they say they will do. Similarly, no one should tolerate incompetence and lack of follow-through from a volunteer any more than they would from a paid person. In a group where everyone volunteers, it is vitally important to create an environment in which people do the work they say they will do.

2. Volunteers have lives beyond the organization. Volunteers should not be encouraged to take on more work than they feel they can do. Suppose you know that Mary Jones would make a great treasurer but she says she hasn't got the time. You talk to her several times, beg her, tell her that no one else can do the job but her; finally she agrees to do it. Don't be surprised when Mary turns out not to be as good a treasurer as you had expected. As part of showing respect for each others' time, it is imperative to create and support an organizational culture that allows people to take on fewer tasks if it also encourages them to finish the tasks they do agree to. Also, some people have more time than others and may be able to take on more work than others. These differences need to be accepted in the group; people with less time must not be made to feel that they are not doing enough if they don't put in as much time as others.

3. Volunteers should use their own and other people's time respectfully. Meetings should start and end on time. There should be an agenda. A facilitator, or the chair of the meeting, or the group as a whole should agree on how long each agenda item will take and try not to take longer than that. There is usually more that can be said on any item, and one more way of looking at things, but unless you are an academic think tank, don't try to explore every possibility.

4. People should take on particular responsibilities. Someone should be the treasurer, someone should prepare the agendas for meetings, someone should be the chair. Organizations working in a collective model can rotate these responsibilities (which need to be rotated occasionally in any structure). No one in the group should have to wonder, "Who is in charge of filing our 990 tax form?" or, "Who has the checkbook?"

5. People should be particularly careful about writing things down. Turnover in all-volunteer organizations is often high, and knowledge easily gets lost, particularly if there is no office or central place to keep files. If you do a special event or a direct mail appeal or write a proposal, keep track of everything someone else might want to know about it in order to do it faster and easier the next time. Preparing reports and narratives for the use of people who will come after you is the best way to ensure that your organization can continue to function well using volunteers and, in fact, helps to ensure that your organization can grow.

6. Volunteers should constantly seek to expand the number of volunteer workers. There is so much work to be done that a few initial dedicated volunteers will burn out quickly. You should be drawing new people into the organization all the time who can help share the work and broaden the organization's thinking and its access to funds.

All-volunteer organizations are not that different from many grassroots organizations that have one or two paid staff people. In fact, in many grassroots groups there are two kinds of staff — low-paid and unpaid. In all other grassroots groups there is one kind of staff — unpaid. The work is still valuable and people's time is invaluable. Keeping these pointers in mind will ensure that your organization is able to do the useful and important work it has set out for itself.

thirty-eight

Being Brand New

Organizations that have just been started are often operating on the donations of their founding members and the energy and enthusiasm these members bring to the cause that has propelled them to action. Soon, however, they realize that they must reach further for support or they will burn themselves out financially as well as emotionally. Someone goes to a fundraising class or reads a book such as this one. Newly inspired to develop a membership base or raise money through any of the other strategies presented, they can also be newly baffled. "But where do I start?" is often the next question. There are so many possible starting places for raising money, but there is little money to meet start-up costs. They now know something about what will attract money, but there is not much room for making mistakes.

First, know that your group will make mistakes. Challenge yourself to make new mistakes and not to fall into predictable and avoidable traps.

Figure out how much money you need for your organization to begin functioning smoothly. Of course you will draw up a budget for a year, but then break it down into what you need for this month and then the month after. See everything in the smallest possible time frame so that you don't get discouraged. If you can raise this much money for one month, then you can continue for that month. Then go on to the next month.

You have probably started by raising money from the founders of the organization — yourselves. Each person should pledge a certain amount per month or per quarter and should bring their pledge check to meetings or mail it to someone designated as the treasurer. This will begin the important practice of developing a culture of giving money among all who work with the group. Next, each founder or core volunteer should assess how much money he or she can raise from friends, family, and acquaintances.

Each person should make a list of all the people they know, without regard to whether these people believe in your cause or give money away. Just list the names of people who would recognize your name if you phoned them. Next to that list, mark all the people who you know believe in the cause your new group represents. If you don't know, put a question mark. Next, for all the people you know who you also know believe in the cause, mark all those who you know for a fact give away money. Now, take all the people whom you know, who you know believe in the cause, and who you know give away money, and note how much you are going to ask each of them for. If you are not sure what to ask them for, keep it small. Is it $50? $100? $35? Remember that some family and friends will give you money just to be supportive of you. Finally, note what method you will use to solicit this money. Will you hold a house party? Send a personal letter and follow up by phone? Set up a personal meeting? If a meeting, will you bring someone else from the new group with you?

Here's what your list might look like:

POTENTIAL DONORS TO OUR GROUP

NAME	BELIEVES IN CAUSE?	GIVES MONEY?	AMOUNT TO REQUEST	METHOD
Francisco	yes	yes	$100	meeting
Edward	yes	?	?	invite to house party
Marianne	?	yes	$35	mail appeal
Gloriano	no	—	—	—
Charmaine	yes	yes	$50	phone call

People sometimes object to raising money in this way for a brand-new group by saying, "You can't just ask people for money without giving them something. We don't have a newsletter or a program or even an office. What are they giving to?" At this point, people are giving to an idea and to the people involved in making the idea an organization — you. They will give for the same reasons you are giving time and money — they agree with you and they think you are the people who can pull this off. Some people enjoy — even prefer — to give money to new groups. Those who prefer to give to more established groups won't give to you right now, but that is not everyone.

The next step is to identify a few people or foundations that will give larger amounts of money ($1,000 or more) for start-up costs. Use the methods described in the section on prospect identification (in Chapter 9) for this step. For information on approaching foundations, go to your local Foundation Center Collection, listed at the end of the Bibliography. You will need to develop a case statement, including a preliminary budget. While your organization has no history, the people who are forming it have history. Each of the founders should be briefly described in order to show that knowledgeable and experienced people are behind this idea.

From the beginning, appoint someone to keep records and ensure that they are accurate. Always write thank-you notes, even before you get organizational stationery. Keep founding donors posted on your progress by sending brief updates or occasional e-mail newsletters.

Being a brand-new organization gives you a chance to do your fundraising the right way from the very beginning.

thirty-nine

The Perennial Question of Clean and Dirty Money

Over the years, I have received several phone calls and e-mails asking about a problem that surfaces at some point in the life of almost every organization. The problem was nicely laid out in the following e-mail:

> Dear Kim:
>
> My group is struggling with what I understand to be a perennial problem: dirty money. The questions are: Should we take dirty money, and how do we decide? A corporation has offered us a large grant for operating expenses, but several people in our group have problems with this corporation because of the way they treat their workers (badly). On the other hand, we need the money and not many places give you money for operating expenses. What shall we do?

This group had indeed stumbled upon the subject that has probably taken up more time in progressive groups than almost any other topic you could name. In fact, had some groups held a "dirty money discussion-a-thon" and sought pledges for each minute they spent discussing the very questions raised in this e-mail, they would be handsomely endowed by now and could change their discussion to "dirty and clean investment policies." However, the writer raises serious questions that are not easy to answer, which is why this debate is perennial.

I would like to divide the questions into two parts and look at them both.

The first part is the idea that there is "dirty money" and "clean money." I don't subscribe to this idea. Money is a tool. Similarly, a hammer is a tool. A hammer can be used to help build a house or it can be used to bludgeon someone to death, but we never talk about dirty and clean hammers. Because we don't credit hammers with power they don't have, we are able to see just what a hammer is and to separate the hammer itself from what it might be used to do. We need to get that kind of perspective on money. Money can be used wisely or squandered. It can be raised honestly or dishonestly. It can be earned, inherited, stolen, given, received, lost, found, and many combinations of all of these. It is not in itself dirty or clean.

If you let go of the idea of dirty and clean money, you can focus on the real questions in accepting money, which are: How does it make you feel to accept money from a corporation whose labor practices you find appalling? How does it make you look to others to accept this money? What will be the cost in goodwill, faith in your organization, or even actual money given to your organization if you accept this money?

I have seen organizations answer this question in various ways. The most sensible one was adopted by San Francisco's Coalition for the Medical Rights of Women in 1980 during a marathon discussion about accepting free printing from Playboy Corporation. As many readers will remember, Playboy Corporation has always been a strong supporter of civil liberties and reproductive rights groups. They used to offer to print stationery, envelopes, invitations, newsletters, and the like for nonprofit groups working for those causes. The group simply had to put "Printing donated by the Playboy Corporation" somewhere on the printed piece.

The Coalition, which was the first place I worked as a development director, had occasionally used Playboy to get some of this printing. Although this was a big help financially, the group always had great uneasiness about taking advantage of Playboy's program. As a collective, we discussed whether to continue taking the free printing. We argued back and forth, with those in favor saying, "Playboy made their money off of women and we should get some." Those against argued that Playboy exploited women and promoted sexism and we would help them in their sex-for-money pursuit by taking their free printing. Late one night, after we had made and re-made every argument several times, one person finally said, "I don't know whether it is right or wrong to take this money. All I know is that the idea of taking Playboy's money or their free printing makes me want to vomit."

From then on, in questions about taking money, we applied the Vomit Test. If a person who was important to the organization — staff, board, volunteer, longtime friend — said, "Taking money from such-and-such makes me want to vomit," then we wouldn't take it, because that person and her continuing contributions to our group were more important than any money.

I have never found a more rational approach to the question, "How does it make us feel to accept money from a source whose practices we do not condone?"

The second question, "How does it make us look to the outside world to take this money?" is a more practical one. Sometimes a source of money will pass the Vomit Test, but fail this second test. For example, a board member of a tiny health center in rural New Mexico was a fraternity brother of the vice-president of a large uranium mining operation that is polluting the entire area around it with radioactive uranium tailings. Through his contact, the board member secured a grant from this mining corporation, which so outraged several major donors to the health center that they stopped giving. The ensuing bad publicity and loss of donations was a major factor in the demise of that group the following year.

When an organization accepts money from a source that is controversial, it needs to think about how its other donors or contributors might react. Of course, others' reactions are sometimes hard to judge, but generally, people will be shocked or offended if an organization accepts money from a place that is perceived to be in conflict with the goals of the organization. So when a mining corporation whose irresponsible practices are causing serious health problems donates to a health center, it can be predicted to cause outrage. Had they donated to the public library, there might have been less outcry.

The other factors in accepting money from a controversial source are the amount of money relative to the budget of the organization and what kind of recognition the source wants for their gift. Though this may have happened, I have never heard of an organization spending hours debating whether to accept a $25 donation from even the most foul corporation or from one of that corporation's employees, because that amount of money cannot buy any influence. Similarly, I rarely hear of an organization refusing to accept even a large gift from an individual who may have made their money from a horrible corporation, because the corporation will not receive any glory for that gift.

Sometimes an organization will accept money from a corporation if they do not have to publicize that gift, but will refuse the gift if it requires public acknowledgment. The hypocrisy of that position can be helpful to groups sorting out whether to take money or not. Ask yourself, "If this gift from this source were to be headline news in our local paper tomorrow, would we be happy or would we be nervous about the consequences?" If happy, take the money. If you would rather people did not know about the gift, then don't.

The issue of clean and dirty money generally comes up in relation to corporations. Since corporations are only responsible for about 5% of all the money given away in the private sector, and only 11% of corporations give away any money at all, I think organizations are better off focusing their fundraising efforts on building a broad base of individual donors. Seeking corporate funds may not be a winning prospect, no matter how you look at it.

Resources

The following list of materials and information is not exhaustive. New resources are being developed daily and published, sent over listservs and distributed in other ways. This list contains the books, magazines, and Web sites I have found most helpful or important for effective fundraising, as well as books and materials I have developed.

One of the most valuable ways to find out more about fundraising is to visit the Foundation Center Collection nearest you. The Foundation Center, headquartered in New York City, is a nonprofit library service supported by foundations, fees for service, products for sale, and other fundraising strategies. The Center collects and disseminates information about funding by foundations, corporations, and government, along with books and other resources on all other types of fundraising and grantwriting. A list of Foundation Centers and their cooperating collections (that is, public libraries or other locations that have materials from the Foundation Center) appears at the end of this resource list. You can also find them online at *www.fdncenter.org*.

Other Titles in the Chardon Press Series:

- *Ask and You Shall Receive: Leader Manual*, Kim Klein
- *Fundraising for the Long Haul*, Kim Klein
- *Grassroots Grants: An Activist's Guide to Proposal Writing*, Andy Robinson

- *Inspired Philanthropy: Creating a Giving Plan*, Tracy Gary and Melissa Kohner
- *Making Policy, Making Change*, Makani N. Themba
- *Raise More Money: The Best of the Grassroots Fundraising Journal*, Kim Klein and Stephanie Roth, Editors
- *Roots of Justice: Stories of Organizing in Communities of Color*, Larry R. Salomon

Also Recommended

- **Achieving Excellence in Fundraising,** by Henry Rosso and Associates. Jossey Bass, 350 Sansome St., San Francisco, CA 941104. 1991. $35.

  The theory and practice of fundraising by one of the best-known fundraising consultants in America. Invaluable.

- **Blueprint for a Capital Campaign: An Introduction for Board Members, Volunteers and Staff,** by Christine Graham. CPG Enterprises, P.O. Box 199, Shaftsbury, VT 05262. 1997. $12.

  Booklet demystifying the process of capital campaign fundraising.

- **Giving USA: Annual Report on Philanthropy.** AAFRC Trust for Philanthropy, 10293 North Meridian St., Suite 175, Indianapolis, IN 46290. $145 per year.

  Analysis of giving and trends in philanthropy.

- **Grantmakers Directory.** National Network of Grantmakers, San Diego, CA, 2000. $40. Available from Chardon Press.

  Information on 200 social-change grantmakers, with a section on writing effective proposals, developing fundraising strategies, and finding Internet resources.

- **The Grassroots Fundraising Book,** by Joan Flanagan. Contemporary Books, 180 North Michigan Avenue, Chicago, IL 60601. Revised, 1992. $16.95.

  Excellent introductory text for small organizations.

- **Grassroots Fundraising: The Kim Klein Video Series.** Headwaters Fund, 122 W. Franklin Ave, Suite 518, Minneapolis, MN 55404 or call 612/879-0602. Purchase price is .1% of your annual budget (minimum $25, maximum $499).

  Seven topics covered in 20-minute sessions in a professionally produced video series with accompanying workbook.

- **Hidden Gold: How Monthly Giving Will Build Donor Loyalty, Boost Your Organization's Income, and Increase Financial Stability,** by Harvey McKinnon. Bonus Books, 160 E. Illinois St., Chicago, IL 60611. 1999. $39.95.

  How and why to start a monthly giving program, with extensive information about record-keeping, set-up, and marketing.

- **How to Produce Fabulous Fundraising Events: Reap Remarkable Returns with Minimal Effort,** by Betty Stallings and Donna McMillion. Building Better Skills, 1717 Courtney Ave., Suite 201, Pleasanton, CA 94588 or call 925/426-8335. 1999. Book and disk, $30.

  How to plan and produce community fundraising events; includes step-by-step guide to a specific event.

- **The International Guide to Nonprofit Law,** by Lester M. Salamon. John Wiley and Sons, 605 Third Ave., New York, NY 10158. 1997. $125.

  Summary of nonprofit laws in 22 countries, making obscure and difficult information accessible.

- **Making the News: A Guide for Nonprofits and Activists,** by Jason Salzman. Cause Communications, 3405 W. Hayward Place, Denver, CO 80211. 1998. $19.95.

  How to shine the media spotlight on any cause or important issue.

- **Philanthropy and the Nonprofit Sector in a Changing America,** C. Clotfelter & T. Ehrlich, eds. Indiana University Press, Bloomington, IN, 1999. $35.

  A series of essays exploring the history and current state of the nonprofit sector by leading scholars and practitioners, including Elisabeth Boris, Eleanor Brown, Emmett Carson, and many more.

- **Planned Giving for the One-Person Development Office: Taking the First Steps,** by David Schmeling. Deferred Giving Services, 614 South Hale Street, Wheaton, IL 60187. 1998. $48.

  Eight steps in making planned giving an integral part of the development process.

- **Planned Giving Simplified: The Gift, The Giver and the Gift Planner,** by Robert F. Sharpe, Sr. John Wiley and Sons, 605 Third Ave., New York, NY 10158. 1998. $34.95.

  Demystifies the complex world of planned giving by one of the nation's foremost experts in the field.

- **Religious Funding Resource Guide,** Eileen Paul, ed. ResourceWomen, 4527 South Dakota Ave., NE, Washington, DC 20017. Updated, 2000. $85.

  Information on 38 faith-based grant and loan programs supporting social service and social change work.

- **Shifting Fortunes: The Perils of the Growing American Wealth Gap,** by Chuck Collins, Betsy Leondar-Wright, and Holly Sklar. United for a Fair Economy, 37 Temple Place, 3rd Floor, Boston, MA 02111. 1999. $6.95.

  Covers the U.S. wealth gap, underlying causes, and proposed solutions.

- **Special Events: Proven Strategies for Nonprofit Fundraising,** by Alan Wendroff. John Wiley and Sons, 605 Third Ave., New York, NY 10158. 1999. $30.

  A masterful guide to producing large special events.

- **Successful Fundraising: A Complete Handbook for Volunteers and Professionals,** by Joan Flanagan. Contemporary Books, 180 North Michigan Ave., Chicago, IL 60601. 1991. $19.95.

  How-to book for large-scale fundraising campaigns.

Other Periodicals

- **Chronicle of Philanthropy.** Chronicle of Philanthropy, 1255 23rd St. NW, Washington, DC 20037. 800/728-2819. Annual subscription, $67.50.

  Bi-weekly publication covering current events in nonprofits, as well as how-to articles and thorough grant listings.

- **NonProfit Times.** NonProfit Times, 240 Cedar Knolls Road, Suite 318, Cedar Knolls, NJ 07927-1621. 973/734-1700. Annual subscription free to executives of qualifying nonprofit organizations.

  Monthly publication with news and analysis, as well as indepth discussion of issues of concern to nonprofits.

Mail and Web Site Addresses for Useful Fundraising Resources

American Association of Fund-Raising Counsel & AAFRC Trust for Philanthropy
37 E. 28th Street, Suite 902
New York, NY 10016
212/481-6705 • www.aafrc.org

Beacon Financial Group, Inc.
1501 Commerce Ave.
Carlise, PA 17013
717/249-8800 • www.bfgi.com

The Chronicle of Philanthropy
1255 23rd Street, NW, Suite 700
Washington, DC 20037
202/466-1000 • www.philanthropy.com

CHI Cash Advance
325 S. Highland Ave.
Briarcliff Manor, NY 10510
212/862-0500
www.chi-cash-advance.com

Contributions
P.O. Box 338
Medfield, MA 02052
508/359-0019
www.contributionsmagazine.com

Council for Advancement and Support of Education
1307 New York Avenue, NW, Suite 1000
Washington, DC 20005-4701
202/328-2273 • www.case.org

Council on Foundations
1828 L Street, NW, Suite 300
Washington, DC 20036
202/466-6512 • www.cof.org

EFT Corporation
2911 Dixwell Ave.
Hamden, CT 06518
800/338-2435 • www.etransfer.com

FINET (Financial Electronic Transfer, Inc.)
500 W. Lincoln Trail, Box 998
Radcliff, KY 40159-0988
800/351-1239 • www.gopay.com

The Foundation Center
79 Fifth Ave.
New York, NY 10003-3076
212/620-4230 • www.fdncenter.org

The Fund-Raising School
Indiana University Center on Philanthropy
550 West North Street, Suite 301
Indianapolis, IN 46202-3162
317/274-7063 • www.tcop.org

Independent Sector
1200 18th Street, NW, Suite 200
Washington, DC 20036
202/467-6100 • www.indepsec.org

National Catholic Development Conference
86 Front Street • Hempstead, NY 11550
516/481-6000
www.amm.org/ncdc.htm

National Center for Nonprofit Boards
1828 L Street, NW, Suite 900
Washington, DC 20036-5104
202/452-6262 • www.ncnb.org

National Charities Information Bureau
19 Union Square West
New York, NY 10003-3395
212/929-6300 • www.give.org

National Committee on Planned Giving
233 McCrea Street, Suite 400
Indianapolis, IN 46225
317/269-6274 • www.ncpg.org

National Committee for Responsive Philanthropy
2001 S Street, NW, Suite 620
Washington, DC 20009
202/387-9177 • www.ncrp.org

National Council of Churches of Christ in the U.S.A.
475 Riverside Drive, Suite 850
New York, NY 10115-0050
212/870-2227 • www.ncccusa.org

**National Council of
Nonprofit Associations**
1900 L Street, NW, Suite 605
Washington, DC 20036
202/467-6262 • www.ncna.org

**National Society of Fund
Raising Executives**
1101 King Street, Suite 700
Alexandria, VA 22314
703/684-0410 • www.nsfre.org

NonProfit Times
240 Cedar Knolls Road, Suite 318
Cedar Knolls, NJ 07927-1621
973/734-1700 • www.nptimes.com

Payment Solutions
P.O. Box 30217
Bethesda, MD 20824
301/986-1062

Philanthropic Advisory Service
c/o Council of Better Business Bureaus
4200 Wilson Boulevard, Suite 800
Arlington, VA 22203
703/276-0100 • www.bbb.org

Other Helpful Resources

The following resources are not specifically about fundraising or philanthropy, but can help with the many other questions common to nonprofit organizations.

- **Accountants for the Public Interest (API)**
  www.accountingnet.com/asso/api/index.html
  Questions and answers as well as materials on accounting for nonprofits.

- **Alliance for Nonprofit Management.** www.genie.org
  "Nonprofit Genie" provides answers to frequently asked management questions.

- **CompassPoint (formerly the Support Center).** www.compasspoint.org
  Classes and consultation on fundraising and management, computer training.

- **Internet Nonprofit Center.** www.nonprofit-info.org/npofaq
  Information, advice, and articles on numerous nonprofit management topics, including how to calculate programs costs or fundraising ratios and how to value donated goods.

- **Professional Support Software.** www.FundraiserSoftware.com
  Excellent software for small nonprofits, samples of which can be downloaded from this site.

- **Technical Assistance for Community Organizations (TACS).** www.tacs.org
  Good place to shop for accounting software.

FOUNDATION CENTER COOPERATING COLLECTIONS   FREE FUNDING INFORMATION CENTERS

The Foundation Center is an independent national service organization established by foundations to provide an authoritative source of information on foundation and corporate giving. The New York, Washington, D.C., Atlanta, Cleveland, and San Francisco reference collections operated by the Foundation Center offer a wide variety of services and comprehensive collections of information on foundations and grants. Cooperating Collections are libraries, community foundations, and other nonprofit agencies that provide a core collection of Foundation Center publications and a variety of supplementary materials and services in areas useful to grantseekers. The core collecti on consists of:

THE FOUNDATION DIRECTORY 1 AND 2, AND SUPPLEMENT
FOUNDATION FUNDAMENTALS
THE FOUNDATION 1000
FOUNDATIONS TODAY SERIES
FOUNDATION GRANTS TO INDIVIDUALS

THE FOUNDATION CENTER'S GUIDE TO GRANTSEEKING ON THE WEB
THE FOUNDATION CENTER'S GUIDE TO PROPOSAL WRITING
GRANT GUIDE SERIES
GUIDE TO U.S. FOUNDATIONS, THEIR TRUSTEES, OFFICERS, AND DONORS

NATIONAL DIRECTORY OF CORPORATE GIVING
NATIONAL GUIDE TO FUNDING IN. . . . (SERIES)
USER-FRIENDLY GUIDE

All five Center libraries and Cooperating Collections have *FC Search: The Foundation Center's Database on CD-ROM* available for public use. Many of our cooperating collections also have the CD-ROM, *FC Scholar: The Foundation Center's Database of Education Funding for Individuals.* Also, many of the network members make available private foundation information returns (IRS Form 990-PF) for foundations in their state and/or neighboring states, as noted by the symbol (✱). IRS returns for all foundations are available for free public reference in all five Foundation Center libraries. Because the collections vary in their hours, materials, and services, it is recommended that you call the collection in advance of a visit. To check on new locations or current holdings, call toll-free 1-800-424-9836, or visit our Web site at http://fdncenter.org/collections/index.html.

REFERENCE COLLECTIONS OPERATED BY THE FOUNDATION CENTER

THE FOUNDATION CENTER
2nd Floor
79 Fifth Ave.
New York, NY 10003
(212) 620-4230

THE FOUNDATION CENTER
312 Sutter St., Suite 606
San Francisco, CA 94108
(415) 397-0902

THE FOUNDATION CENTER
1001 Connecticut Ave., NW
Washington, DC 20036
(202) 331-1400

THE FOUNDATION CENTER
Kent H. Smith Library
1422 Euclid, Suite 1356
Cleveland, OH 44115
(216) 861-1933

THE FOUNDATION CENTER
Suite 150, Grand Lobby
Hurt Bldg., 50 Hurt Plaza
Atlanta, GA 30303
(404) 880-0094

ALABAMA

BIRMINGHAM PUBLIC LIBRARY ✱
Government Documents
2100 Park Place
Birmingham 35203
(205) 226-3620

HUNTSVILLE PUBLIC LIBRARY
915 Monroe St.
Huntsville 35801
(256) 532-5940

UNIVERSITY OF SOUTH ALABAMA ✱
Library Bldg.
Mobile 36688
(334) 460-7025

AUBURN UNIVERSITY AT
MONTGOMERY LIBRARY
7300 University Dr.
Montgomery 36124-4023
(334) 244-3200

ALASKA

UNIVERSITY OF ALASKA AT
ANCHORAGE ✱
Library
3211 Providence Dr.
Anchorage 99508
(907) 786-1848

JUNEAU PUBLIC LIBRARY
292 Marine Way
Juneau 99801
(907) 586-5267

ARIZONA

FLAGSTAFF CITY-COCONINO COUNTY
PUBLIC LIBRARY
300 W. Aspen Ave.
Flagstaff 86001
(520) 779-7670

PHOENIX PUBLIC LIBRARY ✱
Information Services Department
1221 N. Central Ave.
Phoenix 85004
(602) 262-4636

TUCSON PIMA LIBRARY ✱
101 N. Stone Ave.
Tucson 87501
(520) 791-4393

ARKANSAS

WESTARK COMMUNITY COLLEGE—
BOREHAM LIBRARY
5210 Grand Ave.
Ft. Smith 72913
(501) 788-7200

CENTRAL ARKANSAS
LIBRARY SYSTEM ✱
100 Rock St.
Little Rock 72201
(501) 918-3000

PINE BLUFF-JEFFERSON COUNTY
LIBRARY SYSTEM
200 E. 8th
Pine Bluff 71601
(870) 534-2159

CALIFORNIA

HUMBOLDT AREA FOUNDATION
Rooney Resource Center
373 Indianola
Bayside 95524
(707) 442-2993

VENTURA COUNTY COMMUNITY
FOUNDATION ✱
Resource Center for Nonprofit Organizations
1317 Del Norte Rd., Suite 150
Camarillo 93010-8504
(805) 988-0196

FRESNO REGIONAL FOUNDATION
Nonprofit Advancement Center
3425 N. First St., Suite 101
Fresno 93726
(550) 226-5600

CENTER FOR NONPROFIT
MANAGEMENT IN SOUTHERN
CALIFORNIA
Nonprofit Resource Library
606 South Olive St. #2400
Los Angeles 90014
(213) 623-7080

PHILANTHROPY RESOURCE CENTER
Flintridge Center
1040 Lincoln Ave, Suite 100
Pasadena 91103
(626) 449-0839

GRANT & RESOURCE CENTER OF
NORTHERN CALIFORNIA ✱
Bldg. C, Suite A
2280 Benton Dr.
Redding 96003
(530) 244-1219

LOS ANGELES PUBLIC LIBRARY
West Valley Regional Branch Library
19036 Van Owen St.
Reseda 91335
(818) 345-4393

RICHMOND PUBLIC LIBRARY
325 Civic Center Plaza
Richmond 94804
(510) 620-6555

RIVERSIDE PUBLIC LIBRARY
3581 Mission Inn Ave.
Riverside 92501
(909) 782-5201

NONPROFIT RESOURCE CENTER ✱
Sacramento Public Library
328 I St., 2nd Floor
Sacramento 95814
(916) 264-2772

SAN DIEGO FOUNDATION
Funding Information Center
1420 Kettner Blvd., Suite 500
San Diego 92101
(619) 235-2300

NONPROFIT DEVELOPMENT LIBRARY
1922 The Alameda, Suite 212
San Jose 95126
(408) 248-9505

PENINSULA COMMUNITY
FOUNDATION ✱
Peninsula Nonprofit Center
1700 S. El Camino Real, #R201
San Mateo 94402-3049
(650) 358-9392

LOS ANGELES PUBLIC LIBRARY
San Pedro Regional Branch
931 S. Gaffey St.
San Pedro 90731
(310) 548-7779

VOLUNTEER CENTER OF GREATER
ORANGE COUNTY
Nonprofit Resource Center
1901 E. 4th St., Suite 100
Santa Ana 92705
(714) 953-5757

SANTA BARBARA PUBLIC LIBRARY
40 E. Anapamu St.
Santa Barbara 93101-1019
(805) 962-7653

SANTA MONICA PUBLIC LIBRARY
1343 6th St.
Santa Monica 90401-1603
(310) 458-8600

SONOMA COUNTY LIBRARY
3rd & E Sts.
Santa Rosa 95404
(707) 545-0831

SEASIDE BRANCH LIBRARY
550 Harcourt Ave.
Seaside 93955
(831) 899-8131

SONORA AREA FOUNDATION
20100 Cedar Rd., N.
Sonora 95370
(209) 533-2596

COLORADO

PENROSE LIBRARY
20 N. Cascade Ave.
Colorado Springs 80903
(719) 531-6333

DENVER PUBLIC LIBRARY ✱
General Reference
10 W. 14th Ave. Pkwy.
Denver 80204
(303) 640-6200

CONNECTICUT

DANBURY PUBLIC LIBRARY
170 Main St.
Danbury 06810
(203) 797-4527

GREENWICH LIBRARY ✱
101 W. Putnam Ave.
Greenwich 06830
(203) 622-7900

HARTFORD PUBLIC LIBRARY ✱
500 Main St.
Hartford 06103
(860) 543-8656

NEW HAVEN FREE PUBLIC LIBRARY ✱
Reference Dept.
133 Elm St.
New Haven 06510-2057
(203) 946-7091

DELAWARE

UNIVERSITY OF DELAWARE ✱
Hugh Morris Library
Newark 19717-5267
(302) 831-2432

FLORIDA

VOLUSIA COUNTY LIBRARY CENTER
City Island
105 E. Magnolia Ave.
Daytona Beach 32114-4484
(904) 257-6036

NOVA SOUTHEASTERN UNIVERSITY ✱
Einstein Library
3301 College Ave.
Fort Lauderdale 33314
(954) 262-4601

395

INDIAN RIVER COMMUNITY COLLEGE
Learning Resources Center
3209 Virginia Ave.
Fort Pierce 34981-5596
(561) 462-4757

JACKSONVILLE PUBLIC LIBRARIES ✱
Grants Resource Center
122 N. Ocean St.
Jacksonville 32202
(904) 630-2665

MIAMI-DADE PUBLIC LIBRARY ✱
Humanities/Social Science
101 W. Flagler St.
Miami 33130
(305) 375-5575

ORANGE COUNTY LIBRARY SYSTEM
Social Sciences Department
101 E. Central Blvd.
Orlando 32801
(407) 425-4694

SELBY PUBLIC LIBRARY
Reference
1331 1st St.
Sarasota 34236
(941) 316-1181

TAMPA-HILLSBOROUGH COUNTY
PUBLIC LIBRARY ✱
900 N. Ashley Dr.
Tampa 33602
(813) 273-3652

COMMUNITY FOUNDATION OF PALM
BEACH & MARTIN COUNTIES ✱
324 Datura St., Suite 340
West Palm Beach 33401
(561) 659-6800

GEORGIA

ATLANTA-FULTON PUBLIC LIBRARY
Foundation Collection—Ivan Allen
    Department
1 Margaret Mead Square
Atlanta 30303-1089
(404) 730-1909

UNITED WAY OF CENTRAL GEORGIA ✱
Community Resource Center
277 Martin Luther King Jr. Blvd.,
    Suite 301
Macon 31201
(912) 738-3949

SAVANNAH STATE UNIVERSITY
Asa Gordon Library
Thompkins Road
Savannah 31404
(912) 225-5252

THOMAS COUNTY PUBLIC LIBRARY
201 N. Madison St.
Thomasville 31792
(912) 225-5252

HAWAII

UNIVERSITY OF HAWAII ✱
Hamilton Library
2550 The Mall
Honolulu 96822
(808) 956-7214

HAWAII COMMUNITY FOUNDATION
FUNDING RESOURCE LIBRARY
900 Fort St., Suite 1300
Honolulu 96813
(808) 537-6333

IDAHO

BOISE PUBLIC LIBRARY ✱
Funding Information Center
715 S. Capitol Blvd.
Boise 83702
(208) 384-4024

CALDWELL PUBLIC LIBRARY ✱
1010 Dearborn St.
Caldwell 83605
(808) 537-6333

ILLINOIS

DONORS FORUM OF CHICAGO ✱
208 S. LaSalle, Suite 735
Chicago 60604
(312) 578-0175

EVANSTON PUBLIC LIBRARY ✱
1703 Orrington Ave.
Evanston 60201
(847) 866-0300

ROCK ISLAND PUBLIC LIBRARY
401 19th St.
Rock Island 61201-8143
(309) 732-7323

UNIVERSITY OF ILLINOIS
AT SPRINGFIELD, LIB 23
Brookens Library
Springfield 62794-9243
(217) 206-6633

INDIANA

EVANSVILLE–VANDERBURGH PUBLIC
LIBRARY ✱
22 SE 5th St.
Evansville 47708
(812) 428-8200

ALLEN COUNTY PUBLIC LIBRARY ✱
900 Webster St.
Ft. Wayne 46802
(219) 421-1200

INDIANAPOLIS–MARION COUNTY
PUBLIC LIBRARY ✱
Social Sciences
40 E. St. Clair
Indianapolis 46206
(317) 269-1733

VIGO COUNTY PUBLIC LIBRARY ✱
1 Library Square
Terre Haute 47807
(812) 232-1113

IOWA

CEDAR RAPIDS PUBLIC LIBRARY ✱
500 1st St., SE
Cedar Rapids 52401
(319) 398-5123

SOUTHWESTERN COMMUNITY
COLLEGE
Learning Resource Center
1501 W. Townline Rd.
Creston 50801
(515) 782-7081

PUBLIC LIBRARY OF DES MOINES
100 Locust
Des Moines 50309-1791
(515) 283-4152

SIOUX CITY PUBLIC LIBRARY
Siouxland Funding Research Center
529 Pierce St.
Sioux City 51101-1203
(712) 255-2933

KANSAS

DODGE CITY PUBLIC LIBRARY ✱
1001 2nd Ave.
Dodge City 67801
(316) 225-0248

TOPEKA AND SHAWNEE COUNTY
PUBLIC LIBRARY ✱
1515 SW 10th Ave.
Topeka 66604-1345
(785) 233-2040

WICHITA PUBLIC LIBRARY ✱
223 S. Main St.
Wichita 67202
(316) 261-8500

KENTUCKY

WESTERN KENTUCKY UNIVERSITY
Helm-Cravens Library
Bowling Green 42101-3576
(270) 745-6125

LEXINGTON PUBLIC LIBRARY ✱
140 E. Main St.
Lexington 40507-1376
(606) 231-5520

LOUISIANA

LOUISVILLE FREE PUBLIC LIBRARY ✱
301 York St.
Louisville 40203
(502) 574-1617

EAST BATON ROUGE PARISH LIBRARY ✱
Centroplex Branch Grants Collection
120 St. Louis
Baton Rouge 70802
(225) 389-4967

BEAUREGARD PARISH LIBRARY
205 S. Washington Ave.
De Ridder 70634
(318) 463-6217

OUACHITA PARISH PUBLIC LIBRARY
1800 Stubbs Ave.
Monroe 71201
(318) 327-1490

NEW ORLEANS PUBLIC LIBRARY ✱
Business & Science Division
219 Loyola Ave.
New Orleans 70112
(504) 596-2580

SHREVE MEMORIAL LIBRARY ✱
424 Texas St.
Shreveport 71120-1523
(318) 226-5894

MAINE

UNIVERSITY OF SOUTHERN MAINE
LIBRARY
Maine Grants Information Center
314 Forrest Ave.
Portland 04104-9301
(207) 780-5029

MARYLAND

ENOCH PRATT FREE LIBRARY ✱
Social Science & History
400 Cathedral St.
Baltimore 21201
(410) 396-5430

MASSACHUSETTS

ASSOCIATED GRANTMAKERS OF
MASSACHUSETTS
55 Court St.
Room 520
Boston 02108
(617) 426-2606

BOSTON PUBLIC LIBRARY ✱
Soc. Sci. Reference
700 Boylston St.
Boston 02116
(617) 536-5400

WESTERN MASSACHUSETTS FUNDING
RESOURCE CENTER
65 Elliot St.
Springfield 01101-1730
(413) 452-0697

WORCESTER PUBLIC LIBRARY ✱
Grants Resource Center
160 Fremont St.
Worcester 01603
(508) 799-1655

MICHIGAN

ALPENA COUNTY LIBRARY ✱
211 N. 1st St.
Alpena 49707
(517) 356-6188

UNIVERSITY OF
MICHIGAN–ANN ARBOR ✱
Graduate Library
Reference & Research Services
Department
Ann Arbor 48109-1205
(734) 763-1539

WILLARD PUBLIC LIBRARY ✱
Nonprofit & Funding Resource
    Collections
7 W. Van Buren St.
Battle Creek 49017
(616) 968-8166

HENRY FORD CENTENNIAL LIBRARY ✱
Adult Services
16301 Michigan Ave.
Dearborn 48124
(313) 943-2330

WAYNE STATE UNIVERSITY ✱
Purdy/Kresge Library
265 Cass Ave.
Detroit 48202
(313) 577-6424

MICHIGAN STATE UNIVERSITY
LIBRARIES ✱
Main Library
Funding Center
100 Library
East Lansing 48824-1048
(517) 353-8818

FARMINGTON COMMUNITY LIBRARY ✱
32737 W. 12 Mile Rd.
Farmington Hills 48334
(248) 553-0300

UNIVERSITY OF MICHIGAN—FLINT
Frances Wilson Thompson Library
Flint 48502-1950
(810) 762-3413

GRAND RAPIDS PUBLIC LIBRARY ✱
60 Library Plaza NE
Grand Rapids 49503-3093
(616) 456-3600

MICHIGAN TECHNOLOGICAL
UNIVERSITY
Van Pelt Library
1400 Townsend Dr.
Houghton 49931
(906) 487-2507

NORTHWESTERN MICHIGAN
COLLEGE ✱
Mark & Helen Osterin Library
1701 E. Front St.
Traverse City 49684
(616) 922-1060

MINNESOTA

DULUTH PUBLIC LIBRARY ✱
520 W. Superior St.
Duluth 55802
(218) 723-3802

SOUTHWEST STATE UNIVERSITY
University Library
N. Hwy. 23
Marshall 56253
(507) 537-6108

MINNEAPOLIS PUBLIC LIBRARY ✱
Sociology Department
300 Nicollet Mall
Minneapolis 55401
(612) 630-6300

ROCHESTER PUBLIC LIBRARY
101 2nd St. SE
Rochester 55904-3777
(507) 285-8002

ST. PAUL PUBLIC LIBRARY
90 W. 4th St.
St. Paul 55102
(651) 266-7000

MISSISSIPPI

JACKSON/HINDS LIBRARY SYSTEM ✱
300 N. State St.
Jackson 39201
(601) 968-5803

MISSOURI

CLEARINGHOUSE FOR
MIDCONTINENT FOUNDATIONS ✱
University of Missouri—Kansas City
Center for Business Innovation
4747 Troost
Kansas City 64110-0680
(816) 235-1776

KANSAS CITY PUBLIC LIBRARY ✳
311 E. 12th St.
Kansas City 64106
(816) 701-3541

METROPOLITAN ASSOCIATION FOR
PHILANTHROPY, INC. ✳
211 N. Broadway, Suite 1200
St. Louis 63102
(314) 621-6220

SPRINGFIELD-GREENE COUNTY
LIBRARY ✳
The Library Center
4653 S. Campbell
Springfield 65810
(417) 874-8110

MONTANA

MONTANA STATE UNIVERSITY—
BILLINGS ✳
Library—Special Collections
1500 N. 30th St.
Billings 59101-0298
(406) 657-2320

BOZEMAN PUBLIC LIBRARY ✳
220 E. Lamme
Bozeman 59715
(406) 582-2402

MONTANA STATE LIBRARY ✳
Library Services
1515 E. 6th Ave.
Helena 59620
(406) 444-3004

UNIVERSITY OF MONTANA ✳
Mansfield Library
32 Campus Dr. #9936
Missoula 59812-9936
(406) 243-6800

NEBRASKA

UNIVERSITY OF NEBRASKA—
LINCOLN
Love Library
14th & R Sts.
Lincoln 68588-2848
(402) 472-2848

OMAHA PUBLIC LIBRARY ✳
W. Dale Clark Library
Social Sciences Department
215 S. 15th St.
Omaha 68102
(402) 444-4826

NEVADA

CLARK COUNTY LIBRARY
1401 E. Flamingo
Las Vegas 89119
(702) 733-3642

WASHOE COUNTY LIBRARY ✳
301 S. Center St.
Reno 89501
(775) 785-4190

NEW HAMPSHIRE

CONCORD PUBLIC LIBRARY ✳
45 Green St.
Concord 03301
(603) 225-8670

PLYMOUTH STATE COLLEGE ✳
Herbert H. Lamson Library
Plymouth 03264
(603) 535-2258

NEW JERSEY

CUMBERLAND COUNTY LIBRARY
800 E. Commerce St.
Bridgeton 08302
(856) 453-2210

FREE PUBLIC LIBRARY OF ELIZABETH
11 S. Broad St.
Elizabeth 07202
(908) 354-6060

COUNTY COLLEGE OF MORRIS ✳
Learning Resource Center
214 Center Grove Rd.
Randolph 07869
(973) 328-5296

NEW JERSEY STATE LIBRARY ✳
185 W. State St.
Trenton 08625-0520
(609) 292-6220

NEW MEXICO

ALBUQUERQUE COMMUNITY
FOUNDATION ✳
3301 Menaul NE, Suite 30
Albuquerque 87176-6960
(505) 883-6240

NEW MEXICO STATE LIBRARY ✳
Information Services
1209 Camino Carlos Rey
Santa Fe 87505-9860
(505) 476-9702

NEW YORK

NEW YORK STATE LIBRARY
Humanities Reference
Cultural Education Center, 6th Fl.
Empire State Plaza
Albany 12230
(518) 474-5355

SUFFOLK COOPERATIVE LIBRARY
SYSTEM
627 N. Sunrise Service Rd.
Bellport 11713
(631) 286-1600

THE NONPROFIT CONNECTION, INC.
One Hanson Place, Room 2504
Brooklyn 11243
(718) 230-3200

BROOKLYN PUBLIC LIBRARY
Social Sciences/Philosophy Division
Grand Army Plaza
Brooklyn 11238
(718) 230-2122

BUFFALO & ERIE COUNTY PUBLIC
LIBRARY ✳
Business, Science & Technology Dept.
1 Lafayette Square
Buffalo 14203-1887
(716) 858-7097

HUNTINGTON PUBLIC LIBRARY
338 Main St.
Huntington 11743
(516) 427-5165

QUEENS BOROUGH PUBLIC LIBRARY
Social Sciences Division
89-11 Merrick Blvd.
Jamaica 11432
(718) 990-0700

LEVITTOWN PUBLIC LIBRARY ✳
1 Bluegrass Ln.
Levittown 11756
(516) 731-5728

ADRIANCE MEMORIAL LIBRARY
Special Services Department
93 Market St.
Poughkeepsie 12601
(914) 485-3445

ROCHESTER PUBLIC LIBRARY
Social Sciences
115 South Ave.
Rochester 14604
(716) 428-8120

ONONDAGA COUNTY PUBLIC LIBRARY
447 S. Salina St.
Syracuse 13202-2494
(315) 435-1900

UTICA PUBLIC LIBRARY
303 Genesee St.
Utica 13501
(315) 735-2279

WHITE PLAINS PUBLIC LIBRARY
100 Martine Ave.
White Plains 10601
(914) 422-1480

YONKERS PUBLIC LIBRARY
Reference Department, Getty
  Square Branch
7 Main St.
Yonkers 10701
(914) 476-1255

NORTH CAROLINA

PACK MEMORIAL LIBRARY
Community Foundation of Western North
Carolina
67 Haywood St.
Asheville 28802
(704) 254-4960

THE DUKE ENDOWMENT ✳
100 N. Tryon St., Suite 3500
Charlotte 28202-4012
(704) 376-0291

DURHAM COUNTY PUBLIC LIBRARY ✳
300 N. Roxboro
Durham 27702
(919) 560-0100

STATE LIBRARY OF NORTH CAROLINA
Information Services Branch
109 E. Jones St.
Raleigh 27699-4641
(919) 733-3683

FORSYTH COUNTY PUBLIC LIBRARY ✳
660 W. 5th St.
Winston-Salem 27101
(336) 727-2680

NORTH DAKOTA

BISMARCK PUBLIC LIBRARY ✳
515 N. 5th St.
Bismarck 58501
(701) 222-6410

FARGO PUBLIC LIBRARY ✳
102 N. 3rd St.
Fargo 58102
(701) 241-1491

OHIO

STARK COUNTY DISTRICT LIBRARY
715 Market Ave. N.
Canton 44702
(330) 452-0665

PUBLIC LIBRARY OF CINCINNATI &
HAMILTON COUNTY ✳
Grants Resource Center
800 Vine St.—Library Square
Cincinnati 45202-2071
(513) 369-6000

COLUMBUS METROPOLITAN LIBRARY
Business and Technology
96 S. Grant Ave.
Columbus 43215
(614) 645-2590

DAYTON & MONTGOMERY COUNTY
PUBLIC LIBRARY ✳
Grants Information Center
215 E. Third St.
Dayton 45402
(937) 227-9500

MANSFIELD/RICHLAND COUNTY
PUBLIC LIBRARY
42 W. 3rd St.
Mansfield 44902
(419) 521-3100

TOLEDO—LUCAS COUNTY
PUBLIC LIBRARY ✳
325 Michigan St.
Toledo 43624-1614
(419) 418-6000

PUBLIC LIBRARY OF YOUNGSTOWN &
MAHONING COUNTY ✳
305 Wick Ave.
Youngstown 44503
(330) 744-8636

MUSKINGUM COUNTY LIBRARY
220 N. 5th St.
Zanesville 43701
(614) 453-0391

OKLAHOMA

OKLAHOMA CITY UNIVERSITY ✳
Dulaney Browne Library
2501 N. Blackwelder
Oklahoma City 73106
(405) 521-5065

TULSA CITY–COUNTY LIBRARY ✳
400 Civic Center
Tulsa 74103
(918) 596-7940

OREGON

OREGON INSTITUTE OF TECHNOLOGY
Library
3201 Campus Dr.
Klamath Falls 97601-8801
(541) 885-1770

PACIFIC NON-PROFIT NETWORK
Education Resource Center
1600 N. Riverside #1094
Medford 97501
(541) 779-6044

MULTNOMAH COUNTY LIBRARY
801 SW 10th Ave.
Portland 97205
(503) 248-5123

OREGON STATE LIBRARY
State Library Bldg.
250 N.Winter St. NE
Salem 97310
(503) 378-4277

PENNSYLVANIA

NORTHAMPTON COMMUNITY
COLLEGE
Learning Resources Center
3835 Green Pond Rd.
Bethlehem 18017
(610) 861-5360

ERIE COUNTY LIBRARY SYSTEM
160 E. Front St.
Erie 16507
(814) 451-6927

DAUPHIN COUNTY LIBRARY SYSTEM
Central Library
101 Walnut St.
Harrisburg 17101
(717) 234-4976

LANCASTER COUNTY PUBLIC LIBRARY
125 N. Duke St.
Lancaster 17602
(717) 394-2651

FREE LIBRARY OF PHILADELPHIA ✳
Regional Foundation Center
1901 Vine St.
Philadelphia 19103-1189
(215) 686-5423

CARNEGIE LIBRARY OF PITTSBURGH ✳
Foundation Collection
4400 Forbes Ave.
Pittsburgh 15213-4080
(412) 622-1917

POCONO NORTHEAST
DEVELOPMENT FUND
James Pettinger Memorial Library
1151 Oak St.
Pittston 18640-3795
(570) 655-5581

READING PUBLIC LIBRARY
100 S. 5th St.
Reading 19602
(610) 655-6355

MARTIN LIBRARY
159 E. Market St.
York 17401
(717) 846-5300

Participants in the Foundation Center's Cooperating Collections network are libraries or nonprofit information centers that provide fundraising information and other funding-related technical assistance in their communities. Cooperating Collections agree to provide free public access to a basic collection of Foundation Center publications during a regular schedule of hours, offering free funding research guidance to all visitors. Many also provide a variety of services for local nonprofit organizations, using staff or volunteers to prepare special materials, organize workshops, or conduct orientations.

The Foundation Center welcomes inquiries from libraries or information centers in the US. interested in providing this type of public information service, particularly for communities with special need for this information. If you are interested in establishing a funding information library for the use of nonprofit organizations in your area or in learning more about the program, please contact a coordinator of Cooperating Collections: Erika Wittlieb, The Foundation Center, 79 Fifth Avenue, New York, NY 10003 (e-mail: eaw@fdncenter.org) or Janet Camarena, The Foundation Center, 312 Sutter Street, Suite 606, San Francisco, CA 94108 (e-mail: jfc@fdncenter.org).   6/00

Index

A

Accounting errors, 365–366.
  See also Financial troubles

Acknowledging gifts. *See* Thank yous

Acquisition strategies, 23–24

Action plans, 306

Adbooks, 118–124
  timelines for, 97–98

Advertising
  for development directors, 321–323
  Web sites, 288–289

Advertising Age, 29

Advisory boards, 48–50

Alinsky, Saul, 337

Alliance for Choice in Giving, 262

Alternative funds, 262–264

American Association of Fund Raising
  Counsel (AAFRC), 6

American Demographics, 29

American Friends Service Committee, 280

Analyzing donor population, 237–249

Annual dinners, 108–113
  walkthrough of, 111–112

Annual gifts, 19–20, 21.
  See also Major Gifts

Annual reports, 185

Annuities. *See also* Planned gifts
  charitable gift annuities, 228–229
  charitable remainder annuity trusts,
    230–231
  charitable remainder unitrusts, 231

  deferred payment gift annuity, 229

Anxiety
  dealing with, 337–339
  house parties, pitch at, 106

Appointment calendars, 303

Asking for money
  discomfort in, 16–17
  fears about, 152–156
  at house parties, 106–107
  from major donors, 187–188
  by religious organizations, 11

Auctions at annual dinners, 112

B

Barbecues, 125

Beginning-of-year appeals, 85

Benefits programs
  basic packages, 82–83
  direct mail appeal including, 81–84
  for major gifts, 183–184

Bequests, 224–226

Bike-a-thons, 134

Black United Fund, 262

Board of directors, 1, 35–50
  advisory boards, 48–50
  for coalitions, 375–377
  e-mail correspondence with, 287
  evaluation form for, 45
  orienting new members, 48
  recruiting new members, 44–46
  responsibilities of, 36–37, 40–42
  and staff, 37, 44
  statement of agreement for, 38–39

Book sales, 127

Brochures
  as direct mail enclosures, 71
  for major gifts, 184

Budgets, 345–354
  board members and, 46
  in case statement, 32
  case studies on, 353–354
  expenses, estimating, 348–349
  income, projecting, 350–351
  for special events, 96–98

Burn-out, 337

Business reply envelopes (BREs), 69–70

C

Calendars, 303–306

Campaigns. *See* Capital campaigns;
  Major gifts campaigns

Canvassing, 265–271
  materials for, 269–270

Capital campaigns, 207–217
  case statement for, 210–212
  lead gifts, 213–214
  pledge agreements, 215–216
  stages of, 212–217

Capital gifts, 20–21

Career fundraisers, 331–335

Case statement
  for capital campaign, 210–212
  contents of, 27–28
  development of, 33
  financial statement/budget in, 32

goals statements, 30
mission statement, 28–29
objectives, statement of, 30–31

Cash-flow problems, 364

Catalogs, gift, 78–79

Catholic Campaign for Human
Development, 280

Cause-related marketing, 9

Charitable gift annuities, 228–229

Charitable remainder annuity trusts,
230–231

Charitable remainder unitrusts, 231

Charity. *See* Philanthropy

Checks, dealing with, 76

Children's Charities of America, 262

Chocolate tastings, 129

Clinton, Kate, 153

Coalition for the Medical Rights of
Women (San Francisco), 386

Coalitions, 375–377

Cocktail parties, 127–128

Cold lists, 57

Colleges. *See* Universities and colleges

Commission-based fundraising, 320

Commission on Religion in Appalachia
(CORA), 280

Committees
for annual dinners, 108–109
nominating committees, 45
for special events, 95–98

Computers
backing up records, 312–313
database programs, 307–310
information management with, 298–299
in office, 293–294

Concerts, 131

Conferences, 131–132

Confidentiality of donor records, 311

Consultants, 325–330
selection criteria, 327–328

Corporations, 6
controversial donors, 385–387
employee-driven philanthropy, 8
role of, 8–9

Council for the Advancement and
Support of Education, 320–321

Council of Better Business Bureaus, 36

Coupons in adbooks, 119

Crafts fairs, 128

Credit cards, 195–196, 289

D

Dances, 132, 133

Database programs, 307–310
for adbooks, 122

Deadlines, understanding, 302–306

Decorator showcases, 132

Deferred payment gift annuity, 229

Deficit spending, 364–365

Delgado, Gary, 355

Demographics
canvassing and, 268
of donors, 238–241
sample survey, 247

Designated gifts, 78

Development directors, 317–323
executive directors, working with,
341–343
job description for, 321–323

Dinners. *See also* Annual dinners
dinner-dances, 133
progressive dinners, 126–127

Direct mail, 1, 53–87
brief message format, 80
developing lists for, 57–61
enclosures, 70–71
envelopes for, 61–63
evaluating appeals, 77
gift catalogs, 78–79
letters, 63–67
newsletters as appeal, 79
pictures as appeal, 81
promotional items in appeal, 81
for renewals, 73–77
renting lists, 59–61
reply device, 67–69
responses, dealing with, 75–76
return envelopes, 69–70
telephoning after appeal, 147–148
trading lists, 59–61

Directors. *See* Board of directors

Diversifying sources, 13–14

Donor Option Plan, 261–262

Donors, 2. *See also* Benefits programs;
Habitual donors; Major gifts; Personal
solicitations; Renewals
analyzing donor population, 237–249
annual donors, 19
capital gifts, 20–21
controversial donors, 385–387
database information for, 309–310
demographics of, 238–241
e-mail correspondence with, 287
to endowments, 21
goals for, 21
identifying prospects, 244–245
to new organizations, 382
phone-a-thons for, 145–147
pledge programs, 189–196
plotting plans for, 356
psychographic survey of, 242–244
reasons for giving, 14–16
to religious organizations, 10–11
thoughtful donors, 20

Door-to-door canvassing. *See* Canvassing

Drucker, Peter, viii

E

Earmarked gifts, 78

Earth Share, 262

Education organizations, 9, 29

Electronic funds transfers, 192–194

E-mail, 286–287, 302

Embezzlement, 365–366

Employee-driven philanthropy, 8.
See also Corporations

Enclosures with direct mail, 70–71

End-of-year appeals, 85

Endowments, 21, 219

Envelopes, 61–63
personalizing, 62–63
return envelopes, 69–70

Episcopalian United Thank Offering, 280

Estate gifts. *See* Planned gifts

Evaluations
board of directors, 45
of house parties, 107–108
of special events, 99–100

Events. *See* Special events

Executive directors, 341–344
    development directors, relationship
        with, 341–343

Expenses, estimating, 348–349

F

Fact sheets, 71

Famous people
    appeals by, 86–87
    phone-a-thon participation by, 144

Fashion shows, 133

Fee-for-service income stream, 253–257

Filing systems, 298–299

Financial Accounting Standards Board, 173

Financial statement, 32

Financial troubles, 363–366
    accounting errors, 365–366
    cash-flow problems, 364
    deficit spending, 364–365
    embezzlement, 365–366
    mismanagement of funds, 365–366

501(c)(3) status
    benefits of, 35
    one-third rule and, 14

Ford, Henry, 259

Foundation Center Cooperating
    Collections, list of, 395–398

Foundations, 6, 7–8
    religious organizations, giving to, 10

Franklin, Ben, 224

Front money, 1, 93

Fuller, Millard, vii

Fundraising plans, 355–362.
    See also Strategies
        in case statement, 32
        case studies of, 358–362
        sample plan, 357

Fundraising principles. *See* Principles
    of fundraising

Fundraising strategies. *See* Strategies

G

Garage sales, 126

Gift catalogs, 78–79

Gift range chart
    for capital campaign, 210–211
    for major gifts, 181, 182
    for major gifts campaign, 199

*Giving and Volunteering in the
    United States,* 6–7

Giving USA, 6

Goals
    anxiety and meeting, 338
    of capital campaigns, 207
    of direct mail, 56
    for donors, 21
    for fundraising plan, 355
    for major gifts, 180
    for major gifts campaigns, 198–200
    of special events, 89
    statement of, 30

Goldwater, Barry, 53

Guest books, 104

H

Habitual donors, 20, 22
    direct mail for, 54–55

Handwritten thank you notes, 172

Haunted houses, 128

History section of case statement, 31

Holidays
    appeals at, 85–86
    major donors, acknowledging, 185

Honorary committees, 109

Hot lists, 57, 58

House parties, 101–108
    list of invitees, 103
    pitch at, 106–107

Human services organizations, 9

I

Impulse gifts, 19–20, 22, 54

Income, projecting, 350–351

The Independent Sector, 6–7

Individual giving. *See* Donors

Information management, 295–299
    filing systems, 298–299

Insurance, gifts from, 231–232

Internet, 285–290. *See also* Web sites

Invitations
    for annual dinners, 110
    for house parties, 103–104

IRAs, gifts from, 232

IRS. *See also* Taxes
    information management and, 297
    one-third rule, 14
    small business by nonprofits, 274–275

J

Jewish Fund for Justice, 280

Jog-a-thons, 135

L

Lapsed donors, renewing, 55–56

Lead trusts, 231

Legality
    of canvassing, 267
    of raffles, 113
    of voluntary fees for service, 255–256

Letters
    direct mail letters, 63–67
    for personal solicitations, 163, 164–165
    for phone-a-thons, 138–140
    renewal letters, 73

Life insurance gifts, 231–232

Lift-out notes, 70

Lists. *See also* Direct mail
    e-mail lists, 287
    for house parties, 103
    master prospect list, 161
    for personal solicitations, 159–163
    for phone-a-thons, 136–137
    planned gift mailing list, 234–235
    prospect record, 162

M

Mail/mailing lists. *See* Direct mail

Major gifts, 179–188. *See also* Major gifts
    campaigns
        apportionment of, 181–182
        goals for, 180
        materials for, 183–184
        renewals of, 186–188
        in rural areas, 372

Major gifts campaigns, 197–205
  supporting materials, 200–201
  tracking form for, 202
Master task list for special events, 95–96
Matching funds, 8
Mathiassen, Karl, 44
Meetings
  avoiding unnecessary meetings, 305–306
  etiquette for, 167–168
  major gifts campaigns, reporting on, 204
  for personal solicitations, 163, 166–168
Member-to-member appeals, 87
Mentors for fundraisers, 334
Merton, Thomas, 339
Mission statement, 28–29
Money
  clean vs. dirty money, 385–387
  taboos about, 152–153, 333
Month-At-A-Glance calendars, 303, 304

N

National Association of Hospital
  Developers, 320
National Black United Federation of
  Charities, 262
National Society of Fund Raising
  Executives (NSFRE), 315, 320
Needs, 19–21, 22
New organizations, 381–383
Newsletters
  e-mail newsletters, 286–287
  as mail appeal, 79
  as reason for giving, 15
  in rural communities, 370
  voluntary fees for service, 254
Newspapers
  direct mail including articles, 70
  phone-a-thon publicity, 143–145
Nominating committees, 45
Not-for-Profit Corporation Law
  (New York), 36

O

Objectives, statement of, 30–31
Office requirements, 293–294
  information management and, 295
One-third rule, 14

Open houses, 129

P

Pancake breakfasts, 126
Payroll deduction programs, 259–264
Personal solicitations, 151–170
  letters, 163, 164–165
  lists for, 159–163
  meetings for, 163, 166–168
  telephone calls for, 163, 165–166
Personnel. See Staff
Phantom events, 79–80
Philanthropy, 3, 5–11
  employee-driven philanthropy, 8
  trends in, 6
Phone-a-thons, 135–149
  letters for, 138–140
  reminder letters, 143
  scripts for volunteers, 137–138
Pictures in direct mail appeal, 81
Pillsbury, George, 333
Planned gifts, 21, 219–236
  types of, 226–232
Planned Giving Simplified (Sharpe), 236
Plans. See Fundraising plans
Pledge programs, 189–196
  in capital campaigns, 215–216
  credit card charges, 195–196
  electronic funds transfers, 192–194
  sample reminder form, 191
  tracking pledges, 191–192
Pooled income funds, 229–230
Preamble to the Principles of Unity, 28–29
Premiums, 83–84. See also Benefits
  programs
Principles of fundraising, 13–17
  diversifying sources, 13–14
  for planned gifts, 227
Private dinners, 125
Progressive dinners, 126–127
Promotional items, 81
Prospect Identification. See Donors
Prospective board members, 47
Psychographic surveys, 242–246
  sample survey, 248–249
Public figures. See Phone-a-thons

Publicity
  for annual dinners, 110
  board members and, 46
  for phone-a-thons, 143–145
  visibility and, 89–90

R

Radio phone-a-thon publicity, 143–145
Raffles, 113–118
  tickets for, 114–116
Read-a-thons, 135
Recordkeeping. See also Computers
  backing up records, 312–313
  database programs, 307–310
  importance of, 310–311
  updating donor records, 312
Recruiting
  annual dinner volunteers, 109–110
  board members, 44–46
  phone-a-thon volunteers, 141
  volunteers, 337
Religious institutions, 9, 280–282
  donors to, 10–11
Renewals
  direct mail for, 73–77
  lapsed donors, 55–56
  of major gifts, 186–188
  normal rate for, 75
  premiums with, 83–84
  telephoning for, 148–149
Renting direct mail lists, 59–61
Reply device
  for direct mail, 67–69
  for renewals, 73–74
Resources, 389–392
Retention strategies, 24
Retirement plan gifts, 232
Return envelopes, 69–70
Rural areas, fundraising in, 369–374

S

SASEs (self-addressed stamped
  envelopes), 69–70
Seasonal appeals, 85
Seminars, 235
Service clubs, 282–283
Sharing mailing lists, 59–61

Sharpe, Robert, Sr., 236

Small businesses
  as donors, 283
  nonprofits running, 273–283
  in rural areas, 373
  types of, 274–275

Special events, 89–134. *See also* Adbooks;
  Annual dinners; House
  parties; Raffles
    budgeting for, 96–98
    committees for, 95–98
    evaluation of, 99–100
    major gifts campaigns, starting, 204
    master task list for, 95–96
    phantom events, 79–80
    in rural areas, 371, 373

Staff, 1. *See also* Consultants; Development
  directors; Executive directors
    board of directors and, 37, 44
    for canvassing, 268–269
    capital campaign staff costs, 209
    office of, 293
    paid staff, role of, 41–42
    voluntary fees for service,
      discussing, 257

Statement of agreement for board, 38–39

Statement of Purpose, 28–29

Strategies. *See also* Major gifts; Special
  events
    acquisition strategies, 23–24
    for advisory boards, 48–50
    board of directors and, 36–37
    correct use example, 25
    income strategies, 355
    needs and, 19–24
    rural areas, fundraising in, 371–374
    traditional strategies, rethinking, 2
    types of, 23–24

T

Taboos about money, 152–153, 333

Tastings, 129

Taxes
  board of directors and, 35–36
  deductions, 15
  information management and, 297
  small business by nonprofits, 274–275

Telephone calls. *See also* Phone-a-thons
  fees for phone services, 257
  limiting length of, 302
  for personal solicitations, 163, 165–166

Television phone-a-thon publicity, 143–145

Thanksgiving Day appeals, 86

Thank yous, 171–176
  to adbook businesses, 123
  for house party donations, 107–108
  for phone-a-thon donations, 142
  premiums as, 83–84
  for raffle donations, 118
  time management and, 301

Thoughtful donors, 20, 23

Timelines
  for adbooks, 121
  for special events, 97–98

Time management, 301–306

Tomlin, Lily, 345

Trading direct mail lists, 59–61

Trainers. *See* Consultants

Trusts as planned gifts, 229–231

U

Unitarian Universalist Veatch Program, 280

United Church of Christ's Board of
  Homeland Ministries, 280

United Methodist Voluntary Service, 280

United Way, 259–262

Universities and colleges
  capital gifts to, 208
  courses in fundraising, 16

Upgrading donors, 177–178. *See also*
  Major gifts; Pledge programs
    major gifts campaigns, 197–205
    strategies for, 24

Uses of contributions, 9–10

V

Voluntary fees for service, 253–257

Volunteers, 1, 2. *See also* Board of
  directors; Committees
    for adbooks, 124
    all-volunteer organizations, 379–380
    for annual dinners, 108–109
    for canvassing, 268–269

e-mail correspondence with, 287
for major gift programs, 184
for major gifts campaigns, 201–202
for phone-a-thons, 137–138
special events and, 93
voluntary fees for service,
  discussing, 257

W

Walk-a-thons, 135

Warm lists, 57, 58–59

Web sites, 1
  costs of, 289
  developing, 287–289
  foundations maintaining, 7
  pledge page on, 190
  useful sites, list of, 393–394

Weekly time management, 302

Wills, gifts in. *See* Planned gifts; Bequests

Wine tastings, 129

Y

Year-At-A-Glance calendars, 303–305

*Yearbook of American and Canadian
  Churches,* 280

RESOURCES FOR SOCIAL CHANGE

AVAILABLE FROM JOSSEY-BASS AND CHARDON PRESS

Raise More Money
The Best of the Grassroots Fundraising Journal

**Kim Klein and
Stephanie Roth, Editors**
Paper 208 pages
ISBN 0-7879-6175-2 $28.00

This collection offers a wealth of tips and strategies, as well as guidance on how small nonprofits can raise money from their communities, reduce their dependence on foundations or corporations, and develop long-term financial stability.

Fundraising for the Long Haul

Kim Klein
Paper 176 pages
ISBN 0-7879-6173-6 $20.00

In this companion to her classic *Fundraising for Social Change*, Kim Klein distills her 25 years of experience and wisdom to provide practical guidance for sustaining a long-term commitment to social change for organizations that are understaffed and underresourced.

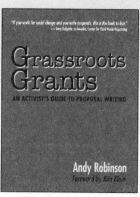

Grassroots Grants
An Activist's Guide to Proposal Writing

Andy Robinson
Paper 208 pages
ISBN 0-7879-6177-9 $25.00

The author describes just what it takes to win grants, including how grants fit into your complete fundraising program, how to use your grant proposal as an organizing plan, how to design fundable projects, how to build your proposal piece by piece, and more.

Ask and You Shall Receive
A Fundraising Training Program for Religious Organizations and Projects

Kim Klein
Paper
ISBN 0-7879-5563-9 $23.00

A self-study course in the basics of grassroots fundraising written specifically for groups raising funds for religious organizations and projects. (Includes a Leader Manual and a Participant Manual.)

Inspired Philanthropy
Creating a Giving Plan

Tracy Gary and Melissa Kohner
Paper 128 pages
ISBN 0-7879-6176-0 $20.00

Learn how to match your giving with your values. No matter how much or little you have to give, you'll learn how to create a giving plan that will make your charitable giving catalytic.

TO ORDER, CALL (800) 956-7739 OR VISIT US AT
www.josseybass.com/go/chardonpress